IN THE LAND OF THE PATH

LATERAL EXCHANGES: ARCHITECTURE, URBAN DEVELOPMENT, AND TRANSNATIONAL PRACTICES

A series edited by Felipe Correa, Bruno Carvalho, and Alison Isenberg

Also in the series

Xiaoxuan Lu, *Shifting Sands: Landscape, Memory, and Commodities in China's Contemporary Borderlands*
Tara Dudley, *Building Antebellum New Orleans: Free People of Color and Their Influence*
Ana María León, *Modernity for the Masses: Antonio Bonet's Dreams for Buenos Aires*
Burak Erdim, *Landed Internationals: Planning Cultures, the Academy, and the Making of the Modern Middle East*
Mary P. Ryan, *Taking the Land to Make the City: A Bicoastal History of North America*
Fabiola López-Durán, *Eugenics in the Garden: Transatlantic Architecture and the Crafting of Modernity*

IN THE LAND OF THE PATRIARCHS

Design and Contestation in West Bank Settlements

NOAM SHOKED

UNIVERSITY OF TEXAS PRESS *Austin*

The Jewish History, Life, and Culture Endowment, which contributed to the publication of this volume, is supported by the late Milton T. Smith and the Moshana Foundation and the Tocker Foundation.

Some of chapter 1 was previously published in "Design and Contestation in the Jewish Settlement of Hebron, 1967–1987," *Journal of the Society of Architectural Historians* 79, no.1 (March 2020): 82–102; and some of chapter 4 was previously published in "Rabbis, Architects, and the Design of Ultra-Orthodox City-Settlements," in *Social Housing in the Middle East: Architecture, Urban Development, and Transnational Modernity*, edited by Mohammad Gharipour and Kıvanç Kılınç (Bloomington: Indiana University Press).

∞The paper used in this book meets the minimum requirements of ANSI/NISO Z39.48-1992 (R1997) (Permanence of Paper).

Library of Congress Cataloging-in-Publication Data

Names: Shoked, Noam, author.
Title: In the land of the patriarchs : design and contestation in West Bank settlements / Noam Shoked.
Description: First edition. | Austin : University of Texas Press, 2023. | Series: Lateral exchanges: architecture, urban development, and transnational practices | Includes bibliographical references and index.
Identifiers: LCCN 2023008527
    ISBN 978-1-4773-2784-5 (cloth)
    ISBN 978-1-4773-2854-5 (paperback)
    ISBN 978-1-4773-2785-2 (PDF)
    ISBN 978-1-4773-2786-9 (ePub)
Subjects: LCSH: Israelis—Housing—West Bank—Design—History. | Human settlements—West Bank—Design—History. | Architecture, Domestic—West Bank—Design—History. | Human settlements—West Bank—Design—Case studies. | Israelis—Housing—Political aspects—West Bank. | Human settlements—Political aspects—West Bank. | Land settlement—Political aspects—West Bank. | City planning—Political aspects—West Bank.
Classification: LCC NA7420.W47 S56 2023 | DDC 307.1/40956942—dc23/eng/20230522
LC record available at https://lccn.loc.gov/2023008527

doi:10.7560/327845

CONTENTS

PREFACE

By the time I had graduated from the School of Architecture at Tel Aviv University in 2006, West Bank settlements had become a major political reality in Israel, but no mention was made of them in the architecture classes I had taken. Instead, the focus was on the modernist history of Tel Aviv and the legacies of the International Style. So naturally I was stunned, on my first day at work after graduation, when I learned that the small firm I had joined, located a block away from the Tel Aviv Port, was kept afloat mainly thanks to its work in settlements. I did not stay there for long. The next firm I worked at, then the largest in the country, had other sources of income at the time, mainly in Eastern Europe, but its history was replete with design commissions in settlements. Settlements, it seemed, were everywhere, but they were nowhere; they were rarely discussed in any academic or professional forum, as if architecture had nothing to do with the settlement project or the Israeli-Palestinian conflict.

Later, after I had moved to North America, and decided to leave practice for a career as a historian of the built environment, I encountered a different reality. In those few times when Israel was mentioned, whether in graduate seminars at Berkeley or in random conversations, the settlements were all people seemed to talk about, and architecture had a lot to do with that. It was seen as a means through which Israel exerted its power over the Palestinians, and thus architects were collaborators of the worst kind. Architecture and architects then, were either completely removed from politics, as was the case in Tel Aviv, or conversely, irredeemably political, as was the case in Berkeley.

So I came back to Israel in 2013 to try to understand exactly what the relationship was between architecture and the settlements. I began by conducting interviews with architects who had worked in settlements. Almost all the architects I contacted agreed to meet with me, even though they rarely expressed much pride in their work in settlements. They were often surprised to hear I was studying settlement architecture. For the most part, I figured, their more impressive body of work was carried out in Israel, not in the West Bank. More importantly, work in the settlements had left many of them bitter and disappointed. "I regret I ever laid a foot there," an architect who designed an entire settlement told me, before he went on to recount the many ways in which a private developer and state officials challenged, tweaked, and ultimately redrew his plans. "What you see there now has little to do with the plans I had drawn." My notebooks are filled with comments of this nature. At times, it was private developers and state officials who undermined the architects' work. Most often, it was the settlers themselves. I soon realized that if I was to understand the architecture of the settlements, I had to expand the scope of my research beyond the profession of architecture, and I began investigating government officials, real estate developers, and the wide range of settler groups who were involved in the settlement enterprise.

The sense of disappointment and bitterness I encountered when conversing with architects, however, continued to loom over my research. It would return in many of the formal interviews and informal conversations I had with settlers. It was also expressed in interviews I conducted with state and military officials. There were exceptions, of course. One settler group was very happy with its new home. So were a handful of architects. But, by and large, few felt as if the design and evolution of settlements reflected their wishes and expectations. Control over the design of settlements has not been localized to the profession of architecture, to settler groups, or to government officials, I learned, but has been in constant flux, shifting from one actor to the other, leaving all parties bewildered and, at times, full of regret.

I explore this haphazard evolution in the chapters of this book. I do not do so with the intention of redeeming architects or the settlement enterprise. As an Israeli who eventually returned to Israel, where I now teach at Tel Aviv University, I am deeply concerned by the spread of settlements, by the ways in which they impinge on the Palestinians' right to sovereignty and undermine Israel's democratic foundations, and by the fact that my students may one day see their work entangled in the messy politics of settlement construction. But unless we understand the interplay between politics and the built environment, unless we understand how power works on the ground, the construction of settlements will go unchallenged, and history will repeat itself.

IN THE LAND OF THE PATRIARCHS

MAP 0.1. Map of Israel and the occupied West Bank (in gray) with locations mentioned in the book. (Map drawn by Yuval Yadlin.)

INTRODUCTION

Few events have shaped the modern Middle East as much as the Six-Day War. Over a period of six days in June 1967, the State of Israel, which had come into existence some twenty years earlier, was transformed into a major regional power, the closest it had come to the kingdom it was said to have been in ancient history some three millennia ago. It decimated the Egyptian air force, pushed back the militaries of Jordan and Syria, and, with not a small amount of bewilderment, tripled in size by capturing the Sinai Peninsula and the Gaza Strip from Egypt, the Golan Heights from Syria, and East Jerusalem and the West Bank from Jordan. In subsequent years, Israel would return the Sinai Peninsula to Egypt in exchange for peace; later, it would withdraw from the Gaza Strip. But Israel would not let go of the West Bank nor would it annex the territory, as it did with the eastern half of Jerusalem and the Golan Heights; instead, it kept it and its native population of Palestinians under a military occupation. In what is arguably the most enduring and controversial legacy of the Six-Day War, the West Bank would become home to a growing population of Israelis, living in settlements built on its rocky hilltops. By the early 2020s, there would be over two hundred such settlements, housing almost half a million Israelis amid close to three million Palestinians.[1]

The political effects of the settlements cannot be overstated. The settlements have generated repeated clashes between Israelis and Palestinians, prompted the seizure of Palestinian lands, disrupted movement (and lives) by cutting off Palestinian towns from one another, and made a territorially viable Palestinian state almost impossible. The settlements have also transformed Israel itself: they have consumed a large fraction of the national budget, sharpened divisions between the Left and the Right, damaged the image of the country abroad, and become home to about 7 percent of its Jewish population.

This book is an account of the design of West Bank settlements, beginning in 1967, when settlements were still an abstract idea, and extending to the present, when they have become one of the most contested housing projects in the world. Because the settlements are so deeply enmeshed in political forces, it is ultimately an account of the complicated relationship between politics and the built environment, of how abstract political ideologies meet the ground.

POLITICS AND THE BUILT ENVIRONMENT

West Bank settlements have a reputation for being monotypic in form, adopting the model of an American suburb. This view is so pervasive that even settlers express it. Ulrich Becker, a German-born urban planner and resident of the settlement of Tkoa, recently bemoaned what he described as the "depressing monotonous uniformity" of the settlements. "They are not building here towns and villages that could keep the Jewish people in its land for the next 500 years but a series of American suburbs," he told a reporter for the daily *Haaretz*.[2] Scholars of the built environment have done little to challenge this perception among the general public. "Although Israel built hundreds and thousands of structures in the West Bank, the number of typologies is very limited," the architectural theorist Eyal Weizman, who is perhaps the most prominent analyst of Israeli architecture, explained to the viewers of Al Jazeera's popular show *Rebel Architecture*. "They are all variations on the single- or double-family houses [*sic*] with red roofs. Very suburban typology."[3]

This presumed uniformity of settlements, even if only at the level of building typology, has lent itself to sweeping interpretations of their design as an instrument of policy. Their lack of formal innovation, some argue, reflects a blatant practice of land expropriation on the part of the state—annexation by real estate.[4] For others, like Weizman, the relative uniform design of settler homes relates to a strategy of military occupation; not only does it protect settlers from friendly fire by making it easy for Israeli soldiers to distinguish friend from foe during an operation, but it also embeds certain building elements designed to dominate the neighboring Palestinians. According to this interpretation, many settler homes were built on hilltops, with their windows and rooms overlooking surrounding Palestinian towns and villages so they would function as optic devices of surveillance.[5] Whether seen as a land grab or as a technology of occupation, the built environment is almost always interpreted as a direct reflection of what appears to be an overdetermined political project.

But when I began visiting the West Bank in 2013 to conduct research on the settlements, I was struck by a staggering diversity in the size and physical organization of settlements, the layout of homes, and the design of public spaces. As I began to speak with residents, I learned that this diversity of settlement forms was matched by a diversity in cultural and political orientation among settlers. In the settlement of Hebron, I met Noam Arnon, a religious Zionist in his midsixties with a thick beard and an assertive style of speech. The settlement of Hebron, housing some eight hundred Jews, was built in the heart of Hebron—a densely populated city of more than 200,000 Palestinians. Noam moved there with his wife some four decades ago because he wanted to live near the Tomb of the Patriarchs, Hebron's most famous shrine, revered by Jews, Muslims, and Christians. Noam's three-story apartment building is a short walk from the old shrine. It includes twelve condos as well as a synagogue and a visitors' center on the ground floor; all units are organized around an enclosed inner court space, where residents can dry their laundry and interact with one another protected from their surroundings. A children's playground was created underneath a neighboring building also occupied by Jewish settlers (figure 0.1). Hostilities between Jews and Muslims in Hebron, one of Noam's neighbors told me, made it unsafe to have a playground out in the open—even with the scores of military checkpoints, fences, and concrete barricades that encircle the settlement. Noam, who raised his eight children in Hebron and now works as the official spokesperson of the settlement, nevertheless refuses to express fear. "[Hebron] is the soul and the roots of the Jewish people," he told a reporter.[6]

Fifty kilometers north of Hebron, in the settlement of Ofra, I met Aharon and Edna Halamish, a soft-spoken couple now in their seventies. Ofra sits on a hill surrounded by rocky fields. It was the first of what came to be called a community settlement (*yishuv kehilati*)—a type of small rural community of residents sharing a commitment to a particular lifestyle or set of worldviews.[7] In Ofra, there are a few hundred pious families. The Halamishes, with their four-year-old boy and twin infants, were among the first to join the settlement in the summer of 1975, shortly after Aharon had emigrated from Wales. They were adventurous and they wanted to live a pioneering life. Most people in Ofra, including Aharon and Edna, live in modest, uniform, detached homes with red-tiled roofs (figure 0.2). It is a design intentionally adopted from the kibbutzim built by the first waves of Jewish immigrants from Europe in the early twentieth century. The kibbutz was an agricultural collective where property was communally owned, and physical labor was distributed among the members. The founders of Ofra claimed the pioneering legacy of the kibbutz, so it was important for them that the settlement

FIGURE 0.1. A kids' playground "sheltered" underneath a settlers' housing compound in Hebron, 2017. Violent clashes between the settlers and their Palestinian neighbors have resulted in the fortification of both settler and Palestinian houses. (Photograph by author.)

reproduce its architectural profile. Edna had in fact grown up in a kibbutz, and the legacy of manual labor appealed to Aharon, an electrical engineer who worked in the aerospace industry. He sought to continue that legacy by founding a construction company in 1981. Urging his fellow settlers to stop hiring Palestinian contractors to build their homes, he wrote in a settler-run magazine, reprising the early Zionist ethos: "We should not create a class of Jews who can only be managers and not laborers."[8] But the legacy of manual labor did not survive the kibbutz, even if the architectural form did, and Palestinians continued to provide the labor that built settlements. Today, Aharon is offering translation services from his home.

Despite the differences between the settlements of Hebron and Ofra—one urban, consisting of apartment buildings, and the other rural, consisting mostly of detached homes—both house Israelis who identify with religious Zionism, an interpretation of Judaism that combines piety with modernity and Jewish nationalism.[9] (Its followers are commonly referred to in Israel as religious nationalists.) For many of them, inhabiting the West Bank—the

FIGURE 0.2. A house in the settlement of Ofra designed to resemble kibbutz houses, 1982. (Berman family, Ofra Archives.)

presumed heartland of the ancient Israelites, the biblical lands of Judea and Samaria ("Judea" denoting the mountainous areas south of Jerusalem, and "Samaria," those to the north)—was at once a moral act of homecoming and a political act of national development. Religious Zionists make up 11–22 percent of Jewish Israelis but about a third of the settlers.[10]

Not all settlers, however, would have such religious or even political motivations. In the settlement of Nofim, just 25 kilometers north of Ofra, near the Green Line that delimits Israel's pre-1967 border, I met Miri Levy, a woman in her sixties with a strongly secular orientation (figure 0.3). Nofim is a suburban hilltop community, built by a private developer who made no claim on the legacy of the kibbutz. Before Miri moved to Nofim in 1987, she had lived in a small condo in one of Tel Aviv's unremarkable bedroom communities, but she wanted more space. In Nofim, parcels of land were available at bargain prices, and she was able to build a luxurious, 300-square-meter, three-story detached house with a flat roof. She designed the interior herself, with a series of arches that flank a large jacuzzi, the centerpiece of the living room, framing breathtaking views of the valley below. "If you have a dream, why not build it," she told me without irony. Her neighbors' houses

FIGURE 0.3. Miri Levy sitting by her private pool in Nofim, 2004. Most houses in Nofim have flat roofs. "From a distance," Levy told me with pride, "you could think it is an Arab village." Regardless of such aesthetic considerations, many settlers like Levy moved to the West Bank to improve their housing conditions. (*Maariv*, September 3, 2004, 19.)

are equally distinctive. All sit on plots of land roughly three times the size of a typical suburban plot in Israel. When a reporter from the daily *Maariv* came to Nofim to explore upscale settlement houses, Miri told him as they stopped by her private pool: "Look around you, where can you find such views from a private balcony? . . . People from the Tel Aviv metropolitan area think I live beyond the dark mountains, but recently I was walking around Schuster Center in Ramat Aviv [a high-end commercial center in Tel Aviv] and I was feeling sorry for these people living in boxes, one on top of the other. And, anyway, I get to the Tel Aviv metropolitan area in 25 minutes."[11]

Some 50 kilometers south of Nofim, and several notches down the economic ladder, Akiva and Esti, an ultra-Orthodox couple in their thirties, were living with their five children in a cramped three-bedroom apartment in Betar Illit when I met them.[12] Betar Illit is a town twenty minutes outside of Jerusalem, just east of the Green Line, designed exclusively for ultra-Orthodox Jews (Haredim). The town's entire population of 65,000

FIGURE 0.4. Apartment buildings clustered around a playground in the ultra-Orthodox city-settlement of Modi'in Illit, 2015. These larger, more visibly "urban" settlements run their own municipal government, finances, and cultural affairs. (Photograph by author.)

live in apartment buildings, some as high as eight stories, densely arranged along streets lined with stores. Small synagogues are scattered throughout the city, and baby strollers are the predominant vehicles. Akiva and Esti, the latter a technical draftsperson, had some reservations when they first considered leaving their Jerusalem apartment for Betar Illit some ten years ago. Some ultra-Orthodox rabbis discourage their followers from moving to settlements because traditional Jewish law prohibits "teasing" non-Jews; moreover, a city designed exclusively for ultra-Orthodox Jews, they feared, might lack certain amenities. But their apartment in Jerusalem was just too small, especially for the large family they planned, and they could not afford a larger one in the city. Ultra-Orthodox Jews are among the poorest demographic groups in Israel, and in settlements like Betar Illit, they enjoy more affordable housing. By the end of 2021, more than 150,000 ultra-Orthodox Jews were living in "city-settlements" tailored to the needs of those abiding by a strict interpretation of Jewish law (figure 0.4). Ultra-Orthodox settlers do not necessarily treat the neighboring Palestinians with hostility. In fact, until a few years

FIGURE 0.5. A settler in the settlement of Revava watching the installation of mobile homes. Many settlements began with the installation of portable buildings, which provided temporary shelter until permanent houses were built. Starting in the late 1990s, mobile homes have come to provide long-term housing for settlers in "unauthorized outposts." (Photograph by Yaron Kaminski, 1995, Government Press Office.)

ago, the residents of Betar Illit regularly did their shopping at the nearby Palestinian town of Husan. "It was our downtown," Esti told me.

In Pnei Kedem, a hilltop community overlooking the Dead Sea that was founded some twenty years ago, Shani and Yotam—a schoolteacher and a carpenter, both in their late twenties—were living with their two children in a mobile home (known as a "caravan," following British usage); it was made of uninsulated aluminum siding with a corrugated metal roof (figure 0.5). It would become a furnace in the summer and an icebox in the winter. They had been wanting to build a permanent house for years, but Pnei Kedem—like most settlements established over the past two decades—was considered illegal when we met, even under Israeli law, and that meant that all structures built there were subject to the possibility of demolition. Of the fifty families or so who had moved to Pnei Kedem by 2015, about two-thirds were living in such mobile homes. Organized in rows, the mobile homes lacked fences, sidewalks, street names, and numbers; the line between public and private space was ambiguous. Children's toys and bicycles were strewn about, marking any open spaces as homogeneous fields shared by

FIGURE 0.6. Yotam (left) and another settler at work on Yotam's octagon-shaped house in Pnei Kedem, 2015. The two are part of a team that had built a couple of structures in Pnei Kedem. In their work (and their dress), they combine 1960s counterculture motifs with Jewish symbols. The design of earlier settlements, they complained, failed to address the spiritual qualities of the land. (Photograph by author.)

the residents. Like residents of other young settlements, known in Israel as "unauthorized outposts," they envisioned developing a "green" community: a small village, limited to perhaps a hundred families, with a lot of greenery, solar energy, and some Eastern spirituality. At our last meeting, Shani and Yotam were building an octagonal house made of locally quarried stones that they envisioned as a "hobbit house" (figure 0.6). In the meantime, they had decorated their mobile home with Eastern rugs and paintings.

These five settlements—Hebron, Ofra, Nofim, Betar Illit, and Pnei Kedem—are as different from one another as are their residents, Noam Arnon, the Halamishes, Miri Levy, Esti and Akiva, and Shani and Yotam. The structures range in style from apartment buildings to single-family homes, from modest high-rises to mobile homes. They represent five different patterns of settlement design and construction. Over the past ten years, I have tried not only to document this heterogeneity but also to understand what it means: what it indicates about the settlement movement and about the country Israel has become since its euphoric victory in 1967, and, more broadly, what it tells us about the production of space in sites of political conflict. I made countless visits to settlements; I interviewed government officials, military attorneys, urban planners, architects, and settlers; I consulted archival materials from both official archives and informal settlement archives; and I even stayed as a resident for a total of twelve months of participant observation in two settlements.

One of the first things this heterogeneity signaled was that government policies toward the settlements changed constantly. Although all Israeli governments, both Left- and Right-leaning, have overseen the construction of settlements, each shaped its settlement policies in response to election campaigns, geopolitical events, domestic economic changes, international pressure, and occasionally the Palestinians' opposition. For example, at the time the lush settlement of Nofim was being built, the Right-wing Likud-led government was encouraging Israelis to relocate to the occupied territories by offering generous subsidies and the promise of a dream house. (Strangely, as the historian Danny Gutwein has noted, the government offered these incentives at the same time as it was reducing public services inside Israel.)[13] Twenty years later, at around the time Pnei Kedem was founded, after the government had signed a set of international agreements in the mid-1990s and, as a matter of policy, stopped authorizing new settlements, mobile homes became the dominant feature in new (unauthorized) settlements.[14] Although shifts in government policy affected the design of settlements, it was not the sole force shaping them.

Paralleling changes in government policy was a change in the demographic profile of settlers. Almost every shift in policy introduced to the West Bank a different group of Israelis, representing diverse political and religious views. In the context of settlement construction, where individual desires were usually unconstrained by preexisting structures, and undeveloped hilltops presented a tabula rasa for the imagination, these groups all made unexpected and occasionally conflicting demands on the built environment that they pursued at times in collaboration with planners and architects and at times in opposition to them. For instance, the residents of Betar Illit worked with planners to adapt the layout of the settlement to the needs of ultra-Orthodox families, which tend to have many children. Buildings were clustered around small playgrounds and were provided with ample ramps, where there might have been stairs, to accommodate baby strollers. In other cases, the design relationship was less congenial, and when settlers found architects unresponsive to their requests, they frequently altered structures to suit their desires. Initially, the houses of Ofra were designed to have flat roofs, but residents replaced these with pitched, red-tiled ones in their attempt to reproduce the architectural style of the kibbutz and fashion themselves as heirs to the Zionist pioneers. The heterogeneous landscape of the settlements—their home layouts, yard furniture, interior decorations, and streets and squares—provides clues to the different and fluctuating ways in which settlers relate to their communities, to Israeli history, and to the occupation itself. At times, the built environment also shaped the settlers' daily life in ways that affected their worldviews.

The heterogeneity of the settlements is symptomatic also of the role of chance in their design and evolution. The combination of shifts in government policy and the array of user demands imposed upon design professionals created an environment characterized by a gap between intention and outcome. Certainly, every architectural commission entails some gap between what is conceived on paper and what is built and how it is used in the world. But in the case of settlements, that gap was exacerbated by a confluence of forces: the sense of urgency among some settlers, the unwinding of the socialist state with its centralized planning apparatus, and, of course, a geopolitical situation in which the Israeli government tried to have its cake and eat it too, shying away from annexing the West Bank but still overseeing its colonization. There were more moving parts than one would expect to find in a usual commission and no strong authority to enforce their coordination. Thus, it sometimes happened that spaces designed with a certain worldview in mind ended up being used in an entirely different way. For instance, when planners designed apartment buildings in the settlement of Hebron around inner courtyards, they thought these courtyards would integrate the settlement with its eastern surroundings, better situating the Jewish settlement in the fabric of the Arab city and even facilitating interactions between the settlers and their Palestinian neighbors. In practice, however, the inward-facing design functioned to further segregate Jews from Muslims. Meanwhile, at the time Miri Levy bought her land plot in Nofim, she was told that the settlement would grow into a suburb of some two thousand families in just a few years. But then the real estate developer went bankrupt, and the outbreak of a Palestinian uprising made the dream of a tranquil suburban life in the West Bank less feasible. Nofim ended up being a small hilltop community that four decades later houses fewer than two hundred families. This kind of adjustment to settlement design in response to contingencies was more the rule than the exception: few settlements were built and inhabited according to how they were envisioned.

In this book, I document the role of contingency in the design, construction, and inhabitation of settlements. In doing so, I seek to challenge a basic assumption that architects, the general public, and even scholars sometimes make about the built environment: that the structures human beings erect are a direct reflection—even unyielding carriers—of political ideologies. This assumption persists even after a number of observers suggested that it may be reductive.[15] The history of architecture is so often narrated in terms of this presumed correspondence between architecture and politics: from the open space of the Athenian agora, which is interpreted as the materialization of democratic engagement (regardless of the agora's exclusionary nature); to Albert Speer's unrealized plans for Germania, capital of the Third Reich, whose wide boulevards and supersized neoclassical buildings are interpreted as a reflection of fascism (even if they might look strangely familiar to anyone who has ever been to the National Mall in Washington, DC); to the uniformity of postwar housing blocks in European countries that, until recently, was seen as a means for achieving social equality. There is, of course, some relation between the architecture and the political formation of a particular historical moment; but the case of West Bank settlements—a case at once mundane and extreme—forces us to confront the fact that this relationship is not so straightforward. Because they are so controversial, the settlements invite closer attention to the process of their production. By closely following that process, I learned that architecture is not so much a direct reflection of political ideologies as it is the product of a dynamic process, shaped by open-ended interactions between a variety of actors with different intentions, some not fully formulated, such that the final structure, its design and use, can rarely be read as an expression of any single intention or carry any uncomplicated political meaning. This book is an attempt to disentangle those interactions.

BEYOND THE DARK MOUNTAINS?

Many Israelis tend to dissociate the settlements from mainstream Israel. As Miri Levy of Nofim put it: "People from the Tel Aviv metropolitan area think I live beyond the dark mountains." In several respects, the settlements are a world apart. They have different political effects, they grew out of different historical moments, and they carry a different legal status—all are illegal according to international law.[16] Indeed, for many of them, access from Israel requires crossing a checkpoint (figure 0.7). Colloquial Hebrew even

FIGURE 0.7. According to Machsom Watch, an NGO that monitors Israeli checkpoints, in 2020 there were twenty-three checkpoints like the one in this picture, monitoring access into and out of Israel. While Palestinians may spend hours at these checkpoints, Israelis usually pass through without being stopped. (Author's collection.)

uses two different words to denote human settlements: *yishuv* commonly denotes any settlement—a town or village—built inside Israel (with *mityashev* denoting a resident); *hitnahalut* denotes any Jewish settlement erected in the West Bank (with *mitnahel* denoting a settler). While the former implies moral legitimacy, the latter does not.[17]

But the idea of "settlement" has been central to the self-definition of Israel from the beginning, when European Jews began to immigrate at the end of the nineteenth century in large numbers to Palestine (which was then part of the Ottoman Empire). In the minds of many early Zionists, the acquisition of land and the construction of new self-enclosed communities were key to achieving national sovereignty, and even redemption, in a territory ruled first by the Ottomans and later under the British Mandate. The organization of these new communities around agricultural production was an essential component of the settlement idea: it was a way not only to secure land for a future Jewish state but also to rejuvenate Jewish society by transforming the effete urbanized Jew of the diaspora into a robust person of the land.[18] Following World War I, that ethical program of Jewish self-reinvention became particularly prominent with the rise of Labor Zionism—a strand of Zionism that combined nationalism with socialism—within the Jewish community of Palestine. It was then that what were called "labor settlements"—whether in the form of the kibbutz or the moshav, a cooperative agricultural settlement model—became widespread.[19] The settlement idea was so central to Zionism at the time that the term *yishuv* (settlement) emerged as the preferred collective reference to the Jewish community in Palestine in the prestate era.[20] In the two decades between the founding of the Israeli state in 1948 and the conquest of the West Bank in 1967, the settlement idea never disappeared; the country was still led by a class of politicians and professionals who had been formed in the crucible of Labor Zionism, and the settlement idea became integrated into the institutions of the state.[21]

That did not mean that the construction of settlements in the West Bank was inevitable. While the construction of West Bank settlements has built on the earlier history of Zionist colonization, it also diverges from that history in a number of ways. First, it reverses a central principle that guided Zionist colonization in the prestate era—to avoid settling in densely populated Arab areas, in order to simplify the purchase of land and to secure a Jewish majority for a future political entity.[22] When Zionist colonists first arrived in Palestine, they learned that the mountainous areas of the West Bank, the heart of the ancient Israelite state, were dotted with Arab villages and towns. Few in that area were willing to sell land to European immigrants. So they focused their settlement efforts on the more sparsely populated areas of the coastal plains and valleys west and north of the West Bank, areas that had played only a marginal role in Jewish history but could nevertheless be used for agriculture-based settlement activity.[23] Later, in 1947, when the United Nations proposed partitioning Palestine into a Jewish state and an Arab state, this early commitment to avoid the West Bank made it easy for the Zionist leadership to cede that area to the Palestinians (excluding Jerusalem and Bethlehem, which were to be governed by an international authority).[24] David Ben-Gurion, Israel's first prime minister, famously noted: "Between the wholeness of the land without a Jewish state and a Jewish state without the wholeness of the land, we chose the Jewish state."[25] But the unplanned conquest of the West Bank in 1967, in a war that Israel launched in order to neutralize what seemed at the time to be an imminent threat to its security posed by Egypt, led some Israelis to reassess Ben-Gurion's calculus, and the "wholeness of the land" became increasingly more important.[26]

In tandem with the abandonment of the early Zionist principle of avoiding areas of dense Arab habitation went a transformation in the demographics of settlement construction. Since the 1920s, Zionist settlement activity was overseen for the most part by an elite circle of secular, quasi-socialist, ethnically Ashkenazi (European-origin) Jews.[27] Other groups, such as religious Zionists and the ultra-Orthodox, had limited political power and little say in planning.[28] After the capture of the West Bank in 1967, however, groups that had been previously suppressed soon erupted onto the political scene. The first ones were religious Zionists, who had previously taken a conciliatory attitude but now began to pressure the government to settle the occupied territories. Then, in the early 1970s, Mizrahi Jews (Jews from Muslim countries) began to hold large demonstrations to protest their poor living conditions and systemic discrimination by the ruling labor parties.[29] Meanwhile, ultra-Orthodox Jews, who had been considered a remnant from the diaspora doomed to disappear under the wheels of modernity, had in the three decades after independence grown from a small minority of about 30,000–35,000 to 140,000, becoming an important political force.[30] (By 2020, there would be 1,175,000 ultra-Orthodox Israelis, making up 12.6 percent of the country's population.)[31] One of the arguments I make in this book is that the West Bank has functioned as a site where some of these groups experimented with new housing and community forms. It was in the West Bank that religious Zionists developed the model of the community settlement, and where the ultra-Orthodox negotiated a city-settlement model that met their unique needs. Both models were imported into Israel proper shortly after they proved successful.

This experimentation in settlement forms, of course, did not occur in isolation from architectural developments within Israel. The West Bank was not a "laboratory," in the way that North Africa offered French architects and planners in the nineteenth and early twentieth centuries an opportunity to experiment with designs that were impossible in terms of scale and execution in mainland France.[32] On the contrary, the experimentation that did take place in the settlements often grew out of trends already forming inside Israel. But in the West Bank—where land was sold to Jewish Israelis for almost nothing, the law was only sporadically applied, and settlements were built from scratch, unconfined by existing infrastructure—conditions allowed for things that were harder to achieve within the country's borders.

The loosening of the constraints that governed the built environment in settlements not only allowed marginal groups to take part in a planning process that had previously been monopolized by elites; the planning process itself was also reshaped in the settlements. Since the 1920s (when Palestine came under British Mandate rule, as part of the resolution of World War I), the labor elite of the Zionist movement worked to create centralized governing bodies to administer its settlements, and those bodies enjoyed a large degree of authority.[33] These governing bodies became the nucleus of the state that emerged with the founding of Israel. After 1948, the labor-led government developed highly centralized planning and building sectors. It nationalized all public lands—including lands belonging to Palestinian villages and towns that had been depopulated during Israel's war of independence

המשתכנים החדשים :

ארגנטינה

טוניס

פרס

חצר־מות

הולנד

ישראל

מרוקו

אנגליה

רומניה

תימן

FIGURE 0.8. A panel entitled "The new tenants" depicts Jewish immigrants from different countries, including Tunisia (top right), Romania (bottom left), and Yemen (bottom right). The panel appeared in a public housing report from 1959. Transforming the newcomers into natives of the new Jewish state was central to government activities. (Haim Drabkin-Darin, ed., *Hashikun Hatziburi: Skirot Vehaarahot al Hashikun Hatziburi Beyisrael Betkufat Haasor 1948–1958* [Tel Aviv: Sifrei Gadish, 1959].)

FIGURE 0.9. Aerial view of Mitzpe Ramon, a development town in the Negev desert. Residents of development towns often found themselves in remote locales. Those who could afford to do so soon left, leaving behind desperate communities with little chance of upward mobility. That their towns safeguarded Israel's borders (which, in many cases, were armistice lines) provided them little comfort. (Photograph by Sa'ar Ya'acov, 1985, Government Press Office.)

(known to the Palestinians as the Nakba [catastrophe])—kept them under state or quasi-state agencies' ownership, and adopted an extensive public leasehold system.[34] With governmental control established over most of the country's lands, state planners embarked upon a massive housing project devised to absorb the masses that flocked to Israel from across the world after independence and integrate them into a cohesive society (figure 0.8).[35] Most notably, they built dozens of new towns, known as "development towns," and scattered them in remote parts of the country to solidify Jewish presence in areas that the Zionist movement had largely ignored.[36] These towns were usually composed of blocks of three- or four-story apartment buildings of uniform design: austere, rectilinear volumes devoid of ornamentation that followed the principles of high-modernist architecture (figure 0.9). The intended future residents were mostly Mizrahi Jews, and they were not consulted about their housing assignment—often located far from employment opportunities—nor about the modest design of the apartments, which often were too small to accommodate the larger families of

Mizrahim. (On average, public housing units built between 1949 and 1958 had just 1.6 rooms, with an area of 35 square meters.)[37] Like many other government initiatives devised to mold the newcomers throughout that era of nation-building, ranging from compulsory military service to free public education, housing was a "top-down" operation.[38]

The same could not be said about the settlements built in the West Bank. Each wave of settlement design would not be engineered so much by the state, as it had been in the development towns, but rather was the result of a moving collaboration—and occasionally collision—between an array of actors: governmental and nongovernmental, public and private, working from above and from below. This dispersal of power in the construction of settlements in the West Bank anticipated, and even stimulated, a decentralization of the building sector inside Israel that began in the late 1970s.

Thus, West Bank settlements do not lie beyond the dark mountains, nor do they form an uninterrupted continuation of pre-1967 Zionist settlement activity. While they grew out of that earlier settlement process, they departed from it not only in the logic governing the choice of location but also in their demographic composition, physical forms, and planning processes. The writer Patrick Wolfe famously noted that settler colonialism is not an *event* but a *structure*.[39] That structure is in part physical: its construction has a history, and it evolves over time. By closely examining the architectural history of five patterns of West Bank settlements, this book details how the settler logic of Israeli society has at once remained durable over the course of more than a century and transformed as Israeli society has changed.

UNTAMED USERS

A striking feature of the settlements, particularly when contrasted with the standardized public housing of the 1950s and 1960s, is the degree to which they have been shaped by the actions of the wide range of Israelis who have made them home: from religious Zionists to upwardly mobile professionals, to ultra-Orthodox wives, to new-age hipsters. These actors, who are often neglected in traditional architectural histories, are the protagonists in the pages that follow. Their participation in the design and construction of settlements was made possible by an evolving set of conditions, including the processes of economic liberalization in the late twentieth century that affected most countries that had some form of centralized planning. Three conditions particular to Israel are worth mentioning here: First is the absence of a clear government policy toward the West Bank in the years immediately following the Six-Day War. In the aftermath of the war, the Israeli cabinet was split three ways: some wanted to return the West Bank to Jordan in exchange for peace; others wanted to give Palestinians political autonomy under Israeli rule; a few wanted to retain the vast majority of the territory.[40] This government stalemate left settlement activity in the hands of not only hawkish ministers but also private citizens. Second, even when settlement expansion became an official policy at the end of the 1970s following the election of the Likud Party, the government refrained from annexing the West Bank. Instead, it courted random citizens and development companies to colonize the land on its behalf. This strategy placed citizens willing to move to the West Bank in a position to make demands they would not have been able to make otherwise. Third, government officials—even those hawkish ministers who were intent on retaining the West Bank and on placing settlements in areas that would make a future withdrawal almost impossible—rarely saw architecture as a means of exercising control over the land. This is not to say that they did not see land requisition as central, because they clearly did, but that they did not see the design of buildings, streets, and public spaces in settlements as relevant.[41] Among other factors discussed in this book, these three—policy gridlock, government delegation, and an indifferent attitude toward design—contributed to a rather haphazard planning process in which settlers came to enjoy relative authority over design of the built environment.

By tracing this process and examining its outcomes, this book adds an important case to recent scholarship in the fields of architectural history and urban studies that has focused on the agency of the user—as opposed to the architect or urban planner—in shaping the built environment. Inspired by Michel de Certeau's notion of "tactics" and the ideas developed by Henri Lefebvre in *The Production of Space*, this scholarship has highlighted how the user, through either temporary, everyday practices or permanent design interventions, can coauthor streets, public squares, and housing projects "from below." These accounts have astutely documented how, in cities like São Paulo, Los Angeles, and Stockholm, the practices of the user facilitate the struggle of subaltern groups to exercise their right to the city, which, in turn, endows them with a sense of active citizenship.[42] Common to many of these accounts is the understanding that these practices make space more inclusive.

The everyday practices and design interventions of West Bank settlers have not, however, made space more inclusive. On the contrary, they have often created spaces of exclusion. Almost all settlements are fortified with gates, and many have set up committees to screen potential residents. The purpose of these committees is not only to keep out Palestinians, who are unlikely to apply for admission in any case, but also to maintain the homogeneity of the community, whether defined by ethnic background, political ideology, or commitment to the observance of traditional Jewish law.[43] In ultra-Orthodox city-settlements, the pursuit of a prescribed style of life also entails regulating space within the community, by means of quasi-official agencies that enforce a strict code of behavior, particularly governing relations between the sexes. Altogether, then, the opportunity to transform space created by the unique conditions that followed the Six-Day War, where settlers enjoyed excessive rights (especially when compared to the Palestinians), did not lead to an expansion of access, but rather to a disciplining of space in line with particular objectives that varied according to the interests of the users involved.

This kind of segregation is not without precedent in the region. Since Zionists started erecting villages in Palestine in the late nineteenth century, they have created homogeneous communities, not mixed communities of Jews and Arabs. Later, under the rule of the British Mandate, Jews and Arabs often lived in segregated urban neighborhoods, worked in separate economies, and participated in different political institutions.[44] In addition, over the years, the kibbutz and the moshav have instituted various mechanisms to screen new residents, including admission committees. In recent decades, rifts within Israeli society have also given rise to other forms of segregation. Most notably, when ultra-Orthodox Jews moved from ultra-Orthodox centers to secular cities, they created homogeneous neighborhoods where rules of modest conduct are enforced, often prompting bitter fights between veteran residents and the newcomers. In Bet Shemesh, a town just west of Jerusalem, these fights have escalated to a point where, in 2011, the then prime minister Benjamin Netanyahu considered dividing it into two municipalities, one ultra-Orthodox and the other non-ultra-Orthodox.[45] The exclusionary practices settlers have developed in the West Bank may have made segregation more common and explicit, even sometimes a matter of policy, but they do not represent a break with local history nor with current trends in Israeli society.

No less important is the fact that, while perpetuating an exclusionary pattern of community formation, the settlements did help precipitate reform in a housing system that was centralized, inflexible, and at times even oppressive in the structural impediments it erected to certain forms of life. The ultra-Orthodox city-settlement and the community settlement offered urban forms that were responsive to the needs of the ultra-Orthodox and religious Zionists—needs that were sometimes ignored by the state-administered housing system, with its melting-pot ideology. Arguably, the exclusionary nature of these settlement forms helped both groups preserve their ways of life by reducing frictions with secular culture, at least in the short run.[46]

As a case study, however, the settlements not only illustrate the exclusionary effects user-led design may have when planning rights are not distributed equitably; they also undermine the analytic opposition between bottom-up and top-down processes that has underwritten much of the scholarship that has focused on the user. In the West Bank, the opposition between user and expert frequently breaks down. As much as settlers clashed with urban planners, architects, and state officials, they also repeatedly collaborated with them, as clients and occasionally as codesigners, even taking on the roles of consultants, construction workers, and planners. This pattern of intermittent contestation and collaboration resonates with what the architectural historian and anthropologist Jennifer Mack has termed "design from below," or the formation of alliances that tend to blur the opposition between planners and users.[47] In this architectural history, the analytic categories of top and down, above and below, expert and user frequently dissolve in the unfolding process of design, construction, and inhabitation.

ARCHITECTS IN THE MIDST OF CONFLICT

While this book considers the built environment as the product of multiple actors rather than the outcome of individual architects, it also offers a vantage point on the architectural profession in Israel. Over the five decades that frame this study, Israeli architects experienced a severe decline in status. During the 1950s and 1960s, when the Israeli building sector was centralized, architects enjoyed unquestioned authority over design.[48] In their work for the government, they typically produced standardized plans for uniform housing blocks that were indifferent to local or individual preferences. The capture of the West Bank opened up a new frontier for building. But in the West Bank, the conditions of practice had been altered, and the authority of the architect was undermined not only by settler-clients who often came with an idea of what they wanted built, but also by undecided government leaders, and later by real estate developers seeking quick profit. This transfer of control over design that took place in the West Bank precipitated a crisis in authority that was subsequently recorded also in Israel proper, where the forces of privatization subjected architects to the new pressures of the market.

This crisis in authority coincided with an ethical impasse that only exacerbated the decline of the profession. Most architects I interviewed for this study told me that they were reluctant to accept design commissions in settlements because they identified with the Left and opposed the occupation; nevertheless, working in settlements was critical to keeping their practice afloat. To overcome this predicament, they came up with various rationalizations. Some insisted that the utilitarian nature of architecture made it apolitical; the buildings they designed could be used by anyone—settlers or Palestinians. Others distinguished between "ideological settlements," located in the depths of the West Bank and inhabited by far-right activists, and "nonideological settlements," located near the border and inhabited by working- and middle-class Israelis who had relocated to the West Bank for economic reasons. Architects have been more inclined to take building commissions in the latter settlements. The architect Yaacov Yaar, for example, refused to take a building commission in the Jewish settlement of Hebron but was willing to design the settlement of Betar Illit, the second-largest settlement in the West Bank.[49] A number of architects, however, insisted that designing settlements, no matter how moderate the residents might be, meant supporting the Israeli occupation. Nevertheless, they argued that there was nothing they could do about it. "Architects are always slaves to [political] structures," one of them told me. "The maximum an architect can do [if he opposes his regime] is not to do, but that is not much."[50]

A number of architects were initially enthralled by the opportunities offered in the West Bank, either to experiment with new architectural forms or to design complete communities from scratch, but they rarely saw their plans realized. If their designs weren't contested by the settlers or by individual politicians and developers, then the execution of those designs was undermined by the eruption of the broader political context—notably, the outbreak of a Palestinian uprising against the Israeli occupation in 1987—or by financial insolvency owing to the fact that the economic model of settlement construction was rarely viable. Even for the most enthusiastic architects, the experience of settlement design was one of repeated disappointments.

And yet in recent decades architecture has become a locus of organized opposition to the military occupation of the West Bank. Professional affiliates like Architects and Planners for Justice in Palestine have issued petitions calling on Israeli architects to turn down design commissions in settlements and pressured the International Union of Architects to suspend the membership of the Israeli Association of United Architects.[51] The architectural theorist Eyal Weizman and the architect Rafi Segal suggested that the work of Israeli architects in settlements might call for legal proceedings to be prosecuted under international law.[52] These efforts have drawn a new kind of international attention to the Israeli-Palestinian conflict, and in particular to the avowedly civilian elements of the occupation. The strength of these initiatives is that they cast a much-needed critical light on the architectural profession and its political ramifications. But that is also their weakness. Architecture, as I argue in this book, involves more than just architects. By singling out architects, these initiatives leave the forces behind the settlements untouched.

To truly halt settlement construction would require disentangling all the social, political, and economic forces in which architecture is enmeshed.

A NOTE ON METHOD

This book builds on scholarly accounts of the settlements written by historians and social scientists. Traditionally, these accounts tended to focus on the messianic ideology and the strategic considerations that motivated settlement construction in the first two decades following the Six-Day War.[53] In recent years, however, a new wave of scholarship began to explore the plurality of settlers' worldviews, the involvement of powerful economic forces, and the roles played by Mizrahi Jews as well as immigrants from the United States and the former Soviet Union in the settlement enterprise.[54] *In the Land of the Patriarchs* contributes to this emerging body of literature, but it also goes beyond it by treating the settlements as architectural formations and by exploring the interactions between the social and the spatial. In analyzing the process of settlement design, it shows how the built environment, its conception and its reception, not only reveals an even greater diversity of actors and ideologies but also interacts with these ideologies.

In this regard, the book takes its method from cultural landscape studies. Cultural landscape studies, according to the geographer and architectural historian Paul Groth, "focus most on the history of how people have used *everyday* space—buildings, rooms, streets, fields, or yards—to establish their identity, articulate their social relations, and derive cultural meaning."[55] By better understanding ordinary environments, cultural landscape studies seek to shed new light on people and on history. Since the 1950s, largely thanks to the writings and teachings of the publisher and philosopher John Brinckerhoff Jackson, this approach has inspired architects and architectural historians to explore the structures of everyday life in North American cities, towns, and villages. They have studied trailer parks, residential hotels, tract houses, mini-malls, and a whole range of everyday built spaces to better understand American culture. In a similar fashion, in this book I study settlement design by examining ordinary spaces—middle- and lower-class houses, yards, playgrounds, and (in the case of religious communities) synagogues, whether designed by high-profile designers or by anonymous Israelis—to understand West Bank settlers and the Israeli occupation.

Treating settlements as ordinary spaces, as if they belong to the same category of objects as North American trailer parks or strip malls, might seem misplaced. After all, there seems to be nothing ordinary about West Bank settlements. One might even object that by looking at everyday spaces in settlements I am normalizing settlements, treating them as benign, as if they were built on neutral ground, as if they do not have the political effects that they clearly have. But that could not be further from my intention. By studying the way that settlers have designed or inhabited settlements in their daily lives, on their way to the grocery store, coming back from work, or when they sit back and relax, I want to understand how an undeniably extraordinary situation—life outside the legal borders of one's country, on seized lands, and against the opposition of both the international community and the local inhabitants—has become relatively ordinary.

GUIDELINE

Organized chronologically, this book traces the design processes that animated five successive episodes in the history of settlement design. Each chapter departs from a major political event: the capture of the West Bank in 1967; the Yom Kippur War of 1973; the 1977 elections that saw the rise of the Right-wing Likud Party; the outbreak of a Palestinian uprising in 1987; and the signing of the Oslo Accords in the 1990s. Nevertheless, the time frame of planning and construction greatly exceeds that of political events, often spanning five or ten years, so it is not political events that distinguish the episodes identified in the book. Rather, each episode is characterized by a different kind of user, the particular demands they made on the built environment, and the pattern of settlement design and construction that resulted. Although none of these patterns constitutes a "pure" settlement type, and overlapping occurs between some of them, each, at least at its time of conception, was characterized by distinct architectural forms, street layouts, programs, modes of governance, and its relationship to the state.

Chapter 1 explores the special interest demonstrated by Israelis, especially religious Zionists, regarding Palestinian towns in the aftermath of the Six-Day War, which ultimately resulted in the construction of the settlement of Hebron. Chapter 2 shows how religious Zionists seeking a form of modern-day pioneering negotiated the rural community settlement in the mid-1970s. In the early 1980s, government subsidies, along with suburbanization trends, paved the way for other Israelis—without particular ideological motivation—to move to large suburban settlements, the topic of chapter 3. Moving forward in time, to the days when the First Intifada was unfolding, chapter 4 explores the design and evolution of ultra-Orthodox city-settlements. Finally, chapter 5 addresses the "unauthorized outposts": the villages where, starting in the mid-1990s, many second-generation settlers have been building their homes, often without government permission.

Although this book covers some five decades of settlement construction, it is not comprehensive. It doesn't account for the small settlements that Israel built in the valleys along the Jordan River and the Dead Sea in the late 1960s and 1970s, mostly as a way of creating a defense line against possible invasions from Jordan. These settlements pose important questions concerning the involvement of the labor-led governments in settlement construction. But since they have had a marginal demographic impact on the West Bank—by the end of 2020, they housed less than 3 percent of the settlers (not including East Jerusalem)—I have left them for future research.[56] In addition, the case studies I discuss in this book do not represent the forty Jewish settlements that Israel built in the Sinai Peninsula and the Gaza Strip, only to evacuate them in 1982 and 2005 respectively.[57] Nor do they include the thirty-two Golan Heights settlements that Israel annexed in 1981; those settlements occupy a different geographical territory, with a different legal status and a different historical trajectory. In a related vein, this study does not cover the architecture of post-1967 East Jerusalem, which, unlike the remaining parts of the West Bank, was annexed to Israel almost immediately after the Six-Day War (despite the opposition of the international community, which, for the most part, considered the annexation invalid). It thus has been subjected to different juridical systems and often designed by different architects for different users, almost none of whom are considered "settlers" in Israel.[58]

In this book, I explore how Jewish Israelis have built their homes outside their national borders, on lands that Israel never annexed, near or in between Palestinian towns and villages. I therefore must ask how these Israelis and their architects see and interact with the Palestinians. To answer this question, I draw on interviews, not only with Israelis but also with Palestinians who in many cases provided the physical labor to build the designs formulated by settlers and architects, or who have engaged in other kinds of commercial relationships with settlers, for example, selling them building materials and furniture. Nevertheless, this study is not about the Palestinians themselves, whose lands were seized to make space for settlements and whose national aspirations have been undermined by their presence. This omission does not stem from a disregard for the suffering of the Palestinians or from any refusal to acknowledge the negative effects of the settlement enterprise. I see these as indisputable truths. The near absence of Palestinians and their architecture from this study is rather the consequence of a structural limitation: as a Jewish Israeli, there are places I cannot go.[59] Moreover, a history of Palestinian architecture under the Israeli occupation, from 1967 to the present, would be a different project. In this study, therefore, my work is confined within the borders of Israeli society.

Finally, this book is not a work of activism. It does not outline a clear line of action. Nor does it offer professional advice for architects or urban planners who may wish to undo or to support settlements. Instead, it takes West Bank settlements as a case study to explore the relationship between politics and the built environment, to understand changes in housing and community forms in Israel, and to analyze the possible consequences of user-led environments. It is my hope that by gaining such a nuanced understanding of the built environment, however, readers may begin to envision a different future for the region.

CHAPTER 1

URBAN TRANSPLANTS

When Zehava Nativ first arrived in the Palestinian town of Hebron, in 1967, she felt that she was returning to a place she had left many years ago. "I had this sharp feeling of: 'this landscape is familiar to me from long ago' even though I was never there," she wrote in retrospect. "I was both surprised and astonished to notice this feeling among many other Jews: soldiers who fought [for] Judea and Samaria, and travelers who flooded the heart of the land in great numbers immediately after the battles ended. . . . [There was] a sharp, crystal clear feeling of returning home, of returning to our childhood landscape."[1]

Nativ was a schoolteacher who had grown up in a moshav, a cooperative agricultural village, in northern Israel; she would spend the next five decades in the area of Hebron. Together with her husband, she would raise their eight children in the settlement of Kiryat Arba, a community of several thousand Jews built right next to Hebron in 1971.[2] Whenever time would allow, she would go on long strolls through the ancient city, walking along its narrow alleyways and colorful markets, sometimes stopping by the Tomb of the Patriarchs, the reputed burial site of the biblical patriarchs and matriarchs—Abraham, Isaac, Jacob, Sarah, Rebekah, and Leah—revered by Jews, Christians, and Muslims. In the late 1970s, she would take part in the founding of another settlement, the Jewish settlement of Hebron that was built in the heart of the Old City, near the Tomb of the Patriarchs.[3] Over the years, however, the city she felt so rooted in would change in front of her eyes, in unexpected ways. As more and more Israeli settlers moved into the settlements of Kiryat Arba and Hebron, tensions between the settlers and the Palestinian residents of the city escalated, reaching deadly violence. These clashes ultimately led to the fortification of the Jewish settlements and their environs. Scores of military checkpoints now dot the city, and a maze of concrete barriers and fences, topped with barbed wire, separates Jews from Muslims.

In this chapter, I explore how this crude form of segregation came into being. I ask, first, who were these Israelis who wanted to settle in the West Bank in the immediate aftermath of the Six-Day War, and how did they envision their life in the occupied territories? I then show how they both confronted and collaborated with government officials, urban planners, and architects over design, first in Kiryat Arba and later in the settlement of Hebron, and how, in the end, they inhabited their spaces in ways that overwrote the intentions of all parties involved.

The settlements of Kiryat Arba and Hebron are unlike other settlements I discuss in this book. These two settlements grew out of a particular moment, in the immediate years following the Six-Day War, when a large number of Israelis took a special interest in Palestinian towns, including Nablus, Bethlehem, and Hebron. In subsequent decades, the idea of settling in Palestinian towns would subside. By chronicling the evolution of design in Kiryat Arba and Hebron, I therefore take us back to a moment that may seem foreign to present-day observers—a time before the settlements had come to be associated with segregated hilltop communities, when Jewish Israelis imagined they could in fact inhabit Palestinian towns in the occupied West Bank.

THE SETTLERS

When Israel captured the West Bank in 1967, it found a relatively underdeveloped territory. Since the 1948 Arab-Israeli War, the West Bank had been under Jordanian rule. Jordanian authorities had officially annexed the West Bank, endowing its inhabitants with citizenship but little material benefit. They invested most public resources in the East Bank of the Jordan River (in present-day Jordan). "Consequently, no industrial progress was recorded" in the West Bank, as the geographer Elisha Efrat noted in a development plan the Israeli Ministry of Interior commissioned in 1967 (but ultimately abandoned).[4] About half of the population were farmers, with another fifth otherwise employed in farmwork. Most were small landholders, cultivating plots of 10–40 dunams (10,000–40,000 square meters). Agricultural production was unmodernized, and the output was low.[5] Moreover, the road network was poor; refugee camps, housing thousands of Palestinians who fled or were forcefully expelled from Israel in 1948, were scattered across the West Bank. Many of the camps suffered from poverty and neglect.[6] On top of that, some 250,000 of the inhabitants of the West Bank—about 30 percent of its population on the eve of the Six-Day War—fled to Jordan during that war and in the following months, leaving behind traumatized communities, faced with an uncertain future (figure 1.1).[7]

FIGURE 1.1. Palestinian refugees cross the Jordan River, which separates the occupied West Bank from the Jordanian East Bank, June 22, 1967. (Photograph by Dieter Hespe, Israel State Archives.)

But that is not what many Israelis saw when they began making visits to the West Bank in the months immediately after the Six-Day War. They saw around them the ancient heartland of the Jewish people. According to the scriptures, the ancient Israelites—to whom Jews trace their ancestry—invaded and settled the region late in the second millennium BCE, and they ruled it for parts of the next thousand years. At first, Jerusalem and the southern highlands of the West Bank functioned as the political center of the Israelite state.[8] The Israelites later split into two political entities, the Kingdom of Judah in the south and the Kingdom of Israel in the north; and now a new capital city called Samaria was established in the northern highlands of the West Bank.[9] Despite some military successes, including the conquest of lands east of the Jordan River, the Israelites ultimately succumbed to foreign powers. After the Roman Empire conquered the region in 63 BCE, and after two unsuccessful Jewish revolts, in 66–73 and 132–135 CE, much of the Israelite population was exiled to the diaspora, where they would spend the next two millennia.[10]

With the Six-Day War, that ancient heartland had once again been captured, and many Israelis were euphoric. That sense of bliss was probably

FIGURE 1.2. Keren Hayesod-United Israel Appeal workers on a tour to Hebron, 1967. The Tomb of the Patriarchs, also known as the Ibrahimi Mosque, is the large stone structure in the background. (From the collections of the Central Zionist Archives, Jerusalem [NKH\452758].)

bolstered by the fact that Israel's sweeping victory in the war caught many by surprise. In the weeks leading up to the Six-Day War, many in Israel had feared that if an armed conflict with the Arab neighbors erupted, Israel would suffer great losses.[11] Now, after that threat was overturned, every weekend, hundreds, if not thousands, of triumphant Israelis would flock to Palestinian towns, including Hebron, the alleged burial site of the biblical patriarchs and matriarchs, and Bethlehem, the presumptive birthplace of King David and burial site of the biblical Rachel (figure 1.2). In the summer of 1967, newspapers reported that some 20,000 Israelis had visited Hebron in just one weekend.[12] For some, these visits were a kind of weekend getaway, a change of scenery, a glimpse into an oriental landscape just a bus ride away from the modern city of Tel Aviv; they walked around old mosques, bought handmade goods in colorful markets, and ate *maqluba* and *musakhan* at restaurants in the centuries-old city centers. For others like Nativ, however, these visits offered something profound. Upon seeing the holy sites that dotted the towns in the West Bank, they experienced a kind of spiritual awakening.[13] With that awakening came a strong sense of attachment.

It was not long before some of these private citizens began to organize into groups to advocate for settling Jews in the West Bank. The most vocal were members of the religious Zionist faction. Until the 1960s, religious Zionists were considered marginal in Israeli society. They abided by a moderate ideology that aimed at closing the gap between secular Zionism and Jewish orthodoxy. Secular Zionists, influenced by modern political thought, for the most part, sought to establish the state of Israel through mundane human initiatives; the orthodoxy, following traditional Jewish laws, saw any worldly attempt to bring about the redemption of the Jewish people as misguided.[14] Religious Zionists embraced Zionism as one step in a larger, nonearthly path to redemption, but insisted that the journey could not be achieved through military force alone.[15] Their conciliatory approach, however, failed to gain much traction beyond a small cohort of followers, and they had little influence on Israeli government agencies after independence.[16]

Yet, in the years leading up to the Six-Day War, some religious Zionists began adopting a less conciliatory attitude—one that elevated the settling of the Land of Israel to the status of a religious commandment. Central to this ideological transformation was Rabbi Tzvi Yehuda Kook, who edited the arguments of his late father, the former chief Ashkenazi rabbi of Palestine Avraham Yitzhak Hacohen Kook, and converted them into a concrete political program.[17] Tzvi Yehuda Kook argued that settling the Land of Israel was a matter of "divine politics" and thus took precedence over mortal and moral considerations.[18] By the 1960s, he had gathered a circle of young followers who shared his views.[19] When the Six-Day War broke out, they saw it as a religious moment, their moment. It was God, they believed, who had secured Israel's victory in the war, paving the way to redemption. And now it was up to them, the people of Israel, to take the next step along that path by populating the West Bank, the heartland of the ancient Israelites, with Jewish Israelis.[20]

At the same time, other groups were forming to advocate settling the occupied territories for more secular reasons. Almost immediately after the war, intellectuals associated with both the Left and the Right founded a movement called the Movement for the Whole Land of Israel, which called for mass settlement of the occupied territories. The group's members believed that settling Jews in the West Bank was a necessary step toward building a strong and durable country.[21] The movement gained the support of notable university professors, artists, writers, military generals, and politicians; its members organized rallies, circulated petitions, and printed journals featuring essays advocating for settlement plans.[22]

Another group, the Canaanites, or the "Young Hebrews"—an ideological affiliation popular among leading Israeli artists since the late 1930s—based their settlement advocacy on mythical origins. They aimed at reviving a long-forgotten Hebrew nation that, before the rise of Judaism, had stretched across the Levant, encompassing multiple ethnic groups. To re-create that imagined nation, they argued, the Jewish people must abandon Judaism and return to a more authentic, place-based culture.[23] The Canaanites believed that settling Jews in the West Bank, the Sinai Peninsula, and the Gaza Strip would be an important step in facilitating not the redemption of the Jewish people but their dissolution into a new regional formation that would combine Israeli and Palestinian cultures.[24]

For a short period of time following the Six-Day War, these diverse groups—representing a broad range of often conflicting ideologies and visions—joined forces to settle Jews in Palestinian towns. Their members met with government officials, toured the West Bank, and even attempted to purchase houses from Palestinian residents.

But on the eve of the Six-Day War, the government had no intention of capturing, much less settling, the West Bank.[25] And so now, after the war, it had no clear idea of what to do with it. Between June 16 and 19, just days after the war ended, cabinet ministers discussed Israel's war gains. They quickly reached a consensus regarding the Sinai Peninsula and Golan Heights: to withdraw from the territories in return for peace with Egypt and Syria; but they decided to defer any decision regarding the West Bank.[26] There were just too many conflicting opinions. Prime Minister Levi Eshkol thought Israel had to exercise military control over most parts of the West Bank, mostly for security purposes, but he didn't want to absorb its population, then about 600,000.[27] "We got a lovely dowry," he commented. "The trouble is that with the dowry comes the wife."[28] Minister Menachem Begin called for annexing the entire territory, regardless of its Palestinian population, basing his argument on the connection between the Jewish people and its historic heartland. Minister of Foreign Affairs Abba Eban thought the territory could be returned to the Jordanians. Minister of Labor Yigal Allon and Minister of Defense Moshe Dayan opposed Eban, but also opposed full annexation.[29] On July 26, 1967, Allon submitted what came to be known as the Allon Plan to the cabinet. The plan proposed annexing the relatively less populated areas of the West Bank—a 10–15-kilometer-wide strip of land along the Jordan River, as well as areas along the Dead Sea and around Jerusalem—while establishing a Palestinian entity on the remaining parts. A few weeks later, Dayan proposed erecting a few clusters ("fists") of Israeli settlements and military bases in densely populated areas near large Palestinian cities, including Hebron, Nablus, Ramallah, and Jenin.[30] Neither of these plans was officially adopted by the cabinet as a guideline for settlement activity, although some settlement activity between 1967 and 1977 surely followed the Allon Plan.[31] "My government has decided not to decide," Prime Minister Eshkol later confessed to President Lyndon Johnson of the United States.[32] And so, for a while, the pleas of Israelis wishing to settle in the West Bank, whether motivated by security, religious, mythological, or artistic sentiments, were met with a bureaucratic stone wall, pending some kind of decision.

FIRST FORAY

The first crack in the government's opposition to settling Jews in the West Bank took place in September 1967, when Prime Minister Eshkol authorized the resettlement of kibbutz Kfar Etzion.[33] Kfar Etzion was one of the four kibbutzim of Etzion Bloc, a cluster of Jewish villages built during the British Mandate in the southwestern part of the West Bank. Under British Mandate rule, Zionists largely avoided settling in the mountainous areas of the West Bank. The four kibbutzim of Etzion Bloc were among the few exceptions to that rule. Kibbutz Kfar Etzion, the first of the four, was founded in 1943 by a group of religious Zionists.[34] The Riga-born architect Meir Ben Uri drew its original master plan. An observant Jew, Ben Uri placed a domed synagogue at the heart of the kibbutz, with housing units, workshops, orchards, and olive groves arranged around it.[35] But, in 1948, five years after the kibbutz was founded, and before Ben Uri's plan was completed, Arab forces conquered the kibbutz, along with the other kibbutzim of the Etzion Bloc, during the 1948 Arab-Israeli War. The women and children had been evacuated to Jerusalem before the fighting escalated. Many of the men who stayed behind were executed. In the following years, survivors were prohibited from returning to the kibbutz that was now under Jordanian rule.[36]

Once the Six-Day War ended, some of the survivors began organizing regular visits to the site they had left nineteen years earlier, where they discovered the remains of an abandoned Jordanian military camp (figure 1.3). Some demanded that the old kibbutz be rebuilt. Seeing an opportunity to establish a first seed in the West Bank, members of the Movement for the

FIGURE 1.3. Descendants and survivors of Kfar Etzion standing by the ruins of the old kibbutz, June 22, 1967. Abandoned Jordanian military barracks can be seen in the background. (Gush Etzion Archives.)

Whole Land of Israel, a few religious Zionists, and the Canaanite Aharon Amir offered their support by arranging meetings between the survivors and Israeli government officials.[37] Government officials were sympathetic but hesitant. "The government is still up in the air on the matter. Soon we'll decide what to do with the territories," Prime Minister Eshkol told the four middle-aged survivors of the Etzion Bloc who came to his office in mid-August of 1967.[38] A couple of weeks later, however, his attitude changed. On September 1, eight Arab leaders gathered for a summit in the Sudanese capital of Khartoum to debate the Six-Day War losses. By the end of that summit, they announced the famous "Three No's": "no peace with Israel, no recognition of Israel, no negotiations with it." The summit's resolution made Eshkol more favorable toward the Etzion Bloc survivors, and soon thereafter they secured government approval for settlement (which, at first, was falsely labeled as a paramilitary outpost so as to avoid international criticism).[39] On September 27, 1967, less than four months after the Six-Day War ended, the site was inaugurated with a ceremony held on the site and attended by parliament member Michael Chasani and Minister of Religion Zorach Warhaftig.[40]

Once the high-profile attendees had left, the new settlers began refurbishing the abandoned camp at Kfar Etzion. One military barrack became the men's sleeping hall, and another barrack served the women. A third was converted into a hub combining a communal kitchen, a synagogue, and a community center. Within a few days, young kibbutz members opened a metal workshop and established a herd of cattle.[41] The ruined camp had become a village.

Soon after, the government commissioned architectural plans for the kibbutz. Since the 1920s, the planning of kibbutzim had been overseen and funded by centralized Zionist organizations. Such planning was entrusted initially to architects and planners at the Israel Land Development Company, and later to the Jewish Agency's Settlement Department. In the 1940s and 1950s, architects and planners working for three umbrella organizations of the kibbutzim joined these planning efforts.[42] But in the late 1960s, the Ministry of Housing established the Division of Rural Planning, taking over some of the planning responsibilities in kibbutzim, including overseeing the design of Kfar Etzion.[43] Israel Goodovitch was asked to administer the project. He was thirty-three, and it was one of his first projects as chief architect at the Division of Rural Planning. The young Tel Aviv–based architect was avowedly secular. He did not associate himself with religious Zionism nor with the Movement for the Whole Land of Israel. Nevertheless, he was moved by Israel's conquest of the West Bank and by the young settlers. "It is hard to explain the feeling I had back then," Goodovitch told me when we met, some five decades later. "There was that amazing feeling of open space after 1967. There were these incredible energies in the air." He did not foresee the negative effects of the settlement movement. Like many at the time, he failed to see the Palestinians as a national collective and believed the occupation could benefit the two populations—that it would create economic opportunities and facilitate new collaboration between Jews and Arabs. And so, he approached the project without misgivings.[44]

On Goodovitch's recommendation, the ministry recruited two architects, Michael Bar and Wladislav Hershkovitz, from the Tel Aviv–based firm Bar-Hershkovitz Architects, to draw up detailed plans for the kibbutz. Under Goodovitch's supervision, they quickly drafted a master plan that reproduced the typical organization of kibbutzim into differentiated living and working zones.[45] The idea of separating the living zones from working zones had emerged in the 1920s and 1930s in the first kibbutzim. The living zone usually included uniform residential units, as well as schools and communal facilities in the center, all laid out on a shared piece of land uninterrupted by lot demarcation lines.[46] In the new settlement of Kfar Etzion, the architects added another component to the kibbutz plan: they

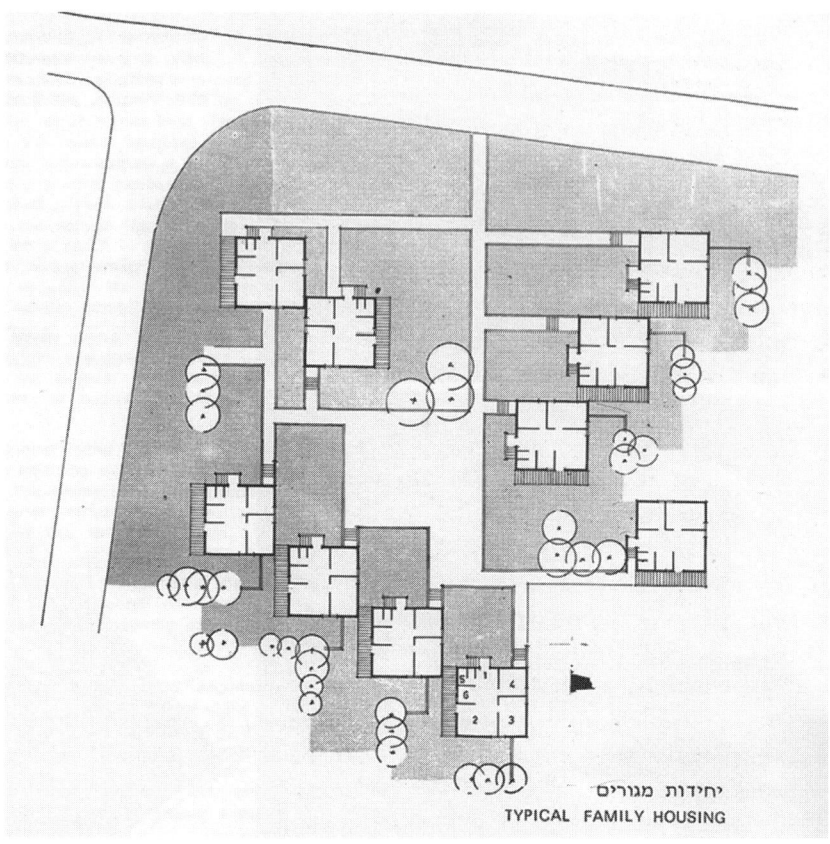

FIGURE 1.4. Michael Bar and Wladislav Hershkovitz, plan of a housing cluster in the settlement of Kfar Etzion, ca. 1968. (*Israel Builds 1977* [Tel Aviv: Ministry of Housing, 1977], 249.)

left untouched the southern edge of the settlement, where the center of the old kibbutz once stood. Dedicated to those who died in 1948, it was to serve as a site of commemoration.[47]

In line with Israeli architects' growing interest in vernacular architecture (a theme with its roots in the late 1950s), the team designed the residential units so that they would resemble the homes of an Arab village from a distance.[48] They organized the settlement into clusters of identical, two-story, flat-roofed buildings arranged around a central courtyard (figure 1.4). Cars were parked outside the clusters.[49] Each building housed two separate units, one on the lower level and one on the upper. Different sets of stairs allowed access to the units. The exterior walls of the lower level were clad

FIGURE 1.5. Housing units in Kfar Etzion. (*Israel Builds 1977* [Tel Aviv: Ministry of Housing, 1977], 250.)

with unrefined rock, while the upper level was veneered with a thin layer of plaster (figure 1.5). "The stone cladding gave the impression that the houses emerged from the rocky landscape," explained Yehoshua Altman, a resident who was in charge of construction work. "From a distance," he added, "it looked like an Arab village."[50]

Security concerns played an equally important role in the design of Kfar Etzion. For a while, the kibbutz was the sole Jewish settlement in the area, so planners feared that the neighboring Palestinians might launch attacks against the settlers, and that the place might fall once again into the hands of the enemy. They therefore designed the houses with thick concrete walls resistant to light artillery and placed underground shelters beneath some of the courtyards.[51] In addition, they placed a large structure housing an educational center and guest house, designed by Bauhaus graduate Arieh Sharon and his son Eldar Sharon, at the southeastern edge of the settlement; they believed the large structure, organized around three inner courtyards that followed the natural topography, could provide a first line of defense in case of an attack.[52] It was "a time of great fear," Altman recalled.[53]

The settlers did not share the architects' interest in vernacular architecture. A number of them were upset by the small size of the residential units, by the architects' decision to arrange the units in two-story structures, and by the plan's crude geometry. But they abided by the established model of architect-client relations, in which the client accepted the architect's design whether they liked it or not. "Back in the 1960s," one of Kfar Etzion's original settlers told me, "you would not fight with the Ministry of Housing about these things."[54] That would change in Hebron, where a new relationship between architect and client would emerge.

"JEWISH HEBRON"

Although many settlement activists saw the foundation of Kfar Etzion as a major milestone, the new kibbutz lacked the deep history of towns like Hebron or Nablus. It was also small and appealed only to people wishing to live in a kibbutz.[55] Those seeking national redemption needed something on a larger scale.

They did not have to wait long. Rabbi Moshe Levinger, an alumnus of Merkaz Harav Yeshiva, the stronghold of the religious Zionist movement as reinvented by Yehuda Kook, joined the settlers at Kfar Etzion. During the first Shabbat dinner in the new kibbutz, only four days after it was founded, Rabbi Levinger began making plans for a settlement in the Palestinian town of Hebron—then the second-largest city in the West Bank (excluding Jerusalem), and home to some 39,000 Palestinians.[56] A few days later, the thirty-two-year-old rabbi met with other activists in Tel Aviv. They elected a committee of seven members to oversee the creation of the Hebron settlement. The committee included religious Zionists as well as members of the more secular Movement for the Whole Land of Israel. That winter, the committee deliberated on settlement tactics; met with government officials, requesting permission to settle in Hebron; and explored the Old City, searching for apartments they could buy or rent.[57]

This plan was not entirely far-fetched. A small Jewish community had existed in Hebron since at least medieval times. Beginning in the sixteenth century, the Jews of Hebron resided in a gated compound.[58] The small compound, about one-quarter of a square kilometer, was walled off by the houses on the perimeter, resembling the Jewish ghettos built in Italian cities at around the same time. Three gates allowed people in and out of the compound during the day. At night and on Shabbat, the gates were closed. The houses inside, some with four stories, were densely built, leaving only narrow alleys and small gathering spaces between them. By the nineteenth century, the compound housed both Ashkenazi Jews and Sephardic Jews (of Spanish and Portuguese origin), who conducted their prayers and religious ceremonies in separate synagogues.[59] In the late nineteenth and early twentieth centuries, families gradually began moving out of this compound—which came to be known as the old Jewish quarter or the Jewish court—into three nearby areas.[60] By the early 1920s, more than four hundred Jews lived in Hebron, scattered across these four zones.[61] The community suffered great losses in 1929, when Arab mobs killed more than sixty Jewish Hebronites and injured many more during the 1929 Arab riots in Palestine; and in 1936, in the wake of an Arab revolt, British authorities permanently evacuated the Jews from the city.[62] After Israel captured the West Bank in 1967, survivors and descendants of Hebron's Jewish community began claiming rights to properties in the city once owned by their parents and grandparents.[63] They founded the Committee for the Restoration of Hebron and demanded that the Israeli government restore the Jewish cemetery that had been vandalized, remove any new structures that had been built on their properties, and re-populate the area with Jewish Israelis.[64]

The Committee for the Restoration of Hebron was a natural ally for Levinger and the committee he had formed to build a settlement in the West Bank town. At one point, Levinger toured the Old City with Avraham Franko, a Jerusalem-based lawyer born and raised in Hebron who, after the expulsion of the Jewish community from the city, was made the legal representative of the Sephardic community's abandoned property in Hebron. Franko, who was keen on renewing Jewish presence in his hometown, was impressed by the activists, and announced that he would give the property to any Jew that the government permitted to reside in Hebron.[65] But the government did not grant such a permit—not to Franko nor to Levinger and his collaborators.

It had good reasons not to give that permission. On top of the opposition (or hesitancy) of some of its own ministers, the mayor of Hebron, Muhammad Ali al-Jabari, mocked the entire idea. "I don't see any reasonable grounds to oppose the return of Jews, now after the war, to their childhood home—on the condition that Arabs will also be granted permission to return to their homes in Israeli towns [which they fled or were expelled from in 1948]," Jabari told a news reporter, striking a sensitive chord among Israelis.[66] It was one thing to get a government permission to resettle the small kibbutz of Kfar Etzion, and quite another to get an authorization to settle in a dense Palestinian town.

In April 1968, after the government repeatedly rejected their requests to settle in Hebron, some settlement activists decided to try an unconventional tactic. They rented all seventeen rooms of the Park Hotel, a Palestinian-owned lodging house located inside Hebron, and once installed there, they refused to leave.[67] In a matter of days, they transformed the hotel into an almost fully functioning settlement. They opened a school in the communal spaces, transformed the kitchen into a kosher one, and even provided work for the residents by setting up an assembly line in the staircase where they constructed prefabricated cardboard boxes.[68] The hotel was now their home.

Many of the hotel residents chose to ignore the predominantly Muslim history of Hebron. As they walked around the streets surrounding the hotel, they imagined that the city's massive stone buildings, with their large arches and vaulted domes, had been there since King David's rule. In other words, they imagined that the architecture of Hebron's Palestinians was really the architecture of the ancient Israelites. This was a view expressed by both secular and religious activists.[69] Rabbi Shmuel Avidor Hacohen, who visited the town, noted the "view of all the houses" and stated: "The beauty of the city, and the way it sits on the natural topography, can perhaps explain why it was chosen to be the capital city of King David."[70] In his mind, evidently, Hebron had remained untouched for three millennia. To restore a connection with this ancient history, however, the settlers would have to move out of the hotel. After all, as Levinger commented, "one cannot live for such a long time in a hotel."[71]

The architect David Cassuto was a recent graduate of Haifa's Technion—the Israel Institute of Technology. He joined the settlers in the hotel for a couple of days and soon proposed a way of expanding their settlement and making it permanent. An observant Jew, Cassuto believed Jewish Israelis had the right to settle in the West Bank, especially in Hebron, the town of the patriarchs. In addition, he welcomed the opportunity to experiment with a historic urban landscape that had long fascinated him. Early in his career, Cassuto had developed an interest in pilgrimage and heritage sites. That same year he joined the settlers in Hebron, he published an architectural survey of the Palestinian town of Bethlehem, the burial town of the biblical matriarch Rachel. Written in the first person, the survey described his journey through the narrow alleys of the old town. Cassuto marveled at its "miraculous alleyways" and its houses "covered with an Eastern atmosphere and memories of ancient times."[72] Cassuto, thus, was keen on the possibility of working in Hebron. Why not, he asked, build a Jewish neighborhood in the heart of the Old City?

Together with his professional partner, Israel Levitt, Cassuto quickly drew up plans for a neighborhood he called "Jewish Hebron" or "Upper Hebron." He arranged settlers' houses there in two sections, and between them he laid out two greenbelts that flanked an area allocated for public buildings. At the outer edge of the neighborhood, he placed an industrial zone.[73] Cassuto thought that individual buildings should replicate those in other neighborhoods in Hebron and follow the mountainous topography of the region.[74]

By late April 1968, Cassuto had sent his plan to Minister of Labor Yigal Allon.[75] At the same time, a settlers' representative shared details of the plan with a news reporter.[76] Minister Allon, who had proposed establishing a Jewish neighborhood in Hebron's area a few months earlier and even paid a visit to the settlers in the hotel just days after they first checked in, took interest in the project.[77] According to Cassuto, other politicians were also intrigued by the plan. But the Ministry of Housing dismissed it. Given the dovish views of architects and other officials at the ministry, Cassuto expected opposition. But he also wasn't surprised that the plan was dismissed because it had not been commissioned; it was not an established practice for private citizens to volunteer plans of this kind. As he later reflected, "It was a plan without a father or a mother."[78]

Nevertheless, Cassuto explained, the plan had a lasting effect: it captured the attention of the public and of several politicians. It amplified the demands of those keen on establishing a stronghold in Hebron. And indeed, not long after the plan had been dismissed, the government ultimately agreed to develop an alternative solution.[79]

RELUCTANT ARCHITECTS

In September 1968, a special ministers' committee commissioned a team of architects and planners to design a Jewish neighborhood near the Tomb of the Patriarchs, not far from the area where Cassuto had planned his "Jewish Hebron."[80] After a preliminary survey of the site, the team members found that it was too small; at best, they reported, it could house 150 to 180 Jewish families, packed into high-density units with minimal communal amenities.[81] To enlarge the neighborhood, the planners suggested leasing available plots from local Palestinians. They also recommended creating a fund that would encourage collaboration between Jews and Muslims on projects in the area of the Tomb of the Patriarchs.[82] But these plans were soon abandoned.

In December, the committee commissioned a different team of architects to "find a site for a settlement, separated . . . [but] at a reasonable distance from the city of Hebron."[83] The team conducted a comprehensive study of Hebron, analyzing social and economic trends prevalent among the Muslim residents of the city, the topographic and climatic conditions of the region, land rights, road systems, building styles, and other urban issues the members deemed important.[84] The team produced a thirty-six-page report that identified three potential sites for a settlement capable of housing 50,000 residents: one adjacent to Hebron, the other two at a distance from the city.[85] But the report also warned that building on any of the three sites would inflict some degree of harm on the local Palestinian community: "Such a settlement, no matter what, will damage the local fabric: At first, the local economy will be damaged, and then, gradually, a change in the relations between the different local Arab settlements, followed by a change in the [cultural] values of the local residents, will occur."[86] The site closest to Hebron, the report noted, was the least suitable, because it would interfere with the existing town's development, require the confiscation of privately owned Palestinian lands, instigate conflicts with the Islamic religious trust, and result in a "clash of cultures."[87]

To the architects' dismay, this was the site that government officials selected and where they soon found themselves at work.[88] To reduce the settlement's potentially negative impact on the region, the architects tried to integrate it with Hebron. If handled correctly, they believed, an integrative design approach might encourage a cultural melding of adjacent sites—one for Jews, the other for Muslims, a pairing they had originally opposed.[89] They divided the new Jewish settlement, designed to house some 50,000 Jews, into seven neighborhoods, the first one extending to the Tomb of the Patriarchs in the Old City (figure 1.6).[90] They placed each neighborhood on a different hilltop, with valleys separating it from the other neighborhoods. It was a common practice among state planners in the 1950s and 1960s to organize new towns around well-defined neighborhood units of 5,000–10,000 residents each, surrounded by greenbelts.[91] Inspiration for this design came from Britain, where planners sought to avoid urban congestion and anonymity by erecting new towns of modest size outside large city centers, preferably in rustic settings, and dividing them into neighborhood units. Inside the neighborhood unit—a planning concept that originated in the United States and was enthusiastically adopted by British planners—residents were to enjoy face-to-face neighborly relations and, along the way, develop a sense of solidarity (at times, at the price of excluding many others).[92] Although Israeli cities were hardly as polluted and overcrowded, the atomized urban layout of the British new towns—which, in the postwar years, had spread to many other cities across the world—to some degree matched the Labor Zionists' preference for nonurban environments. The socializing function of the neighborhood unit also seemed to correspond with the government's melting-pot ideology, devised to absorb Jewish immigrants who came from different parts of the world after independence.[93] In any case, in Kiryat Arba planners connected the neighborhood units with a grand boulevard that was

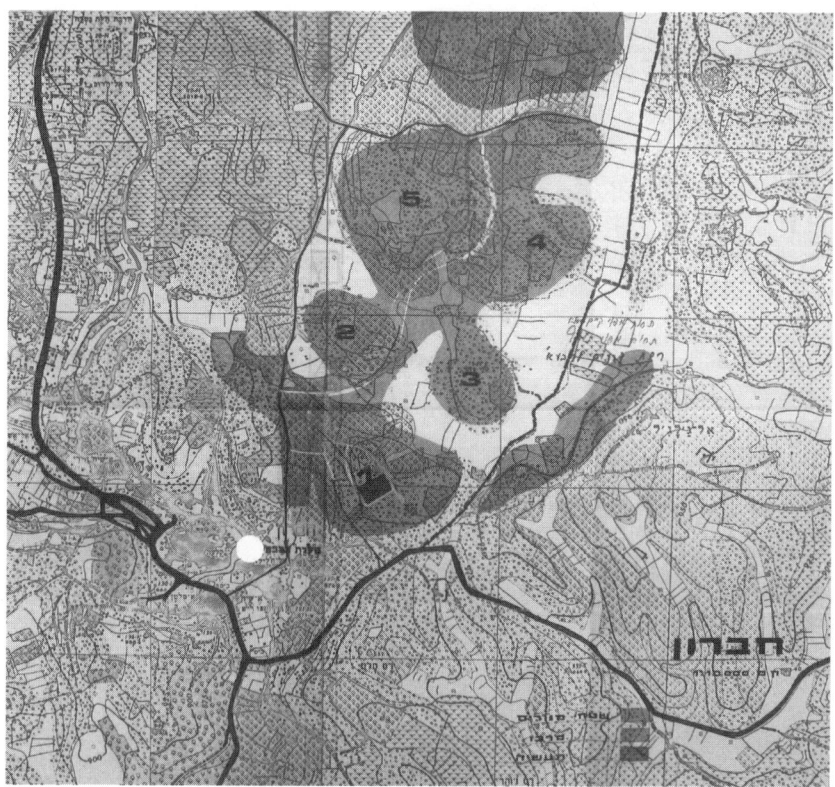

FIGURE 1.6. Plan for a settlement for 50,000 Israeli residents, June 24, 1970; neighborhoods of the Jewish settlement are shaded, and the white dot marks the location of the Tomb of the Patriarchs. (Israel State Archives.)

to start at the Tomb of the Patriarchs in the heart of the Old City and proceed northward through the settlement to its northernmost neighborhood, ultimately joining the two cities. One of the architects, Rita Dunsky-Feuerstein, named it "400 Shekels Boulevard," for the amount of money that Abraham was asked to pay for the tomb, according to the biblical story.[94]

When the mayor of Hebron, Muhammad Ali al-Jabari, was shown the architects' plans, he was outraged. The proposed integration of the new Jewish settlement with the Palestinian town was offensive, potentially even incendiary. In a meeting with Israeli officials that included the ministers of housing and defense, Jabari warned that it would not only undermine municipal governance, but it also risked inciting the local population. In response, the Ministry of Housing eliminated the plan to integrate the settlement with the town.[95]

FIGURE 1.7. Aerial view of Kiryat Arba and Hebron, 1984. (Photograph by Werner Braun, from the collections of the Central Zionist Archives, Jerusalem [PHIS/1467467].)

In what was likely a symbolic gesture aimed at reinforcing the separation between the two, it was soon decided that the Jewish settlement would be named not Upper Hebron or Jewish Hebron but Kiryat Arba (Town of Four), a name that appears in the Bible as a nickname for Hebron.[96] According to the biblical archaeologist Benjamin Mazar, the name refers to the four geographic sections that constituted the ancient city. Nevertheless, as Mazar explains, and as the officials must have known, the name Kiryat Arba does not carry the same significance as Hebron: the name is not as old, and it appears less commonly in Jewish scriptures.[97]

Over the next few months, architects at the Ministry of Housing drafted new plans for a settlement that would be separated—both physically and aesthetically—from Hebron (figure 1.7).[98] In stark contrast to the vaulted domes and tall minarets of Hebron—a cityscape beloved and familiar to the settlers—all 250 units of the settlement's first neighborhood were organized in repetitive, prefabricated, multistory apartment buildings set amid pedestrian-oriented green spaces (figures 1.8, 1.9, and 1.10). The apartment buildings followed the design principles of high modernism: austere, functional, and devoid of ornamentation. This style, which was

FIGURE 1.8. Aerial view of Kiryat Arba, 1984. (Photograph by Werner Braun, from the collections of the Central Zionist Archives, Jerusalem [PHIS/1467472].)

brought to the country by émigré architects, had dominated Israeli architecture since the 1930s. In the prestate era, high modernism had particular
appeal in the minds of these émigré architects: according to the architectural
historian Alona Nitzan-Shiftan, its negation of detail seemed to parallel the
political project of Labor Zionism, which sought to negate class differences,
the history of diaspora, and the oriental setting of the Jewish state.[99] After
the establishment of the Israeli state in 1948, high modernism was also an
expedient form of design to quickly construct housing for the hundreds of
thousands of Jews who flocked to the country. So, by the time Kiryat Arba
was built, it had become standard design at the Ministry of Housing. In a
nod to the thick stone walls common in Hebron, however, ministry architects clad the buildings in Kiryat Arba with thin stone sheathing.[100] Other
than that detail, one of the architects involved in the settlement's planning
concluded, "the design of Kiryat Arba, its shapes and forms, did not draw
anything from Hebron, not a single element."[101]

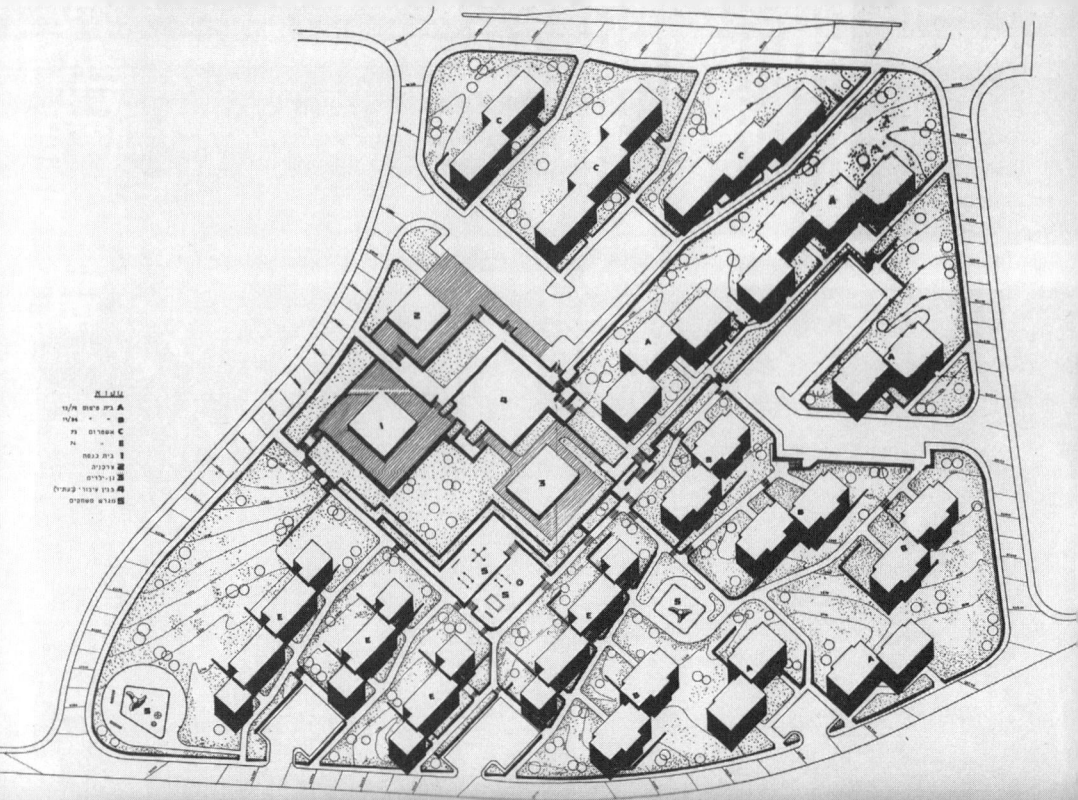

FIGURE 1.9. Bitush Comforti, site plan of Kiryat Arba's first neighborhood, ca. 1971. (*Israel Builds 1973* [Tel Aviv: Ministry of Housing, 1973], 128.)

It was not only that the architects had ignored the settlers' aesthetic preferences; they also took little account of the settlers' material needs. Much of the new settlement's design was adapted from an earlier ministry project for low-income Palestinian refugees who had been forced to leave the Old City of Jerusalem in 1967 (figure 1.11). The refugees, the ministry explained, "were unable to procure suitable living quarters through their own endeavors."[102] To better understand the refugees' special needs, architects at the ministry had consulted with representatives of the Palestinian community. The resulting units, said a ministry publication, "were planned according to the Arab way of life, i.e., their layout was based on enclosed spaces with a maximum amount of privacy" and minimum open or in-between spaces.[103] The small and claustrophobic units may have suited the immediate needs of the Palestinian refugees, but the same design was at odds with the needs of the predominantly middle-class Jewish settlers in Kiryat Arba.

The repetitive multistory apartment blocks of the new settlement were especially inadequate for the religious settlers, who had been gaining influence

FIGURE 1.10. Apartment buildings in Kiryat Arba, 1972. (From the collections of the Central Zionist Archives, Jerusalem [PHG/1066158].)

in the months leading up to the project's construction. Following the initial squatting activity at the Park Hotel, the government had moved the settlers to a nearby military base while planning (and later also the construction of housing) proceeded.[104] During their time at the base, Levinger, the rabbi of Moshav Nehalim who had taken a leading role in the initial settlement efforts, functioned as the settlers' secretary. Levinger took special care of his followers' religious needs. Under his command, for example, the settlers were able to operate a yeshiva (a religious educational institute) for thirty students at the military base. The new apartments, however, could not easily accommodate the large families common among religious Jews.[105] They also lacked basic features required for religious practices, such as the double sinks needed for kosher cooking, one for meat and the other for dairy, as well as a third sink for certain hand-washing rituals, and balconies that could accommodate sukkahs—temporary outdoor ritual huts where the father of the family can sleep and host guests—during the Jewish holiday of Sukkot.[106]

On top of that, the architects had arranged the housing units in ways that made the settlement dense and bleak. They had added a third floor atop all two-story buildings, initially designed to hold only four units, so that each now accommodated six units. In addition, while in the original refugee

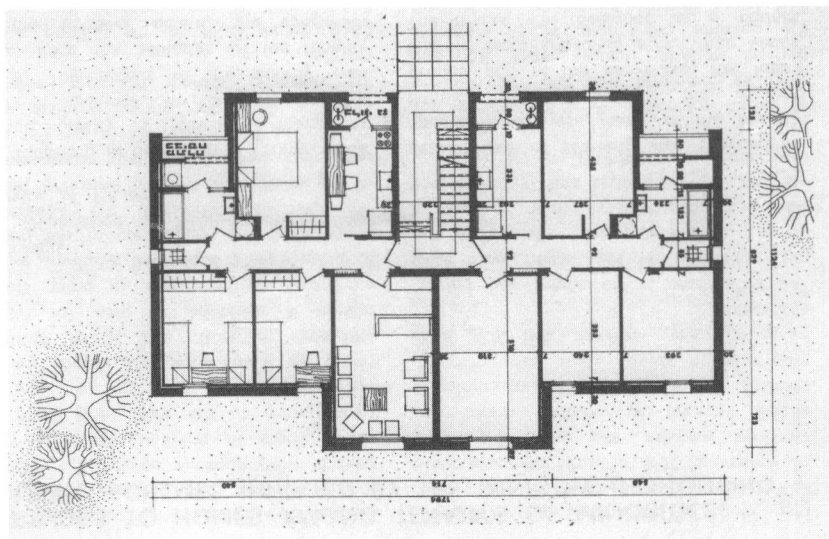

FIGURE 1.11. Floor plan of an apartment building designed for Palestinians forced from the Old City of Jerusalem and relocated to Wadi al Joz, ca. 1968. (*Israel Builds 1970* [Tel Aviv: Ministry of Housing, 1970], 4.101.)

neighborhood on which Kiryat Arba was partially based, the buildings were to be scattered "so as to create framed views of the natural and built up landscape," in Kiryat Arba, the buildings were attached to one another.[107] In this way, architects blocked the views of the Tomb of the Patriarchs and the Old City—which was precisely what drew the settlers in the first place.

REBELLIOUS USERS

Trouble began almost immediately after settlers moved into the new neighborhood in 1971. The settlers complained that the housing complex was problematic not only because it was removed from the Old City but also because the apartments were too small for their needs. Two large families, the Nahliel family with ten members and the Nachshon family with eleven, found themselves in three-bedroom units.[108] Further, many of the middle-class settlers found the simplicity of the design beneath them. As one explained to a visiting journalist: "Among us are people of means, who came here because of our dedication to the idea of renewing the Jewish settlement in the town of the patriarchs. . . . Many [of us] don't want to live in standardized public housing apartments."[109] What may have been accepted by other, more passive or more vulnerable ministry clients who had little recourse did not satisfy the new residents of Kiryat Arba.

The settlers were equally frustrated with the fact that the Ministry of Housing had instituted an admissions process. Since all apartments in the settlement were built by the ministry, anyone interested in renting one—excluding the original squatters from the Park Hotel—had to submit an application to an admissions committee managed by the ministry.[110] Favoring smaller families (with no more than three children), young couples, and individuals with the professional skills required for settlement maintenance, the committee effectively privileged secular Jews over religious ones, undermining the wishes of many settlers who envisioned a pious community.[111] "Not letting the settlers take part in Kiryat Arba's admissions committee," the activists complained, "is like stealing the fruit of a tree that was planted and nurtured over the course of three years by others."[112]

Settlers also complained about the lack of adequate public buildings, especially those needed for religious practices. Architects had not allocated space for a mikveh—a public bath for Jewish purification rituals—in the first neighborhood, and they had designed a 150-seat synagogue, which was too small to allow the entire community to worship simultaneously.[113] Residents therefore began conducting prayers in informal spaces, such as in the underground shelters built to provide protection in the event of an attack or in temporary shacks.[114]

Moreover, legal constraints seemed to be standing in the settlers' way of setting down roots in the place. For a while, because the lands on which Kiryat Arba was built were seized by military orders—granting Israeli authorities usage rights rather than ownership—the settlers could rent their units but not purchase them.[115] No less important, the settlement's master plan could not be officially approved. This meant that the architects had to work on one section of the settlement at a time, with no clear and comprehensive vision for the whole.[116] Settlers feared that this lack of formal approval signaled the government's lack of interest in the project, and that Kiryat Arba might be nothing more than a small-scale, one-off experiment.[117]

As doubts emerged, the settlement's founders began to wonder if the planners and the architects had intentionally sabotaged the settlement. "These are houses built by the Ministry of Housing like a fortress," one settler wrote across a drawing she made of the apartment buildings (figure 1.12). "These are apartments built [in such a way] so no one would live in them." Above the sketched settlement she drew seven single-story Palestinian houses. Between these houses she wrote: "This is a beautiful valley that separates Hebron, the city of the patriarchs, from the 'housing solution' known

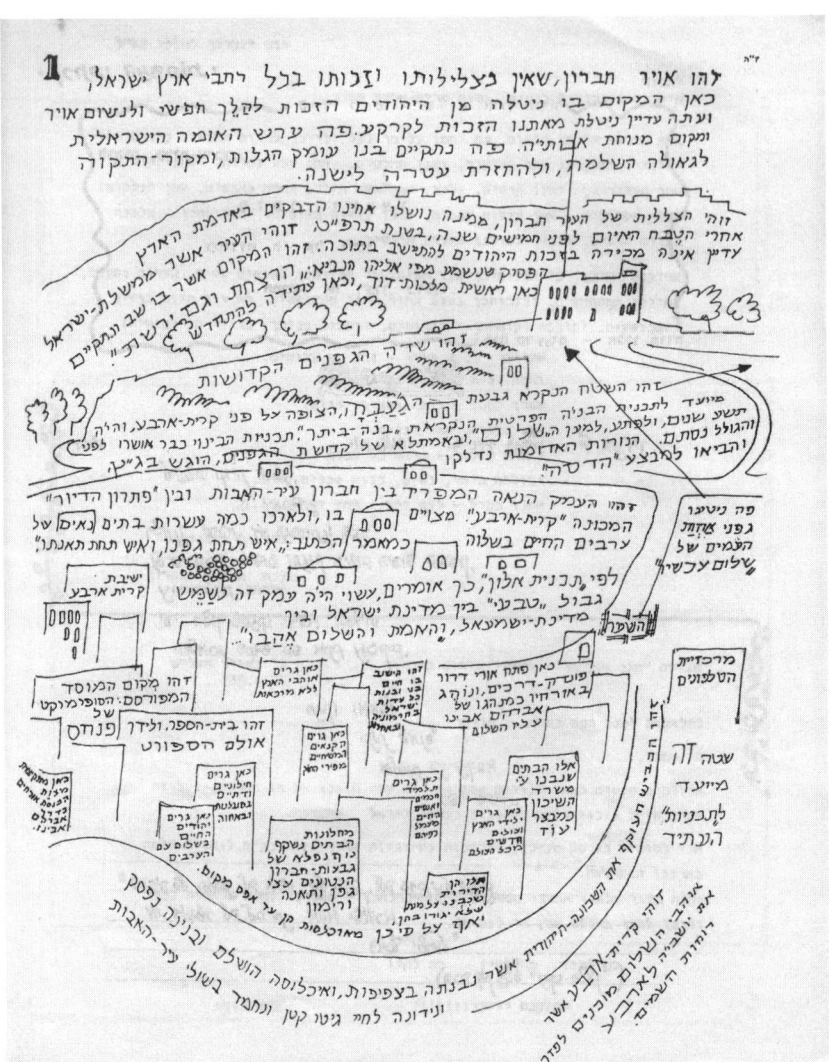

FIGURE 1.12. Annotated drawing of Kiryat Arba (bottom) and Hebron (top) by a Kiryat Arba settler, ca. 1979. (Israel State Archives.)

as 'Kiryat Arba.' " Above a serrated line marking the skyline of Hebron, she wrote: "This is the air of Hebron, the clearest and purest in the land of Israel. This is the place where Jews are not allowed to walk and breathe freely."[118] Similarly, already in February 1972, one of the founders, Elyakim Haetzni, wrote a letter to the daily newspaper *Maariv* in which he lamented that

"Kiryat Arba has no hope" and wondered, "If Kiryat Arba was so unwanted, why did the government decide to build it in the first place?"[119]

These suspicions were not without cause, nor were the conditions that raised them unique. During the 1960s and 1970s, the Ministry of Housing designed many similar housing projects, including the neighborhoods of French Hill and Neve Yaacov in East Jerusalem and Sanhedria Murhevet near the pre-1967 border between Israel and Jordan.[120] Architects working for the ministry rarely gave much consideration to residents' unique needs—religious or otherwise—before the late 1970s.[121] This was true even though some architects working for the ministry actively supported the settlement movement. Israel Levitt, who was involved in the planning of Kiryat Arba, had helped David Cassuto draft the initial plan for "Jewish Hebron," and he would later draw plans on a pro bono basis for the settlement of Ofra, in the central mountainous region of the West Bank, some 20 kilometers north of Jerusalem.[122]

The residents of Kiryat Arba, however, were either unaware of these factors or indifferent to them. They turned a blind eye to similar treatment that the ministry's other projects received. In their minds, the ministry was intentionally targeting and mistreating them. Some religious settlers saw this as related to the largely secular government's tendency to marginalize religious Zionism.[123]

The settlers of Kiryat Arba expressed their dissatisfaction in petitions to architects and government officials, in which they requested a number of changes, including the enlargement of residential units, relocation of the synagogue to a more prominent site, and an increase in the number of worship spaces. They also pressed for changes in the composition of the admissions committee and for individuals to be allowed to purchase plots inside Hebron.[124] They complained about the lack of commercial amenities and asked for permission to open small stores and restaurants in their residential units.[125] When their requests were denied or went unanswered, some settlers became more aggressive, organizing rallies and petition drives to prohibit ministry employees from entering their settlement.[126] At one point, the residents of Kiryat Arba went on strike, shutting down all health, commercial, and educational facilities.[127] They formed an alternative admissions committee, squatted in empty units, and began drafting their own plans for the settlement.[128] They also began enforcing religious laws and blocked the entrance to the settlement on Saturdays, making it a vehicle-free, Shabbat-observing zone.[129]

These efforts were short-lived and failed to yield lasting results. Ministry planners, architects, and officials refused to surrender to the settlers' demands. As one newspaper story asked, "The funds invested in the neighborhood were state money, so why should [a small group of] yeshiva students, followers of Rabbi Levinger, be given the right to decide on the nature of the place?"[130] At one point, Prime Minister Golda Meir intervened and expressed unwavering support for the ministry's employees. They would continue working according to their plans, she told the settlers, and the government would not tolerate any squatting attempts.[131]

By 1973, the settlers and their supporters seemed to have arrived at a dead end. As a reporter for the newspaper *Davar* wrote, they could no longer "ignore the enormous gap that stretched between their original vision and the reality taking place in front of their eyes."[132] Within a couple of years, some seventy families from among the original setters would leave the settlement.[133] In their absence, one secular settler warned, more religiously radical settlers were gaining influence over Kiryat Arba.[134] Only those driven by an extremist ideology, it seemed, could endure life in the settlement. By 1977, approximately 400 of the 877 units in Kiryat Arba were unoccupied.[135] When asked about the large number of empty apartments, settlement activists blamed the ministry and its architects, "who have been given too much authority in city planning."[136] Said one activist: "One should wonder how 350 families actually survive here."[137] The first settlement attempt in Hebron, everyone seemed to agree, had failed.

A FOOTHOLD IN THE OLD CITY

In the summer of 1973, as many other settlers were giving up, David Cassuto, who five years earlier had made the first design for a Jewish neighborhood in Hebron, began plotting a new venture. From his office in Jerusalem, together with two other settlement activists, he researched the old compound that once housed Hebron's Jewish community, and by then was in ruins. Some of its houses had been severely damaged by an earthquake in 1927, and following the massacre of Jews by local Arabs during riots in 1929 and the Jewish community's expulsion from Hebron in 1936, the site was left abandoned. Most of the abandoned buildings had been seized by the Jordanian Custodian of Enemy Property and demolished in the early 1950s.[138]

Among the demolished buildings was the Avraham Avinu Synagogue, a domed, centuries-old temple that had once functioned as the spiritual center of the Jewish community in Hebron. By the time Israeli forces took the city, in 1967, no one knew where the synagogue had stood, so the Israeli Military Governorate leased out the destroyed enclave to Palestinians. Cassuto and his two collaborators were confident that they could determine where the synagogue had been located, and that if they did so, the government would be forced to rebuild it or at least confiscate the site. It would be difficult, they believed, for the government to oppose the preservation of one of the city's holiest Jewish sites.[139] Where resettlement strategies had failed, archaeology and heritage conservancy might yet prevail.

Using aerial photographs taken during the 1920s and architectural drawings made in the 1930s by the architect and archaeologist Jacob Pinkerfield, Cassuto and his two allies were able to identify the synagogue's approximate location. Without wasting time, they drove to the site and surveyed the area, looking for remnants. After wandering around for a while, Cassuto found an old Hebrew plaque covered with sand and dirt, buried underneath a sheepfold. Next to it, he detected remnants of a thick stone wall that matched Pinkerfield's plan drawing. Cassuto was convinced that he had discovered the lost synagogue.[140]

Cassuto's findings thrilled the residents of Kiryat Arba. They were enchanted by the synagogue's glorious past and angry that it was now in a state of neglect.[141] One of them, a recent immigrant from the Soviet Union named Ben Tzion Tavger, demanded that something be done to restore the site.[142] Although the site had been leased to a Palestinian shepherd, in December 1975 Tavgar began going to the site daily to clear layers of dirt and rubble, conducting his own unofficial excavation. Police officers repeatedly arrested him for conducting an illegal dig and disturbing the neighboring Palestinians.[143] Nevertheless, inspired by his dedication, yeshiva students from Kiryat Arba soon joined him. Within a few months, they had excavated large portions of the synagogue and the adjacent housing complex that had once accommodated worshippers.[144] With these findings in hand, Cassuto approached a special ministers' committee and demanded the synagogue's restoration (figure 1.13).[145] By the end of 1976, the committee acceded to his request.[146] Jewish settlers had achieved a foothold in the heart of Hebron, "and it was a big victory," Cassuto later recalled.[147]

However, when Cassuto was asked to oversee the restoration project, he refused, deeming it inappropriate. "I didn't fight this war in order to get a design commission," he later explained.[148] The government instead commissioned another architect, Dan Tanai, an expert on synagogue design, to oversee the work. But Tanai soon found that he had little control over the project. Excavation and construction were carried out by a group of settlers from Kiryat Arba, who expanded the excavations to nearby plots and dug in areas that Tanai had insisted should remain undisturbed. He could do little to rein them in on his weekly visits to the site.[149]

With construction under way in September 1977, settlers already began conducting religious rituals on the synagogue site. Military officials would

FIGURE 1.13. Ministers' committee visiting the site of Avraham Avinu Synagogue, Hebron, 1976. (Photograph by Sa'ar Ya'acov, Government Press Office.)

FIGURE 1.14. Avraham Avinu Synagogue (domed structure behind the figure), Hebron, 1983, reconstruction overseen by Dan Tanai. (Photograph by Yisra'el Simionski/Israel Sun Ltd., from the Judaica Collection of the Harvard Library, Harvard University.)

sometimes stop them, citing safety concerns. At one point, soldiers forcefully removed the settlers from the site.[150] Nevertheless, by 1980, the restoration was almost complete, and settlers took full control of the synagogue (figure 1.14).[151] Praying there daily, they had now become an undeniable part of the city's fabric.

RENEWING THE JEWISH QUARTER

After the right-wing Likud Party came to power in 1977, settlers living in Kiryat Arba felt emboldened and began relocating to houses in the area surrounding the synagogue.[152] They wanted to live in the Old City, not just pray there.[153] In March 1980, after an Arab resident of Hebron shot and killed Yehoshua Salome, a Danish-born yeshiva student from Kiryat Arba, Israeli government officials decided to extend the synagogue project. At first, they agreed to erect a yeshiva next to the synagogue and to install another educational center in a nearby building that once catered to the old Jewish community of Hebron.[154] Yet, over time, and following another Palestinian attack against settlers that took place in May 1980, the government expanded its plans and ultimately commissioned the renovation of the adjacent housing compound, Avraham Avinu Quarter, along with several other buildings in the Old City.[155]

Planners and architects working for the Ministry of Housing—which was renamed the Ministry of Construction and Housing in 1977—again found themselves drafting plans for the settlers of Hebron. This time, their clients were more active. Having learned from their experience of Kiryat Arba, when they left the design of the settlement in the hands of the government, the settlers now followed the design process carefully. Upon seeing preliminary plans for the Avraham Avinu Quarter, they complained that the proposed buildings looked too modern and were foreign to Hebron's biblical landscape. They demanded that the ministry start over and hire Saadia Mandel, a Tel Aviv–based architect with an impressive record.[156]

Born in Yugoslavia, Mandel had immigrated to Mandatory Palestine at the age of seven. After spending his youth in Tel Aviv and Jerusalem, he traveled to Europe, where he took architecture classes first at the École des Beaux-Arts in Paris and later at the Architectural Association in London. Eventually, Mandel obtained his architecture diploma from the Technion in Haifa. In 1960, he opened his own practice in Tel Aviv, and soon thereafter he became involved in a number of preservation projects, including the redevelopment of old Jerusalem, Jaffa, and Acre.[157]

The settlers had never met Mandel, but given his interest in historic preservation, they thought he would be a sympathetic collaborator. What most probably did not know was that Mandel was among the Ministry of Construction and Housing's favored architects, and that he had worked on several of its flagship projects. No less important, in the government's initial decision to expand Jewish presence in the heart of Hebron, in March 1980, it was in fact noted that "the planning will be done in keeping with the style of the [city's] fabric and in its spirit."[158] So, after going through the motions of some perfunctory negotiations, ministry officials acceded to the settlers' demands and commissioned Mandel—along with Erol Paker, a Turkish-born architect and occasional collaborator of Mandel's—to take over the project.[159]

Mandel and Paker were keen to work in Hebron. They belonged to a generation of architects who, as Nitzan-Shiftan has observed, sought to supplant the high modernism that had dominated Israeli architecture. Members of this generation were especially troubled by the high-modernist housing blocks—repetitive, crude, and without local particularity—that had mushroomed across the country in the first two decades after independence. Inspired by criticism of the modernist movement, including the post–World War II work of Team 10 and the New Brutalism in Europe, they argued that the standardized forms of high modernism failed to take into account the cultural diversity of those who immigrated to Israel from places as different as Morocco, Poland, and Iraq. They also contended that high modernism hampered the immigrants' efforts to develop emotional attachments to their new land. Thus, they wanted to replace the universal and blank forms with a more rooted language drawn from local building traditions, which often meant those of the Palestinians. By the 1970s, these architects had gained significant influence over the Israeli architectural scene. They oversaw many projects that incorporated Palestinian building elements, such as arched entryways and stone details, including several in Jerusalem.[160] For Mandel and Paker, Hebron—at once Palestinian, Jewish, and a site of modern settlement—was the perfect setting to experiment with the kind of architecture that they had been developing. It provided them with an opportunity, as Paker later described it, to connect to "the spirit of the place."[161]

Before they would draw up any plans, however, Mandel insisted that he and Paker meet with the settlers. "I had to understand these strange people who wanted to live in a place surrounded by hostile Arabs," he later explained. Despite opposition from the head of the Jerusalem region within the Ministry of Construction and Housing, he contacted the settlers' representatives and scheduled a meeting with them in Hebron's Old City. Sitting with them on a dilapidated rooftop overlooking the city, Mandel asked how they imagined themselves living in the ancient city, with its population of

Arabs. "What did you come to do here?" he asked. "Did you come to live with the Arabs? Next to the Arabs? Instead of the Arabs?"[162] The settlers told Mandel and Paker that they thought they could live alongside Palestinian residents, buying groceries at the Old City's market, taking their babies to the local clinic, using facilities operated by their Arab neighbors. But they wanted to preserve their privacy, even if that required keeping some distance from the Palestinians.[163]

In response, Mandel and Paker developed an introverted scheme, organizing all the housing units in their plans around a couple of courtyard spaces. They thought that an enclosed compound fit the urban fabric of Hebron, and that it resonated with the traditional courtyard house—a private residence organized around a patio space closed off from the street that can be found throughout North Africa, the Middle East, and Asia—which they associated with Arab culture.[164] (In fact, the introverted plans resembled other recent projects designed by their peers elsewhere in the country, including the settlement of Gilo in East Jerusalem that was also organized around enclosed courtyard spaces.)[165] Mandel and Paker used small alleys to connect the compound's courtyard spaces to the city beyond; the alleys branched out from the two roads flanking the compound on the north and south. The southern road was the Old City's main thoroughfare, crowded with vendors, kiosks, and shops. The architects imagined that it would link the compound to the Tomb of the Patriarchs and to other settler housing projects.[166] It was obvious, Paker later noted, that he and Mandel would rely on Hebron's existing infrastructure and road system.[167]

When considering building materials, Mandel and Paker faced an obstacle: the head of the Civil Department at the Israeli State Attorney's Office, Plia Albeck, insisted that the architects use lightweight, modular, prefabricated housing components. The site, she told them, was divided into small subplots, and although Jordanian records registered some of these as Jewish-owned, it was unclear who owned the remaining ones. The titles of several subplots were listed under the names of Muslim families, but government officials had been unable to find the families.[168] Light construction was necessary, Albeck explained, so that it could easily be moved if any title-holders were suddenly to come forward and demand the removal of anything standing on their property.

Mandel and Paker drew some sketches for prefabricated units, but it soon became clear that another solution was needed.[169] Such units reiterated the mistakes of Kiryat Arba and were at odds not only with settlers' preferences but also, this time, the architects' preferences. After consulting Albeck again, they decided to convert all subplots whose owners were unknown into patio

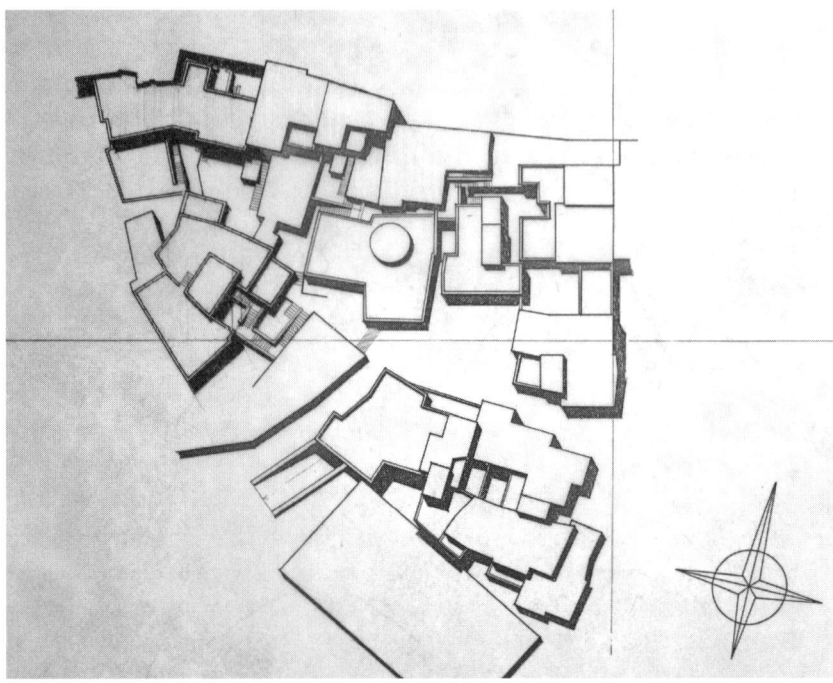

FIGURE 1.15. Saadia Mandel and Erol Paker, site plan of Avraham Avinu Quarter, Hebron. Units arranged around small patio spaces, 1986. (Private collection of Erol Paker.)

spaces. This way they avoided the risk of future demolition and at the same time rendered the project part of Hebron's urban fabric. The project now followed historical subdivision lines, with an irregular pattern common to other areas of the city (figure 1.15).[170]

Blending the settlement into its surroundings was a key element of Mandel and Paker's vision. To this end, they also employed flat roofs and covered the external walls of the enclave with thin stone veneers (figure 1.16). Some units were designed so that one room hung over an inner courtyard or alley, to resemble housing forms that the architects associated with Arab culture. In some areas, they modeled the ceilings after three-dimensional shapes that echoed traditional domed structures (figure 1.17).[171]

In designing residential units, Mandel and Paker were particularly attentive to the religious needs of the future residents. On the advice of settler representatives, who served as project managers and construction workers, they provided each unit with a balcony, a sink outside the washing room for hand-washing rituals, and two sinks in the kitchen for kosher cooking. The

פרספקטיבה

FIGURE 1.16. Saadia Mandel and Erol Paker, drawing of Avraham Avinu Quarter, Hebron, 1985. (Private collection of Erol Paker.)

living rooms of most units were replaced with expansive dining spaces to accommodate large Shabbat dinners.[172] According to Paker, the project had nothing in common with the standardized housing projects the Ministry of Construction and Housing typically commissioned.[173]

By the end of 1987, families began to move into the complex. An inauguration ceremony, attended by the architects and the minister of Housing, was held in June 1989.[174] After the ceremony, a female settler approached Mandel with two little kids, one in her arm and the other holding her hand. She reminded him that she had been among the group of settlers who had met with him before construction began, when he tried to understand what form of life the setters imagined for themselves. She admitted that she had been skeptical, never imagining that an architect would listen to the settlers' requests. But the complex, she said, was exactly what they needed.[175]

That settler had other reasons to feel satisfied. Around the same time, the Ministry of Construction and Housing was overseeing the restoration of other Jewish properties in the heart of the city. Most notable of these was Beit Hadassah, a mixed-use complex of approximately twelve residential units, with a synagogue and a museum, located 600 meters from the Tomb of the Patriarchs. This time it was Cassuto who oversaw the design. Like Mandel and Paker, Cassuto saw the project as "an opportunity to connect with history."[176] He thus drew on original building elements he found on the site. He arranged the units around an inner courtyard, in reference to

FIGURE 1.17. Domed passageway in Avraham Avinu Quarter, Hebron, 2016. (Photograph by author.)

the traditional courtyard house; clad the walls with stone; and ornamented the façade with a large arched window. Beit Hadassah had been finished a couple of years earlier, in 1986. So, when the residents of Avraham Avinu moved into their new housing units, they were joining a growing community of Jewish settlers in the heart of Hebron. They felt strong and reassured in a way that the residents of Kiryat Arba did not. After two decades of protesting, of signing petitions, and confronting state officials and planners, they finally got to see Jews populating the town of the patriarchs, and, fittingly, the modernist architecture of Kiryat Arba had been superseded by a more vernacular one. It was exactly what they needed, they thought.

Perhaps this was not exactly what they needed. Perhaps it came too late. While construction was under way in 1987, the First Intifada—a Palestinian uprising against the Israeli occupation—broke out. Clashes between settlers and Palestinians became an everyday occurrence in Hebron. By the time the Avraham Avinu Quarter was completed, many of the original settlers had left the area. Far more radical ones took their places, which led to even greater violence between the two populations. The most notorious act of violence was carried out in 1994 by Baruch Goldstein, a settler from Kiryat Arba, who shot dead twenty-nine Muslims during the dawn prayer inside the Tomb of the Patriarchs.[177]

To limit interaction between the two sides, authorities asked Mandel and Paker to block some of the alleyways connecting the settler compound to the city at large. Ironically, while their enclosed layout had been intended to blend the project into the city's fabric, it now served the opposite purpose: the alleys could easily be blocked to separate the two groups. Arguably, the compound's inward-facing layout heightened the settlers' sense of alienation from the Palestinians. This alienation paved the way for the site's ultimate fortification, achieved by sealing off some of the small gates on the pathways branching out from Avraham Avinu's patio spaces.

The architects initially thought the conflict would be temporary, that things would calm down and the blocked entryways would be reopened. Paker optimistically called one of these the "Peace Gate."[178] But peace never took hold. In 1997, Israel and the Palestinian Authority (which was established in the mid-1990s to manage the Palestinian population in the occupied territories) signed the Hebron Protocol, which divided the city in two: about 80 percent of the city (and 115,000 Palestinians) would be under Palestinian security control, and the remaining parts, including the Jewish compounds (and some 35,000 Palestinians), under Israeli security control.[179] Both sides agreed to keep movement between the two parts uninterrupted so as "to keep the unity of the city of Hebron."[180] But violent incidents between Palestinians

FIGURE 1.18. Military checkpoint near a settler compound in Hebron, 2017. (Photograph by author.)

and the settlers continued, and eventually, the entire area surrounding Avraham Avinu and the other Jewish compounds was closed to Palestinian motor traffic; some areas were also closed to pedestrians.[181] Israeli forces also closed hundreds of Palestinian stores near the settler compounds, citing security concerns. The economic decline of the area, caused by the military blockades and long curfews that were placed on the Palestinians during the Second Intifada in the early 2000s, dealt a blow to the remaining stores. By 2007, 1,829 Palestinian businesses in the area had been closed. Palestinian residents who could afford to, moved out of the area, leaving behind them scores of vacant buildings.[182] The Hebron Rehabilitation Committee, a Palestinian organization founded in 1996, has been fighting the deterioration of the Old City (and its takeover by Israeli settlers) by renovating abandoned Palestinian-owned structures and developing public spaces that cater to Palestinian residents.[183] These efforts could do little, however, to restore the area's economic viability; nor could they remove the military barriers and checkpoints Israel had installed across the Old City to separate the two populations (figure 1.18). By 2020, according to some reports, there were more than one thousand Israeli soldiers and police officers protecting the roughly eight hundred settlers in Hebron's Old City.[184] The settlers are barred from entering areas under the control of the Palestinians.

Meanwhile, Kiryat Arba has been struggling with high poverty rates and negative migration, with more people leaving the settlement than moving into it.[185] Like the Avraham Avinu compound, it is also guarded by fences and armed soldiers. With approximately 7,300 settlers—surrounded by hostile Palestinians and removed from Israeli economic centers—it is home to barely 15 percent of the original projected population.[186]

CONCLUSION

In 2015, I made regular visits to the Jewish settlement of Hebron. I would usually walk along the main street that connects Avraham Avinu Quarter and the other settler compounds (figure 1.19). The settler compounds were sandwiched between the one- to three-story Palestinian-owned buildings that flanked the street. It was once a bustling street, filled with Palestinian stores and kiosks on the ground floor. But now the stores were all shut with rusting metal panels that haven't been opened in years. Above some of the sealed stores were Palestinian residential units. Most seemed abandoned, but here and there I could sometimes see a person or hear sounds coming from inside. The windows of the units, however, were shielded with dense metal grates installed to protect the residents from settler violence.[187] Some of the alleyways and roads branching off the street were blocked with fences and concrete slabs topped with barbed wire. Some were covered with Hebrew graffiti announcing the coming of the Messiah. I would rarely see other civilians walking down the road—only the soldiers stationed in front of settler compounds. The soldiers would carefully follow my steps, sometimes walking out of their booth, only to retreat inside after I greeted them in Hebrew. It was not a place to wander around.

A large gap stretches between that "sharp, crystal clear feeling of returning home" that Zehava Nativ recorded on her first visit to Hebron in 1967, or the hybrid culture that the Canaanites wanted to forge in the city, and what ultimately came to be the Jewish settlement of Hebron—a segregated landscape, sustained by walls and barbed wire. An equally large gap stretches between the appearance of the settler compounds and their political effect. The building elements that the architects adopted from the Palestinians—in an attempt to merge the settlement with its surroundings—in practice serve to block the Palestinians. The inner courtyards and narrow alleyways of Avraham Avinu Quarter are an eerie reminder that architectural forms do not have intrinsic political meaning. They are always open to change and to unanticipated uses.

FIGURE 1.19. Closed Palestinian-owned stores on the main street that connects settler compounds in Hebron, 2017. (Photograph by author.)

But it wasn't only the political meaning of architectural forms that took unexpected turns over the course of planning and inhabitation in Hebron; it was also the design process itself. In the 1950s and 1960s, when housing the masses of immigrants who flocked into Israel after independence was a prime national task, the government gave state architects unquestioned authority over design. In Hebron, after government ministers agreed not to decide—or, as the historian Gershom Gorenberg has noted, "more than deciding on settlement . . . [they] drifted into permitting settlement"[188]—the planners and architects at the Ministry of Housing saw their plans for a settlement separated from Hebron undermined by amateur archaeologists and volunteer architects. Later, Mandel and Paker—and perhaps even Cassuto—saw radicalized settlers undo their vision of urban coexistence. Such a haphazard planning process was at odds with previous Israeli planning procedures. So was the involvement of religious Zionists, who had previously been marginal to Israeli polity. It was among the first cracks in what was until the 1970s a centralized and inflexible planning regime ruled by the labor elite.

We usually think about architectures of power and domination in terms of top-down planning, with powerful politicians and planners smoothly manipulating the built environment to advance their political goals. The architectural history of the settlement of Hebron offers a different perspective. It shows that a landscape marked by excessive use of power, with significant political effects, can also grow out of a much messier process, with unexpected negotiations between multiple actors working from above and below, promoting contending ideologies and aesthetic visions.

While these negotiations were taking place in Hebron, however, a number of settlers were beginning to consider new settlement venues. Already in the mid-1970s, as I discuss in the next chapter, they began to shift their focus away from dense city centers and toward the more isolated hilltops of the West Bank, where they would formulate a different settlement model. The dream of settling inside Palestinian towns like Jericho or Nablus would continue to linger in the minds of religious settlers, but with time, it would subside. Today, Hebron is the only Palestinian town in the occupied West Bank, outside Jerusalem, where settlers have established a residential neighborhood. The settlement of Hebron thus stands alone: the sole realization—distorted, disappointing, and volatile as it might be—of this early settlement model evoked in the aftermath of the Six-Day War, before the term "settlement" had a clear social meaning, and when multiple paths were still open.

CHAPTER 2

COMMUNITY SETTLEMENTS

In the years after the settlement of Kiryat Arba opened on the outer fringe of Hebron in 1971, the settlement movement seemed to be losing steam. More than half a decade had passed since the conquest of the West Bank, and yet, by 1972 the total number of settlers was only 1,500, and it seemed unlikely that that number would increase much anytime soon.[1] Israelis wanting to move to the West Bank had two main options, neither of them especially promising: they could settle in Kiryat Arba, which had failed to attract Israelis; or they could move to small cooperative settlements designed to accommodate only a few dozen families. (After inaugurating kibbutz Kfar Etzion in 1967, Israel built another kibbutz in the Etzion Bloc, as well as eleven cooperative villages along the Jordan River valley.)[2] It became clear that the *form* of the settlement mattered. What form of settlement would both appeal to a large number of Israelis and, equally important, evade government officials' opposition was a matter of discussion and debate. Some settlement activists continued to advocate for settlement plans in Palestinian towns like Nablus and Jericho.[3] Others envisioned a network of small agricultural settlements, where Israelis would work the land of the West Bank.[4] There was no consensus about the "right" settlement form.

A decade later, by the mid-1980s, dozens of small settlements had sprung up across the West Bank. Most of them were neither urban nor agricultural. Located on nonarable hilltops, they were smaller than agricultural settlements and often did not have an agricultural or industrial area at all. Each housed a few hundred residents who shared a number of communal facilities. Almost all of them resided in single-family houses that were often capped with red-tile rooftops. This new form of settlement came to be known as the "community settlement" (*yishuv kehilati*); its layout and management were without precedent either in the West Bank or in Israel.

These settlements puzzled state architects, who struggled to understand them years after they had first appeared. "In spite of its popularity, there is still little information about the Community Oriented type of settlement," Shmuel Horwitz, deputy director of the Ministry of Construction and Housing's Rural Building and New Settlements Administration, admitted in 1988. This lack of information on the community settlement model stemmed not only from its novelty, Horwitz explained, but also from "the fact that the model was largely developed by the settlers themselves and not 'from above' by planners and organizers in the public establishment."[5] Until the 1970s, physical planning in Israel had almost always been "from above," orchestrated by centralized public agencies. Two agencies were especially powerful: the Ministry of Construction and Housing, established as an independent department in 1961 (and known as the Ministry of Housing until 1977); and the Settlement Department of the Jewish Agency, a nongovernmental body dating from the prestate era that continued to collaborate with the government on the construction of scores of villages.[6] Neither of these bodies, however, had much control over the emergence of the community settlement model. It was a new vernacular.

Over the 1970s, plans to reinhabit West Bank towns with a biblical legacy, or to reconnect to the land through agricultural communities, were replaced by community settlements. For many settlers, the creation of the new settlement form marked a triumph over state planners, who had previously ignored their wishes. But what was it about small enclaves of private houses, which had so little in common with the models they had previously preferred, that satisfied the settlers' desires? And, equally important, how could a settlement model have taken form "from below" in the first place? What role did professional planners play in its conception and development, and how would this trend affect the country's centralized planning regime?

This chapter traces the emergence of the community settlement. It reconstructs the debates that accompanied the design and construction of the settlement of Ofra between 1975 and 1987. Ofra was where many of the planning principles of the community settlement model were first negotiated. It was also where some of the most vocal settlement activists had assembled. They engaged several different design professionals to draft the planning principles for the settlement, but on each occasion, they reformulated the designs presented to them, adapting them to their own vision for the kind of settlement they wanted to live in. Over the years, these activists also helped popularize these planning principles among other settlers across the West Bank such that, for a number of years, Ofra served as a model for subsequent settlements.

The outbreak of a war in October 1973 ushered in a period of political unrest in Israel. On October 6, a coalition of Arab states led by Egypt and Syria attacked Israel. Launched on Yom Kippur, among the holiest days in the Jewish calendar, the war—which quickly came to be known as the Yom Kippur War—caught the country off guard. With Egyptian forces invading from the south and Syrians from the north, the Israeli military suffered several defeats in the first days of the war. With massive support from the United States, Israel was able to strike back, but the large number of casualties on both sides left many Israelis disillusioned about the state of the country. They realized that their military advantage over the neighboring Arab countries was anything but permanent.[7] A wave of intense discontent swept the country in the aftermath of the war, as the political scientist Ian Lustick has noted, producing various grassroots organizations that questioned the existing political structures.[8]

One such organization was Gush Emunim (Bloc of the Faithful). Gush Emunim was founded in early 1974 by activists in the settlement of Kfar Etzion. It was initially conceived as an ideological group within the National Religious Party, which had represented religious Zionism in the Israeli parliament since 1956.[9] Until the Six-Day War, the National Religious Party was considered moderate, participating in labor-led government coalitions and focusing on domestic issues. Gush Emunim, however, was far less moderate: its stated goal was to bring national redemption to the Jewish people. Under the spiritual leadership of Rabbi Tzvi Yehuda Kook, it promoted the idea of Greater Israel or "the whole Land of Israel." The whole Land of Israel refers to the territory conquered by, or promised to, the ancient Israelites. According to the halakhah (Jewish law), this territory has a special religious significance. Its borders, however, are somewhat elusive. At certain points in the biblical narrative, for example, the Jordan River marks the eastern boundary of the Land of Israel, while at others it is the Euphrates (in modern-day Iraq).[10] Moreover, the terms used to delineate this territory are often imprecise (e.g., "from the desert to the river").[11] Despite these ambiguities, the idea of the whole Land of Israel—though referring to various different geographical boundaries—had long informed the thinking of several Zionist leaders. In the first half of the twentieth century, those associated with revisionist Zionism—a hawkish strand of Zionism—invoked the idea of the whole Land of Israel to argue that the borders of the Jewish nation-state should encompass not only Palestine but also Transjordan. "Two banks the Jordan [River] has, this is ours and that one as well," went the chorus of a 1930 poem written by Vladimir (Ze'ev) Jabotinsky, the leader of revisionist Zionism.[12] When the activists of Gush Emunim took up the banner of the whole Land of Israel in the 1970s, they emphasized the connection between the Jewish people and the territories Israel captured in the Six-Day War, a connection they considered not only historical but divine. Withdrawal from the occupied territories was thus out of the question.[13] Moreover, they believed that the erection of new Jewish settlements on these lands was a religious command, if not a redemptive act.[14]

The activists of Gush Emunim presented an enigma to outside observers. Dressed in modern clothes, preferably military jackets, the men did not look like orthodox Jews. But one could see the tassels of their traditional Jewish undergarments trailing beneath their jackets, and knitted skullcaps covered the tops of their heads. Their thinking, too, as the journalist Akiva Eldar and the historian Idith Zertal have noted, was a mash-up of modern, rational political thought combined with a mystical, irrational worldview. But perhaps it was precisely this mixture of modernity and radical religiosity, of rationalism and messianism, that ultimately rendered them powerful in their interactions with the government.[15]

Gush Emunim was keen on settling Jews in the densely populated mountainous areas of the West Bank, especially those north of Jerusalem. But government officials expected the region to become part of a future Palestinian political entity, so they opposed the idea.[16] The activists of Gush Emunim therefore struck out on their own, employing multiple tactics aimed at establishing a Jewish presence. They organized hikes to strategic destinations and performed religious ceremonies at sacred sites. More daringly, the activists began squatting at locations around the West Bank. In one instance, about a hundred activists locked themselves inside a stone cave near one of the highest hills in the region, where, according to their belief, God had promised the Land of Israel to Abraham a few millennia ago.[17] More well known were the squatting attempts carried out in the abandoned Ottoman railroad station near the Palestinian village of Sebastia, 10 kilometers north of Nablus (figure 2.1). Time after time, the activists—initially operating under the auspices of an overlapping settler group called Elon Moreh—would arrive at the station and erect an instant settlement of temporary structures, or simply barricade themselves inside the station, only to be forcefully evacuated by Israeli soldiers a few hours (or sometimes days) later.[18]

The idea of erecting instant settlements in frontier areas, somewhat clandestinely, was not new to Zionist history. To a degree, the activists' attempts to settle near Sebastia resonated with "stockade and tower" (*homa umigdal*), a settlement method that Zionist colonizers devised in the mid-1930s. This

FIGURE 2.1. Makeshift camp erected by settlement activists near the Palestinian village of Sebastia, 1975. (Photograph by Moshe Milner, Government Press Office.)

method entailed the construction of new outposts in record time. As its name indicates, it required two main building elements: a protective wall made of prefabricated wooden parts designed to enclose an area of about 1,225 square meters; and a prefabricated wooden watchtower installed inside the walled area (figure 2.2). Both elements would be installed, usually along with a couple of shacks, in the space of a day. Later, after these bare-minimum elements had become a fact on the ground, the place would be developed into a fully functioning settlement, usually taking the form of a kibbutz.[19] This method had emerged in response to two challenges. First, the Arab Revolt in Palestine between 1936 and 1939, which included violent attacks against Jewish agricultural colonies, had made it especially difficult to erect new settlements. Second, in the late 1930s, British authorities began to seriously consider partitioning Palestine between Jews and Arabs—prompting Zionists to increase settlement activity to create facts on the ground before the final borders were decided.[20] Stockade and tower delivered the goods; between 1936 and 1939, more than fifty new outposts were erected using this method.[21] In subsequent decades, stockade and tower came to enjoy a mythic status in Zionist history. Seen as a symbol of resistance and triumph, it was featured in elementary school texts and youth movement activities.[22]

FIGURE 2.2. Two men by a model of kibbutz Sha'ar HaGolan, 1938. The kibbutz was initially built according to the stockade and tower method. (Photograph by Zoltan Kluger, Government Press Office.)

In their attempts to establish strongholds in the West Bank, Gush Emu- nim activists would sometimes invoke this legacy of surreptitious Zionist colonization. Critics, however, called attention to the contrast between the prestate settlements and Gush Emunim's squatting attempts. A reporter writ- ing for the daily *Al Hamishmar* in August 1974 argued: "The pioneering and settlement activity of the prestate [era] were not in the style of guerilla. All the ascents to the land [i.e., founding of new settlements] were planned and executed by the elected institutions of the *yishuv* [the Jewish community in Palestine] and the Zionist movement. . . . The classic settlement activity of the [prestate] pioneers was carried out with force but without confiscating lands. The lands were bought with good money, and they were bought, in most of the cases, in areas that were available, on pristine land, without houses or else sparsely populated." The same could not be said about Gush Emunim's settlement attempts, the reporter concluded. "They are provoking the title of Zionism and pioneer-ship for nothing."[23]

It is unlikely that Gush Emunim activists were troubled by such criticism. They were concerned with a different question: would these pseudo-stockade and tower settlement attempts suffice to bring about a change in state policy? On the one hand, with each squatting attempt, which drew significant media attention, Gush Emunim gained more supporters.[24] On the other hand, the encampments were short-lived, leaving some of the group's supporters unsure what exactly its members' intentions were.[25] It became clear to some of the activists that other tactics would have to be found.

OCCUPATION

Among those eager to find more effective settlement tactics was Yehuda Etzion. Etzion had spent his early childhood in Ein Tzurim, a kibbutz 45 kilometers west of Jerusalem founded by religious Zionists who had been expelled from an earlier kibbutz of that name in 1948, when Jordanian soldiers seized the West Bank during the first Arab-Israeli War. He had grown up hearing about that painful defeat and yearning to return to the lost kibbutz. When the Six-Day War broke out, he was sixteen years old. Less than two years later, in 1969, he moved to the settlement of Kfar Etzion, where he attended Har Etzion Yeshiva and met some of the leading figures in the settlement movement.[26] While attending the yeshiva, Etzion teamed up with Menachem Felix and Benjamin Katzover, both settlers from Kiryat Arba, and together they began making plans to build a settlement near the Palestinian town of Nablus. When the Yom Kippur War broke out, however, Etzion was drafted, and their plans were put on hold. After the war, Etzion and his collaborators joined forces with Gush Emunim.

Now twenty-three, Etzion immersed himself in the group. He spent hours debating settlement tactics with other activists. At one point, he moved into Gush Emunim's headquarters, sleeping on a mattress on the floor. He was fully committed to the cause of settling Jews in the West Bank, and over time, he grew frustrated with the unending debates and the failure of Gush Emunim's much-publicized squatting attempts to yield any results.[27]

One day, an activist named Hanan Porat returned from a long hike in the West Bank with a new idea. On his hike he had passed a military camp under construction, 9 kilometers south of the Palestinian town of Ramallah. Porat was accompanied by Rachel Yanait Ben-Zvi, the widow of the former president of Israel Yitzhak Ben-Zvi, who had a daring idea. She suggested that Gush Emunim members could pose as construction workers, take over the project, create a work camp, and then transform it into a settlement. She explained to Porat that this was how a number of Jewish colonies had been established during the prestate period.[28] If head-on confrontation with government officials had failed them, deceit, she argued, might still prevail.

Yanait Ben-Zvi's suggestion drew on what the political scientist Ehud Sprinzak has identified as a culture of illegality. According to Sprinzak, Israeli society has developed a high tolerance for illegal activity that can be traced to the early twentieth century, when Palestine was under British rule and Jews had to negotiate their right to immigrate and settle with British officials. They believed their cause justified transgressing the law, so they sometimes arranged for Jews to immigrate into Palestine without the necessary permits, or, as Yanait Ben-Zvi recalled, erected illicit settlements.[29] This kind of disrespect toward state laws has evolved over time, but it did not disappear after the founding of the State of Israel. For Yanait Ben-Zvi, there was now a moral obligation to settle the West Bank, and that trumped civil obligation to follow the laws of the state.

This attitude toward state laws would become a leitmotif in Etzion's career. When Porat shared Yanait Ben-Zvi's idea with him, Etzion was intrigued. He managed to schedule a meeting with the contractor in charge of construction on the site.[30] The contractor, who had been appointed through the Ministry of Defense, told Etzion he was looking for a group of workers to build a 4-kilometer-long, 1.8-meter-high fence around the military camp. Etzion and his friends lacked the required skills. Nevertheless, they said they would be happy to take the job; after a brief conversation, they were hired.[31]

For the next few months, Etzion drove from Jerusalem to the construction site every morning. At first, other activists joined him. But the work proved more difficult than they expected, and many of them gave up. They had also questioned Etzion's plan from the beginning.[32] But on April 20, 1975, some eight months after he first arrived on the site, he was joined by twenty-two other activists, who came along not with the intention of working but with the intention of staying. When evening came, instead of heading back to Jerusalem, they settled into deserted Jordanian military barracks near the construction site and refused to leave. The barracks were part of an army base Jordan began building in 1966 but abandoned during the Six-Day War.[33] Etzion and his collaborators were now claiming them as workers' lodgings. The Israeli military governor of Ramallah brought the matter to the attention of Defense Minister Shimon Peres. After some negotiations, Peres agreed to let the settlers stay, on the condition that the settlement would be treated as a workers' camp and kept secret.[34]

FIGURE 2.3. The abandoned Jordanian military camp shortly after Etzion and his collaborators took over the site. (Photo by Yisra'el Simionski/Israel Sun Ltd., from the Judaica Collection of the Harvard Library, Harvard University.)

Etzion spent the first night along with the other activists in one of the concrete military barracks. The next morning, they woke up to the sizable task of transforming the abandoned military base into a Jewish settlement. Straightforward solutions were not available. Not only was the place designed for military training, but since construction on the base had begun shortly before the Six-Day War broke out, none of the structures had been completed. The barracks had been abandoned at different stages of construction; they lacked windows, doors, and restrooms. Paved roads and other basic infrastructure were also missing (figure 2.3).[35]

Unsure about the future prospects of the place, the settlers began transforming the camp. They first blocked out the window frames, installed a water tank, and connected the electrical system to a generator (figure 2.4).[36] Quickly, they also agreed to name the place after one of the biblical capitals of the region, Ofra.[37] In the following weeks, as word about the mysterious workers' camp began to reach a broader public in Israel, people from across the country started donating furniture and building materials. Some came to the site and offered to help renovate the place. One Jerusalem-based contractor came every night to Ofra, after a long day's work in the city, to work in the military camp for a couple of hours before heading back home.[38]

FIGURE 2.4. Settlers renovate a military barrack in the abandoned Jordanian military camp. (Ofra Archives.)

The settlers realized, though, that they needed a professional architect. One of them suggested contacting his friend Zalman Deutch, an American-born architect living in Jerusalem who happened to be a supporter of Gush Emunim. Trained at the Pratt Institute in New York, Deutch had immigrated to Israel after the Six-Day War.[39] At the time, he was working for the architects Yosef Sheinberger and Tuvia Katz. An observant Jew, Deutch considered himself fortunate to be working for Sheinberger and Katz. Both were religious and both were known for their work on worship spaces. Working in that studio, Deutch gained valuable experience designing synagogues, yeshivas, and mikveh structures.[40]

When the settlers of Ofra approached Deutch, he immediately agreed to their request. In fact, he even offered to do the work pro bono.[41] Without wasting any time, he began designing residential units for the settlers. He first converted the existing barracks into livable spaces, adding partitions, openings, kitchen fixtures, and other basic elements. Each barrack was designed to house one or two families. For single men, Deutch designed several long rectilinear structures made from prefabricated storage containers. He divided them into small rooms of 15 square meters, each designed to accommodate four bachelors. Although the renovation budget was extremely tight—"maybe good for buying a shoelace," as he told me a few decades later—Deutch was committed to transforming the dilapidated military base into a temporary but livable settlement.[42]

Official planning agencies were absent throughout the design process. Both the Ministry of Housing and the Jewish Agency's Settlement Department opposed the settlement. Planners from the Settlement Department did survey the area, under the auspices of a new entity called the Settlement Division, but they concluded that it was impossible to erect a residential quarter on the site. Not only was it too small, but its location on a hilltop also rendered it vulnerable to hazardous weather.[43]

The Settlement Division was established by the World Zionist Organization in 1971 specifically to facilitate work in the West Bank. Lawyers had determined that the Jewish Agency's work in the West Bank, through its Settlement Department, would undermine its ability to receive tax-exempt donations from American philanthropists. (The Settlement Department's budget came from both the Jewish Agency and the government.) The Settlement Division was thus created to take over the Settlement Department's responsibilities in the occupied territories, with its budget coming from the government. This was mostly a formal gesture, however: until 1992, the staff of the Settlement Department carried out a significant portion of the Settlement Division's operations, using the Settlement Division's budget.[44] (In this chapter, I use the two terms interchangeably.)

In any case, the Settlement Department's report probably never reached the settlers of Ofra—and if it did, it had little effect on the settlers. By the time the report was published, the settlers had already transformed the camp into a relatively functioning civilian settlement (figure 2.5). When Yehiel Admoni, second in command at the Settlement Department, visited the site for the first time a few weeks later, he was "amazed and perplexed at the same time." On seeing the converted barracks and new infrastructure, he wondered why "without any help from the Settlement Department . . . [the settlers'] achievements were significantly superior to those settling seeds that enjoyed massive support from the [Settlement] Division."[45]

Etzion and his friends were well aware of their achievements. Working outside the purview of official planning agencies, they realized, could actually be empowering. While government agencies were debating whether Ofra had the right to exist, the settlers continued developing the settlement over the next few months. To speed up the process, they would soon create their own planning and design agencies that would have a lasting effect on the settlement enterprise.

FIGURE 2.5. Postcard of Ofra, 1976. ("Palphot" Hertzlia, Ofra Archives.)

A SETTLEMENT MODEL "FROM BELOW"

Once there were enough temporary housing units to accommodate the immediate needs of the embryonic population of the new community, the settlers
of Ofra went on to develop guidelines and a plan for a permanent settlement.
At first, Ofra functioned like a quasi-kibbutz: many of the residents received
modest salaries from the settlement, all ate at a communal dining hall, and
everyone took part in the various voluntary committees that oversaw each
aspect of daily life. But as the community started to take root, the model of
the kibbutz seemed inappropriate. A kibbutz, the settlers feared, could not
attract large masses of Israelis to the West Bank. It was limited in size, and,
equally important, since the founding of the State of Israel in 1948, and
more so after the Six-Day War, the kibbutz had been losing its status as the
paradigm of Israeli nation-building.[46] In addition, many residents of Ofra had
grown up in urban centers and were unaccustomed to economic cooperation.[47] Some of them maintained jobs outside the settlement, commuting daily
to Israel. In one of the many assembly meetings where the settlers debated

their future, one resident bluntly stated: "Had any one of us wanted to live in a kibbutz . . . he would have done so long ago. . . . Personally, I prefer a settlement-form where one doesn't intervene in the life of his neighbor. . . . I am against any form of cooperation." Another resident chimed in, "Whenever I hear about cooperation, I get nauseous."[48] The model of the kibbutz, almost everyone agreed, did not fit.

Finding an alternative model, however, was not so simple. Each night during the summer of 1975, the residents would meet and discuss different alternatives. They debated the size of the settlement, the level of cooperation between the residents, and the type of industries that could fit the site. These debates often lasted for hours, but they were rarely productive. Some wanted to have Ofra turned into a large urban settlement, while others preferred limiting its size to a small village. A few maintained that some economic cooperation was essential, despite the opposition of many others.[49] For a while, the settlers seemed unable to reach a consensus.

To ease the process, and to solve related problems in other settlements, three Gush Emunim activists paid a visit to Uzi Gdor, an urban planner based in Bet HaLevi, a village 30 kilometers north of Tel Aviv. They were joined by Yehuda Harel, a friend (and a settlement activist based in the Golan Heights) who had recommended Gdor as an urban planner with an unconventional approach.[50] Indeed, Gdor had extensive experience developing new regional models for state planning agencies. After graduating from the Hebrew University, where he studied agriculture and economics, Gdor had worked at the Settlement Department as lead planner for the Negev region. He also took part in the reconstruction of a rural area in Iran devastated by an earthquake. In 1967, he was appointed chief planner for the Golan Heights region after it was seized from Syria during the Six-Day War.[51] In the early 1970s, he had also been involved in the master planning of the Sinai Peninsula.[52]

The settlers who met with Gdor found an energetic forty-year-old who, despite his impressive resume, was humble and friendly.[53] Sitting in his living room, the activists explained their situation: they already had several settlements on the ground, but they lacked planning guidelines that would structure their development, and, equally important, they encountered difficulties when communicating with state institutes. They felt they needed a centralized planning body that would oversee the settlements and work with government officials. They asked him to take on the task of constructing and managing such an agency. An avowedly secular man, Gdor was hardly a supporter of Gush Emunim, but he agreed to the request because, like many Israelis in the 1970s, he did not fully understand the political significance of the settlements. "Back at the time," Gdor told me when we met in 2015, "people saw the settlement movement in a totally different way. It is not like today when you have those who are in favor of it and those who are against it." He did have one condition—that the settlers get official government approval before undertaking any project. "I am not going to run on the hilltops of the West Bank in the middle of the night," he told the young settlers.[54]

Shortly after that meeting, Gdor wrote a short text he entitled "The Community Settlement." In that text, he delineated the main principles of a new kind of rural settlement that would change the face of the West Bank.[55] When drafting his text, Gdor first considered existing rural settlement models. Rural settlements had played an important role in the history of Zionist colonization. The Zionist movement often favored the village over the city, especially after the labor division of the Zionist movement rose to power after the First World War (figure 2.6). Labor Zionists sought to overturn the urban lifestyle and employment patterns that had been associated with Jews in Europe, and instead create a new society based on agricultural production and manual labor. They thus directed great efforts toward the development of innovative forms of agricultural settlements, the most celebrated of these being the kibbutz and the moshav. For a while, these settlement forms were seen as the fountainhead of Zionist ideology.[56] But agricultural production, Gdor knew, was virtually impossible on the hilltops of the northern region of the West Bank. And equally important, by the 1970s, agrarian lifestyles were becoming less popular in Israel.[57] In fact, starting in the 1950s, kibbutzim themselves began to industrialize, setting up factories that complemented their agricultural produce.[58] (Altogether, the share of agricultural production in Israel had sharply declined from 14.2 percent of GDP in 1955 to 7.9 percent in 1970.)[59] So the agricultural work that had once been the organizing center of the kibbutz and the moshav could not be a focal point for new rural settlements.

Other rural settlement models based on industry or services rather than agriculture were also inadequate, Gdor observed. In the early 1970s, the Settlement Department had developed the "Industrial Village," which was centered around in-house factories.[60] But there were no factories in Ofra to anchor the settlement; many of its residents were commuters who worked in city centers.[61] Equally inadequate was the "Rural Center," a settlement type designed to provide general services, such as education and healthcare, to nearby agricultural settlements. The problem with this settlement type was that "right of residence" in the Rural Center was limited to service workers, such as teachers and nurses, during the period of their employment. Once they ceased to be engaged in that work, residents had to leave the place.[62] Rural Center residents, in other words, were considered temporary, and they

בצלאל / בית ספר לאמנות ולאומנות ,ירושלים   BEZALEL / SCHOOL OF ARTS AND CRAFTS / JERUSALEM

FIGURE 2.6. "From the City to the Village," an award-winning poster designed by Dan Reisinger, 1953. In subsequent years, the General Organization of Workers in Israel produced posters bearing the same title to encourage Israelis to move to rural communities. (The Shenkar Institute for Research and Documentation of Design in Israel.)

could not become homeowners. This model was therefore at odds with the settlers' desire to set down roots in the West Bank. (Another settlement, the settlement of Allon Shvut, which housed a number of Gush Emunim activists, had been designated as a Rural Center, and it was, in fact, one of the concerns the settlers raised in their meeting at Gdor's house.)[63] A new model had to be devised to accommodate a permanent community of commuters in a rural area.

Central to that new model, Gdor insisted, would be a strong sense of community among homeowners who worked in remote urban centers and did not share either their income or means of production. He therefore limited the model to 250 or 500 families. This way, Gdor explained, everyone would know everyone else in the settlement.[64] He also insisted it was important to have some homogeneity among the residents. As long as the residents shared a system of beliefs, like the ideology of Gush Emunim, the settlement could function as a close-knit society. A shared ideology, he thought, would encourage residents to organize community events and provide services, such as extracurricular school and youth movement activities and home-care for the elderly.[65] To ensure this homogeneity, Gdor designed his model as a closed system. All residents would be members of a cooperative union, and anyone wanting to move in would have to be vetted by the union.[66] As Gdor later recalled, the settlers were especially intent on having a screening mechanism, since they worried that Palestinians might move to Ofra.[67]

The settlers were hardly the first to take an interest in screening mechanisms. Screening mechanisms had played an important role in the rise of co-ops, or cooperatives, as a popular housing form in North America in the late nineteenth and early twentieth centuries. At a time when American cities were becoming more ethnically diverse, co-ops offered middle- and upper-middle-class Americans some control over their milieu by excluding those they deemed socially unfit, including Jews and Catholics.[68] But Gdor didn't need to look that far for other references. Over the years, cooperative villages in Israel had developed their own screening mechanisms. Some kibbutzim went as far as to put candidates through a trial period, sometimes lasting a year or two, before members voted on whether to accept the applicant as a full member of the kibbutz.[69] The community settlement model was not an outlier in its quest for homogeneity.

Gdor did not give much attention to questions of aesthetics and physical form when delineating his model. Nevertheless, in meetings and personal correspondence, he underlined the importance of uniformity. Since the social structure of the community settlement allowed economic stratification, it would be important to have some sense of equality among the residents, at least on the level of aesthetics. Houses therefore had to look the same, Gdor explained. If needed, a community settlement could develop a couple of alternative models of homes, but not more than that. "It was important not to allow residents to build whatever they wanted," Gdor later emphasized. He also insisted that model homes should be relatively small. The community settlement wasn't planned for multistory houses, especially since plot sizes were significantly smaller than those in older rural settlement types like the moshav.[70]

Uniformity was already a common feature in the Israeli landscape. After independence, in the 1950s and 1960s, the government erected scores of repetitive, modernist housing blocks. Some were built on the outskirts of existing cities; others defined new towns in the periphery of the country. Uniformity allowed cheap and fast construction at a time when masses of immigrants were flocking to the nascent country from around the world. In addition, it seemed to correspond to the government's melting-pot policy, devised to assimilate the new immigrants and make them natives of the new Israeli state. Architectural uniformity, according to the architectural theorists Rachel Kallus and Hubert Law-Yone, was a means of establishing some kind of social coherence in the early years of statehood.[71] The future residents of these uniform housing estates were rarely consulted.

The settlers of Ofra, however, *were* consulted, and they did not feel comfortable at first with Gdor's overall conception. When he drove to Ofra to present his model to the general assembly in November 1975, Gdor encountered some opposition. Some residents told him they wanted something bigger and more open—something that would resemble an urban center. They considered rural settlement models only because they lacked land tenure and funds needed for a large settlement. Other residents showed no interest in professional planning, or in having a settlement model at all. One bluntly explained, "Most of the people here came to Ofra not in order to erect some kind of a community model. . . . We came here to settle the land of Judea. . . . And for this cause I am willing to have some chaos if it advances the settlement and the development of the land." Another dismissed the entire discussion, complaining, "This is all about the distant future. It doesn't solve our immediate problems. Our main problem is to enlarge the settlement by a few dozen members (and even that's a stretch)." Gdor was perplexed by the residents' criticism. As if to mock their indecisiveness, he ironically replied, "I know of one settlement where everyone is constantly preoccupied with ideological debates and instead of growing larger, they only end up splitting [into smaller and smaller pieces]."[72]

Gdor's relationship with Gush Emunim activists soon began to deteriorate.

As he later recalled, he could no longer ignore the huge gap between his professional interest as a planner and the ideas that motivated the settlers. "My approach was a planning approach. I am a planner," Gdor explained. "But Gush Emunim [activists] were busy founding as many settlements as possible. So we had conflicts."[73] Gdor also found the activists too aggressive, too contemptuous of the law, and too dismissive of his planning guidelines to sustain a working relationship. And so, some six months after he first met the activists, he resigned.[74]

In subsequent years, dozens of settlements would be built in the West Bank, based loosely on the model of the community settlement that Gdor had proposed. Today he believes his work had little to do with that. The propagation of the model was part of the political project of Gush Emunim, not the planning guidelines he drafted. "I gave them a formula. Politics had nothing to do with it," he told me when we met.[75] But politics certainly had an impact on the way Gush Emunim used Gdor's formula. As he suspected, they cared more about populating the West Bank with Jewish Israelis than planning guidelines. They did adopt some of his recommendations, like the closed nature of the community, secured by an admissions process; its commuter base; and the name "community settlement" (which became a legal category that state planners have come to recognize). Beyond this, the activists changed many of Gdor's planning guidelines. For example, they expanded the size of community settlements and ignored his suggestion to build uniform, modest houses. "Today, there are so many community settlements," he concluded. "[But] the majority of them, almost all, are distortions of the community settlement model."[76] Like other planners and architects who would soon work with the settlers of Ofra, Gdor left the West Bank feeling he had only a limited influence over the form of the settlements.

GIVING FORM TO THE COMMUNITY SETTLEMENT

Shortly after the settlers of Ofra parted ways with Gdor, they reached out to the architect Israel Levitt and asked him to develop plan drawings for the settlement.[77] Born in Poland in 1925, Levitt had grown up in Jerusalem. He served as an officer in the military and then studied architecture at the Technion. After graduating in 1950, he returned to Jerusalem, where he would open his own practice a few years later.[78] Colleagues described Levitt as short, gregarious, and energetic.[79] These qualities made him likable to many, and he quickly took on leading roles in the Architects and Engineers Association and the Rotary Club. Thanks to his strong social skills—which, according to his peers, exceeded his design skills—he started receiving large building commissions shortly after opening his firm. Notable among these was a residential quarter in Eshkol Heights, the first Jewish neighborhood Israel built in East Jerusalem, almost immediately after the Six-Day War.[80]

By the mid-1970s, however, Levitt was struggling to get building commissions in Jerusalem. The government still dominated the construction of the built environment, and as the architectural historian Alona Nitzan-Shiftan has shown, a new generation of Israeli architects, born in Palestine and socialized into the Zionist ethos, had taken over at the Ministry of Housing in the years following the Six-Day War. Inspired by postwar critiques of high modernism, these young architects rebelled against the high-modernist ethos of their predecessors—the very ethos Levitt had been trained in—and sought to transform Jerusalem into a testing ground for emerging design trends.[81] They had little interest in Levitt's work, which was now seen as dull and dated.

It was at this point in his career, in the face of an unfavorable market in his hometown of Jerusalem, that Levitt encountered the settlers of Ofra. Unsurprisingly, he took on the job. Levitt died in 1990. When I met with David Cassuto, Levitt's employee and later his business partner, who drew the first plans for a settlement in Hebron, he told me that Levitt volunteered to do the work at first, without charging a fee, because he probably saw Ofra as a potentially lucrative planning commission. Sooner or later, he must have assumed, the government would authorize the settlement and commission whoever it was that had already drafted plans for the place. As for any ideological concerns, they took a secondary place. An avowedly secular man, Levitt did not share the political vision of Gush Emunim, but, like Gdor, he was not an opponent of Gush Emunim either. In a refrain that I would hear frequently over the course of my research on this period, Cassuto reminded me, "At that time, unlike what's happening today when we have people who are in favor of [keeping] the [occupied] territories and people who are against it—then it wasn't like this."[82] It was a time when few could foresee the scale or the political consequences of the settlement movement.

It wasn't simply that Levitt, like many others, underestimated the political effects of the settlements. At the time, many in Israel believed that the occupation would improve living conditions in the occupied territories—that it would open up employment opportunities and bring economic prosperity to the Palestinians. To a degree, this had actually happened in the first years following the Six-Day War. Soon after the war ended, the government incorporated many Palestinians from the occupied territories into the Israeli workforce, where salaries were significantly higher. By 1974, 69,400 Palestinians were employed inside Israel, making up 33 percent of the Palestinian workforce of the occupied territories. As a result, between 1970 and 1974,

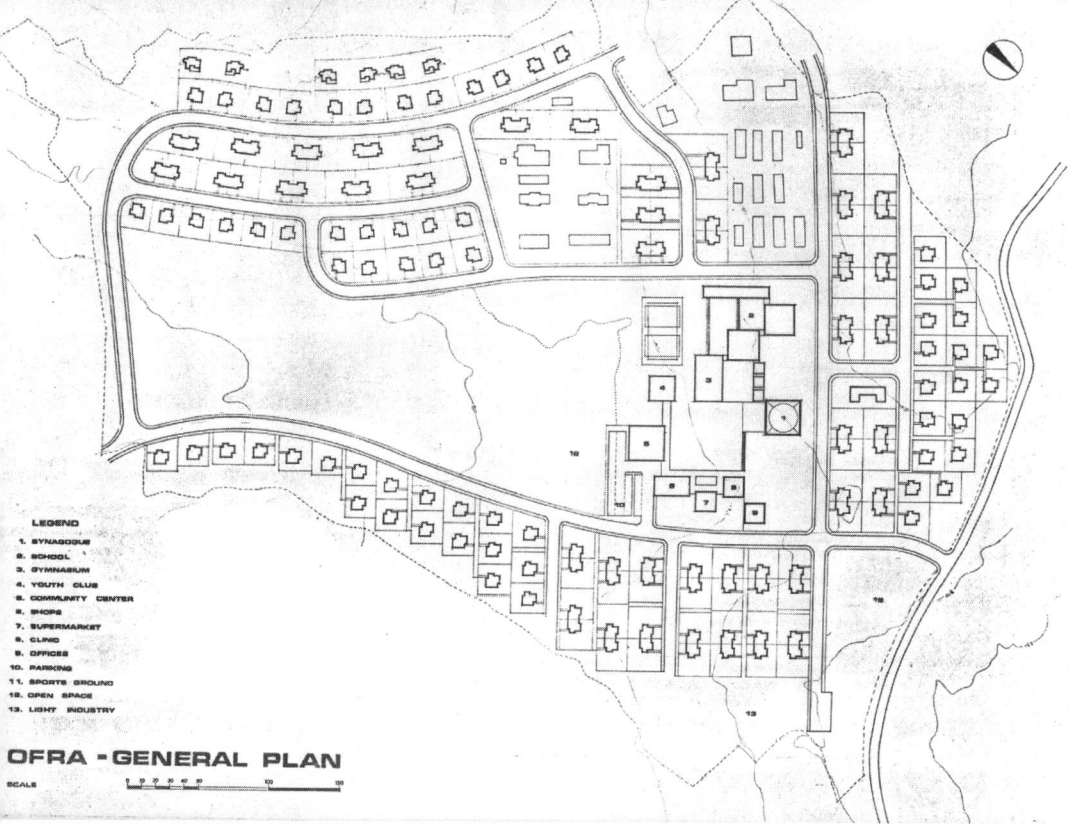

OFRA - GENERAL PLAN

SCALE

FIGURE 2.7. Israel Levitt, site plan of Ofra, 1977. (Ofra Archives.)

the average daily wages of all West Bank workers rose 35 percent. This economic growth, according to the writer Neve Gordon, ultimately had negative effects. It rendered the Palestinians more dependent on Israel, kept them in low-skilled manual jobs, and discouraged them from developing their own economy in the West Bank.[83] Nevertheless, at the time, it made the occupation appear somewhat benevolent. And it was probably with a sense of optimism, naïve as it may appear in retrospect, that Levitt took on the job at Ofra.

By April 1977, Levitt had completed a preliminary master plan for Ofra (figure 2.7). Designed for some two hundred families, it was organized around an area for public buildings. Among the public buildings were a synagogue, a school, a gymnasium, a youth club, a community center, and some shops. None of these installations exhibited any notable design innovation. They were modest single- or double-story flat-roofed structures. According to one of his colleagues, Levitt copied some of the designs from other architects, as he did in many of his projects. The community center, for example, resembled a library building recently inaugurated in Tel Aviv, designed by the architects Moshe Lofenfeld and Giora Gamerman. Adjacent to these public buildings was a large plot left open for outdoor recreation. All houses were placed on 500-square-meter plots and arranged around these two public areas, leaving the southeastern part of the settlement open.

Levitt gave careful attention to questions of parking and transportation, which were important for a rural commuting settlement, the first of its kind in the country. In contrast to existing rural settlements, which often enjoyed large vehicle-free areas, most houses in Levitt's plan had direct access to one of the main roads. There were barely any pedestrian-only pathways. In addition, Levitt placed a parking lot next to the community center that allowed easy access to the synagogue and other public buildings. Altogether, though the plan was not innovative in the design of individual buildings, it followed Gdor's planning principles, and it had little in common with other rural settlements in Israel.[84]

While Levitt was developing his plan, the settlers formed a voluntary building committee charged with overseeing his work and communicating it to the settlers. In a letter they attached to Levitt's drawings and circulated among the residents, they expressed their approval of the plan, explaining that the layout—the network of roads and subdivisions—could be built pretty much as is.[85] The only things stopping the settlers, however, were government authorization and funding, without which not much could be done.

PLANNERS "FROM BELOW" MEET PLANNERS "FROM ABOVE"

A few weeks after Levitt shared his drawings with the settlers, in the spring of 1977, things began to change in Ofra. On May 17, 1977, the Right-leaning Likud Party won the elections. Two months later, on July 26, the settlement of Ofra was on the agenda of a meeting held by the Joint Settlement Committee of the Israeli Government and the World Zionist Organization. The Joint Settlement Committee was then composed of seven ministers and seven board members of the World Zionist Organization; it had been founded in 1970 to decide on the establishment of new settlements on both sides of the Green Line. The committee, as the official approving body, was responsible for deciding on the size of the new settlements and for designating the planning agency responsible for their development—whether this would be the Settlement Department or the Ministry of Housing.[86] By the end of the meeting on July 26, the Joint Settlement Committee had authorized Ofra and two other West Bank settlements.[87] A week later, it assigned the planning and development of Ofra to the Settlement Department.[88] The settlers were ecstatic. After years of uncertainty and being turned down by government officials, their settlement was now in the hands of the same planners responsible for the design of most other rural settlements in the country.[89]

Within just a few weeks, however, the settlers' initial euphoria gave way to seemingly endless debates and negotiations with planning institutes. From the beginning, officials at the Settlement Department were uncomfortable with the project; a number of them strongly opposed the construction of settlements.[90] That feeling of discomfort grew after architects and planners from the Settlement Department met with the settlers and, later, with Levitt. The design principles of the community settlement had little to do with the established models for rural settlements—the kibbutz and the moshav—that architects and planners at the Settlement Department were familiar with. Partially reflecting a certain pastoral and communitarian ideal, the kibbutz and the moshav were generally characterized by modest houses, pedestrian-only pathways, and large agricultural fields. These elements were somewhat absent in Levitt's commuters' settlement, which was organized around private plots and dominated by roads, with almost no space for agricultural fields. On seeing Levitt's plan, Gavriel Krien, the chief architect at the Settlement Department, who himself had grown up on a kibbutz, described it as "extremely superficial." The program upon which the plan was based, he complained, was immature.[91] Officials agreed it had to be changed.

The settlers, however, were adamant about keeping intact some of the features of the community settlement, especially its commuter basis and the absence of any form of economic cooperation. Having spent two years on the site, long before official planning institutes had arrived, they had developed a sense of ownership over the place. "We got used to having this independence to decide over the settlement," one settler told a journalist who visited the site.[92] The architect Lou Gelehrter, who was hired by the Ministry of Construction and Housing to oversee the landscaping and development of Ofra, was struck by how assertive the settlers were. Normally, he communicated exclusively with the Ministry of Construction and Housing or with private developers and contractors; the future tenants played only a passive role. But now he found himself serving people who were already living on the site.[93]

Government planners and architects came to accept that it was too late to turn back time and establish a more conventional planning process in Ofra. Still, they tried. The settlement activist Yoel Bin-Nun later recalled an instance when officials from the Settlement Department met with several activists at Ofra. For an entire day they tried to convince the settlers to change their plans and have the settlement designed according to existing guidelines. But by the end of the day, he recalled, the officials had given up: "After we explained to them how the settlement works, told them about the building code, that we were here for almost three years already and had 30 families, they understood that it was impossible to turn back the wheel. I remember they said, 'It is impossible to take this baby back into the womb.' "[94]

In December 1977, the Settlement Department commissioned Levitt, as he had calculated, to develop his master plan for Ofra.[95] (In the preceding month, the military had issued an expropriation order seizing 265 dunams in the area to make space for the settlement.)[96] Over the next couple of months, Levitt redrew the plan. In particular, he increased the number of residential units from 200 to 275 and distributed them along identical roads. Approximately ten streets branched off from each of these roads. The streets ended in cul-de-sacs, creating ample parking space for the houses. In addition, Levitt added an industrial area near the settlement. Between the residential and the industrial areas, he allocated a small land plot for agriculture.[97] Not everyone wanted these agricultural fields; many settlers considered it a waste of space. But Yehuda Etzion, the original founder of Ofra, who was born on a kibbutz, insisted on having agriculture. Eventually, he convinced his fellow activists that some agriculture would help make their stay in Ofra more permanent.[98] Admittedly it also rendered the plan more agreeable to the government planners, who were baffled by the commuter settlement model.

In March 1978, Levitt presented the revised plans for evaluation by a special review committee at the Settlement Department.[99] Members of the review committee were not entirely satisfied. The private land plots, they complained, were too large, and the roads took up too much space. In an attempt to make Ofra look more like a kibbutz, the committee members asked Levitt to eliminate some of the roads he drew, remove the cul-de-sacs, and replace them with pedestrian-only paths and centralized parking areas.[100] Regardless of their discomfort, however, the review committee approved the master plan at the end of that meeting.[101]

The settlers must have been satisfied. They could now move on to construction. Architects and planners at the Settlement Department, by contrast, were anything but happy. They were hardly convinced by the model of the community settlement and by Levitt's plan. They resented the paucity of agricultural fields, the car-dominated layout, and the overall absence of so-cialist ideals. Altogether, according to the geographer David Newman, until the 1970s, Israeli centralized planning agencies looked down on the idea of commuting communities, seeing it as "anti-ideological," especially when compared to communities of agricultural laborers.[102] "I am allergic to your [community settlement] model," the head of the Settlement Department told Gdor when he saw him in his office.[103] Some of them resent it even today.

When I met Gavriel Krien in 2015, he was frankly perplexed by my interest in writing an architectural history of Ofra. Leave it, he advised. There is nothing to look for there. Reflecting on the community settlement model, he added, "It is not a sophisticated thing. . . . It is just a collection of houses sitting on a mountain. . . . Sometimes it may have a little agricultural land and a small service center . . . that's it."[104] It was devoid of all the Labor Zionist ideals that he and many other planners at the Settlement Department believed in.

"TRUE SOCIALISTS"

Once officials had approved the master plan, the settlers shifted their focus to the design of permanent houses. Levitt had designed a model home for the settlement even before the government authorized Ofra (figure 2.8). Residents, he thought, could choose between two iterations, one with two bedrooms and the other with four.[105] Settler representatives asked Levitt to design the first model to be expandable so that families with moderate incomes could purchase the smaller iteration and then easily transform it into a four-bedroom house once funds became available to them.[106] He capped the homes with flat roofs and clad the walls with horizontally arranged stone tiles to highlight the sense of connectedness to Jerusalem that many of the settlers shared. As long as the settlement was unauthorized, though, no one would take Levitt's model homes too seriously.

Now, settler representatives shared Levitt's model home designs with planners at the Ministry of Construction and Housing.[107] Neither the settlers nor the government planners, however, were impressed by the model homes. "Gentlemen, these are not our models," planners told the settlers, and explained that developing Levitt's models would take a lot of time and money, as opposed to replicating one of the model homes that the ministry had already built elsewhere.[108] The settlers, for their part, were keen on having their homes built as quickly as possible. By that point, they were tired of living in temporary structures, and, equally important, they feared that any delay in construction might endanger the future of the settlement. But members of the settlers' building committee had also been unsure about Levitt's model homes from the beginning, particularly their flat roofs. They preferred pitched roofs.[109]

Inspired by European conceptions of rural landscapes, Zionist settlers were building pitched-roof houses in rural settlements in Palestine from the late nineteenth century.[110] In the early twentieth century, the pitched roof functioned as a sign of modernity and progress, in contrast to the old Palestinian domed roof. Even after modernist émigré architects had popularized

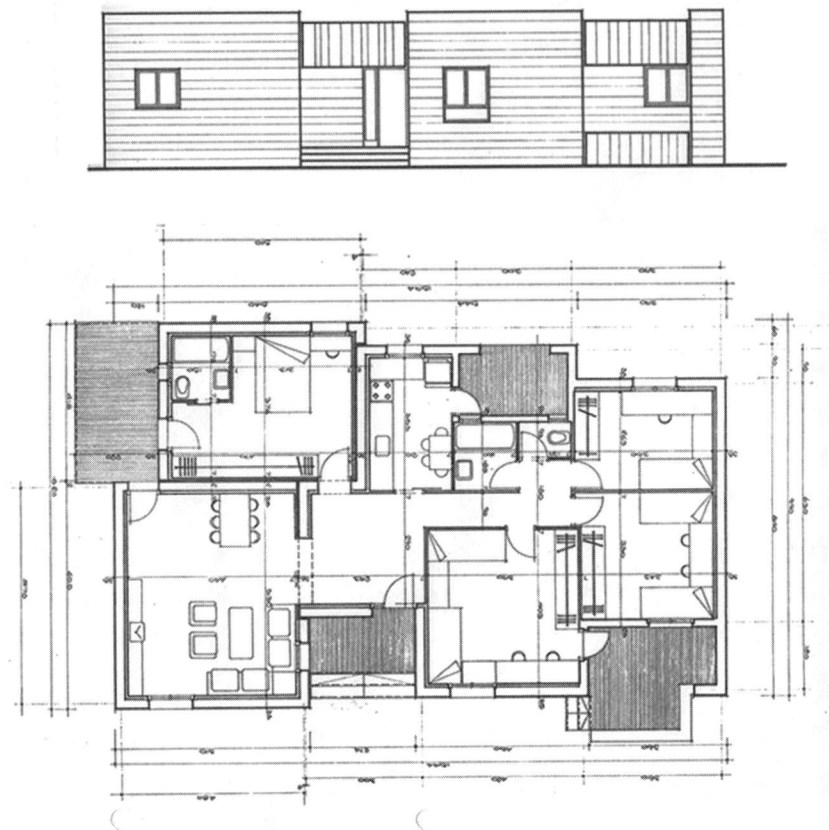

FIGURE 2.8. Israel Levitt, plan and façade drawings of a four-bedroom home designed for Ofra, 1977. (Ofra Archives.)

the flat roof in Jewish towns, architects working in the kibbutz and the moshav continued designing pitched-roof houses. They continued doing so even as they designed public buildings in rural settlements—dining halls and community centers—with flat roofs.[111] By the mid-twentieth century, therefore, the pitched roof had become an undisputed marker of the moshav and the kibbutz.

Although the settlers had no interest in the collectivist life of the kibbutz, and the community settlement model had been stripped of most of its co-operative elements, Ofra's representatives still wanted to be associated with the kibbutz. As David Newman has argued, Gush Emunim activists from the beginning portrayed themselves as modern-day pioneers, on a par with prestate Zionist settlers.[112] Moshe Merhavia, who had served as the secretary of Ofra at the time, told me that by linking the settlement with the kibbutz, they hoped to bolster a sense of pioneer-ship among the community itself and, equally important, help legitimize the community in the eyes of the planning institutes.

> Because we didn't have economic cooperation [that was common in the kibbutz] we had to solidify this thing through other supports. And we sometimes went into the innards . . . like deciding on the roofs. . . . Such esoteric things [the pitched roofs] were very important at the time in giving an expression to heart yearnings, to the idea of social cooperation, that we are like a kibbutz. . . . It was also part of the thing to express rural-ness, so that they [official planning bodies] will swallow us up. I remind you that we knocked on their doors . . . and said . . . "we are like you."[113]

When I met Etzion, the original founder of Ofra, he concurred: "The image, I mean the graphic image—at the level of posters and ads—of the kibbutz [house] . . . had its effect on us, also on me. It talked to me. I don't remember how vocal I was about the pitched roofs, but I am sure this image had an impact on me, and . . . others."[114] Aside from signaling a genealogical relation with the kibbutz, the sloped roof also had the added practical benefit of increasing the square footage of the houses. As another resident of Ofra explained to me, the attic space created by the sloped roof could be used as an extra bedroom, an important feature in light of the relatively large family size typical of religious families.[115]

The settlers' desire to resemble the kibbutz went hand in hand with their wish to differentiate themselves from the Palestinian village, where flat roofs were abundant. Unlike the settlers of Hebron, who were enthralled with Palestinian architecture, Ofra's settlers were geographically removed from any dense Palestinian urban fabric. In addition, by the time the master plan had been approved and the settlers began negotiating the design of their model homes, a number of violent clashes had occurred between settlers and Palestinians.[116] Such clashes tended to harden the Gush Emunim activists' view of the Palestinians.[117] They also seem to have disabused many settlement activists of their early fantasies in which Palestinian architecture was identified as the architecture of ancient Israel. As Merhavia explained to me, they now saw the Palestinian village as primitive and backward—not something they wanted to emulate. "We were freed from that dream of looking like an Arab village in order to be authentic," he clarified with pride, and with some scorn for his predecessors. "We wanted to resemble the pioneers who founded the kibbutz and the moshav."[118]

FIGURE 2.9. Pitched-roof house that state planners presented to the settlers, undated. Most houses that were eventually built in Ofra had steeper rooftops. All also had their ground floor leveled. (Ofra Archives.)

For these reasons, when Ministry of Construction and Housing planners showed the settler representatives the pitched-roofed homes they had built in other kibbutzim, the settlers agreed to drop Levitt's model homes, without even consulting him. Together they selected a model produced by Ashtrum, a private company that the Ministry of Construction and Housing had collaborated with (figure 2.9). Compared to other ministry models, this model home was relatively large and could be easily expanded from a two-bedroom into a three- or four-bedroom house.[119] Merhavia and members of Ofra's building committee made some changes to Ashtrum's model home so that it would fit their religious lifestyle. Most importantly, they moved the kitchen from its original location, which was open to the living room.[120] While appropriate for secular users, many of the settlers preferred having the kitchen closed off from the living room. This way the living room could serve as an additional bedroom.[121] An extra bedroom was usually needed during the holidays, when distant family members would come visit, or if the family grew and needed more space. Furthermore, moving the kitchen allowed it to be enlarged to serve large holiday dinners. The settler representatives also added two sinks, required for a kosher kitchen, and added another sink outside the washroom for hand-washing rituals.[122] In addition, they added a thin layer of stone cladding, emphasizing their sense of connectedness to Jerusalem.[123]

Not everyone was satisfied with the new model home. When Merhavia and members of the building committee presented it to the settlers' assembly, they encountered harsh criticism. Some settlers complained that the model home lacked the needed insulation and was of very poor quality altogether. Their concerns were not unfounded. Even the people at Ashtrum warned the settlers' representatives that the model home had been designed for a coastal climate and did not fit the weather conditions of the mountainous region of the West Bank, where winter temperatures were lower and harsh winds were recorded throughout the year.[124] The assembly therefore voted against the model home. Although Merhavia and his collaborators agreed with the assembly's concerns, they decided to ignore the vote, and signed the contract for the model home the following day. "We understood that if these homes will not be approved, construction would get stuck," one of them later explained. Delays, he feared, could have detrimental effects on their entire enterprise.[125] As much as the design process expressed the settlers' desire to establish themselves as the forebearers of pioneering Zionism, it also reflected their fear that the government would reverse its decision and remove the settlement.

By October 1980, construction of the first fifty houses was in full swing. By September of the following year, they were all occupied (figures 2.10 and 2.11).[126] With time, the settlers learned to love the model home, even those who had previously opposed it. The model home accommodated their religious needs and expressed some of their ambitions, making them feel as if they were part of a longer lineage of pioneering Zionists. "We are the true socialists," one settler proudly told Edna Solodar, a Member of Parliament and kibbutz member, when she visited Ofra shortly after construction was completed. "We did not want to have one [resident] envy the other," he explained, pointing at the repetitive, pitched-roofed houses.[127] It was ironic, if not preposterous, for the settlers to claim the legacy of the kibbutz after removing all of its communitarian and agricultural features and keeping only the red roofs. Leaders of the kibbutz movement publicly disassociated themselves from the settlers, and the luminary writer Amos Oz called them out as nothing but religious radicals masquerading as pioneering Zionists.[128] But still the settlers continued to see themselves as the heirs of Zionism. From now on, they decided, all new houses in Ofra would have to follow the model home's design principles—namely the pitched roof and stone-clad walls (figure 2.12).[129] And a number of subsequent settlements would follow suit.

FIGURE 2.10. Settlers repairing houses in Ofra, 1981. (Berman family, Ofra Archives.)

FIGURE 2.11. Houses in Ofra, 1984. (Photograph by Herman Chanania, Government Press Office.)

FIGURE 2.12. Aerial view of Ofra, 1993. (Ofra Archives.)

A DIMINISHED SANCTUARY

Levitt, the architect of record, was disappointed to see the houses the settlers chose for themselves.[130] They didn't resemble the houses he had designed. Nevertheless, he continued to work on the settlement's next major project: Ofra's synagogue. By the end of 1981, Levitt had completed two detailed design alternatives for the building. The first version showed a two-story structure crowned with four crystal-shaped towers. These vertical elements, combined with a rather dramatic floor plan featuring two identical superimposed square shapes, made the building eye-catching. The second alternative showed a slightly smaller two-story structure. Taking the shape of a hexagon, it was capped by a Star of David and could accommodate some four hundred guests (figure 2.13). The Jewish tradition calls for the sexes to be segregated during worship, and both alternatives observed that ritual practice by allocating the ground floor of the synagogue for men and the upper level for women. Levitt decided the second alternative was more appropriate for the settlement. He therefore built a model of the hexagon-shaped synagogue and placed it inside Ofra's temporary synagogue so the residents could observe it.[131]

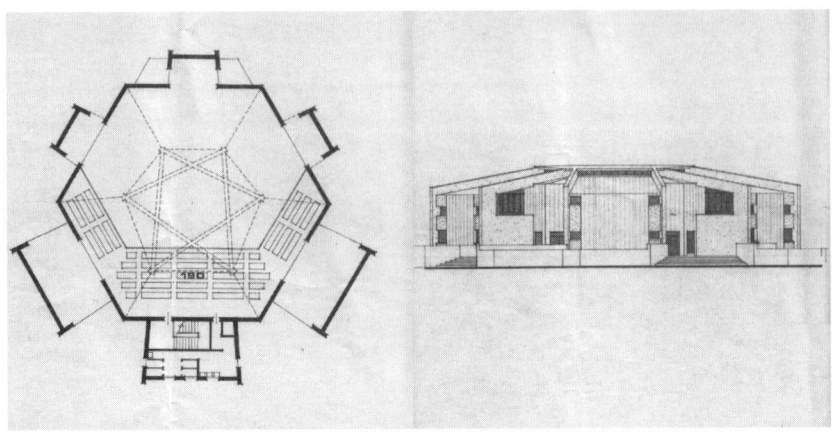

FIGURE 2.13. Israel Levitt, Ofra's synagogue, second alternative, 1981. (Ofra Archives.)

When the settlers saw Levitt's model, they were outraged. "It doesn't seem right that the synagogue at the center of the settlement (at the physical center and the spiritual center of the settlement), would be imposed on us by an outside force," one complained.[132] Yehuda Etzion, the yeshiva graduate who had founded Ofra six years earlier, was especially concerned. In a letter he circulated among the settlers, he insisted that the design lacked [the right kind of] beauty, and "even if there was any beauty in Levitt's plan, other than the Star of David, created by the beams of the ceiling, its beauty was arbitrary."[133] By arbitrary beauty, Etzion was referring to the plan's complex geometry, which had little to do with the building's function. To his belief, "A synagogue structure should have simple lines so they would match the simplicity and honesty a prayer should express."[134] And, as for the Star of David, Etzion lamented, it was a symbol the Jewish people had adopted at a relatively late stage in history. It definitely wasn't something "worth casting in dozens of cubic meters of fortified concrete."[135] Levitt's design, several settlers agreed, had to be replaced.

The settlers elected a residents' committee charged with redesigning the synagogue.[136] The committee was composed of three members, with Etzion among them. The committee drew inspiration for the new design from the ancient Jewish Temple (known as Herod's Temple) that stood on Temple Mount in Jerusalem until 70 CE, when it was destroyed by the Roman army. In a letter he published in *Et Ofra* (a magazine the settlers began to produce regularly in 1982), Etzion wrote on behalf of the committee that any modern-day synagogue was merely a substitute for the Temple—a "diminished temple" (mikdash me'at).[137] Ofra's synagogue, therefore, had to remind the residents of the old Temple. Nevertheless, Etzion emphasized, it should not be an exact replica of the Temple but an incomplete copy exhibiting intentional design mistakes.[138] An incomplete copy, he later explained, "had the power to encourage the people of Israel to build the actual place of gathering—the Holy Temple [in Jerusalem]."[139]

Etzion's brief required studying the old Temple. The Temple itself had of course been destroyed, so the committee members searched for synagogues that were built shortly after the destruction of the Temple and were now in ruins. They were hardly the first to look for traces of Jewish life from ancient times for purposes other than archaeological curiosity. Secular Zionists in the first decades of the twentieth century were eager to identify biblical sites and structures associated with the ancient Israelites in Palestine. These sites provided a much-needed collective past for people who had recently immigrated to Israel from many other parts of the world.[140] Later, to further national cohesion, David Ben-Gurion, Israel's first prime minister, gave speeches that drew on the Bible and emphasized attachment to the Land of Israel.[141] In the aftermath of the Six-Day War, as the sociologist Michael Feige has shown, the passion for seeking evidence to show the connection between the ancient Israelites and the Land of Israel transferred itself, so to speak, from the secular Zionists to religious Zionists. Bar-Ilan University, an academic institution associated with religious Zionism, opened its Department of Land of Israel Studies and Archaeology in the early 1970s. In subsequent years, Gush Emunim activists would open educational centers in a number of settlements, dedicated to biblical archaeology and local geography and geared toward high school students. Although the scientific value of these centers is questionable, they served to strengthen the activists' sense of belonging to the land.[142]

In Ofra, the search for ancient sources led the synagogue committee members to visit the Galilee region in the northern part of Israel to examine the ruins of old synagogues. These old synagogues, they explained in a letter circulated among the settlers, were the closest one could get to the original: the Jewish Temple. Etzion and his collaborators drew plans of these synagogues and used them as a source of design principles for Ofra's synagogue. The committee was especially intrigued by the old synagogues' rectilinear scheme: this, they thought, could remedy one of the flaws in Levitt's plan. The hexagonal shape of Levitt's plan, the committee understood, made it virtually impossible to enlarge the synagogue as the population of the settlement grew. The rectilinear shape, by contrast, would allow for future expansions; as they showed in a diagram attached to the letter, new aisles could simply

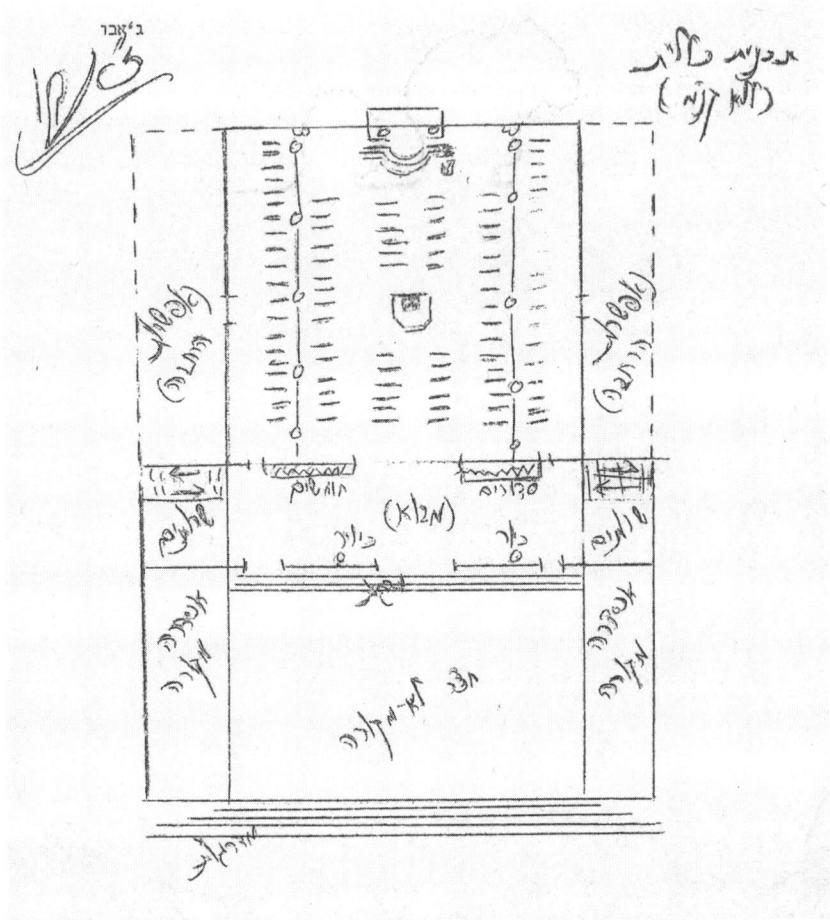

FIGURE 2.14. Ze'ev Hanoh Erlih (member of Ofra's synagogue committee), sketch of a rectilinear synagogue, showing how new aisles (marked in dashed lines) could be added to the building, August 1982. (Ofra Archives.)

be added to the sides of the main hall (figure 2.14). The committee members also took interest in a courtyard they documented at an ancient synagogue in Mount Hebron. Such a courtyard could host wedding ceremonies and serve as a reception space, they wrote. Equally inspiring, they noted, were the pilasters common in many old synagogues. If replicated correctly, they argued, these elements "would remind us, the people coming to pray, of the glorious days of the people of Israel."[143]

To assemble these elements into a detailed design proposal, Etzion recruited one of his friends, Gideon Charlap. Charlap was a graduate of a far-right yeshiva in Kiryat Arba and a supporter of Gush Emunim, and he happened to be a fifth-year architecture student at the Technion. At the time, Charlap was working on a design thesis about Ofra. Architecture students are often required to produce a thesis in which they develop plans for prospective building projects. For his thesis, Charlap developed a new public center for the settlement, a revised model home, and a synagogue design. He was therefore excited about the possibility of working with Etzion and the other members of the synagogue committee. Based on Etzion's guidelines, Charlap drafted a set of drawings that incorporated numerous references to the old Temple and its successors.[144] Notably, he recessed into the wall the closet where the Torah scrolls were to be kept and surrounded it by five glass slits, referencing the five wooden gates that surrounded the Torah Ark in the old Temple. In addition, Charlap replicated the three monumental gates that once welcomed visitors to the old Temple. But to highlight the structure's incompleteness, he blocked two of the gates and designed the central one so that it would be taller than the synagogue's walls and break through the ceiling. "Here lies a first expression of the pending wholeness we have not reached yet," Etzion wrote, reflecting on the blocked gates.[145] By the end of 1982, Charlap had completed the design and passed it to Etzion, who presented it to the residents' assembly.

The settlers took great interest in Etzion's idea of a diminished temple. Nevertheless, they had doubts about Charlap's competence, due to his youth and lack of experience. The general assembly therefore dismissed Charlap and paired Etzion with Meiron Poliakin, a Jerusalem-based architect who had previously done some design work for three of the settler families.[146] Poliakin was relatively young at the time, and although he did not share the ideological project of the Gush Emunim, he was open to Etzion's vision for the synagogue.[147]

Etzion and Poliakin soon became close friends. "It was truly an intimate relationship, the most intimate a friendship can be," Etzion recalled. The two would spend hours at Poliakin's office drafting sketches for the synagogue. Poliakin would listen carefully to Etzion and flesh out his ideas with architectural solutions. Together, for example, they agreed the Torah Ark should be placed in one of the corners, framed by a wall with three unequal gates that echoed the main façade of the old Temple.[148] By June 1983, the two had completed a design for a 560-seat synagogue (figure 2.15).

A few months later, construction began. Etzion was ecstatic. Every day he would spend hours on the site with the construction workers. But then, on a spring day in 1984, a group of police officers arrived at the construction site.

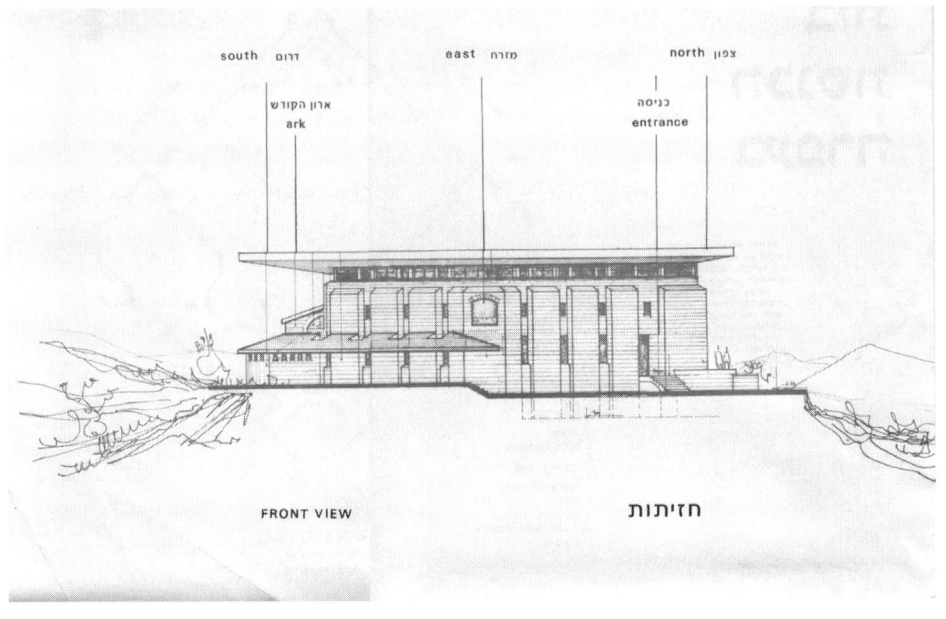

south ‏דרום‏   east ‏מזרח‏   north ‏צפון‏

‏ארון הקודש‏   ‏כניסה‏
ark   entrance

FRONT VIEW   ‏חזיתות‏

FIGURE 2.15. Meiron Poliakin, elevation of Ofra's synagogue, 1983. (Ofra Archives.)

At the time, Etzion was not only preoccupied with a "diminished temple" but was also developing plans for a real Temple. And unlike the one in Ofra, the second one was to be built on the ruins of the Dome of the Rock—among the holiest sites in Islam, where the Prophet Muhammad is believed to have ascended to heaven during a night vigil. Etzion, along with other members of what came to be known as the Jewish Underground, was planning to blow up the site. Between 1980 and 1984, members of the Jewish Underground were involved in a series of terror attacks against Palestinian civilians and officials.[149] When the police showed up at the construction site, it was not to halt construction of the settlement but to take Etzion to prison, where he would spend the next seven years.

Still, Ofra proceeded with the design, and in 1987 the synagogue was opened to the public (figure 2.16). Poliakin, the architect of record, did not show up for the inauguration ceremony. He was hardly happy to see the building complete—not because the settlers had undermined his authority or gutted his design, as they had done previously with other design professionals. On hearing about Etzion's arrest, Poliakin was terrified. He could never have imagined that one of his closest friends, a pious man with whom he had been sharing his artistic vision and innermost thoughts, was in fact a terrorist.[150]

FIGURE 2.16. Interior view of Ofra's synagogue. (Photograph by author.)

Like Gdor and Levitt, Poliakin could not see the settlement movement for what it was. He, too, it seems, envisioned an "enlightened occupation" that would benefit both Jews and Muslims. Now, it occurred to Poliakin that his endless talks with Etzion about the Temple and about redemption were not innocent speculation. Etzion and the Gush Emunim were not just playing with abstract ideas. They had a concrete political program, and Poliakin, unwittingly, had put his professional skills at their service. Offended and perplexed, Poliakin never returned to the construction site. Still today, he refuses to talk about the synagogue and the design process. "It is personal and it is painful," he told me over the phone and asked me not to contact him again.[151]

The settlers, on the other hand, gladly attended the inauguration event. Even though Etzion's criminal activity seemed to cast a shadow over the synagogue, the pious settlers were pleased with the design. Almost every detail in the building was loaded with religious meaning. Etzion, together with his many collaborators, had managed to generate a formal language that originated in the scriptures. And even though some outsiders criticized the overt symbolism and grandiose scale of the building, almost all residents were enthusiastic about the finished product.[152]

By the time the settlers gathered to celebrate the new synagogue, something else had happened: the model of the community settlement they had vigorously fought over was replicated across the West Bank. In the spring of 1978, there were eight community settlements in the West Bank at different stages of development.[153] Just two years later, in 1980, there were more than twenty.[154] Although planners at the Settlement Department had initially opposed the community settlement model, a few of them had come to embrace it. In 1978, shortly after the Likud Party came to power, the Settlement Division was assigned a new chairperson, Matetyahu Drobles, specifically to counterbalance the Settlement Department's dovish planners. Almost immediately, Drobles proposed erecting scores of community settlements across the West Bank.[155] To encourage the new settlements to develop according to their model, Ofra's settlers occasionally sent representatives to oversee their construction and development.[156] Some of Ofra's residents assumed leading roles in Gush Emunim, gaining considerable influence. In 1980, one of them founded *Nekuda*, a monthly publication that further assisted in disseminating the residents' ideas.[157] Even though many of these subsequent community settlements did not ultimately look like Ofra—most notably, they rarely shared Ofra's modest model home—they maintained some of its features. Almost all had a relatively similar curvilinear road system, regular division into private plots, and admissions committees in charge of keeping the homogeneous nature of the settlements. Some also reproduced the pitched red-tile roofs. It was not long before the community settlement model was also imported to Israel, where it became equally popular. Starting in the 1970s, with the unwinding of the nation-building era, a growing number of Israelis came to prioritize high living standards rather than the pioneering spirit that had inspired previous housing forms in the country. They yearned to leave their modest public housing units, and they had little interest in agricultural work. For some, the community settlement provided a much-needed outlet.[158] For religious Zionists, whether in Israel or in the West Bank, it also offered a refuge from the largely secular urban centers, allowing them to preserve their religious way of life in a self-segregated environment.[159] By 1987, only ten years after the government authorized Ofra, there were some one hundred community settlements in Israel and the West Bank.[160] Standing together by the new synagogue, on that summer day when the building was first opened to the public, the settlers of Ofra had many reasons to be satisfied.

CONCLUSION

In 2015, a strange thing happened: Ofra began building monuments to itself. On the occasion of the settlement's fortieth anniversary, after more than sixty-five community settlements had been built in the West Bank, the settlers erected plaques next to the Jordanian camp and the makeshift shacks where Ofra's founders had first settled in 1975.[161] Each plaque bore a short description detailing the history of a structure. "This building contained Ofra's administrative offices in its early years," said one plaque. "Important decisions were made here, and when major issues had to be decided, the people were alerted by means of a PA system." Underneath the plaques were old photographs from the mid-1970s, showing Etzion and his fellow settlers standing by the rudimentary structures. They were all young and full of ambitions. The small shacks have not changed over the years. After the settlers moved to their permanent houses in 1981, the shacks housed different public facilities, including a post office, art gallery, health clinic, and school classrooms. Now, Hemdat Shani, the archivist of Ofra, proudly told me, they were designated for preservation, set to be frozen in time.

The fact that the settlers have begun historicizing their own existence just four decades after founding Ofra is symptomatic of an important shift. The commemoration of the past often functions to provide a source of identity at times of change, when that past seems especially distant.[162] In the 1970s and 1980s, the settlers of Ofra had a clear sense of who they were, and that sense of identity proved to be a source of power, especially when communicating with official planning agencies and design professionals. Architects like Levitt and Poliakin, who were struggling to get design commissions in Israel and did not fully grasp the political significance of the settlement movement, were helpless in the face of the strong-willed settlers who had a clear vision of what they wanted. Over the course of a decade, the settlers had contested, twisted, and redrawn their plans. Notably, they selected red rooftops that emphasized their identification with prestate Zionist pioneers and they moved the synagogue to the highest point in the settlement and modeled it after the old Temple in ways that resonated with their sense of piety.[163] The result was perhaps what one could have expected from the pairing of second-tier architects with zealot settlers without basic training in architecture: banal, rudimentary, and, in the case of the synagogue, out of scale. But to a degree, it also reflected the settlers' self-image, an image that other settlements, like Kokhav HaShahar and Ma'ale Michmash, were eager to replicate. For a while, then, it seemed as if the settlers had found the ultimate settlement form, and that from now on, Israelis wishing to live in the West Bank would all relocate to pseudo-kibbutz settlements where they would reside in identical houses that were fairly modest and maybe attend Shabbat services at a synagogue that was almost fantastic.

But by the time I began researching this book, many of Ofra's long-standing residents had come to feel that the new generation had lost the founders' spirit of pioneer-ship and their political commitment to the idea of the whole Land of Israel. Houses in Ofra had gotten bigger and, in a couple of cases, even flashy. The few agricultural plots Etzion had cultivated to reinforce a connection to the kibbutz had been replaced by relatively large single- or double-family houses. Also lost was the sense of social solidarity that Uzi Gdor had made the foundation of the community settlement. In 2020, Ofra housed about three thousand settlers, and few knew their neighbors. In other community settlements, these changes have become even more pronounced. Some even attracted private developers and investors.[164] Other than the desire to create a closed community that excludes the Palestinians, little remains of Ofra's founding vision.

The settlers of Ofra were not naïve. All the residents I interviewed for this study indicated that, at the end of the day, they were happy that the number of Israelis in the West Bank had increased, even if that came at the price of ideological diminution. Some added that perhaps these changes are a sign that the settlement movement has matured, that it has been normalized. But still this is not what they had in mind some four decades ago.

When I asked Etzion about the present state of settlements, he couldn't hide his frustration: "If I compare this to the dreams and aspirations we had in the past, then it hurts. It is sad."[165] The Jordanian shacks, standing by the large plaques, are a matter of the past, he knows. They no longer speak to the spirit of Ofra nor to that of other settlements. They have become museum objects.

Ironically, the vision of Etzion and of the Gush Emunim went the way of Gdor, Levitt, and perhaps even Poliakin, whose plans had been twisted and turned. However, neither the settlers of Ofra nor their disappointed planners were the last to see their vision upended, bulldozed by the haphazard, relentless engines of the settlement enterprise. In fact, already in the early 1980s, long before plaques commemorating Ofra's history were installed, as I discuss in the next chapter, a new group of settlers arrived: lower- and middle-class Israelis who loved the cheap real estate and beautiful vistas of the West Bank but had little interest in Labor Zionism or the divine relation between the Land of Israel and the Jewish people. This new group would negotiate yet a different settlement form that would become the new vanguard of the settlement enterprise.

CHAPTER 3

QUALITY-OF-LIFE SETTLEMENTS

On March 30, 1983, an exhibition opened in Tel Aviv in which plans and photographs documenting construction projects under way in thirty West Bank settlements were presented to the general public. The show, entitled *The Achievements of the Settlement of Judea and Samaria Exhibition*, was held at the Israeli Center for Building. It was curated by Israel Goodovitch, the former chief architect at the Division of Rural Planning of the Ministry of Housing (renamed the Ministry of Construction and Housing in 1977), who had overseen the construction of the first settlements in the West Bank. Goodovitch had since left the ministry, but he had been carefully following the construction of settlements.[1] The show was in part a documentary exhibition charting the progress of the settlement enterprise and in part a sales expo, intended to expand the market for West Bank real estate among the population of Israel's metropolitan center.

Unusual for an architectural exhibition, visitors were welcomed by a row of Fiat 127 cars upon their arrival. All were wrapped with red gift ribbons as if the exhibition center was the set of a game show. Indeed, anyone who bought a house in one of the settlements on view would be given a car. Behind the Fiats, the visitors passed through a series of four identical gates, shaped like the silhouette of a pitched-roof house. A poster at the side of each gate indicated the number of settlements that had been built since 1967. If there were only twenty-four settlements in 1977, by 1983 there were more than sixty, the posters indicated.[2] The message of these posters was clear: everyone is moving to the settlements; don't miss out!

After passing through the four gates, visitors entered the main exhibition hall, where they encountered a large-scale model of the West Bank made of sand and rocks brought in from the bare hilltops of the occupied territories. Rising from the rocky landscape of the model were street signs with names of settlements. A gift ribbon stretched from each sign to a large map of the

FIGURE 3.1. Minister of Construction and Housing David Levy (left) by one of the models on view in the exhibition, Tel Aviv, 1983. (Photograph by Yisra'el Simionski/ Israel Sun Ltd., courtesy of Israel Goodovitch, the architect, Tel Aviv.)

West Bank that sat in the corner of the hall. On the map, each settlement was marked with a small light bulb.

Moving past the sand model, visitors arrived at a large courtyard, where ten projection screens displayed images of construction projects in the West Bank. Dozens of sales booths were scattered around these screens and in the adjacent exhibition spaces (figure 3.1; see also figure 3.7). Operated by private developers, the booths invited potential homebuyers to examine the architectural plans and three-dimensional models of hundreds of new settlement houses, all for sale.

The houses on view were radically different from the rudimentary model home of Ofra or the repetitive modernist units of Kiryat Arba. They were significantly bigger and were offered in a range of styles, from neo-Orientalist, adorned with arches, stucco, and tile, to modernist cubic shapes with plaster cladding. They boasted lush lawns and fruit trees and amenities like swimming pools. A few had been designed by prominent Tel Aviv–based architects, but most were the work of less well-known architects. The settlements where these houses were being built, in turn, had little in common with the modest community settlement model developed by the religious members of Gush

Emunim. They were much larger, housing hundreds if not even thousands of families; they lacked admissions committees; and some had generic names like "Tree Tops" or "Scenery" that made no reference to biblical history. There was no connection between the architecture of these new settlements and the messianism that had motivated the establishment of religious Zionist settlements a decade earlier.

Indeed, the visitors who attended the exhibition were quite unlike the activists of Gush Emunim. They were mainly middle- and lower-income young couples looking to purchase a suburban home, in order, as Goodovitch put it, "to live the American dream."[3] The "true star of the show," according to a reporter for the weekly newspaper *Ha'ir*, was Minister of Construction and Housing David Levy, a Moroccan-born Jew and former construction worker who came from a struggling development town in northern Israel, and who was well known for his alienation from the labor elite. At the opening of the exhibition, Levy hopped from one sales booth to another, posing for the cameras with developers and contractors. The minister, the reporter explained, wanted to make sure no one else would get the credit for the construction boom on display.[4]

The show marked a high point in the process of settlement development that began in the late 1970s. It was fueled by a new kind of settlement that emerged with the rise of the Right-wing Likud Party, catering to a new kind of settler.[5] These settlements were large, suburban, and located near the border with Israel; and they were built for Israelis in lower- and middle-income brackets who wanted to improve their housing conditions. Few of these buyers held any strong ideological conviction about living in the West Bank or establishing a Jewish population there, or any strong emotional attachment to the sites of biblical history. Yet they flocked to the new settlements that are sometimes referred to as "quality-of-life settlements." (This term is used to refer also to community settlements that have taken a suburban façade.)[6] Between 1977 and 1984, the number of settlers increased from 4,000 to 35,000, populating some seventy-one new settlements.[7] Although some of these settlements were small or remote, the settlements that starred in the 1983 exhibition absorbed a larger share of the newcomers.[8] This exponential growth, however, began to slow toward the end of 1984, after the Likud Party failed to win enough votes in an election and was forced to form a national unity government with the more Left-leaning Alignment Party.[9] Between 1984 and 1987, only eight new settlements were founded.[10] Then, when the First Intifada broke out in December 1987, it became more difficult to attract Israelis to the West Bank just to improve their housing situation.[11] By that point, however, there were approximately 60,000 Israelis living in settlements, making the settlements a major fact on the ground.[12] Arguably, then, the decade between 1977 and 1987 marked the heyday of the settlement movement.

In this chapter, I explore how, during that decade, the messianic vision that guided the development of settlements like Ofra and Kiryat Arba in previous years was eclipsed by another motivation: the desire for space and privacy on the part of Israelis who were not (or were no longer) well served by the Israeli housing system. Accordingly, in this chapter, the focus shifts away from the messianic Jews, who are often singled out in historical and sociological accounts of the settlements. Although religious Zionist activists played important roles in establishing settlements in the first decade following the Six-Day War, they were somewhat marginal in the construction of settlements in the 1980s. At times, they expressed concerns about their construction. The construction of settlements was now led by the Ministry of Construction and Housing, which, for the most part, no longer commissioned in-house architects to produce designs, but preferred to outsource projects to private developers and contractors.[13] Although the state initiated the construction of most settlements, it did not exercise full control over their design; the wave of economic liberalization that swept through Israel in those years opened up the architecture of the new settlements to an array of contingent forces. This chapter details the experimentation in housing and community forms that resulted from this new conjuncture and that was driven by the aim of attracting Israelis without any political ideology to the West Bank.

My discussion of this experimentation focuses on three cases: Ma'ale Adumim, where Ministry of Construction and Housing officials employed new environmental design techniques; Alfe Menashe, where architects experimented with Palestinian architecture; and Nofim, where a private developer commissioned some of the most ostentatious houses in the West Bank. Each of these three settlements represents a different moment in the privatization of the design and construction of settlements: in Ma'ale Adumim, which was officially inaugurated in 1982, the Ministry of Construction and Housing was involved in most of the planning and construction stages; in Alfe Menashe, opened in 1983, the ministry outsourced the detailed planning and construction to a large consortium of private developers and construction companies; and in Nofim, opened in 1987, state officials allocated almost the entire enterprise to a single small developer. These three case studies cannot, of course, account for all the settlements built during this decade of intense construction, but they do illustrate a number of reoccurring themes that animated the construction boom of the 1980s: the shaky alliance between state officials and private developers, the fascination of local architects with global trends, and the cultivation of a new species of settlers who, as one visitor to the 1983 exhibition remarked, "discovered they can have the same quality of life as in California."[14]

PRIVATIZATION AND SUBURBANIZATION UNDER A LIKUD GOVERNMENT

The election of the Right-leaning Likud Party in 1977 marked a turning point in Israeli history. For three decades, the labor parties had enjoyed unquestioned control over the country. Under their command, the construction of settlements was relatively slow and inconsistent, and few government ministers openly supported the settlement movement. But now the government was in the hands of explicitly Right-wing politicians, many of whom actively supported the settlers. Two days after the elections, Menachem Begin, the head of the Likud Party, paid a visit to an outpost of Gush Emunim, where he proudly announced that soon there would be many settlements in the West Bank. A few weeks later, the government began authorizing a number of wildcat settlements associated with Gush Emunim. In September 1977, Minister of Agriculture Ariel Sharon, among the settlement movement's greatest supporters, proposed a twenty-year plan for settling some two million Israelis in scores of new settlements along the Jordan River, on the top of the mountain ridge of the northern West Bank, around Jerusalem, and across other areas he deemed important for Israel's security.[15] Then, in November 1979, the government officially decided, as a matter of policy, to expand the settlement project: to enlarge existing settlements and erect new ones.[16] In so doing, the sociologist Erez Maggor has argued, it flipped the logic of settlement construction. While bottom-up pressures had previously animated key parts of the construction of settlements, now top-down initiatives would take the lead.[17]

Under the guidance of the state, the construction of settlements entailed a number of preliminary projects that had not necessarily concerned the Gush Emunim and other activists. Most notably, the government established a legal framework for appropriating vast spans of land in the West Bank. Previously, settlements were occasionally built on privately owned Palestinian lands that were confiscated through temporary military orders, officially for security purposes.[18] A landmark court ruling of 1979, however, ruled the confiscation of privately owned Palestinian lands for settlement construction illegal.[19] To pursue its settlement plans, therefore, the government launched a mapping project aimed at locating uncultivated land parcels in the West Bank.[20] As an occupied territory, the West Bank inherited the Ottoman Land Code of 1858 that had remained almost intact under Jordanian rule. The Ottoman

Land Code instituted a system of land tenure according to which ownership was determined by acquisition *or use*. Any unregistered land located at a reasonable distance from existing communities, as well as land that had been left uncultivated for three years (or that had been cultivated for less than ten consecutive years), could revert back to the state.[21] Now, Israeli officials invoked the Ottoman Land Code to claim uncultivated parts of the West Bank as "state lands" (basically, public lands) and thus available to serve as sites for settlement construction.[22] By 1984, state officials had "found" tens of thousands of dunams of such "state lands," paving the way for grandiose settlement plans.[23] In addition, the Israeli Military Governorate and the Civil Administration issued a number of military orders that extended Israeli law to settlements while keeping Palestinians under military rule.[24]

Equally important, the new government provided generous funding packages to settlements. These packages included mortgages at favorable interest rates, as well as education, health services, and physical infrastructure often superior to that provided in Israel proper.[25] The historian Danny Gutwein has argued that such incentives were designed not only to populate the West Bank with Israelis but also to preserve the Likud Party's popularity among the working classes at a time when they had good reason to break ranks. Originally, in the 1940s and 1950s, Israel had instituted a robust welfare system. State agencies provided housing for tens of thousands of immigrants who flocked to the country after independence, as well as healthcare, education, and other services. Following the 1977 elections, the Likud government gradually reduced many of these services, including the housing provision.[26] Whereas in 1975 the government oversaw the construction of more than 27,000 residential units across the country, in 1983 that number fell to just 7,320 units.[27] The gradual withdrawal of public services—housing being one of many—had devastating effects on lower-income Israelis, the very constituency who voted in large numbers for the Likud. The funding packages allocated to West Bank settlements, according to Gutwein, functioned as a form of compensation through which the Likud could keep its base of voters. To continue enjoying state services, however, Israelis would have to move to the West Bank, where a quasi-welfare state was preserved by a neoliberal government.[28]

Relocating to a settlement became all the more appealing in light of suburbanization processes already in effect in Israel. As the architectural historian Shanee Shiloh has shown, during the 1950s and 1960s, suburbs were built on the outskirts of Tel Aviv, where a small elite class of mostly white-collar Ashkenazi Jews exchanged the apartments of socialist housing for relatively large single-family houses.[29] This trend increased in the 1970s and 1980s as Israelis took a growing interest in the suburban lifestyle. They were especially keen on purchasing detached or semidetached houses with private lawns and car garages. In 1971, one- or two-story structures accounted for only 11.2 percent of residential construction projects in Israel and West Bank settlements; by 1991, they accounted for 52.4 percent.[30] This trend had a number of causes. First was wealth. In the decades leading to the 1970s, the Israeli economy had grown at an accelerated pace. If in 1950 Israel's per capita GDP was 35 percent of US GDP, by 1972 it amounted to 62 percent.[31] This meant that more Israelis could adopt lifestyles that were previously limited to the elite.[32] Second, by the 1970s, after Israel had become a regional force, the nation-building project had begun to wither. A growing number of Israelis had come to feel alienated from the presumed Israeli national unity promoted by labor-led governments and were instead seeking physical and social privacy.[33] This sort of privacy was hard to achieve in the repetitive public housing blocks that had mushroomed in previous decades, with their shared spaces and the uniformity they enforced. Other factors that contributed to this trend toward suburbanization in Israel included improvements in transportation, making it easier to commute, and the experience of Israelis living abroad in countries where suburban culture was well established.[34] Regardless of their motivations, however, Israelis seeking life in the suburbs encountered an impasse: land on the periphery of Israeli cities was scarce and expensive.[35] Under the government's new policies, land in the West Bank, by contrast, was abundant and relatively cheap—and, in areas near the Green Line, still within commuting distance to Tel Aviv and Jerusalem.[36] And so the West Bank became Israel's suburb.

MA'ALE ADUMIM: SOLAR HOUSES ON CONFISCATED LANDS

The first major settlement the Likud government built was Ma'ale Adumim. The seeds of Ma'ale Adumim were laid in 1974, three years before the Likud Party came to power, when the Labor government decided to build an industrial zone between Jerusalem and Jericho on Palestinian lands that Israel had seized in 1973. In addition to factories, the zone included a small workers' camp that housed a few dozen employees.[37] In February 1977, the Ministry of Housing commissioned a team of planners to examine the possibility of erecting an urban settlement in the area. The team produced a 147-page report analyzing five possible sites. Based on their examination, the team singled out two sites they deemed promising: one not far from Jerusalem, and the other farther away, closer to the Palestinian town of Jericho. The team endorsed the latter location, despite the fact that it required seizing more land, because it enjoyed a number of advantages, including excellent views of Jerusalem.[38] Views of Jerusalem were important, they later explained, because "they could give [settlers] the feeling of belonging to the big city. A feeling that is important for an isolated settlement."[39] The team recognized that a Jewish settlement on the site might impede the natural growth and expansion of the nearby Palestinian villages and towns, but such concerns, they explained in the report, were beyond the scope of their work, and, in any case, their report was exploratory.[40] Years would go by, the planners seemed to think, before the Labor government would move forward with the project.

A few days after the team submitted the report, however, the Likud came to power in one of Israel's most dramatic elections, and the project gained an unexpected momentum. In a matter of weeks, ministers of the new government announced that a city would be erected in the area.[41] In July 1977, the Ministry of Construction and Housing hired the Tel Aviv–based architect Thomas Leitersdorf to develop plans for the site closer to Jericho.[42] Leitersdorf had international experience in urban planning and design. After graduating from the Architectural Association in London in 1964, he had worked on a number of urban and suburban developments in Florida and the Ivory Coast in Africa. Upon his return to Israel in the 1970s, he came to be associated with a number of prominent politicians, including the new Likud-appointed Minister of Housing Gideon Patt, who recruited him to the project.[43]

Leitersdorf quickly realized he was faced with a difficult task. "Ma'ale Adumim is in a relatively isolated area, it is located in a hostile environment and it exhibits harsh natural conditions," Leitersdorf wrote in a letter shortly after he was hired. "If developed according to a conventional public housing scheme, it would have scarce chances of attracting residents and of keeping them on the site." Other, less conventional schemes, he argued, had to be considered. Among other ideas, he proposed making Ma'ale Adumim a pilot project for novel solar energy systems.[44]

Leitersdorf's recommendation would fall on fertile soil. In the years after World War II, as the architectural historian Daniel Barber has shown, architects and scientists in North America and Europe had been experimenting with solar energy technology. Motivated by fears of resource scarcity, they had tried to engineer new building materials like solar absorption roof panels, and to design more energy-efficient structures by incorporating passive cooling elements.[45] Some of these experiments also reached Israel, where a couple of building climatology centers were founded in the 1950s.[46] But the oil crisis of 1973 gave the search for more energy-efficient design a new urgency in the country. In protest of the Israeli occupation, Arab oil producers launched an oil embargo that sent the price of crude oil soaring. In this context, the Ministry of Construction and Housing in Israel began to take the climatology experiments more seriously. "The oil crisis," as a ministry publication explained, "has turned the problem of energy saving into a matter of great concern across the world, and especially in Israel, where most fuel required for energy is imported."[47]

To come up with alternative energy systems, the ministry had been collaborating with the Technion's Department of Building Climatology on several research projects. In 1976, the ministry appointed a team of experts, chaired by Baruch Givoni, the former head of the Department of Building Climatology, to develop a "Master Plan for Research and Development" on saving energy in building.[48] "The planning and construction of Ma'ale Adumim," the ministry's coordinator of research explained, "offers an exceptional opportunity to put to the test that knowledge that has been accumulated, and make [Ma'ale Adumim] a 'model city.'"[49] The ministry therefore recruited Givoni and other leading figures in the field to conduct a survey and prepare climate-sensitive design guidelines for the settlement.[50]

By the time he was invited to take part in the planning of Ma'ale Adumim, Givoni had already established himself as a world-renowned expert on solar energy. After obtaining a degree in architecture from the Technion in 1953, Givoni spent some time at the Central Research Laboratory of the American Society of Heating and Ventilating Engineers in Cleveland, Ohio, where he developed a special interest in human comfort, especially thermal comfort. He then attended graduate school at the University of Pittsburgh, where he studied the cooling efficiency of sweat evaporation, before obtaining a doctoral degree in environmental physiology from Hebrew University. In 1969, he did some research on the physiological effects of work and climatic conditions at the US Army Research Institute of Environmental Medicine in Natick, Massachusetts.[51] That year, Givoni published a book entitled *Man, Climate, and Architecture*, which explored thermal comfort in indoor environments, with a focus on hot climates.[52] The book, which was based on his research findings at the Technion's Department of Building Climatology, won him international attention. In Ma'ale Adumim, he had the opportunity to test some of the cutting-edge solar energy technologies he had been experimenting with in his laboratory on the scale of an entire settlement.

Following a preliminary survey of the site closer to Jericho, Givoni and his collaborators concluded that the location was climatically less than optimal. It was exposed to strong winds, harsh weather conditions, and air pollution from the nearby industrial area. Givoni's team argued that the other site proposed in the 1977 report, the one closer to Jerusalem, had better climatic conditions. It had relatively pleasant temperatures, low humidity, and a moderate wind regimen.[53] Leitersdorf agreed with the climate consultants' assessment, and he urged officials to change the location of the settlement.[54]

This assessment presented a rather new set of criteria for evaluating the suitability of settlements. Some officials at the Ministry of Construction and Housing with other priorities initially opposed the idea. The site closer to Jerusalem, one official noted, was strategically unfavorable. It would stimulate Palestinian construction in the area and would leave the settlement surrounded by hostile neighbors.[55] But that opposition quickly subsided. By January 1978, ministry officials agreed to move the settlement to the site advocated by the climate consultants, despite its strategic inferiority, and Leitersdorf began drafting plans for a 5,000-unit settlement.[56]

The advisory team that oversaw the initial 1977 report suggested laying out the settlement along four narrow ridges that extended like long fingers from one central ridge—"the palm of the hand," as it was referred to in a ministry publication (figure 3.2).[57] These finger-like ridges were to house residential neighborhoods, with the valleys between them serving as sites for recreational activity and doubling as "green lungs." The town center, with most of the public facilities, would be located on the central ridge.[58] Leitersdorf concurred with the team's recommendations. To overcome the large distances between the farthest residential areas and the town center, he proposed developing a trolley system—"like in Disney"—that would run at 10 kilometers per hour, every fifteen minutes, along a pedestrian-only pathway. These trolleys, Leitersdorf and his consultants proposed, could be powered by solar energy and made to run automatically, without a driver, to respect the Jewish prohibition against operating machinery on Saturdays.[59] In proposing the installation of trolleys, Leitersdorf no doubt drew on his work experience in the United States, home to Disney World, as well as in the city of Abidjan in the Ivory Coast, where, together with the Los Angeles–based architect William Pereira, he had worked on an aerial tramway and a monorail that was supposed to connect a set of tourist attractions.[60] To adapt the idea to local conditions, transportation experts at the Ministry of Construction and Housing contacted Chance Manufacturing Co., a Texas-based company that produced amusement park trolleys, and began testing their trolleys' suitability to Maʻale Adumim's settings and its budget.[61]

At the same time, Givoni's team drafted a number of climate-sensitive design guidelines for Maʻale Adumim. The team based its guidelines on data gathered from climatological stations at the site and on interviews with residents of a housing development in East Jerusalem, which had relatively similar climate conditions. By April 1978, Givoni had sent the initial guidelines to

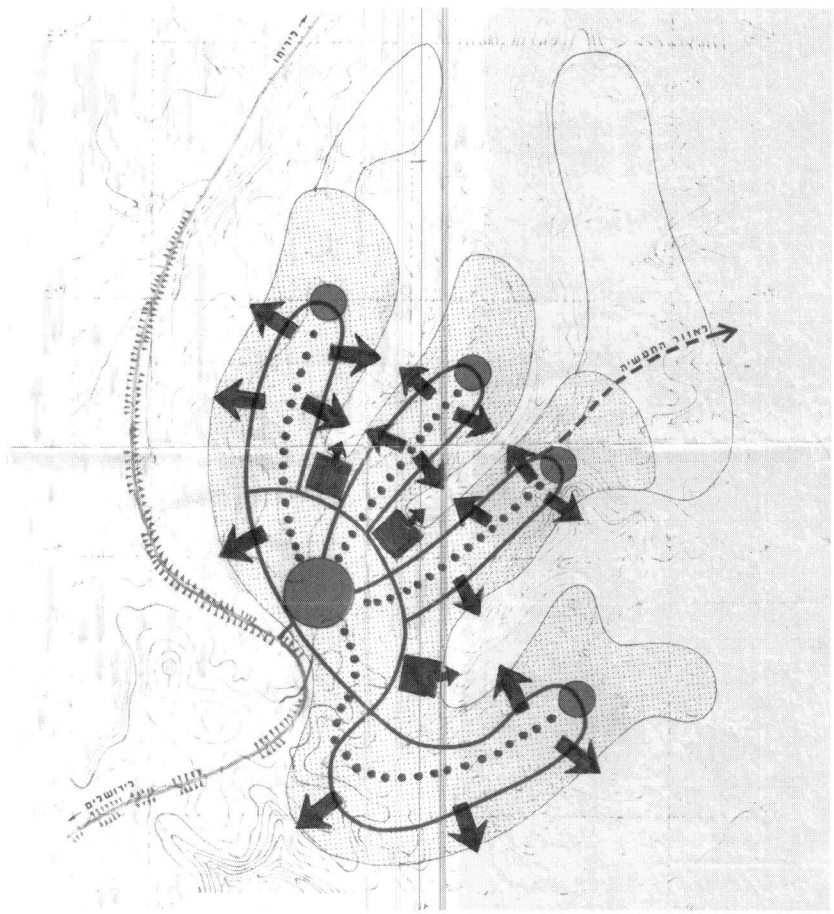

FIGURE 3.2. Mahon Urbani, site plan of Ma'ale Adumim showing the four ridges of the settlement, 1977. Dotted lines indicate pedestrian walkways, circles indicate settlement centers, and arrows indicate views from the settlement. (Ma'ale Adumim Archives.)

the ministry. First and foremost, Givoni noted in the document, low-rise residential buildings (preferably two-story row houses) were best suited to the site. Low-rise buildings would allow for the direct sun exposure needed to charge the solar panels installed on each. Multistory apartment buildings, he explained, would create shadows, and that would require large gaps between neighboring buildings, resulting in lower occupation density. Tall buildings would also create wind funnels. To maximize sun exposure and to protect the row houses from strong winds, Givoni proposed orienting them toward the south and layering them on top of one another. And to mitigate the heat created by the direct sun exposure, he proposed placing a layer of gravel underneath each unit that would absorb cold air during the night and help cool the building during the day.[62]

Givoni's data-based and climate-sensitive design guidelines accorded with Leitersdorf's own architectural sensitivity to design trends. From the beginning, he did not want to reproduce in Ma'ale Adumim the multistory apartment buildings that were prevalent in Israel. "The standard four-story building, so common in Israel, is on its way out throughout the world," he told a news reporter, referring to modernist housing blocks that mushroomed in the 1950s and 1960s (see figure 0.9).[63] Ministry of Construction and Housing officials similarly recognized that low-rise structures were more appealing to Israelis, given recent suburbanization trends, and would likely draw homebuyers to the settlement.[64] Nevertheless, to also attract lower-income populations from Jerusalem, they decided to include a few more affordable units in four-story buildings. These buildings, however, constituted a small portion of the total buildings in Ma'ale Adumim. More than 90 percent of the buildings had fewer than three stories, and about 40 percent had two stories.[65] More than 50 percent of the units had a private yard.[66] Leitersdorf distributed the low-rise housing units along the sides of the ridges and concentrated taller buildings on the ridges' tops.[67] In addition, Leitersdorf designed a ring road that flanked a number of residential developments, leaving generous pedestrian-only areas in each.[68]

To expedite the construction process, the Ministry of Construction and Housing began issuing commissions to design and build several of the residential areas even while Leitersdorf was still finalizing the master plan.[69] Each area was assigned to a different construction firm and a different team of architects.[70] All were required to collaborate with Givoni and his team so they could adapt their designs to the climate profile of the site.

Among the architects were Yaacov and Ora Yaar, a pair of Tel Aviv-based architects who came to be known for their innovative housing projects, which included a celebrated design of a low-income neighborhood in Tel Aviv as well as a number of residential compounds in the Old City of Jerusalem.[71] The Yaars, as Nitzan-Shiftan notes, took a special interest in regionalism, an approach to architecture that aspired to authenticity, often by reinterpreting local building styles. In a neighborhood they designed in the northern district of Israel in the late 1950s, for example, they organized all housing units into rows of two-story buildings along narrow streets that followed the natural topography.[72] Yaacov Yaar would later say that they had been hesitant to accept a design commission in Ma'ale Adumim, and that they had previously refused to work in settlements outside Jerusalem for political reasons, but they eventually accepted the job because Maʻale Adumim was relatively close to Jerusalem and not in the depths of the West Bank.[73]

The Yaars welcomed the opportunity to collaborate with Givoni and the other climate consultants. It offered them an opportunity to develop a place-based architecture, something they had been preoccupied with for a number of years. Following the consultants' guidelines, they developed two terraced quarters of approximately three hundred one- to two-story units that exhibited a number of climate-responsive features. The units were layered on top of one another in ways that created shaded, wind-sheltered private yards and public walkways. Each unit had a "climate tower," or solar chimney, popping out of the roof and facing south. The tall chimney absorbed solar energy from the south and allowed winds to enter the house from the north (figures 3.3 and 3.4).[74] These designs were without precedent in Israel.

The public buildings in the town center were outfitted with alternative cooling and heating systems that relied on the thermodynamic properties of building materials as well as the strategic positioning of structures that created shade. The architect Dror Haruvi designed the "Solar Kindergarten," for instance, with special solar-energy-absorbing walls and supported them with adjustable shading elements.[75] Equally innovative was Maʻale Adumim's civic center, designed by Shimon Powsner and Gideon Powsner. Housing public and commercial facilities as well as some 150 residential units, the civic center was organized around a series of enclosed patio spaces and shaded walkways designed to protect residents from desert winds and sun exposure.[76]

Not everyone at the Ministry of Construction and Housing was enthusiastic about the new design process governed by climatology. In June 1981, while construction was in full swing, ministry planners from the Programs Division at the Urban Planning Unit authored a report warning against what they perceived to be "a broken urban fabric." They worried that Maʻale Adumim lacked public spaces like streets and squares, where residents could congregate and interact. They acknowledged the environmental concerns that informed the design of low-rise buildings and small, sheltered patio spaces, and the decision to leave the valleys between the ridges relatively undeveloped. They also acknowledged the future residents' wish to enjoy a quiet, "pastoral" atmosphere. But these alterations, the planners wrote, came at the expense of public spaces, without which residents may experience "a feeling of loneliness and alienation." Most open spaces were private, or semiprivate, they explained. There was no "main street." They also described "a feeling of alienation and foreignness separating one building site from the next." This feeling, it seems, stemmed not only from the paucity of certain kinds

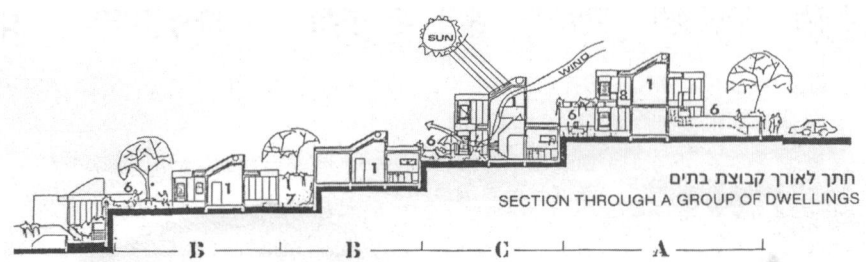

FIGURE 3.3. Yaar Architects, section drawing of a residential quarter in Maʻale Adumim showing how solar chimneys would cool off the units and absorb solar energy, early 1980s. (*Israel Builds 1988* [Tel Aviv: Ministry of Construction and Housing, 1988], 172.)

FIGURE 3.4. View of a residential quarter designed by Yaar Architects in Maʻale Adumim, 1983. (Photograph by Harnik Nati, Government Press Office.)

of public spaces where residents could gather, but also from the ministry's decision to issue separate commissions to different architects to design the various residential quarters. The incoherence created by this practice would further estrange residents from their neighbors, according to these critics within the ministry.[77] In direct contrast to Israelis' growing desire for social and physical privacy, the ministry's report continued to emphasize the importance of shared urban spaces and uniformity.[78] As in the case of Ofra, some state planners could not see past their own assumptions about what constitutes "good" planning. But the warnings issued in the report about the evaporation of public space fell on deaf ears.

The planners' concerns had little impact on homebuyers. Toward the end of 1980, the Ministry of Construction and Housing began selling residential units in Ma'ale Adumim. Many of the units were marketed to first-time buyers and were thus affordably priced; the government also financed the mortgages with loans at favorable interest rates.[79] Apartments in Ma'ale Adumim were sold for less than a third of the price of similar apartments in Jerusalem.[80] Unsurprisingly, the first 1,300 units were sold in a matter of days.[81] Each development company sold the units it had built. In some cases, the demand for units outnumbered their availability: the Yuval-Gad building company reported that over 224 families had applied for the eighty-nine units it was selling.[82] Smaller units, especially two-bedroom apartments, were the most popular.[83] In particular, Jerusalemites who were unable to purchase an apartment in their hometown were eager to move to the new settlement.

Occupants began to move in to their new apartments in Ma'ale Adumim in 1982; by the end of 1983, 1,500 families were living in the settlement.[84] Almost all were young couples in their late twenties and early thirties.[85] Eighty percent of them came from Jerusalem.[86] A large number of the new residents were Mizrahi Jews. Until that time, according to the sociologists Uri Cohen and Nissim Leon, Mizrahim—who were excluded from the labor elite and often employed in manual labor—were largely confined to three main geographic areas, all with more affordable housing: "development towns," built by the government in the 1950s and 1960s to absorb the large number of immigrants who flocked to the country after independence; immigrant moshavim located in the periphery; and underdeveloped but not suburban neighborhoods at the outskirts of large cities.[87] Some had joined community settlements in the West Bank, but, according to *Nekuda*, a settler-run magazine, the community settlement's screening mechanisms blocked Mizrahim from settling in large numbers.[88] Ma'ale Adumim, in contrast, was one of the first places that offered them a much-needed alternative: suburban life, near the city and with good infrastructure, at a bargain price. According to a 1995 survey, Mizrahim would come to constitute no less than 32 percent of Ma'ale Adumim's population, exceeding their proportion in Israeli society.[89] In the years following the founding of Ma'ale Adumim, a growing number of upwardly mobile Mizrahim would join other suburban settlements.[90]

Although some complained about the lack of public amenities, like health and telephone services, and although the Texan trolley system was never installed, Ma'ale Adumim's residents were largely pleased.[91] "I could not have enjoyed this quality of life, a private house and a small yard, in the city," a settler who moved from Jerusalem told a reporter in 1986.[92] The settlement's name, Ma'ale Adumim ("red ascent" in English), was taken from the Bible, where it refers to the red-hued limestone nearby. One resident commented that the name of the settlement should be changed to "Gold. [It should be called] Ma'ale Gold and not Ma'ale Adumim. Quality of life, good services, good municipality."[93] The availability of an exceptional quality of life at bargain prices would continue to draw Israelis to Ma'ale Adumim. By 1987, the population grew to 11,100, making it the most populous settlement in the West Bank, and it would remain the largest settlement for some two decades.[94]

Despite the concerns raised by the Programs Division about the absence of public space, officials at the Ministry of Construction and Housing considered the settlement a success. Not only did the settlement create affordable housing for thousands of Israelis, but the money poured into Ma'ale Adumim made it possible to experiment with new forms of design and planning. Elinoar Barzaki, who oversaw the planning of Ma'ale Adumim as head of the Jerusalem Region of the Ministry of Construction and Housing, told me: "It was perhaps the last, or second to last, city with a utopian vision."[95] Architects responsible for the design of individual buildings were also satisfied. Their experiments with solar energy were indeed groundbreaking.

Ma'ale Adumim was one of those rare instances, if not the only instance, in the architectural history of West Bank settlements where government officials, architects, and settlers were all satisfied. As in Ofra, however, it seems that few were able to see the political consequences of building a major settlement on land that would increasingly be claimed as the territory of a Palestinian state. In fact, the emphasis on climatology in the design of Ma'ale Adumim may have helped obscure the political tensions that would erupt at the end of the 1980s but had been lurking beneath the appearance of an affordable suburban community with environmentally friendly architecture, just a fourteen-minute drive from Jerusalem.

ALFE MENASHE: AN "ARAB VILLAGE" FOR MIDDLE-CLASS ISRAELIS

The success of Ma'ale Adumim was largely based on the allocation of large state subsidies and the presence of a sizable lower-income population in Jerusalem who could be lured by high-quality affordable housing. Arguably, it did not establish a sustainable funding model for subsequent settlements. To save public money—and in keeping with the Likud's privatization program—in

1979, the government started allocating more building rights to private developers in the West Bank.[96] At the same time, it began directing organized
groups of socially homogeneous middle-class Israelis looking to live together
in a suburban environment to the West Bank. These groups often consisted
of young households headed by employees of large governmental organizations like the Israel Aerospace Industries or military officials. Members of
each group sometimes knew one another from work or from social events,
held in private homes or the outdoors, where they had socialized prior to
settling together.[97] In the past, such groups, especially groups of households
headed by military officers, had played an important role in the expansion
of the Tel Aviv metropolitan area; in the immediate years after the founding
of Israel, when public money was scarce, they sometimes received land that
was leased to them for free as a supplement to their salaries.[98] In the early
1950s, for example, a group of military personnel and their families received
generous mortgages to settle in what was then the northern edge of Tel Aviv,
where they formed the neighborhood of Zahala that soon evolved into a rich
suburb.[99] Now, such groups were going to assume an equally important role
in the founding of West Bank settlements.[100]

The phenomenon of groups of households wishing to create housing developments for themselves is not limited to Israel. In the immediate years after
World War II, in the face of a national housing shortage, groups of veterans
and labor union members organized to build housing cooperatives in New
Jersey, San Francisco, and Los Angeles, among other places. At times, these
groups embraced a pioneering political character, as when groups in Los
Angeles and the San Francisco Bay area sought to create racially integrated
communities when segregation still prevailed.[101] The Israeli groups sent to
the West Bank, in contrast, often showed no interest in pioneering political
programs, not even the settlement movement. They did not oppose it, but
what mattered most to them was the higher standard of living they could
enjoy in the West Bank.

In 1979, one such group, composed of military officers and Ministry of
Defense employees, began to take form. The Ministry of Defense, the main
force behind the initiative, started to pressure government agencies to have
a suburb built especially for them.[102] Describing the security personnel who
joined the initiative, a reporter noted a few years later: "They were not young
couples looking for a shelter, and willing to reside in a prefabricated house.
For all of them this wasn't even their first apartment. They sold former
apartments or left rented ones in order to fulfill the private, though common
to all Israelis, dream: a lovely villa, with a yard, even if small, attached to
their house, at a place that is outside of the city, but close enough to the

center."[103] Like many Israelis in the 1970s, the ones who signed up for the initiative were hoping to improve their living conditions, and they were avowedly secular. They had little in common with the starry-eyed activists who wanted to settle in Hebron or with the ideological Gush Emunim members who had founded Ofra.

By the end of 1979, the Joint Settlement Committee of the Israeli Government and the World Zionist Organization had allocated to the initiative a tract of land in the northern part of the West Bank, about 8 kilometers east of the Israeli town of Kfar Saba.[104] At first, planners and architects at the Ministry of Construction and Housing's Rural Building and New Settlements Administration were asked to prepare drawings for the settlement, with instructions to "create an attractive settlement with a high quality of life."[105] But there were disagreements about what exactly "quality of life" meant. For the prospective residents, this meant that all the houses should have private yards, even though planners warned that this would increase costs significantly, due to the steep topography of the site. Ministry of Defense officials, who represented the future residents, also objected to the planners' suggestion to have the settlement moved to another site, a few kilometers eastward (i.e., farther from Israel), where existing conditions would allow fast and cheap construction of some five hundred units.[106] The prospective residents were commuters, and so it was important to have the settlement located closer to Tel Aviv.

In 1981, after it became clear that the costs of building a settlement on the site would exceed standard budgets, ministry officials decided to outsource the detailed planning and construction to Tzavta, a consortium of six commercial construction companies and two development firms.[107] To ensure the success of the settlement—which was now planned for some two thousand families—government officials offered the developers a generous support package: the Custodian for Government and Abandoned Property (which manages "state lands" in the West Bank) allocated them the land plots, while the Ministry of Construction and Housing installed the infrastructure and funded the construction of public buildings. The government also committed to purchasing half of the five hundred units planned to be built in the first phase of construction if they remained empty after completion, and to subsidizing the mortgages of homebuyers.[108] A steering committee at the Ministry of Construction and Housing was assigned to supervise the planning and construction process.[109]

The prominent architect Avraham Yaski was hired to lead the design.[110] Yaski was one of the most prolific architects of his generation. Since graduating from the Technion in 1951, he had overseen the design of many original housing projects that received wide acclaim in the local architectural community. Notable among these projects were a four-story, quarter-kilometer-long housing slab in Be'er-Sheva and a series of housing clusters in the settlement of Gilo, in East Jerusalem.[111]

Yaski and Yossi Sivan, a partner in his office who was assigned to the project, were committed to the ethos of New Brutalism and its emphasis on authenticity. Like other architects of their generation, they believed that the repetitive housing blocks that had mushroomed across the country after independence, built under the supervision of the state, had failed to form a connection between Jewish immigrants and the land.[112] "We wanted something local, something place-based," Sivan explained to me when we met some three decades later.[113] And, like many architects working in Israel at the time, they found their "place-based" architecture in the architecture of the Palestinian village. The turn to the Palestinian village—which, by the late 1970s, was often coded as Mediterranean—was a common theme among Israeli architects of that generation, as Nitzan-Shiftan has explained. In their minds, the Palestinian village was an expression of a native intimacy with the landscape, the very intimacy they sought to establish. In the previous decade, this theme had inspired Israeli architects working in East Jerusalem.[114] Now, in the settlement of Alfe Menashe, Yaski and Sivan had the opportunity to model an entire settlement after a Palestinian village.

The architecture of the Palestinian village in particular offered solutions to the design problems posed by the site's steep topography. Conventional housing schemes would have required flattening large parts of the hilltop. In Palestinian villages, by contrast, houses were adapted to the terrain by being broken into interlocking cubic shapes, Sivan observed.[115] To emulate that effect, albeit with modern building technologies, Yaski and Sivan arranged most of the residential units in the first phase of construction in two-story row houses of two to four units that followed the natural topography; they carved public passageways between some of the houses, connecting the upper levels with the lower ones. They broke up large building masses into small, box-shaped units, and layered one on top of the other. Each was capped with a flat roof and left unclad (figures 3.5 and 3.6).

Yaski and Sivan thought that organizing most of the residential units in cascading row houses would also help meet the residents' demand for private yards without having to build a large number of detached houses. Having too many detached houses, Sivan knew, would have resulted in greater expense, exceeding the project's budget. Although the settlement was geared toward middle-class Israelis, and many of the units were indeed significantly larger than those built in Ma'ale Adumim, it was hardly a luxurious one. The cascading row houses were thus a compromise between standardized

FIGURE 3.5. View of Alfe Menashe, 1984. (Photograph by Harnik Nati, Government Press Office.)

FIGURE 3.6. Cascading, flat-roofed row houses in Alfe Menashe, 1984. (Photograph by Harnik Nati, Government Press Office.)

public housing units and the stand-alone houses with private yards that so many Israelis were seeking at the time.

Despite having a private yard, the units were not as luxurious as the military officers and civilians at the Ministry of Defense had been imagining, perhaps because the units were piled on top of one another and the yards were small. The price was also a lot higher than expected.[116] They were still cheaper than equivalent homes in nearby Israeli cities, but in the context of the West Bank, where, since 1981, as a matter of policy, land was leased to settlers for a fraction of its value, they seemed overpriced.[117] (Parcels of land are generally leased—not sold—to homebuyers in Israel.)[118] After seeing the drawings, many canceled their plans to move to the West Bank. Of the approximately five thousand candidates that had registered for the settlement before the planning phase, only 110 families ended up purchasing a home in Alfe Menashe.[119]

In September 1982, once it had become clear that security personnel were not going to purchase the remaining 390 units of the first phase of construction, the government gave Tzavta permission to sell the houses to anyone, regardless of their association with the military or the Ministry of Defense.[120] Tzavta launched a sales campaign marketing Alfe Menashe as the ideal suburban community: "Just Five Minutes from [the Israeli city of] Kfar Saba," where "Dreams Become Reality," "A place where you can mix high quality of life with high latitude" (figure 3.7).[121] Prospective homebuyers were offered mortgages with relatively low down payments and low interest rates. In 1983, a house priced between $84,000 and $115,000 could be purchased for a down payment of $10,000, a little over the average annual income of Israeli households whose main breadwinner was a salaried employee at the time.[122]

But Alfe Menashe struggled to attract middle-class Israelis. Nine months after the settlement opened, more than 150 units—about a third of the units built in the first phase of construction—remained unsold.[123] According to an article in the newspaper *Koteret Rashit*, the reason for poor sales was not people's reluctance to move to the West Bank, outside the borders of the country, but rather the architecture of the settlement: "Sales are going very slow. It is understandable. The settlement is not beautiful." Specifically, the article noted, "the units are large and spacious, but the entire settlement is built very densely. The [private] yards built in front of and in-between the houses are pretty small."[124] The row houses with small yards did not match the suburban ideal advertised by Tzavta. Many of those who did buy houses in Alfe Menashe were disappointed. "We had wanted to create a high-quality settlement, not a socialist one," one resident told a local magazine, complaining about Yaski and Sivan's design.[125] Some thought that the gray unadorned

FIGURE 3.7. Sales booth exhibiting drawings, photos, and a model of houses in Alfe Menashe. The sales booth was installed at *The Achievements of the Settlement of Judea and Samaria Exhibition*, Tel Aviv, 1983. (Photograph by Yisra'el Simionski/ Israel Sun Ltd., courtesy of Israel Goodovitch, the architect, Tel Aviv.)

façades were merely a way for the developers to avoid expense.[126] Altogether, the row houses were just too modest, especially when compared to the dream of the detached houses of American suburbs.

The outbreak of the First Intifada, a grassroots Palestinian resistance to the Israeli occupation, in 1987, would render Alfe Menashe's row houses even less adequate. The intifada included occasional attacks against Israeli civilians. In the wake of these attacks, as Nitzan-Shiftan has argued, Tel Aviv–based architects began to see Palestinian architecture differently: no longer as a benign native building tradition but as the architecture of a rival national project.[127] The residents of Alfe Menashe seemed to share that change of heart. Not only were their houses too similar to public housing units; they were also too similar to the houses of the people who were now attacking them. The intifada made it somewhat necessary to alter the architectural profile of their homes, and many tried to do that, perhaps unwittingly, by adding balconies and attics, replacing the flat roofs associated with Palestinian architecture with pitched ones that came to be associated with affluence

FIGURE 3.8. Pitched roofs that residents have added on top of their flat-roofed units in Alfe Menashe, 2015. (Photograph by author.)

(figure 3.8).[128] The flat roof, the archivist of Alfe Menashe explained to me, suddenly seemed "unsophisticated" to the residents.[129]

The pitched roofs, however, did little to increase the settlement's desirability. In addition to the new security threat posed by the Palestinian uprising and what residents saw as unsightly design, there were other shortcomings. The settlement lacked a community center, a cinema, or a restaurant; there was not even a coffee shop. One resident bluntly told a reporter from *Haaretz*, who visited Alfe Menashe in 1989 to report on the escalation of violence and its effects on the settlers: "If they [Alfe Menashe's residents] were honest with you, they would have told you about the choking mortgages [with which the government had initially attracted residents]. They would have told you that there are people here who would have left [Alfe Menashe] long ago, if they were only able to sell their units. But there is no one to sell them to. There are no buyers for houses in Alfe Menashe."[130]

In subsequent years, after political tensions had subsided, and new

FIGURE 3.9. Detached houses in Alfe Menashe, 1997. (Photograph by Amos Ben Gershom, Government Press Office.)

neighborhoods were built with detached and semidetached homes designed by much lesser known architects, Alfe Menashe became popular among middle-class Israelis (figure 3.9). It became especially popular after the Israeli government, in 2002, decided to build the separation fence (known to the Palestinians as "the apartheid wall"), which monitors entrance from the West Bank into Israel. To the relief of Alfe Menashe's residents, the separation fence deviates eastward from the Green Line when it reaches the settlement, encircling it and keeping it on the "Israeli side," despite the protests of the neighboring Palestinians (from the villages of a-Ramadin, Abu-Farda, Wadi a-Rasha, Ma'arat a-Daba, and Hirbet Ras a-Tira), whose mobility has been undermined by the meandering fence.[131] In 2020, about eight thousand Israelis lived in the settlement.[132] But the original neighborhood that Yaski and Sivan designed remains relatively undesirable to this day. Few wish to reside there, and a number of its residents have left for new neighborhoods. The vernacular design of the eminent architects did not pave the way for nonideological Israelis to flock to the West Bank. The row houses with small yards failed to fulfill the suburban dream, and the references to the architecture of the Palestinian village only brought the emerging conflict "home."

More affluent settlements, the kind that Alfe Menashe's original residents had in mind, became available shortly after Alfe Menashe was founded, after the government granted permission in April 1982 to commercial developers to build settlements from scratch, with only marginal intervention from state planners.[133] Developers could receive "state lands" from the government; indeed, by the end of 1982, no fewer than fifty companies had filed official requests for "state lands."[134] But they could also purchase privately owned lands from the Palestinians at a relatively low price.[135] Whether on "state lands" or privately owned lands, settlements could be built cheaply, fast, and with a handsome return, given what one journalist described as the "ravenous hunger" of Israeli homebuyers for property.[136] By July 1983, the Joint Settlement Committee approved nine private initiatives to found new settlements.[137]

One developer who was especially intrigued by the economic prospects of settlement construction was Danny Weinmann. The owner of an insurance company, said to be "capable of selling ice to Eskimos," and former deputy mayor of the city of Givatayim, Weinmann enjoyed easy access to government officials.[138] In 1981, he went on a tour of the West Bank with a few high-profile acquaintances. At one point during the trip, the assistant to Minister of Agriculture Ariel Sharon, Uri Bar On, pointed at a bare hilltop and urged Weinmann: "Take this mountain and plan [something on] it."[139] And Weinmann did.

Upon returning from the West Bank, Weinmann visited the office of the architect Haim Katseff. Katseff was not a prominent architect like Yaski, nor was he friends with Likud Party members like Leitersdorf. After spending a year at the École Spéciale d'Architecture in Paris, Katseff had earned his architectural diploma at the Technion. Following the Six-Day War, as a junior associate at the influential architecture firm of Ram Karmi, he took part in the design of the Hebrew University's new campus on Mount Scopus in Jerusalem. In the mid-1970s, Katseff opened his own practice in a basement apartment in Tel Aviv. He worked on a number of commercial projects and was able to get enough building commissions to maintain a team of six employees, but few in the local scene took much interest in his work.

Katseff recalled the first time he met Weinmann: "He walked into my office and just said, 'Hello, I am Danny Weinmann, I am an insurance agent [and] I want to build a city.'" Katseff was perplexed. He had never imagined someone would just knock on his door and commission a city. That's not how cities are founded, he thought to himself. And, in any case, his office was small; it was not the kind of office anyone wanting to build a city would go to. But Weinmann was determined. He bluntly told Katseff that he had found a way to get a lot of land in the West Bank and he needed an architect. Katseff needed the work, and, as he later recalled, he thought it was a rare opportunity to develop "something completely new, something different." He therefore agreed to take on the project. On Katseff's advice, Weinmann also hired Shmuel Shaked, who had worked as chief architect at the Ministry of Construction and Housing, and who might use his contacts at the ministry to expedite the process. Nevertheless, they agreed that Shaked would not intervene in the design.[140]

Katseff drafted a master plan for a two-thousand-family settlement. He divided the settlement into three main residential areas that followed the natural curve of the ridge on the site. Between the residential areas, he allocated a large area for office space, community centers, a school, a clinic, and municipal services. Other public buildings, like kindergartens and youth centers, were distributed across the residential quarters. The residential plots were exceptionally large, measuring 1,000 square meters—two or even three times the size of private plots in earlier settlements. To secure approval of the large plot size, Katseff divided each plot into two areas: one zoned for construction and the other designated as "private open space," on which construction was prohibited.

After examining the master plan, by the fall of 1982, government officials gave Weinmann permission to develop the first four hundred plots in the northern part of the settlement, all as detached single-family homes. The schedule Weinmann agreed to, however, was tight. Construction of the residential units and appropriate infrastructure would start in April 1983; the first two hundred units as well as several public facilities were to be completed within a year of that date, and the remaining parts were to be built by 1986.[141]

Katseff designed a number of relatively similar model homes for homebuyers to choose from (figure 3.10). During the decade that Katseff had worked in the office of the architect Ram Karmi, New Brutalism and regionalism were in vogue in Israel, and Karmi was one of their biggest advocates. But Katseff was now inspired by the postmodern tendency toward stylistic heterogeneity that was surfacing in the 1980s. The model homes he designed combined elements from different sources. He took the motif of the arch from the Palestinians, which he integrated into the elevation of the house, but for some reason, he extended the arched façade beyond the building's envelope, as if to disintegrate it from the building. In addition, Katseff punctured the façade with a cylindrical shape. The rounded shape, he thought, could serve

FIGURE 3.10. One of the model homes that homebuyers in Nofim could select. The home, designed by Haim Katseff, exhibited a number of elements drawn from different sources, including an arched wall, a pitched roof, and a rounded dining space. (*Maariv*, December 24, 1982, 146.)

as a dining space, separated from the kitchen. He saw such dining spaces in the United States, he told me.[142] Some of the homes were capped with pitched red-tile roofs. The steep pitch of the roof and the red tiles, it seems, were intended to cater to a growing preference for pitched roofs, especially steep ones, among aspirational Israelis wanting to project high economic status.[143] All the houses were rather spacious, with the largest one measuring 250 square meters.[144]

Large houses exhibiting diverse formal elements, like the model homes Katseff designed, had begun to appear in Israel proper in the early 1970s as part of a Ministry of Housing initiative that came to be known as Build Your Own Home. Build Your Own Home, which was first tested in the 1960s in a Negev town, allowed individuals to design and build detached homes according to their own stylistic preference, on land plots leased from the state. The scheme was conceived to reinvigorate so-called development towns.[145] These towns were often built at a distance from the metropolitan areas of Tel Aviv and Jerusalem, and usually consisted of three- and four-story modernist housing blocks (see figure 0.9). Over the decades, they had grown impoverished, and Build Your Own Home was an attempt to breathe new life into the languishing towns.

When the Likud came to power, it extended that program beyond the development towns to include the West Bank, where it proved especially popular. In some cases, developers designed entire settlements offering a selection of lavish model homes from which homebuyers could choose. Alternatively, they sold empty land plots to homebuyers who were then free to design their own house with their preferred architect. Such statement houses—large, eclectic, and almost never modest—soon began to appear also in the community settlements that followed some of the planning principles formulated at Ofra. In the community settlement of Neve Tzuf, for example, all of the houses incorporated wooden elements, imported from Finland, Sweden, and the United States (figure 3.11). Some were built almost entirely from wood—a rather rare and expensive building material in Israel. "Since we were surrounded by all this greenery here," one of Neve Tzuf's founders explained to me, "we thought to ourselves: why not make a little Switzerland here?" In another flight of fancy, some of the homes in the settlement of Beit Horon were built behind a miniaturized Roman aqueduct (figure 3.12). Many of those purchasing these houses, according to a report by Danny Rubenstein for the daily *Davar*, were Israelis fleeing modest public housing estates.[146] The story Rubenstein told was one of (consumer) captivity and liberation. In the West Bank, he wrote, freed from the modernist housing blocks built by the Ministry of Construction and Housing, they could finally voice their true desires and realize their "dream houses."[147] These "dream houses," as the architectural theorist Tula Amir has noted, sharply diverged from previous building styles in Israel, building styles that, under the rule of the labor elite, had prized modesty and uniformity. The appearance of these "dream houses" was symptomatic of larger societal changes in Israel, with the rise of individualism and the decline of the older labor elite.[148]

These new settlement houses baffled members of the labor elite. Ora Namir, a parliament member and prominent figure in the Labor Party, was appalled upon visiting the settlement of Ari'el, a fifteen-minute drive from Nofim. "I was at Ari'el and there was one thing I couldn't understand," she complained. "How [do] you build a new town and make it so ugly? I saw the Build Your Own Home [there]. . . . Why [do] you need to build like this? There is no unifying style, a window blocks another window, house right next to house. Where is the Ministry of Housing?"[149] Other observers, going beyond questions of taste, criticized the settlement movement more broadly.

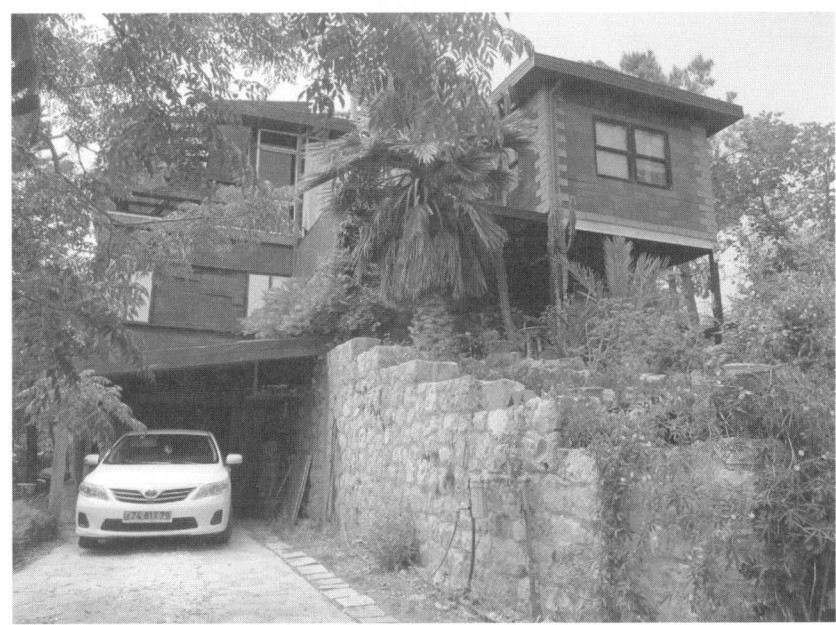

FIGURE 3.11. Houses with wooden elements in Neve Tzuf, 2015. These houses were unlike most previous housing forms in Israel, where wood construction was uncommon and uniformity prevailed. One of the residents proudly told me that Neve Tzuf still has the largest concentration of wooden houses, both in the settlements and in Israel proper. (Photographs by author.)

FIGURE 3.12. Houses in the settlement of Beit Horon behind a miniaturized aqueduct. (Photograph by author.)

In a short piece that appeared in the newspaper *Yediot Aharonot* in 1984, the columnist Boaz Evron ironically commented:

> I regularly get all the issues of *Nekuda*, Gush Emunim's journal. Browsing through the pages of the journal, I get worried, and not only because of the political attitude that guides it, but by the spiritual self-portrait it expresses . . . of [settlers] being an elite group guiding the people of Israel, on "Zionism," on "Idealism." . . . And all this "idealism" is accompanied by large advertisements for "Italian porcelain tiles," and "natural marble floor tiles" . . . exquisite furniture, cabinet rooms, kitchens, cladding materials. . . . And you see these double-story villas, all this luxury built at my and your expense, all, of course, in the name of galvanized "idealism." No kibbutz, even after decades of hard work, ever reached such levels of luxury . . . [and] the reason for that is obvious: Kibbutz people made their money out of hard labor. The "settlers" are building their palaces at our expense. [So] the next time you hear the words "idealism," "sacredness," and "Zionism"—watch over your wallet.[150]

The flashy new houses did not square with pioneer-ship, at least not in the Labor Zionists' concept, and their grandeur encouraged some Israelis to question the ideological grounding of the settlement movement itself.

Such criticism had little chance of deterring hundreds of Israelis determined to buy their dream home at a bargain price. In Nofim, the large, lavish houses designed by Katseff went for as little as $100,000, with some $20,000–$40,000 of the original cost subsidized by favorable government loans and mortgages. To secure a house, homebuyers needed to put down only $15,000.[151] This discounted pricing was coupled with an extensive publicity campaign orchestrated by one of Tel Aviv's most famous advertising agencies. In dozens of full-page newspaper ads, Nofim was marketed as the cure for the malady of the claustrophobic and monotonous urban jungle. Nofim's houses, an ad from 1982 announced, were the solution for those "living in the big city . . . [and] tired of living in a box, tired of being part of unending rows of boxes . . . [who] want to see the horizon, to breathe fresh air."[152] The anti-urban rhetoric was paired with signing incentives, such as a new Fiat 127 or free tickets to the musical *Fame* (figure 3.13).[153] "Such a sales campaign was unbelievable," one homebuyer told me some three decades later. "It had no precedent in this country. It was like in America maybe."[154]

Within just a few months, more than two hundred houses were sold in Nofim.[155] Katseff was bewildered by the pace of the sales. He insisted he needed more time to finalize his plan drawings, which were still in a rather incipient stage. But there was little he could do in the face of Weinmann's ambitions and his sales campaign. Nor did it help that Weinmann organized sales events on the site, and people came to them in droves.[156]

Miri Levy, whom I mentioned in the introduction of this book, was one of those people. An elegant lady in her sixties with a somber demeanor, she is still a resident of Nofim. She told me about the day she drove with her husband to Nofim's hilltop to attend a sales event. It was the Sukkot holiday of 1982. They were a young couple, living in Tel Aviv but eager to move out of the city. Once they arrived at the site, they were welcomed by cheerful sales representatives. The entire site was festive. It was dotted with flags and billboards that showed Katseff's plan drawings under the slogan, "Nofim—Life is Beautiful." Miri was struck by the landscape; it appeared to her untouched by man. "I immediately fell in love," Miri recalled. Two days later, she and her husband purchased two units in Nofim.[157] For some time, a mental barrier had kept Israelis like Miri from even considering moving to the West Bank. They considered it a foreign territory. But something had changed. Neither Miri nor other homebuyers seemed to be concerned now by the fact that Nofim was built in the occupied territories, outside the national borders. Katseff's luxurious homes, combined with the massive campaign, helped repress such concerns. As Weinmann proudly announced, after a number of such successful events: "The [mental] barrier was broken. It is no longer weird to live in Samaria."[158]

FIGURE 3.13. Advertisement for houses in Nofim promising a Fiat 127 to anyone buying a house. One thousand tickets to the musical *Fame* were to be distributed to visitors to Nofim's sales centers. (*Yediot Aharonot*, April 1, 1983.)

Not long after Israelis removed their mental barriers and construction had begun, however, Weinmann's company ran into financial trouble.[159] In February 1984, after their repeated requests for additional funding from the Ministry of Construction and Housing had gone unanswered, the company ran out of money, and construction was stopped.[160] About 126 homes were left unfinished. A reporter who visited the site described it as "a huge cemetery for fancy villas."[161] Several homebuyers filed a lawsuit against Weinmann, claiming that he misused their money.[162] About a year later, an investigation by the Israel Police confirmed some of the complaints; it concluded that Weinmann faked documents, misused homebuyers' property, and obtained their money by fraud.[163] The police also suspected that he had never, in fact, intended to build a settlement.[164] But the investigation and its findings did little for homebuyers who were left in the lurch, unsure whether they would ever live to see their dream homes completed.

When word about the fall of Nofim made it into the news, hundreds of Israelis who had considered moving to the West Bank got cold feet.[165] The Weinmann scandal was hardly the first of its kind. According to Plia Albeck, legal adviser to the government, the permission granted by the state for Israelis to buy privately owned Palestinian lands, coupled with the allocation of thousands of acres of "state lands" in the West Bank to private developers, had opened the door to multiple cases of fraud.[166] Early settlement activists, including the ones who founded Ofra, were especially concerned by these cases. In 1986, the journal *Nekuda* observed that "private initiative settlements have become a synonym for failure. The money of hundreds of families had gone down the drain. Many of the developers found themselves in the accused dock in court. The collapse of Nofim and other private developments has given a bad name to the entire settlement [enterprise]."[167]

To homebuyers' relief, in 1987, the Ministry of Construction and Housing stepped in to complete the unfinished houses in Nofim and to install needed infrastructure.[168] Katseff, however, was not involved. He was angry, disappointed, and ridden with guilt.[169] Within a year, a number of families were able to move in.[170] The houses were lavish, and the views were spectacular. They were everything most Israelis moving to the West Bank in the 1980s dreamed of. Their splendor easily surpassed that of their predecessors in Alfe Menashe or Ma'ale Adumim.

But relief had come too late. By the time the settlers of Nofim moved into their luxurious homes, the Palestinian uprising had broken out. Israelis could no longer feel physically safe in the West Bank, and some who might have considered moving to Nofim or similar settlements—despite the economic risk—clung to their old, modest apartments in Israel.[171] In 1992, a year before the intifada ended with the Oslo Accords peace process, there were only 223 people living in Nofim instead of the two thousand families it had been designed to accommodate.[172] In 2018, it housed only around 800 settlers.[173] Nofim was arguably the apex of the building boom that began shortly after the election of the Likud Party. It saw the largest and most lavish houses—but it also laid bare the limitations of that period and its promise of tranquil suburban life in an occupied territory.

CONCLUSION

In 1983, a radio host and a reporter for the daily *Yediot Aharonot* met with Eldar Sharon, a leading architect and son of Arieh Sharon, a Bauhaus graduate and winner of the prestigious Israel Prize, to discuss the state of architecture in the country. When the reporter commented on the construction boom occurring in the West Bank and asked Sharon why he was not taking part, Sharon was dismissive. "Construction in the [occupied] territories is done without any imagination. It does not introduce anything new. . . . If there was any professional challenge there, a chance to do something innovative, I might have ignored the political issue [and worked in settlements] . . . but for the time being, I am not interested, politically or professionally."[174] Sharon had in fact taken part in the design of the first settlement, Kfar Etzion, in the previous decade. Working with his father, he designed an educational center with a guest house at the southeastern edge of the settlement. But he saw no merit in the architecture of the new settlements that mushroomed in the aftermath of the 1977 elections, because he saw no opportunity there for creativity. Sharon's view became the standard line about the new settlements among the prominent architects of his generation.[175]

The architectural history recovered in this chapter, in part from the documentary record and in part from interviews, suggests the opposite. In each of the three case studies presented above, architects experimented with new designs. In Ma'ale Adumim, Leitersdorf developed new models of housing based on the climatological research conducted by Givoni and his team. In Alfe Menashe, Yaski and Sivan tried to fuse vernacular building elements inspired by the Palestinian village with the North American backyard, in an attempt to update public housing models by bringing them in line with a new suburban ideal. In Nofim, Katseff experimented with diverse aesthetic references in lavish houses. All three designs responded in different ways to a growing sense of individualism and a desire for privacy among Israelis. Although the election of the Likud Party made the construction of settlements a government policy, there was no consensus concerning the architectural form settlements should take. That lack of consensus—combined with generous subsidies from the state and the gradual privatization of planning—created the conditions for architects to experiment with a wide range of design solutions and housing schemes. Each architect took into consideration the desires of developers and consumers in a new way, some more successfully than others. The resulting landscape was anything but unimaginative.

Sharon's inability to see the architectural innovation that was taking place in the West Bank speaks to a dramatic transition in the local architectural culture and building market. Sharon belonged to a small circle of elite architects who, thanks to their close collaboration with the Ministry of Housing, had dominated Israeli architecture until the 1977 elections.[176] Although members of that circle may have shifted their aesthetic preferences over the years, they remained committed to a number of tenets, including the goal of supporting national cohesion and solidarity and an adherence to Labor-Zionism's ethos of modesty. These principles were somewhat apparent in Kiryat Arba's identical housing blocks, in Ofra's modest model homes, and, to a degree, even in Alfe Menashe's row houses. Most Israelis flocking to the West Bank in the 1980s, however, had no interest in these uniform housing schemes that erased markers of social difference, or in the collectivist vision of society that those schemes perhaps sought to promote. Instead, they wanted detached single-family houses in the suburbs, with lush lawns, garages for their cars, and preferably some aesthetic references to Tuscany, Scandinavia, or the United States. While these desires were quite common within Israel, they were particularly visible in West Bank settlements, where land was plentiful, where government funding was available, and where entire communities could be built from scratch, unconfined by existing infrastructure and building styles. And once design and construction had been outsourced to private developers, who were keen on making a quick profit, architects working in settlements had to adjust their design principles. Gone were the days when architects of Sharon's circle could rely on their connections at the Ministry of Housing to secure design commissions. And quickly, many of them were left behind, staggered by a landscape of settlements that seemed so foreign, so out of touch, and at times so offensive to those values they had championed. It marked the end of an era when a small group of elite architects enjoyed a centralized, state-led building market.

Elite architects, however, were not the only ones who felt uncomfortable with the new suburban settlements that mushroomed in the 1980s. As much as the expansion of the settlement enterprise pleased the religious Zionist settlers of Gush Emunim—the people widely considered the indisputable leaders of the settlement movement—some of them watched these developments with concern. A number of the activists complained that the new settlements were located too close to the border with Israel to further their ultimate goal of annexing the West Bank in its entirety.[177] The activists who founded Ofra and devised the community settlement model also worried that the lavish houses that sprung up in the 1980s posed risks. Moshe Merhaviya, the secretary of Ofra, warned in 1981 that many of these large houses seemed beyond the means of the people buying them. There was thus a risk that they would be left unfinished, creating a landscape of arrested development.[178] Some worried that the lack of stylistic uniformity and the overall ostentatiousness signaled moral defects in settler society. The community settlement, as it was developed in Ofra, had been based on the recognition of a relationship between architecture and identity, and they saw the new eclecticism of settlements like Nofim through that lens. What they saw was monstrous. Yisrael Har'el, a resident of Ofra, wrote: "If architecture and gardening attest to a group's culture, then we have created in our settlements an image that attests to a defected interiority. It is enough to take a glimpse at our settlements. Usually what we see is a random collection of shapes, built without any planning or taste. We have scarred the landscape and you can see it everywhere."[179] In similar fashion, Yehuda Etzion, the founder of Ofra, wrote of the new settlement houses: "The villas and the castles—built in wood and stone—that rise in many of Judea and Samaria's settlements . . . they sting the eyes of the beholder from the outside, and might also harden the heart of the person inside. . . . Let's build in a modest way! Modesty is beautiful . . . not just at the level of the building but also, and mostly, in the hearts."[180] For Etzion and many other members of Gush Emunim, there was a fundamental link between architecture and subjectivity. For the homebuyers, it seems, it was about consumer choice and having a backyard.

Arguably, the main concern of the early settlement activists was that these luxurious houses damaged the reputation of the settlement movement among the general public. The activists had invested great effort to position the settlement enterprise within the longer history of pioneering Zionism by adapting the community settlement to resemble the kibbutz and the moshav. As described in the previous chapter, the settlers of Ofra built their homes with pitched red-tiled rooftops, instituted a strict building code, and altogether aimed at modesty and uniformity, even if they insisted on a degree of privacy and financial autonomy that had been absent on kibbutzim. By drawing an architectural link, if not an ideological one, between the settlement and the kibbutz, they had sought to reframe the settlement enterprise in terms that most Israelis could recognize and few would dare to oppose. But now, as settlers were buying large houses like the ones in Nofim, it was becoming increasingly difficult to maintain this image. As an activist from the settlement of Psagot complained in the Gush Emunim journal *Nekuda*: "This [building] style had created an absurd formula: 'Villa Settling' . . . something kept only for the rich!"[181]

Some settlement activists fought the new trend. In 1983, Uri Ariel, director of Amana, an official settling agency founded by Gush Emunim in 1976, warned in the pages of *Nekuda* that the leaders of the settlement movement were about to make changes to the building codes that would prohibit the construction of what he referred to as "unreasonably large houses."[182] Such attempts, however, came to nothing. They had little chance of standing in the way of those Israelis wishing to improve their living standards and escape their modest apartments and a collectivism they perhaps never really wanted. These Israelis, for the most part, didn't care very much about Gush Emunim and its views. In fact, according to Haggai Segal, a *Nekuda* reporter and resident of Ofra, by 1986, there were fewer than three thousand settler families residing in community settlements associated with Gush Emunim.[183] Meanwhile, tens of thousands of settlers—many with no relation whatsoever to Gush Emunim—resided in the new, large suburban settlements.[184] The religious activists of Gush Emunim had lost their privileged position as the vanguard of the settlement enterprise.

Soon, however, construction in new settlements would become far less flashy, though not because of Gush Emunim's directives or grievances aired by its activists in the media. While the First Intifada was still going on, a new segment of Israelis, namely, non-Zionist ultra-Orthodox Jews, would start flocking to the West Bank. They would soon outnumber both the religious radicals of Gush Emunim and the newer, lower- and middle-class profiteers. And as had happened before, the introduction of a new public would place new and unexpected demands on the shaping of the built environment.

CHAPTER 4

FAITHFUL CITIES

The settlement of Modi'in Illit is unlike any other settlement I have described in this book thus far. With a population of more than 75,000, it is much larger than the settlements of Kiryat Arba, Ofra, or Ma'ale Adumim. Individual buildings, in turn, are also much larger. Some rise up more than eight floors, and each is studded with balconies that project out in different patterns. In addition, where most settlements are dominated by vehicle traffic, Modi'in Illit has an elaborate network of pedestrian-only pathways and ramps that crisscross the city, connecting dozens of playgrounds that seem to sprout up on almost every block. Some blocks have two or even three playgrounds. They are almost always overcrowded with young ultra-Orthodox kids, recognizable by the locks of hair covering their ears. Groups of three or four young women, dressed in modest clothes that cover their forearms and legs, gather at the benches nearby. They chat with one another while they look after the kids. Here and there, older men dressed in black coats and black broad-brimmed hats, often with books in their hands, pass by the playgrounds on their way to the synagogue, the yeshiva, or the mikveh. At night, almost everyone is outside. Few cities can compete with Modi'in Illit's street life. And yet, as urban as it may seem, Modi'in Illit is closed in on itself in the way of a small village. Everyone who lives there, without exception, adheres to an ultra-Orthodox interpretation of the Jewish tradition.[1] Outsiders are rare. They are so rare that when I visited Modi'in Illit for the first time, a group of ten young boys gathered around me and stared at me silently, in my T-shirt and chinos, with both wonder and suspicion, until one of them dared to ask "Are you a Gentile?"

Modi'in Illit belongs to a species of settlements that took shape in the late 1980s and early 1990s, while the Palestinian uprising was unfolding. A push from the Israeli Right to increase the number of Jewish settlers in the West Bank, combined with a housing crisis, had resulted in an influx of ultra-Orthodox Jews to the West Bank. The ultra-Orthodox, who made up about 5 percent of Israelis in 1995, had largely avoided settling in the West Bank in previous decades.[2] But once they began migrating in large numbers to the West Bank, their religious beliefs and practices made a new kind of demand on the construction of settlements. In response to this demand, a new kind of settlement emerged—the ultra-Orthodox city-settlement. Among the ultra-Orthodox community, these new cities, composed of large multistory apartment buildings, were initially called, not without both irony and pathos, "the Projects." Some three decades later, however, almost half of the new construction in West Bank settlements takes place in these cities, and the ultra-Orthodox have come to form about one-third of the total population of Jewish settlers.[3]

The architects who were tasked with designing settlements exclusively for the ultra-Orthodox community faced unfamiliar challenges. The rules of life that the ultra-Orthodox abide by call for a particular organization of space, something the architects came to realize only later. At first, they aestheticized the religious attachments of the user; they tried to develop a formal language that would reflect the customs of the ultra-Orthodox community. Some drew on Jewish symbolism; others explored new urban schemes, inspired by emerging postmodern tendencies. But when many in the ultra-Orthodox community began to resent the Projects, and it was unclear whether young ultra-Orthodox couples would set roots in the West Bank, architects rethought their designs. They began to study and accommodate the unique practical needs of the ultra-Orthodox community. Although these needs proved to be more complex than the architects had imagined, and some of their attempts failed, these architects opened a dialogue between secular design professionals and the ultra-Orthodox community that dislodged the practice of architecture from its secular assumptions.

This chapter unpacks the short history of these city-settlements and the design debates that accompanied their development. Focusing on the settlement of Betar Illit and its predecessor, Immanu'el, it shows how these negotiations between the planners and the residents resulted in paradoxical outcomes. These paradoxes—perhaps more than any other episode in the architectural history of settlements—problematize the prevailing narrative of the history of settlement design as the direct reflection of military strategy. Instead, these negotiations and their outcomes point to the intricate relations between top-down and bottom-up design processes in engendering the urban formation around which great parts of the Israeli occupation are built. In turn, they also complicate intellectual frameworks that foreground the emancipatory nature of bottom-up design processes and force us to think differently about user-led design.

UNLIKELY SETTLERS

Ultra-Orthodox Jewry is unlike other modern-day branches of Judaism, and it is different from the religious Zionism of the Gush Emunim that drove the construction of key settlements in the 1970s. It adheres to a different set of religious and cultural practices. The origins of ultra-Orthodox Jewry can be traced back to Europe of the eighteenth and nineteenth centuries, when forces of modernization, whether compulsory secular education, urbanization, or the first stirrings of modern nationalism, combined with increasing acculturation (in some cases complete assimilation) to provoke a backlash in the Jewish community. A number of pious Jews saw such modern transformations as heretical. In response, they adopted an uncompromisingly conservative ideology, calling on other Jews to resist these changes.[4] In some cases, according to the historian Michael Silber, they drew on marginal texts and traditions. Nevertheless, they succeeded in shifting parts of mainstream Jewry toward a more rigid observance of Judaism, laying the foundations for modern-day ultra-Orthodoxy. In subsequent decades, over the course of the first half of the twentieth century, Jews who opposed the increasingly secular culture of modern life established large communities that were committed to this hardened form of orthodoxy in places like Israel and the United States, becoming a distinct (though not unvaried) religious movement.[5] Although they are sometimes referred to as "ultra-Orthodox," many Jews have come to favor the Hebrew term Haredim (or Haredi in the singular), which means "those who tremble" (at God's word).[6]

The opposition of Haredim to nationalism made them unlikely candidates to take part in the settlement enterprise. Just as they had rejected European nationalism, so they also rejected Zionism. Their rejection of Zionism, however, also stemmed from theological reasons. They believed that the State of Israel would be reconstituted only after the coming of the Messiah. To many Haredi leaders, therefore, the founding of modern Israel, and later the occupation of the West Bank, appeared to be religiously insignificant and even flawed: it was an attempt to bring about redemption through mundane human activity, to arrogate to humankind what belonged to God.[7] Their opposition to the occupation of the West Bank in particular was informed by another tenet of the Jewish tradition. In light of other countries' opposition to the settlement enterprise, they saw the construction of settlements as "teasing the goyim [Gentiles]," which is strictly prohibited according to some rabbinic traditions.[8] In the first two decades after the conquest of the West Bank, most leaders of the Haredi community had thus prohibited their followers from moving to the occupied territories.[9]

The lifestyle and customs of Haredi Israelis are also at odds with the commuter-based pattern of most settlements. The Haredim cling to certain ways of life that had developed in Eastern Europe during the eighteenth and nineteenth centuries. Many Haredi people therefore lack professional skills, leaving them dependent on services provided by those outside their community.[10] This, combined with the fact that many Haredi men in Israel dedicate their time to the study of rabbinic literature, and the tendency to have large families—an average of 6.5 children per family[11]—has meant that the Haredim have consistently suffered from high poverty rates.[12] Accordingly, many families do not own a car, and thus must live within walking distance of businesses, synagogues, and schools.

Until the 1960s, Haredim in Israel primarily lived in two major urban areas: the northern neighborhoods of Jerusalem, and the city of Bne Brak on the outskirts of Tel Aviv. But by the 1960s, these areas became too small for the rapidly growing community, and many young couples were forced to move out. At first, some moved to nearby cities, but the rising cost of living made these cities too expensive. By the 1970s, Haredi families began moving to the remote towns built originally to accommodate the masses of Jews who immigrated to Israel during the 1950s.[13] But these remote towns were already economically distressed, and they were often too small; moreover, their secular residents often expressed hostility toward the Haredi tenants. By the early 1980s, as more and more Haredi couples were trapped in small apartments with rocketing rent prices, a more comprehensive solution was needed.[14]

It was this housing crisis that would reverse the Haredi position on settlements. But the lifestyle of the Haredim would in turn prompt a reformulation of settlement design.

THE RISE AND FALL OF IMMANU'EL

The first serious attempt to solve the Haredi housing crisis came from a rather unexpected source. Following a series of government decisions, made between 1979 and 1982, that opened the settlement enterprise to private developers, Haredi developers decided to build a settlement exclusively for Haredi Israelis in the heart of the West Bank.[15] Planned for 200,000 residents, it would be an entire city, the first of its kind, whether in the occupied territories or in Israel itself.[16] It was named Immanu'el, after a figure in the book of Isaiah. Even though the Haredi developers lacked extensive experience with large-scale construction projects, and indeed failed to satisfy some of the preliminary requirements demanded by government officials, they were able to obtain the required approvals.[17] By the end of 1982, construction was in full swing.[18]

The developers commissioned a master plan from the architect Thomas Leitersdorf, who had been overseeing the design of the settlement of Ma'ale Adumim. It may have been because of the experience Leitersdorf had gained working on Ma'ale Adumim that he was selected to design the master plan for Immanu'el. In any case, one day, a young Haredi man, carrying an old map, came to his office and asked Leitersdorf to plan the city. The man had not identified any particular site, nor had he secured any building rights, but he was glowing with enthusiasm. Leitersdorf was at first doubtful, but the young man assured him that he would take care of any needed approvals. Leitersdorf was so moved by the strong will of the gentle man that he agreed to take on the project.

Before drawing any plans, Leitersdorf wanted to know more about the future residents. So he asked to meet with the spiritual leader supporting the initiative, and soon thereafter he was introduced to the rebbe (spiritual leader) of the Kretshnif Hasidic court, a twenty-eight-year-old man who seemed to exercise magical control over his followers. The rebbe explained to Leitersdorf that families in his Hasidic court were often large, with each couple having at least four kids, and that they often had meager sources of income, for usually only the wife had paid employment. After that first conversation with the rebbe, Leitersdorf realized that these people had needs unlike those of secular Israelis with whom he had previously worked and that there were no precedents he could follow or relevant guidelines from the Ministry of Construction and Housing that he could consult.[19]

Previously, Haredim had received little attention from local architects. In the immediate decades after the founding of the State of Israel, under the reign of the labor parties with their melting-pot ideology, the Haredim remained a small minority with marginal political power. Many among Labor Zionists had, in fact, expected the Haredim to abandon their ways and assimilate into Israel's secular culture. And so, as late as the early 1980s, architects and planners at the Ministry of Construction and Housing did not recognize the distinct needs of the Haredi population.[20] There were a few minor exceptions to this rule. Most notably, in the 1970s, the ministry had overseen the design of a small neighborhood for Hasidic Jews in Hatsor HaGlilit, a peripheral town in northern Israel, which took into account the needs of the Haredim. The design of the neighborhood allowed the individual units a high degree of privacy, with each having a separate entryway, and it included large open spaces among other features. But this was a very small neighborhood. Inaugurated in 1976, by the early 1980s it housed about ninety families. (By 2020, it had grown to two hundred families.)[21] It could hardly have served as a model for an entire city designed exclusively for

Haredi Jews. Leitersdorf therefore commissioned a study aimed at coming up with some guidelines, which concluded that what a Haredi city mainly needed were large, yet affordable, units.[22]

With that information in hand, Leitersdorf approached the drafting table. To minimize construction costs, he laid out all the roads and the buildings according to the topography of the site so as to avoid the need to erect large retaining walls. He also replicated a number of elements from Ma'ale Adumim, including a driverless trolley system imported from Texas as well as the terraced townhouses that opened out toward the surrounding landscape.[23] Leitersdorf drafted plans for one thousand residential units in which he attempted to accommodate the strict segregation of the sexes observed by Haredim as well as their regular rituals. To this end, he divided the interior spaces into areas accommodating the wife and children and those serving the husband and his male friends (see figure 4.5.1). In addition, he designed the units with balconies that were big enough to serve as sukkahs (temporary ritual huts) on Sukkot, a seven-day holiday during which the husband is required to dine, host friends, and sleep in the sukkah. To satisfy what he perceived to be the residents' aesthetic preferences, he also added some arches to several of the public buildings he interspersed among the residential buildings.[24]

Other architects were also invited to design buildings in Immanu'el, and they drew inspiration from a variety of sources. The Tel Aviv–based architect Eli First, who was moved by the piety of the future residents, turned to Jewish symbolism, and designed one of Immanu'el's main synagogues in the shape of an extruded Star of David (figure 4.1). The Star of David shape, the avowedly secular architect explained, was to be seen only from the sky, just like a prayer aimed at God.[25] Other architects drew inspiration from the neighboring Palestinian towns and villages. As discussed in the previous chapters, since the late 1950s a cohort of leading Israeli architects had turned to the architecture of the Palestinians as a means of both challenging the high modernism of their forefathers and establishing themselves as natives of the land.[26] Now, in Immanu'el, a number of them continued experimenting with that vocabulary. Notable among these architects were Avraham Yaski and Yossi Sivan, who had also worked in the settlement of Alfe Menashe. Together with the architect Yaacov Gil, they designed one of Immanu'el's neighborhoods, which they organized around multistory apartment buildings ornamented with prefabricated concrete arches and covered with a thin layer of stone. At their feet, as if woven into the natural topography, the architects installed seventy-two cottages also featuring concrete arches; these were staggered one on top of another, enclosing multiple inner courtyards in ways

FIGURE 4.1. Star of David–shaped synagogue designed by Eli First in Immanu'el, ca. 1984. (Star of Samaria offices in Immanu'el.)

that echoed the traditional courtyard house (figure 4.2). In like fashion, in an adjacent neighborhood, another architect designed a series of double-story cottages with arched entryways and stone cladding.[27]

While the architects were drafting their plans, the developers encountered opposition from some influential rabbis. According to a reporter for the daily *Davar*, leaders of two Haredi communities in Jerusalem were angry at those

FIGURE 4.2. Housing units partially inspired by Palestinian architecture, designed by Yaski-Gil-Sivan Architects for Immanu'el, 1983. (City Planning Division in Immanu'el.)

"self-proclaimed Haredim, wishing to erect 'Kollels' [religious schools] on lands the Zionists have stolen from the Arabs, against their opposition."[28] In their view, the construction of Immanu'el, like other settlements, was in defiance of the traditional Jewish law prohibiting pious people from teasing non-Jews. For this and other reasons, Rabbi Elazar Shach, among the most influential rabbis at the time, boycotted Immanu'el and discouraged his followers from moving there.[29]

To overcome the rabbis' opposition and to downplay the settlement's remote location, the developers launched an extensive marketing effort, not unlike the campaigns for other settlements at the time. The campaign included free round-trip tickets to anywhere in the world for potential homebuyers, as well as guided tours, lectures about the place, and a Hasidic music festival held on the hilltop site that was attended by over 10,000 Haredi people.[30] The city, as it was promoted in these events, was to bring the newest technologies from abroad and adapt them to suit traditional Jewish customs. Describing his plans for the city, one of the developers explained, "I have seen this in the US: a computer in each house. You press a button and you order a cottage cheese . . . you want to order a babysitter—you press [a button]; you have a question about halakhah [traditional Jewish law]—you ask and the halakhic computer . . . replies. . . . I even plan a video recording studio that will broadcast Gamara and Judaism classes."[31] Futuristic but also traditional,

Immanu'el was set to transform residents' everyday life while leaving their religious beliefs and customs uncompromised.

References to events in Jewish history and to sites of Haredi interest also played an important role in promotional materials (figure 4.3). In advertisements, graphic designers underlined Immanu'el's resemblance to the Old City of Jerusalem. In one rendering reproduced in large numbers, Immanu'el's skyline is dominated by domed buildings and large arches (figure 4.4). In some ads, the developers also emphasized Immanu'el's proximity to Jerusalem, falsely claiming that, with the completion of a new road, slated for 1986, it would be a thirty-five– to forty-minute drive instead of the seventy-five minutes it takes today.[32] Equally important were references to the religious significance of Immanu'el's immediate surroundings. According to one ad, Immanu'el was just north of the burial site of Moses's successor, Yehoshua Bin Nun, and adjacent to an ancient and especially sacred vineyard that once provided the wine used in rituals at the old Temple.[33] By establishing ties to Old Jerusalem and to biblical times, the developers were attempting not only to appeal to religious homebuyers but also to downplay Immanu'el's actual context—an occupied territory, surrounded by a potentially hostile population.[34]

Once construction got under way, however, the developers encountered financial difficulties and began pressuring the architects to work under an extremely tight budget. Under the new constraints, most of the elaborate designs for houses with decorative arches and stone cladding were cut. Instead, the few buildings that were actually built in Immanu'el were basic. As the architect David Nofar, who designed some of the residential buildings, explained to me: "We did . . . the simplest and most banal design one could think of . . . [that is,] as many units as possible for as little investment possible."[35]

In the end, many residential buildings showed little consideration of either vernacular aesthetics or the special needs of the Haredi community. The budget cuts merely compounded the original challenge of designing a modern Haredi city. Some of the architects completely ignored the special needs of this community. The windows of many of the units, for example, were positioned in such a way that left the interior spaces exposed to outside passersby, forcing women to adhere to modesty rules that regulate their appearance in public (like wearing long-sleeve shirts and covering their hair) inside their own home.[36] Likewise, the floor plan for a standard unit that was replicated in large numbers across the settlement was too small to accommodate the large Haredi families and lacked a partition between the entrance door and the living room that would allow the women of the house to avoid interacting with men sitting in the living room (figure 4.5.2). In another case,

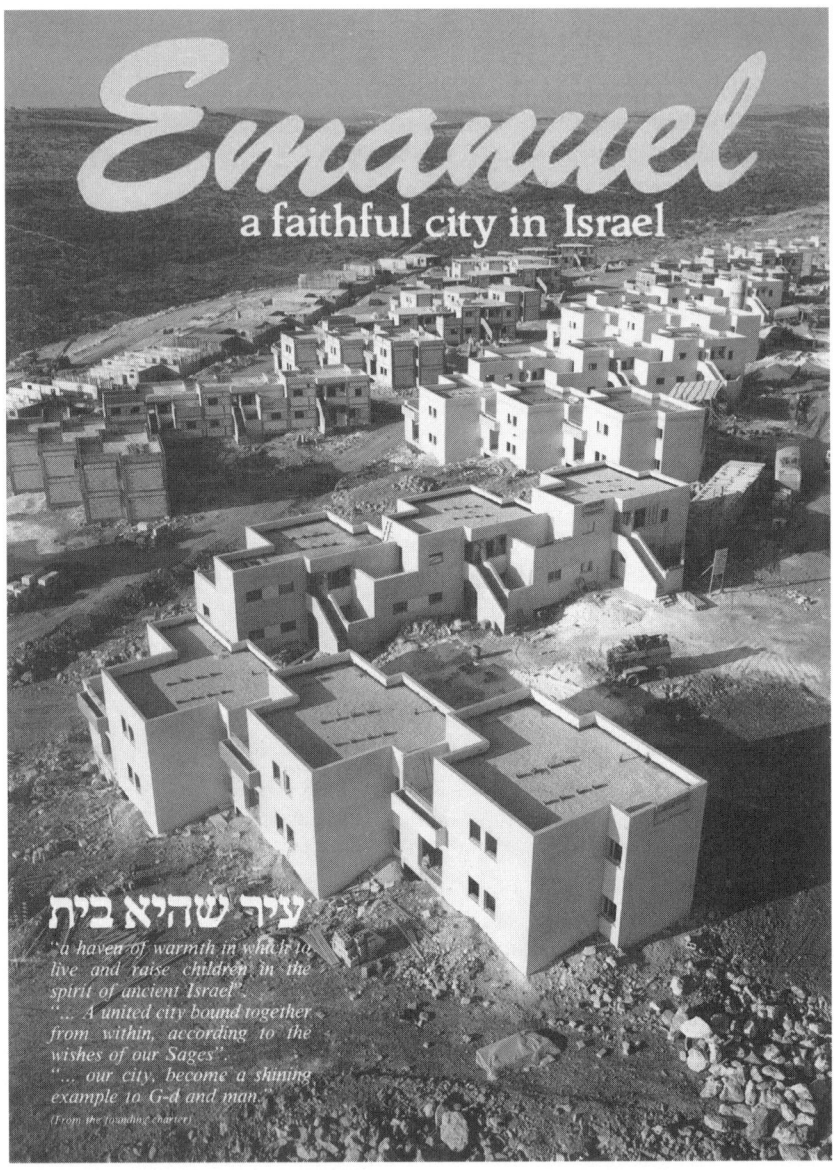

Emanuel
a faithful city in Israel

עיר שהיא בית

"a haven of warmth in which to
live and raise children in the
spirit of ancient Israel".
"... A united city bound together
from within, according to the
wishes of our Sages".
"... our city, become a shining
example to G-d and man."
(From the founding charter)

FIGURE 4.3. Ad for Immanu'el (spelled as Emanuel) describing the city as "a haven of warmth in which to live and raise children in the spirit of ancient Israel," 1983. (Star of Samaria offices in Immanu'el.)

FIGURE 4.4. Drawing of Immanu'el inspired by representations of the Old City of Jerusalem, entitled "Immanu'el: A City That Is a Home," 1982. (City Planning Division in Immanu'el.)

a multistory house that was built after the first stage of construction had rounded balconies that rendered them too small for a sukkah and lacked any partitions dividing the living room from the kitchen or the parents' bedroom. Adding to this, the apartments had in-between spaces, such as small family corners, that were considered wasted and unusable space. Furthermore, the placement of the bathroom door in the parents' bedroom made it almost impossible to lay out two twin beds, undermining Haredi couples' ability to follow the strict gender segregation rules requiring them to sleep in separate beds, at least when the woman menstruates and during the immediate days following menstruation (figure 4.5.4).[37] Unsurprisingly, many Haredi people found the units unattractive.[38]

FIGURE 4.5. Apartment layouts in Immanu'el: (1) a three-bedroom unit, showing partition walls that separate the living room from the entrance space, the kitchen, and the bedrooms (original plan by Leitersdorf Goldenberg Planning and Architecture, ca. 1982); (2 and 3) units lacking partitions between the entrance door and the living room, planned by the architect David Nofar (2) and the architect Israel Levitt (3), ca. 1983; (4) unit with no partitions dividing the private from the public spaces of the house, and with a balcony too small to serve as a sukkah, plus a family corner and a master bedroom that cannot easily accommodate two twin beds. (All plans drawn by the author based on original plans available at the City Planning Division and Star of Samaria offices in Immanu'el.)

Things got even worse in March 1984, shortly after the first residents had moved in. The developers lacked the funds needed to pay the construction companies working on the site. So, one after the other, building sites were left abandoned at various stages of development.[39] Meanwhile, tensions between the developers over management issues had erupted. Then, in 1985,

FIGURE 4.6. Apartment building left unfinished in Immanu'el, 2015. (Photograph by author.)

the development company collapsed and went into receivership. At that point, construction came to a complete halt. Some one thousand units were left unfinished, waiting for a savior (figure 4.6).[40] Many homebuyers now found themselves paying mortgages for apartments they might never own.[41]

Meanwhile, homebuyers who had already moved in—some 450 families of about eight to nine people each[42]—were left isolated in the middle of the West Bank, with almost no public facilities or basic infrastructure.[43] The residents directed their frustrations at the Ministry of Construction and Housing. "It is impossible that we will continue in this embarrassing situation, especially now that winter is about to arrive," one of the residents wrote to the Ministry of Construction and Housing, while complaining about the lack of sidewalks on his street. "Women, men and children would have to trudge through the sludge and the water."[44] Others complained about the lack of telephone service and unfinished public buildings, including a fifty-family synagogue catering to Jews of Yemeni origin, who found themselves unable to congregate.[45] "We are now temporarily housed in a room, where the density and the duress are unbearably painful," three of the congregation members pleaded to the minister of Construction and Housing.[46] Meanwhile, some found the Star of David–shaped synagogue inefficient, if not even offensive. As one resident of Immanu'el explained to me: "We clearly didn't ask for this. It is unpractical. This [star of David] shape is very wasteful. It has these sharp corners, and we [Haredi people] care the most about functionality. For us it is all about using as much space as possible. We don't need this shape. . . . And this shape, not only is it seen only from the sky, from an airplane, but we have rules about how to build synagogues, and it is prohibited [to use figures]." In some cases, homebuyers whose units were not finished were housed in apartments bought by others, without the latter's permission, resulting in growing conflicts within the community.[47] If all this was not enough, in 1987, the Palestinian uprising broke out and dealt another blow to Immanu'el. Within a few years, those who could afford it moved out, leaving behind them a poor community that some three decades later, in 2020, made up barely 2 percent of the city's originally projected population.[48]

SIENA ON THE HILLS OF JUDEA

After the fall of Immanu'el, one might have assumed that the Haredi community could not again be recruited to the settlement enterprise. But by the late 1980s, the housing shortage facing the Haredi community had reached a critical point.[49] At the same time, as the Palestinian uprising continued to discourage some middle-class Israelis from moving to settlements, someone, preferably with a high fertility rate, it seems, had to ensure the growth of Jewish presence in the occupied territories. A second attempt to settle Haredi people in the West Bank—where land was cheap, and the political stakes were high—was almost inevitable.

In the mid-1980s, planners at the Ministry of Construction and Housing were informed about a possible site for a new settlement: three bare hilltops located a few hundred meters from the Green Line. Joe Rosenberg, a (non-Haredi) Jewish developer who had emigrated from South Africa, had been trying to establish a suburban settlement on these three hilltops since 1982.[50] Rosenberg had named it "Aliza Hill" after Aliza Begin, wife of Prime Minister Menachem Begin.[51] Later, the settlement's name was changed to Hadar Betar. With the help of Hanan Porat, the settlement activist who had scouted the site where Ofra was built, Rosenberg brought several mobile homes to the site. He thought the settlement might cater to the kind of religious Zionist settlers who had moved to Hebron and Ofra. But very few Israelis were willing to move to Hadar Betar, where the winds were especially strong. And those who did quickly found themselves stuck in rudimentary mobile homes that failed to protect them from the harsh weather conditions. Soon, they began leaving the settlement. At one point, only two settlers remained on the hilltop.[52] Rosenberg's plan, it seemed, was reaching a dead-end.[53]

Planners at the Ministry of Construction and Housing saw the site's potential (primarily its proximity to Jerusalem, climate notwithstanding), and by the end of 1985 they had begun drafting plans for a city-settlement catering also to Haredi Israelis. It would be called Betar Illit and would house thousands of families.[54] The first move-in date was scheduled for May 1990. At first, planners thought the city could also accommodate religious Zionist settlers.[55] But the two groups refused to share the settlement. "You are too Zionist for us," Haredi people told the religious Zionist settlers of Hadar Betar, who had hoped to become part of the new city-settlement.[56] Ministry of Construction and Housing officials thus shelved their initial plans to incorporate religious Zionists and focused their efforts on the first hilltop that was planned exclusively for Haredi residents.

The Ministry of Construction and Housing outsourced the planning and construction of Betar Illit to Ashdar, a large building company. Hoping to avoid the planning mistakes that arguably contributed to the failure of Immanu'el, Ashdar hired Ora and Yaacov Yaar, a pair of well-known Tel Aviv–based architects, who had a long history of designing housing, including more recently a large residential quarter in the settlement of Ma'ale Adumim, which was probably the most successful settlement to that date. Whereas a few years before this the Yaars had been hesitant to accept a design commission in the West Bank, the combination of general economic instability and government subsidized construction of settlements left them no real choice, Yaacov Yaar later argued in his memoir. "In the mid-1980s, to plan or not to plan beyond the Green Line was a question of 'to be or not to be,'" he wrote, referring to the disproportionately favorable budgets allocated to settlements at the time.[57] And so the Yaars began to work on the first hilltop of Betar Illit, designed for 3,400 families.[58]

Unlike some of their predecessors in Immanu'el, the Yaars did not draw on the Palestinian village as a source of inspiration. At the time, they had been interested in the work of postmodern thinkers who reasserted the importance of preindustrial European cities, in particular the work of the architect and theorist Léon Krier. Since the 1970s, Krier had come to be known for his criticism of the kind of modernist urbanism promoted by Le Corbusier and codified in the Athens Charter of 1933, which had emphasized functionalism, at times with a reckless disregard for the historic urban fabric of cities. Krier called on architects to recover that historic urban fabric by reconstructing preindustrial urban patterns and types, such as the traditional square, narrow street, and arcade.[59] "We must go back and take up the work of imitation of the most beautiful preindustrial examples in their proportions, dimensions, and morphological simplicity," he stated in a text he coauthored with the Belgium-born architect and theorist Maurice Culot.[60] Yaacov Yaar had heard Krier lecture at a meeting of the International Union of Architects in Cairo in 1985, and though he found Krier's rhetoric too forceful, he admired his embrace of historic cities. "There is no one like Krier when it comes to expressing and perceiving urban spaces," Yaar noted in his memoir. "His urban drawings had been an inexhaustible source of inspiration for me." The Yaars also found inspiration in the work of the Catalan architect Ricardo Bofill, whom they met in Paris. Bofill had produced urban plans for a number of housing projects near Paris that readapted neoclassic forms. Yaar visited many of them and was deeply moved: "Bofill's work shone like diamonds in a pile of gravel," he wrote.[61]

In the early 1980s, inspired by these architects' reappraisal of preindustrial cities, the Yaars began exploring elements they associated with history and tradition in their designs for Pisgat Ze'ev, a settlement in East Jerusalem.[62] In contrast to modernist schemes that separated automobile from pedestrian traffic, the Yaars integrated the two throughout the neighborhood, which also eliminated large parking lots. The streets were lined with multistory apartment buildings. On the ground floor of the buildings bordering the main street, they allocated spaces for small stores. "Here dwelling and shopping facilities were interwoven at the center of the city, as is the case in traditional cities," the Yaars noted in a Ministry of Construction and Housing publication. "As a result, the street in Pisgat Ze'ev recovers its traditional meaning."[63] In 1992, the architectural critic Aba Elhanani heralded Pisgat Ze'ev as an indicator of the arrival of a new kind of urbanism—the kind of urbanism Krier and his contemporaries were trumpeting—to the local scene.[64]

Betar Illit, a city designed for people known for their hostility to modernity, must have seemed like the most appropriate place to explore "traditional" urban forms. Indeed, in one of the earliest meetings concerning the planning of Betar Illit, the Yaars agreed to model the city, with some modifications, on the design principles of Pisgat Ze'ev.[65] They thus designed Betar Illit with mixed-use streets, lined with three- to four-story buildings with a shopping arcade occupying the ground floor (figure 4.7). Curving along the steep topography, the arcade lent Betar Illit the image of an older hillside town in Italy or southern Spain, Yaar later noted.[66] The architects enhanced the Mediterranean atmosphere by capping all the houses with red roofs. "The most urban cities in Europe—Siena and Florence—they have red roofs," Aviv

FIGURE 4.7. Apartment buildings with a shopping arcade on the ground floor, Betar Illit, 1996. (Photograph by Reuven Milon, from the Judaica Collection of the Harvard Library, Harvard University.)

Yaar, the project architect, explained to me without irony. "We wanted to achieve the same urban feeling with the red roofs in Betar [Illit]."[67]

The Yaars combined their formal approach to designing Betar Illit with a research-based one that focused on the specific needs of Haredi people. To study these needs, they made trips to the Haredi neighborhoods of Jerusalem accompanied by David Lev, an American-born civil engineer assigned to the project who happened to be Haredi. Together, they walked around the crowded streets of Jerusalem and discussed the residents' lifestyles and the building elements unique to the Haredi apartment. The residential units they drafted on the basis of this research were unconventional. The balconies were enlarged, small sinks were added outside the restrooms for hand-washing rituals, and careful attention was paid to the gendered division of the house. Whenever possible, the living room was closed off from the rest of the house so that it could function as a study room for the husband (figure 4.8).[68] Proud of the design process, Yaacov Yaar later concluded: "Planning a city for the Haredi population is, first and foremost, an original challenge. When approaching it, planners have to carefully study the unique needs [of

FIGURE 4.8. Yaar Architects, residential unit with a living room closed off from the rest of the house, Betar Illit, ca. 1989. (Drawn by author based on original plan available at the City Planning Division of Betar Illit.)

the people]. . . . And indeed, we did it, in the design of both the residential buildings and the rich variety of public buildings."[69]

To attract Haredi families to the city, the Ministry of Construction and Housing offered homebuyers financing so good it was almost impossible to turn down. In 1989, two-bedroom units, for example, sold for $54,000, of which only $6,000 had to be paid in advance. The remainder was financed with favorable loans.[70] To reach Haredi families, the Ministry of Construction and Housing collaborated with Mishkenot Yerushalayim (Jerusalem Residence). Founded in the early 1980s by a group of nineteen Haredi men, Mishkenot Yerushalayim provided informal assistance to Haredi families seeking housing inside Jerusalem. They contacted landlords, and they provided homebuyers with information about mortgage programs and legal advice. Now, with the backing of the Ministry of Construction and Housing and Ashdar, they advised, screened, and registered applicants for units in Betar Illit.[71] In addition, the Ministry of Construction and Housing established a special steering committee of rabbis and community leaders in charge of promoting the city among young Haredi couples (figure 4.9).[72] The kind of promotional events that private developers had pioneered a few years earlier were also held on the construction site. On the holiday of Sukkot in October 1989, Ashdar erected a large sukkah (a ritual hut) that hosted thousands of

FIGURE 4.9. Betar Illit's steering committee with Ministry of Construction and Housing officials by the entrance to the city. A master plan showing Betar Illit's three hilltops is printed on the billboard in the background. (*Hadshot Betar*, October 1989, 5.)

potential homebuyers on the site, with Hasidic music and dances performed inside.[73] A number of special guests, including influential rabbis and the manager of the Ministry of Construction and Housing, visited the sukkah and delivered speeches celebrating the city that was about to become a reality.[74] With the blessing of both religious leaders and government officials, Betar Illit seemed set for success.

Yet, when residents started moving into the first neighborhood, things took a different turn, and Moshe Leibovitz, the first head of Betar Illit's local government, found himself struggling to somehow keep the town from falling apart.[75] At the time, Leibovitz was thirty-four years old, a former military officer whose strong sense of piety was matched by his unapologetic pragmatism. He thought he had seen it all after witnessing the fall of Immanu'el, where he had worked as a junior adviser to the developers. But nothing had prepared him for what awaited him in Betar Illit. "The architects got every-thing wrong," he told me with a thick accent, left over from his childhood in Romania. "Whatever planners should not do when planning for the Haredi community—they did."[76] Most significantly, he complained, they clustered the main public facilities—the central synagogue, school, community center, and park—in one area. In doing so, they failed to account for the multiple groups and subgroups that make up the Haredi community.[77] Each group conducts its own ceremonies, daily prayers, and education system, and each follows its own traditions. Mixing between groups is unacceptable. (It is so unacceptable that Raphael Dankner, the former manager of the Planning Division at Betar Illit's local council, told me that in 1990, when he tried to convince a resident to send his three-year-old daughter to a kindergarten that catered to children of another sect, the man was appalled and asked, "You think their girls are like mine?")[78] Not surprisingly, many of the spacious public buildings the architects designed remained empty. Furthermore, Lei-bovitz complained, the architects failed to accommodate the large number of children in the city, and there was a severe shortage of playgrounds.[79]

The architects' assumptions about the community's shopping habits and labor patterns were also flawed. Given the scarce resources available to most Haredi families, very few could afford to rent the large ground-floor commercial spaces the Yaars had borrowed from European towns, and many of them remained empty.[80] In addition, Leibovitz lamented, the planners did not think that the Haredi residents were likely to take real jobs. They planned only one industrial area and placed it on a small site with inhospi-table topography, thus limiting much-needed employment opportunities and damaging the city's economic prospects.[81]

Equally troubling, Leibovitz complained, was the lack of an adequate public transportation system. "Planners thought this was just going to be another settlement," he lamented. They assumed that most residents would have cars, as was common in other settlements. They therefore planned only one bus line connecting Betar Illit to Jerusalem. The bus made three daily trips: in the morning, afternoon, and evening. But, as Leibovitz recalled, few Haredi fam-ilies in Betar Illit owned a car at that time, and almost everyone commuted to Jerusalem on a daily basis. Government officials also refused to offer low-fare bus tickets to Betar Illit's disproportionately high number of low-income families. As a result, many found themselves disconnected from Jerusalem.[82]

As for the residential units, even though the Yaars and their team had conducted research trips to Jerusalem's Haredi neighborhoods and tried to ac-commodate some of the needs of Haredi families, they never really consulted with Betar Illit's future residents, and thus most of the units were inadequate in the end. Most importantly, according to Tamar, a thirty-something resident and draftsperson of ultra-Orthodox faith, the architects failed to account for the exceptionally large Haredi family size:

> In the original neighborhood you mainly have three-room [two-bedroom] units. But what are three rooms for a Haredi family? That's nothing! You can't live in that. It really doesn't help the people of Betar. Here, two or three years after you buy your place, usually, your family expands and can no longer live in three rooms. The average here is around six or seven kids per family. . . . If in the general public, they say that it is all about "location, location, location!" here it is "[square-] meter, [square-] meter, [square-] meter!" People here need more space.[83]

In fact, among the first families that moved in was a family of seventeen people.[84] Planned for standard families, the units in the first neighborhood were too small and allowed little space for future expansion.[85] Besides not taking into consideration the growth of families over time, the Yaars also misunderstood how Haredim use the living room. Their insistence on designing the living room as a secluded study space for the husband worked against the main purpose of the Haredi living room: accommodating Shabbat dinners for the extended family. Avishai Meiron, the manager of the City Planning Division in Betar Illit, observed that such dinners require an elongated space, with enough room for an exceptionally long dining table and easy access to the kitchen.[86] Replacing this space with a study room was unnecessary in the eyes of many of the residents. As one of them explained to me, the men spend the entire day in the Kollel—a Talmud and rabbinic literature school for married men—so they do not actually need a study space at home.

The small, rudimentary units also discouraged middle-aged and potentially more affluent residents from moving to Betar Illit. According to Leibovitz, the absence of middle-aged Haredi people in the settlement disrupted the important intergenerational support networks that were common among Haredi families. Normally, young Haredi couples rely on their parents for moral guidance and general coaching in life. For example, Leibovitz explained, a young wife will constantly consult her mother about how to raise a family, cook, and comport herself in intimate situations with her husband. "If the [Haredi] daughter has a problem with her husband, she wouldn't go to a psychologist," he told me. "She would go and talk to her mother about it." For this reason, many young couples prefer residing near their parents. But planners seemed to be unaware of the role this support network plays in the lives of Haredim, and they designed the city with only young couples in mind.[87]

With overcrowded apartments, inadequate public transportation system, and dysfunctional public spaces, many in the Haredi community worried that Betar Illit, which quickly came to be known as the Projects, was doomed to end up like its older sister Immanu'el.

FROM PUBLIC PARTICIPATION TO SELF-GOVERNANCE

Frustrated with secular planners and the conventional housing programs they drew upon, the leaders of the local Haredi community decided to take a more active role in the design of the other neighborhoods. Leibovitz scheduled a meeting with Prime Minister Yitzhak Rabin, shortly after Rabin was elected in 1992. Leibovitz took to the meeting a copy of the master plan of the city, in which he had blacked out all the residential areas, leaving only public buildings and green spaces in white. The plan was almost entirely black. In the meeting, Leibovitz recounted, he showed the blacked-out plan to Rabin and shouted, "I am not going to be part of this mistake the state is about to make. Look at how it all looks here? All looks black! You will place blacks [i.e., Haredi men, who usually wear black clothes] in black areas, and you will mark the state with black. . . . Where do you think kids could play here? Would you send your grandkids to live here?" When the prime minister laughed, Leibovitz insisted, "Don't laugh, Mr. Prime Minister, they may be Ba'aley Teshuva [become pious] and live in Betar."[88] It is hard to imagine that Rabin was convinced by this argument—and the meeting's transcripts remain undisclosed—but by the end of that meeting the two had agreed that the design must be changed.

Granted oversight of all design decisions in the following months, Leibovitz and his team of community representatives transformed what was coming to be called the Projects. At their request, the architects added more public buildings and green spaces, subdivided existing ones into smaller plots, and distributed them across the city.[89] In addition, the team insisted that the architects draw clusters of buildings that enclosed small public courtyards, allowing vehicle-free playgrounds for the disproportionately high number of children living in the city (figure 4.10).[90] Furthermore, they supervised the redesign of the residential units. Apartments surrounding the playgrounds were designed with their kitchens facing out onto the courtyard, so that mothers could watch over their kids playing below while they cooked meals or breastfed an infant. To accommodate the growth of families over time, Leibovitz and his team also insisted that in order to get building permits, architects must include plan drawings outlining future additions of at least two rooms to each new unit. To strengthen the city's connection to

FIGURE 4.10. A playground enclosed by residential buildings in Modi'in Illit, a Haredi city-settlement that followed some of Betar Illit's design principles, 2015. (Photograph by author.)

Jerusalem, they even initiated a low-fare "kosher" transportation system, the first of its kind.[91]

Other design ideas emerged as architects and planners began to seriously consider the lifestyle of residents. For example, they designed many multistory buildings with front and back façades: a flat one facing the street and a cascading one facing the surrounding landscape. The latter allowed exceptionally large, unroofed balconies needed for the Sukkot traditions. Many of Betar Illit's residents do not use elevators on Shabbat (just like they do not drive or turn on electrical appliances on the holy day).[92] To help those families purchasing units on upper levels, who would otherwise have to climb many flights of stairs each time they left the house on Shabbat, architects positioned tall, eight-story buildings next to near-vertical slopes in such a way that the upper four stories of each would rise above the street level, where the main entrance is, while the lower stories descend below. This way, no resident would have to climb (or descend) more than four stories. In addition, ramps were installed across the city to accommodate the movement of baby strollers, perhaps the main means of transportation in Betar Illit.[93]

Looking back at the early years of Betar Illit, Leibovitz, who has since assumed a number of key positions in the public sector, could not hide his pride, and some amusement, at his own audacity. "These were some serious wars I had with the architects. We screamed at each other, screams that made it all the way to the skies," he admitted. "I once even kicked Ministry of Housing officials out of my office."[94] Leibovitz's "wars" were well known throughout the settlement. By 1994, residents of Betar Illit had come to refer to him as the "prime minister."[95] One secular news reporter who visited the city could not help but wonder, and not without concern, whether Leibovitz was building his own Haredi kingdom in the settlement.[96]

Residents also helped transform the city in more direct ways. Instead of renting the commercial spaces the architects had installed on the ground floor, they opened small stores in their apartments (usually in one of the bedrooms) or in public spaces, like the building's staircase and corridors (figure 4.11). These stores are illegal according to municipal law, but the ordinance prohibiting commercial spaces in residential buildings has rarely been enforced in Betar Illit, and many storeowners brazenly decorated their balconies with signs advertising their products.[97] In 2014, the manager of the City Planning Division of Modi'in Illit, a Haredi city-settlement that was built a few years after Betar Illit, issued an ordinance specifically allowing residents to use parts of their units for commercial purposes.[98] It is reasonable to assume that Betar Illit will do the same in the near future. In similar fashion, different subcommunities in Betar Illit created small synagogues and other public facilities in portable structures and private apartments.[99]

In an extraordinary twist, women in the settlement also took control of the community's architecture. To relieve the overcrowding in apartments in the first neighborhood, a number of Haredi wives, most with a two-year diploma in architectural engineering, oversaw the expansion of almost all the units (figure 4.12).[100] "Those who do not get a building addition get fined here," one of them, a pious lady in her mid-thirties, explained, laughing, as she described to me the high volume of work she has overseen in Betar Illit.[101] The experience they gained in the first years encouraged many others to acquire professional skills, and today some of them occupy leading positions in the city. In Modi'in Illit, the manager of the City Planning Division and her entire staff are Haredi wives. The division's manager also teaches architectural drafting at a community college in Jerusalem where many young Haredi wives are her students.[102] Other Haredi wives are involved in the design of a new industrial zone in Betar Illit, intended to create new employment opportunities. According to Meiron, who oversees its planning, it is the first industrial area with all the needed services to be planned exclusively for Haredi women.[103]

FIGURE 4.11. Menswear store in a building's staircase, Betar Illit, 2015.
(Photograph by author.)

These activities by the women of Betar Illit were part of a longer process
of change in women's status in Israel's Haredi community. During the first
quarter of the twentieth century, Haredi women received minimal education
in Palestine. With the arrival of immigrants from Germany and Poland in

FIGURE 4.12. Building additions planned by ultra-Orthodox draftspersons, Betar Illit, 2015. Additions highlighted in white. (Photographs by author.)

the 1930s, a couple of educational centers for Haredi women were opened in Palestine and prepared their graduates for careers in schoolteaching. For a while, these centers had little impact, as few could afford to attend them, and their graduates struggled to find employment. The change came after the founding of the State of Israel, when the government began funding Haredi schools as part of its mandatory public education system, creating a great demand for Haredi teachers.[104] Around that time, in the early 1950s, as the sociologist Menachem Friedman has shown, a new labor division became the norm among Haredi Israelis: men were to dedicate their time studying the Torah, while the women were to provide the family with money.[105] For these reasons, in the 1950s and 1960s, many Haredi wives became teachers. After a couple of decades, though, teaching jobs became scarce as the market was inundated with Haredi teachers. By the 1980s, some turned to small-scale entrepreneurship, opening souvenir and clothing stores.[106] In subsequent decades, they would explore other fields, including computer programming, administration, and laboratory work. This process, in which

Haredi women explored various fields, was an empowering one. It exposed them to secular culture and education.[107] The emergence of the Haredi city-settlement further contributed to this process of empowerment by opening more employment opportunities to women in such fields as planning and management. (Tech companies also opened headquarters in Betar Illit and in Modi'in Illit, where Haredi women work in computer programming, often earning below-market salaries.)[108] It may seem ironic that their empowerment has been advanced through taking part in a political project and an ideology that many of them initially opposed. But irony is hardly foreign to the architectural history of the settlements.

Other changes to the settlement were more mundane. Apartments have been extended into corridors and toward the staircase. Residents have placed wardrobes and cabinets in the corridor outside their entrance door, or stored strollers and bicycles in the stairwell. It can be difficult to say where exactly public space ends and private space begins.

In newer neighborhoods of Betar Illit, community representatives have had a greater influence also on the planning and allocation of public buildings (figure 4.13). Over the course of the 1990s, Haredi politicians assumed key roles at the Ministry of Construction and Housing. In 1996, for instance, Meir Porush, a Haredi politician, became deputy to the minister of Construction and Housing. Having Haredi people inside the establishment surely made state planners more sympathetic toward Betar Illit's representatives. Indeed, just in 2003, they scattered more than twenty synagogues in one neighborhood.[109] In the previous year, city officials allocated more than thirty plots for synagogues and distributed them across the city. This way, a representative explained, each sect would be able to conduct its own rituals without having to mix with others. Equally important, each of these synagogues was to be built on top of a kindergarten, creating mixed-use, multistory buildings.[110]

These spatial tactics and strategies were continuous with forms of self-governance and management that had emerged in the settlement. In 2002, leading rabbis decided to close off the gates of the settlement on Saturdays to preclude the entrance of outsiders, who did not observe Shabbat and would disturb the Shabbat-observing residents.[111] The residents of Betar Illit founded a number of community organizations that took over many of the Ministry of Construction and Housing's responsibilities. Most notable was a "Populating Committee," created shortly after the first residents moved in. This committee was composed of rabbis and community representatives, and it was mainly in charge of securing the religious nature of the settlement. Among other things, it enforced new property laws, requiring all potential

FIGURE 4.13. Officials discuss the allocation of synagogues in one of Betar Illit's new neighborhoods, 2003. (*Zo Irenu*, May 2003, 3.)

homebuyers and renters to submit an application specifying their religious affiliation and family status. In addition, the committee initiated an unofficial call center to receive residents' complaints about "spiritual hazards," as well as a plethora of community-based charity funds.[112]

THE TYRANNY OF THE USERS

In a short period of time, the Populating Committee and other informal groups gained a significant amount of power, and their activities transformed the city in unexpected and sometimes controversial ways. For instance, the Populating Committee has been accused of applying discriminatory practices, favoring applicants from certain Haredi groups or ethnic backgrounds over others.[113] Families in which one of the children refuses to follow religious customs, it was reported in the daily *Yediot Aharonot*, have been denied residence in the city.[114] In addition, after gaining control over the city's building laws and real estate market, the committee gave unofficial, disproportionately generous building permits to several individuals. Their decisions, I was told, were based on an arbitrary logic, and more often than not, these permits were given at the expense of open public spaces or other individuals. A young Haredi couple, for example, complained to me that a grocery store in their building had received an unofficial permit to expand into what is officially public space. The store now blocks the entryway to their building, but there is little they can do, the husband told me. "They will irritate you, they will post *pashkevilim* [posters pinned to public walls] and stuff like that if you complain," he added. "There are things you can't do here." Making things all the more complex, it was reported that the identities of Populating Committee members have been kept secret and remain unknown to residents.[115]

Equally unexpected was the establishment of informal police forces that had been patrolling the city and penalizing residents who did not follow the city's unofficial laws. Among these were females caught wearing jeans or other clothing items that did not adhere to a strict dress code, men who associated with unmarried females, and anyone who used the wrong entrance to the bus (men at the front, women at the back).[116] To ensure women's adherence to the Haredi dress code, a "Female Rabbis Committee" was founded and put in charge of surveying all clothing stores in Betar Illit. Among the rules the committee enforced was a prohibition against red, pink, and orange dresses, or any other clothing item with "loud or flashy patterns."[117]

These residents' organizations extended their reach into what is considered the private sphere. For instance, the Populating Committee took it upon itself to make sure residents did not have television sets or an internet connection in their homes. Because enforcing this rule would require access to all units in Betar Illit, something that the committee did not have, they encouraged residents to report any suspicious satellite dishes their neighbors might have installed or any television sets they might have noticed.[118] Residents who felt uncomfortable with these laws developed tactics that afforded them some freedom. I met residents who had succeeded in installing an internet connection in their homes without being reported. Yoel, a man in his twenties who grew up in Modi'in Illit (where relatively similar laws have been applied), recalled how he had once convinced his parents to host martial arts classes, which were prohibited in public space, in their apartment.[119] But those found violating such city laws, as Yoel knows, are likely to be deprived of basic public services and to become the subject of public condemnation.[120] According to news reports, some residents have even been imprisoned or violently attacked by agents working for the city's informal police forces.[121] Yoel, who now works at a pizza place in Modi'in Illit, explained to me: "You have to be very careful here . . . if you don't strictly follow their norms, they would simply cancel you."[122] Therefore, while many residents have found these committees favorable, allowing them to adhere to Jewish laws in their strictest form, some view them as oppressive and exclusionary.

Neither the residents who found themselves disempowered by these groups nor officials at the Ministry of Construction and Housing have been able to balance the committees' increasing influence. In 2007, following multiple resident complaints, the Ministry of Construction and Housing attempted to end the Populating Committee's unlawful activity. After all, not only did the committee apply discriminatory measures in allocating apartments to certain groups, but these apartments were in many cases the property of the Ministry of Construction and Housing, at least in theory. Since committee members' identities were unknown, making direct contact with them impossible, ministry officials decided to circulate a warning underlining the illegality of the committee and its land laws. However, residents and local newspapers refused to cooperate and did not publish the warning. When asked for his assistance, the former mayor of Betar Illit seemed unable or unwilling to fight the Populating Committee.[123] In fact, a few months later, when the deputy mayor of Betar Illit submitted an application for a new apartment to the Populating Committee, it was rejected.[124]

If those who did not obey the city's laws or did not belong to the right Haredi group were unwelcome, the Palestinian residents of neighboring villages were subjected to greater offenses. Even though many residents of Betar Illit do not identify with the settlement movement, it is impossible to ignore the fact that Betar Illit sits on lands that were seized by Israel and declared "state lands" despite the protests of the Palestinians.[125] It is also impossible to ignore the military watchtowers and checkpoints erected in its vicinity. Built to secure the uninterrupted daily activities of the residents of Betar Illit, they have severely undermined the mobility of the Palestinians and subjected them to periodic security checks. And while it was military officials and politicians who ordered these measures, it was often the residents of Betar Illit and their representatives who pressured for them and later even oversaw their enforcement (figure 4.14).[126]

Over time, the benign attitude of Betar Illit's residents toward their Palestinian neighbors changed dramatically. Initially, as non-Zionist residents of the West Bank, they frequently visited the nearby Palestinian town of Husan, where they did most of their shopping. "It was the downtown of Betar Illit," one resident told me. Leibovitz even signed multiple peace agreements with the residents of the neighboring Palestinian villages. "We, the sons of Abraham" were the words that opened most of these agreements. The agreements were signed to curb stone-throwing attacks on the few cars that residents had, and in some cases to channel electricity and water from Betar Illit to its Palestinian neighbors.[127] In 1994, Leibovitz collaborated with Jordanian officials on a daily helicopter line that was to connect Betar Illit with Wadi Moussa in Jordan, where biblical Aaron is said to be buried. He thought residents of Betar Illit would flock to the pilgrimage site (figure 4.15).[128] But

FIGURE 4.14. Betar Illit's steering committee by a new tunnel road that goes underneath the Palestinian town of Beit Jala. (*Hadshot Betar*, October 1992.)

FIGURE 4.15. Moshe Leibovitz (on right) and Jordanian officials discuss a daily helicopter line that was planned to connect Betar Illit with Wadi Moussa. (*Maariv*, May 23, 1995, 16.)

as political tensions grew, these agreements were increasingly cast aside and forgotten, and the settlers stopped going to Husan.

Life in the West Bank seems to have hardened the views of the Haredi community. In a survey conducted in 2014, some 87 percent of Betar Illit residents indicated that they identify with the political Right in Israel.[129] In recent years, they have also become more directly involved in actions common in other settlements. For example, at times of political tension in 2015, the leaders of Betar Illit decided to expel all the Palestinian laborers working at the city's numerous construction sites.

Betar Illit, along with other Haredi settlements, has, in fact, contributed to a broader shift toward the Right among Haredi Israelis. In the past, leading Haredi rabbis—such as the chief Sephardic rabbi of Israel, Ovadia Yosef—publicly denounced the settlement movement, but by 2021, they would refrain from such criticism. This change in attitude resulted from a number of developments, including the growing distrust between Israelis and Palestinians, but it cannot be disassociated from the construction of Haredi settlements. The fact that some 160,000 Haredi Israelis live in settlements (about 13 percent of the Haredi population in Israel) has made it difficult for Haredi Israelis to support calls for a withdrawal from the West Bank, which could have devastating economic effects on their public.[130] In 2003, the settlement activist and resident of Ofra Pinhas Valershtein observed, "Even if they [Haredi settlers] didn't arrive here for ideological reasons, they will not give up on their houses so easily."[131] Some two decades later, it is also clear that none of their representatives inside Israel would support any suggestion of evacuation without significant compensation to the settlers.

CONCLUSION

In 2005, the Ministry of Construction and Housing commissioned Geocartography Knowledge Group, a private research and consultancy company, to conduct a survey of Betar Illit residents to assess their economic status, special needs, and overall satisfaction with their city. Geocartography conducted a phone survey of about 320 residents. The results surprised officials at the ministry: 80 percent of the settlers indicated they were "very much satisfied" with life in Betar Illit. Arguably, they may have been the most content citizens in the country.[132] A few months later, the municipality of Betar Illit commissioned another survey, and the results were similar: 79 percent of the 501 residents surveyed expressed unequivocal satisfaction with their housing conditions and the municipal services available in the city.[133] The residents' satisfaction was not without cause. In the 2000s, Betar

Illit won awards for its design and maintenance in a number of national competitions.[134] More importantly, it was the product of their own efforts. Over the course of about a decade, together with their representatives, they had succeeded in transforming a poorly planned public housing project and adapting it to their unique needs. Not surprisingly, Betar Illit came to form a model that informed the planning of towns and neighborhoods not only in the West Bank but also inside Israel.

Recently, scholars of the built environment have carefully studied the ways in which nondesigners, whether working in opposition to or in collaboration with official planning institutes, have been able to transform the built environment, making it more suitable to their own needs. The anthropologist and urban historian Jennifer Mack has shown how, through tactical and material interventions, Syriac immigrants transformed standardized welfare state spaces in Stockholm's periphery into the global capital of the Syriac Orthodox Christian diaspora.[135] The urban historian and theorist Margaret Crawford has shown how random individuals have taken over spaces, through street vending and yard sales, inserting themselves into the city's fabric and creating new economic possibilities.[136] In most of these accounts, the interventions authored by the users have ultimately rendered spaces more inclusive.

The case of Betar Illit presents a different scenario. On the one hand, the material interventions of the settlers and their representatives have afforded the Haredim a space that allows them to follow a certain form of life, which in a secular world has become increasingly hard to maintain. On the other hand, their interventions ultimately created what appears to be a highly exclusionary space. Those who do not abide by the strictest interpretation of Jewish law, whether by failing to adhere to Betar Illit's dress code or by installing a television set, often find themselves subjected to disciplinary measures and ultimately excluded. Meanwhile, the Palestinians, who at first may have had a more relaxed relationship with the settlers, have been subjected to heavy restrictions. The right to shape their city afforded the Haredi settlers a realm of autonomous space where basic social contracts can be ignored.

The activities of the settlers and their representatives, however, did not take place in a political vacuum. Although some of their interventions took place outside the purview of official planning agencies, they also worked with the establishment, enjoying easy access to high-profile politicians, as when Leibovitz met with Prime Minister Yitzhak Rabin or when Haredi politicians assumed key positions at the Ministry of Construction and Housing. In the final analysis, the government and its planning agencies endowed the people of Betar Illit with disproportionate rights (while largely ignoring the rights of the neighboring Palestinians). As a case study, therefore, Betar Illit is not so much a cautionary lesson illustrating a pathology inherent to bottom-up design processes. Rather, it points to the unexpected turns a user-led environment can take when the distinction between top-down and bottom-up processes becomes blurred, and when planning rights are not distributed equitably among the people affected.

Whether they worked from above or below, the triumph of the users over the planners in Betar Illit also illustrates the often slapdash nature of design and construction in West Bank settlements. It points to a chain of contradictions, a process unforeseen by its founders that resulted in paradoxical outcomes, including non-Zionist settlers, architects modeling a Haredi city-settlement after a medieval town, and a public housing project over which the government has only partial control. These contradictions, in turn, point to a gap between military strategy on the one hand and the design of settlements in the West Bank on the other. The two are hardly of the same order.

Despite these contradictions—or perhaps because of them—Betar Illit has continued to grow rapidly. In 2021, there were more than 63,000 residents in Betar Illit.[137] Meanwhile, there were some 80,000 Haredi settlers in Modi'in Illit.[138] As of 2022, they are the two largest settlements in the West Bank. Tel Zion, another Haredi settlement north of Jerusalem (officially part of the settlement of Kokhav Ya'akov), houses some 6,000 settlers and has plans to reach 35,000.[139] Haredi people have thus become major actors in the settlement enterprise. In 2015, some 40 percent of all new settlers—15,523 in total—were Haredim (the majority of whom were babies born to Haredi settler families).[140]

The growth of the Haredi population in the West Bank, however, is for the most part limited to existing settlements. The Israeli government largely stopped authorizing new settlements in the West Bank after signing the Oslo Accords in the 1990s and after facing growing international pressure. As a result, in the last two decades, it has become almost impossible to build new Haredi city-settlements. In their place, small, unauthorized settlements—developed by much younger and far less conservative Israelis—have emerged, setting a new vanguard of settlement construction.

CHAPTER 5

OUTPOSTS

By the early 2000s, Israel had put in place a procedure to legalize West Bank settlements. To get authorized, a settlement had to meet four criteria: it had to have land; an initial green light from the government; a military order defining its area of jurisdiction; and a master plan detailing land uses, building rights, and codes.[1] When the residents of Pnei Kedem, a settlement of about fifty families located 20 kilometers south of Jerusalem, met one evening in April 2015 to discuss the settlement's pending master plan, they were unable to agree on a final version. Some of them had already been living on the bare hilltop for fifteen years—in mobile homes or, more recently, in single-family houses made of concrete and stone—and yet they could not agree on the basic planning principles that underpin any master plan. Hila, a pious woman in her thirties who had moved to the settlement after an unsuccessful career in theater, stood up and presented some images from Tuscany and other rural areas, saying that this is how she and some other residents would like to see Pnei Kedem develop. "We were thinking of something more natural, perhaps a network of pedestrian-only walkways, so people could walk freely," she explained. "Vehicles would not be allowed to enter the center. We also thought of planting some ecological structures in between." Other participants expressed discomfort. Some got angry, and raised their voices, explaining that they would much rather live in a denser settlement, similar to the ones founded in the 1980s. "I did not come here to live in a Tuscan village," one laughed. Another resident, who worked as an inspector for a national forestry company, dismissed the entire enterprise, stating that he would rather not commit to any future plan. After about an hour and a half, it became clear that, as had happened in previous meetings over the past few years, a decision was not going to be made, and the meeting was brought to an end. The legalization process, it seemed, was stalled.

Pnei Kedem is not the only settlement in which settlers have been clashing over the formulation of a master plan. Since the mid-1990s, more than a hundred settlements have been built, each usually housing no more than sixty families. Most of them lack an approved master plan and are considered illegal even according to Israeli law. In many of these settlements, settlers have been debating their master plan for years, often without reaching a consensus. In one case, a settlement was almost entirely abandoned after clashes over the matter had escalated into physical violence.[2]

Until the early 1990s, things had worked differently. Settlements rarely remained in a such state of illegality for more than a couple of years. Settlers residing together in one locale often shared some kind of an aesthetic vision—and if they did not, they were willing to swallow their individual preferences for the sake of having a functioning settlement. They did not argue over planning for such a long time, not among themselves, at least. Why, then, did settlers in these new settlements turn against one other? Why did some settlers in Pnei Kedem wish to eschew previous settlement models and replace them with a more "natural" one? And how have these settlements taken shape over the past two decades without government authorization? What does planning and design look like outside the law?

In this chapter, I try to answer some of these questions by focusing on the design and evolution of the settlement of Pnei Kedem, from its founding in the late 1990s through 2020. Using Pnei Kedem, I shed new light on processes common in other settlements built over the last two decades: the retreat of professional planners, the rise of participatory design, and the emergence of new architectural forms. These processes continue to unfold as I write this book.

A large part of the history of Pnei Kedem and its contemporaries is informal and thus undocumented. In this chapter therefore, I supplement archival documents with ethnographic sources. Over the course of ten months, I resided in Pnei Kedem, where I joined a construction team, took part in the settlement's planning and synagogue committees, and attended general assembly meetings. In addition, I became part of the social life of the settlement. I attended synagogue services, Shabbat dinners, and holiday celebrations, and I formed strong friendships with a number of residents. I went on night walks, did my grocery shopping, and dined with them.[3]

In Pnei Kedem, I was both an outsider and an insider. As a secular Israeli who had been living abroad for almost a decade, without a wife or children, I was not the kind of person the residents of Pnei Kedem were used to. My lifestyle, body language, manners, and speech marked me as an outsider. I didn't try to hide the gaps between us. I always introduced myself as a scholar of the built environment studying the architecture of settlements, and aside from times when I attended services at the synagogue, I did not wear a yarmulke. Nevertheless, most settlers warmly greeted me. As much as I was an outsider, I was also an insider. I was born and raised in Israel. In addition, even though I am not familiar with many religious rituals, I am Jewish—an important fact in the minds of many of my informants. It made me one of theirs.

THE EMERGENCE OF "UNAUTHORIZED OUTPOSTS"

The early 1990s marked a turning point in the history of settlement construction. In 1992, Yitzhak Rabin won the elections and formed a Left-leaning government. It was the first government without a single supporter of the settlement movement since 1977.[4] Within a year, Rabin and his ministers had significantly reduced government support to existing settlements and, at least officially, paused all plans for new ones.[5] In 1993, government officials embarked on initial peace negotiations with the Palestinian Liberation Organization (PLO). These negotiations culminated in the Oslo Accords that were signed over a period of six years, starting in 1993. Setting a roadmap for a future peace agreement between the two peoples, the Oslo Accords created the Palestinian Authority and divided the West Bank into three areas. Area A in 2018 consisted of 18 percent of the lands and housed 26 percent of the Palestinian population; Area B consisted of 22 percent of the lands and housed 70 percent of the Palestinians; and Area C housed all Jewish settlements and just 4 percent of the Palestinians (map 5.1). Varying degrees of control over Areas A and B were transferred to the Palestinian Authority, while Israel retained control over Area C.[6] Even though the exact future geographic borders of the Palestinian Authority were undetermined, and the fate of most Jewish settlements was undecided in the accords, settlers now found it increasingly difficult to get building permits for projects in the West Bank.[7]

Despite these developments, new settlements mushroomed in subsequent years. According to Talia Sasson, a former senior attorney at the Ministry of Justice, about 105 settlements were erected in the West Bank between the mid-1990s and 2005.[8] These settlements, Sasson highlighted in a 2005 report, were not neighborhoods adjacent to existing settlements where construction had continued anyway; they were new and autonomous settlements.[9] Yet unlike older settlements, the latter were built without the official support or approval of the Israeli government.[10] All were built illegally even under Israeli law, which—in contrast to international law—considers most other settlements legal. Accordingly, these new settlements came to be known in Israel as "unauthorized outposts" (*ma'ahazim bilti murshim*), or just "outposts" (*ma'ahazim*).[11]

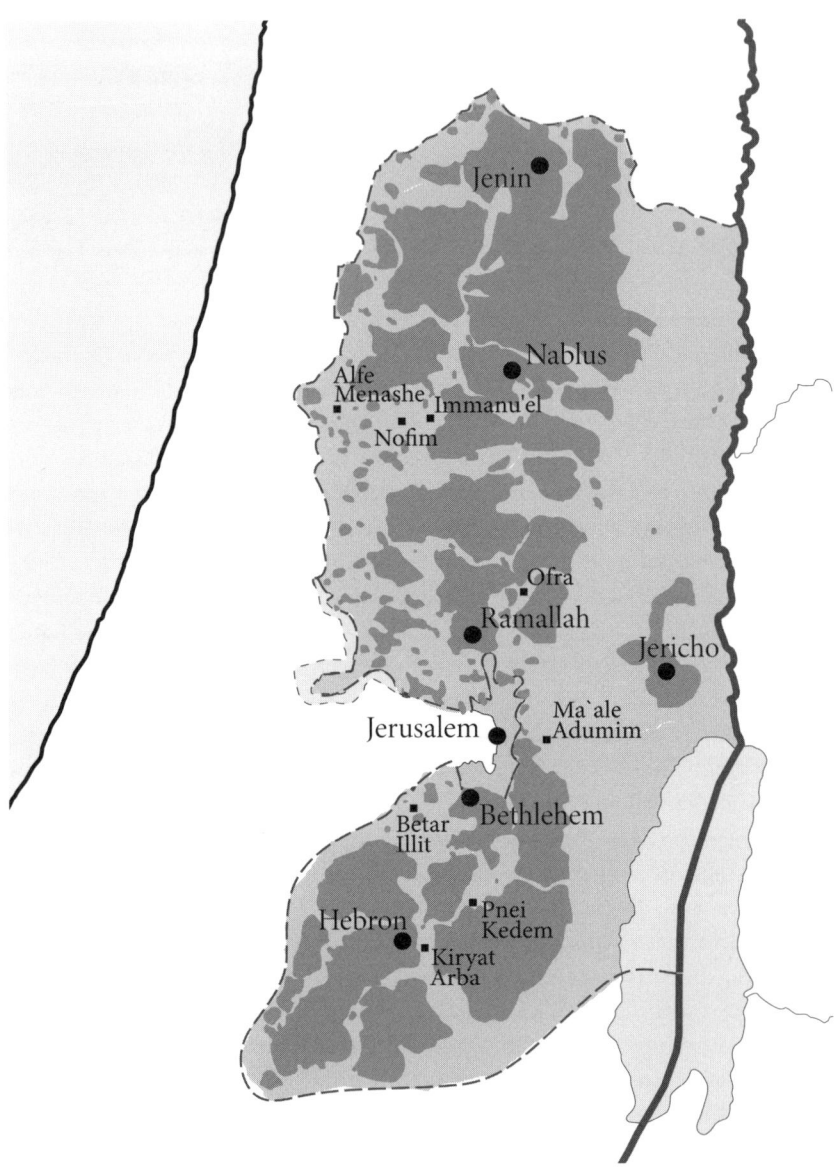

MAP 5.1. Map of the West Bank with Areas A and B marked in dark gray. Area C is marked in light gray. (Map drawn by author based on a map produced by Peace Now.)

Illegal as they may be, very few of these unauthorized outposts have faced demolition or any kind of legal proceeding in the last two decades. In part this is because the composition of the government has changed since the initial signing of the Oslo Accords. As Niv Ya'ari, a young attorney at the Civil Administration—the governing body responsible for the West Bank—explained to me, the Israeli government has taken an ambivalent attitude toward unauthorized outposts. "On the one hand, the state does not want to evacuate them," he bluntly admitted. Some government ministers support the settlement enterprise and would oppose the destruction of any settlement, legal or illegal.[12] (In 1998, Ariel Sharon, then minister of Foreign Affairs, for instance, went as far as to urge settlement activists to "grab as many hilltops as possible.")[13] "But, at the same time," Ya'ari explained, "it is difficult for the state to formalize and legalize them for a number of reasons. For one thing, some outposts sit on privately owned [Palestinian] lands. In addition, legalizing them would have [negative] effects on Israel's international relations. So basically, outposts are caught in a legal limbo."[14] The illegality of these outposts, in other words, is not as fatal as it might seem at first glance.

Accordingly, even though the government cannot allocate public funds for the planning and maintenance of outposts, support from the state reaches them indirectly through various channels. For example, according to Sasson, outposts have received money from regional councils (municipal entities, each of which governs a number of small settlements) and the Settlement Division of the World Zionist Organization, both of which receive funding from the government. In some cases, Sasson revealed, outposts have even enjoyed the direct support of the Ministry of Construction and Housing.[15] Thanks to these informal funding networks, many outposts have been able to sustain themselves economically, enjoying basic infrastructure and, in some cases, occasional planning services.

Equally important, the legal status of these settlements can change dramatically in a matter of days. Eli Tobeli, another young attorney at the Civil Administration, explained to me that the government could decide to authorize outposts at any given moment. "And if there is such a decision, I could process thirty new settlements within days . . . so you cannot really know," Tobeli argued.[16] Indeed, the government of Benjamin Netanyahu oversaw the legalization of several outposts. According to a report issued by Peace Now, an NGO monitoring settlement activity, by 2018, the government had already legalized thirteen outposts, and thirty-five other outposts were in different stages of legalization.[17] Reflecting on the meeting I had witnessed in Pnei Kedem, Tobeli commented: "It is not as if these people in Pnei Kedem are laboring for nothing over their master plan. There is a chance. But you cannot know. You cannot tell when and if legalization would happen."[18] It is in this state of perpetual waiting that many outpost residents operate.

A NEW GENERATION OF SETTLERS

According to most accounts, the people residing in unauthorized outposts are largely young, unruly Right-wing fanatics, whose ideology seems troubling even compared to Yehuda Etzion and the Gush Emunim, who founded some of the earliest settlements in the aftermath of the Six-Day War.[19] These accounts are bolstered by terror attacks against Palestinian civilians carried out by youth groups, known as Youth of the Hills, that came to be associated with outposts. Some of these attacks have had devastating effects on the Palestinians. In 2015, while I was doing fieldwork, a Palestinian couple and their eighteen-month-old baby were murdered in an arson attack by Amiram Ben-Uliel, a twenty-six-year-old resident of the outpost of Adei Ad. Ben-Uliel was later convicted and sentenced to life in prison.[20] Clashes also occasionally break out between outpost residents and the police forces deployed to demolish illegal structures. These clashes have further colored the reputation of outpost dwellers among the general public. In 2006, a confrontation between a few thousand activists, who came to protest the demolition of nine structures in the outpost of Amona, and police and military forces resulted in hundreds of injuries.[21] For many, the news reports about these attacks on Palestinians and altercations with the military confirmed what they had always suspected: young, unpredictable, and unmoved by state authorities, outpost residents were the worst of settler society, if not Israeli society altogether.

To my surprise, however, when I began visiting outposts, and later resided in the outpost of Pnei Kedem, I mainly encountered relatively ordinary people. I also encountered some young zealots, whose hatred toward the Palestinians was indeed deeply troubling, but they constituted a minority of the settlers I met in outposts. There were usually no more than fifty families in each outpost. Most of them were young couples in their twenties or thirties with at least three children. Usually, though not always, they were observant and associated with religious Zionism. Many of the women I met worked as schoolteachers or social workers. The men had more diverse career paths; some worked as lawyers, computer programmers, construction workers, or real estate agents in Jerusalem and Tel Aviv, while others opened small businesses, such as restaurants, vineyards, and wineries, in the outposts or in nearby commercial centers.

Many of the people I met were second-generation settlers. They had grown up in the West Bank; it was home. Many assumed that the illegality of their outpost was temporary. After all, as they explained to me, some of the settlements their parents had erected a few decades ago, such as Ofra or Kedumim, also started out as quasi-legal encampments. Some went a step beyond that and insisted that the history of planning in Israel was a history of illegal construction. "There is almost not a single town in the land of Israel that was not founded in defiance of the then prevailing legal system," argued Dan, a settler in his thirties who had grown up in Ofra and later helped found the outpost of Ma'ale Rechav'am. "Whether it was 'stockade and tower' under the British Mandate . . . or later [after statehood], when state authorities simply acted too slowly and too hesitantly, all were founded illegally."[22] Illegality, then, did not feel so abnormal or alarming to many of the people I met in outposts.[23]

More importantly, though, a house in an outpost was the best many of the outpost residents I met could have afforded. Real estate in older and more established settlements had become expensive, and beyond their means.[24] Coming from religious families, they usually had more than three siblings, so they could not rely on the support of their parents when buying a home. In addition, since they themselves usually had a few children, they needed large homes with at least three bedrooms. Outposts offered them an easy solution. Land leaseholds in outposts—managed by grassroots residents' unions without much intervention from the regional council—are relatively cheap. In 2015, a 500-square-meter plot in the outpost of Pnei Kedem went for about $10,000. For the same plot in an established settlement, home-buyers would pay at least $50,000. In addition, construction costs significantly less in outposts. Many settlers hire Palestinian contractors, who pay their employees comparatively low salaries, below the minimum wage in Israel, and are unburdened by the taxes Israeli contractors have to pay. On average, in 2015, Palestinian contractors charged around $80,000 to build a three-bedroom, single-family home in outposts. Under these conditions, one settler told me, buying a home in an outpost becomes a wise investment, even at the risk of getting a demolition order.

The financial calculation that partially motivates the creation of outposts has caused resentment among an older generation of settlers who see their own motivations for moving to a settlement as "pure." One settler from Ma'ale Mikhmas, a settlement founded in 1981, complained to me about the residents of Pnei Kedem:

The second generation of Judea and Samaria is very different from my generation. We were very ideological and we cared about our beliefs and about the settlement movement. Now, the new generation, they take everything for granted. They think that they simply deserve to be here. And the way they build is terrible. . . . I went there [to Pnei Kedem] last month, and each resident just builds there whatever he wants with no thought whatsoever. . . . And almost all of these [young settlements] call themselves "ecological settlements." You know what "ecological" means? It means that each resident takes a 2.5 dunams [2,500-square-meter] plot without paying, and then asks the state to fund infrastructure reaching his home. That is outrageous! This is not how we were. We worked hard and we cared about our settlements. . . . I hate what the young generation is doing. . . . They are greedy and have no ideology.

Surprisingly, some of the people I met in outposts agreed. For example, a twenty-four-year-old resident of the outpost of Tkoa Dalet, who had been working in construction, once admitted to me: "My parents were idealists. They had money, but they chose to move to [the settlement of] Talmon and live in a shack. In a mobile home! I was born the year after they moved in. They chose to move there because they had ideals. Today you won't find this kind of idealism. People don't build outposts because of ideals. You had that in the past; not today."

It would be a mistake, however, to attribute the existence of outposts to sheer greed. People living in outposts do have ideals, but these ideals are different from the ones that guided their parents' generation. As the sociologist Michael Feige has noted, some outpost residents have questioned the bourgeois homes of their parents, and, along the way, developed an interest in a variety of New Age practices.[25] They do yoga, attend laughter and poetry workshops, and dance in music festivals. Many share a desire to live in a more immediate relation to nature and seek a more community-oriented way of life. Many follow the preaching of the late Rabbi Menachem Froman, a longtime settlement activist who encouraged singing and dancing, and even advocated a strange kind of coexistence with the Palestinians. Froman's commitment to coexistence was skin-deep; he seemed relatively ignorant of Palestinians' claims to land conquered by Israel, and he repeatedly made homophobic comments. But his growing popularity among outpost residents speaks to their search for a new settlement ideology, one that might be less militant than that which guided their parents' generation.

Outpost residents' interest in community-oriented life and their desire to get closer to nature were in keeping with wider trends. During the 1990s, a handful of Americans, following earlier models in Scandinavia, began to organize into so-called cohousing communities—urban, suburban, or rural communities of like-minded individuals that combine private and collective ownership along with community social obligations. Motivated by a desire to escape urban or suburban alienation, these communities usually foster regular communication and collaboration between neighbors, as well as a shared concern with environmentalism evident in the construction of low-impact, resource-efficient homes.[26] Similarly, in the early 2000s, middle-class Germans began to form construction groups (*Baugruppen*) that combined their private resources to commission multistory buildings, usually in city-center areas, where each member (or family) owned and occupied a unit. In line with American so-called cohousing communities, these multistory buildings encourage neighborly relations, usually in the form of meeting rooms and common roof terraces, and adhere to a high standard of energy efficiency. Although these non-Israeli groups tend to lean politically to the Left, they nevertheless share a certain political attitude with outpost residents. Neither seeks to overthrow the norms of their respective societies; rather, they seek to create a desired way of life for themselves by piecemeal interventions.[27]

One thing outpost residents clearly do not seek to overthrow is their parents' pioneering spirit. Many outpost residents I met admired the settlement movement of the 1970s and 1980s, and they saw themselves as its successor. They were fascinated by their parents' ability to create something out of nothing. Their parents had been pioneers in the best tradition of Zionism, they thought. And now, many believed, it was up to them, the younger generation, to find new frontiers for pioneering in the West Bank.

THE FOUNDING OF PNEI KEDEM

David is a soft-spoken man in his forties—pious, gentle, and reserved. He grew up in England, in a modern Orthodox community, where he would hear stories about the adventures of his uncle, who immigrated to Israel from England after the Six-Day War and was one of the founders of the settlement of Ofra. They were stories about the wildcat settlement that changed the face of the West Bank, and they left a strong impression on him. After graduating from Queen Mary University of London in 1994, David joined his uncle in Ofra. Soon after, he began planning to found a new settlement, just as his uncle had done. By the summer of 1995, he had gathered around him three other residents of Ofra, recent immigrants from the United States and Australia, who were also eager to found a new settlement. They called themselves Garin Ofni (Ofni Seed), after the biblical town of Ofni that allegedly stood on a hilltop near Ofra where they wanted to settle.[28]

In 1998, after a few more couples joined Garin Ofni, David and his collaborators began working on a master plan. Reflecting the settlers' interests, the plan was marked by an emphasis on ecological design. In an English-language brochure (figure 5.1), they explained:

> The Garin [Ofni] wishes to establish a village in harmony with its natural surroundings. A plan is being drawn for an initial community of 150 families with an emphasis on building with the natural contours of the hill rather than resorting to flattening and leveling the hill. It is hoped that the infrastructure will be laid along these lines too, despite the additional cost and time that may be entailed. The Garin is eager to promote reforestation of the surrounding area. This will enhance the beauty of Ofni[,] providing recreational space and shade for its residents. At the same time, reforestation will prevent erosion, improve the quality of the soil, providing a natural habitat[,] and also, it will act as a natural windbreak. The Garin is interested in further examining renewable and sustainable energy sources.[29]

According to the plan, each house would sit on a plot large enough to allow the cultivation of extensive gardens on all sides. A network of cul-de-sacs, with large grass verges on each side, was designed to allow easy access to the houses.[30] According to Moshe, a religious Zionist who emigrated from Australia and joined Garin Ofni, they imported most of the planning principles, especially the ecological ones, from abroad.[31] "We brought this model from Australia and the US," he explained to me. "At the time, it wasn't so common here in Israel," he added while reflecting on the mixed reactions they encountered from their Israeli-born counterparts in other settlements.

Despite the ambitious plan and the support the group received from Amana (an official settling body founded by Gush Emunim in the 1970s), Garin Ofni failed to secure government authorization to construct the settlement.[32] Faced with repeated rejections, David and his friends—in keeping with the time-honored Israeli practice of ignoring the law—decided to settle the hill anyway regardless of its legal status. They arranged to have a couple of metal containers delivered to the site, and without anyone noticing, they moved in. For four weeks, they were able to survive on their own. But then, David told me, when he approached the secretariat of the settlement of Ofra and asked for their help, things started falling apart. To David's surprise, some of Ofra's officials worried that an unauthorized outpost in the vicinity of Ofra might attract unwanted media attention and, in turn, endanger other illegal construction projects in the settlement of Ofra. To avoid this situation,

O F N I

BUILDING FOR THE FUTURE

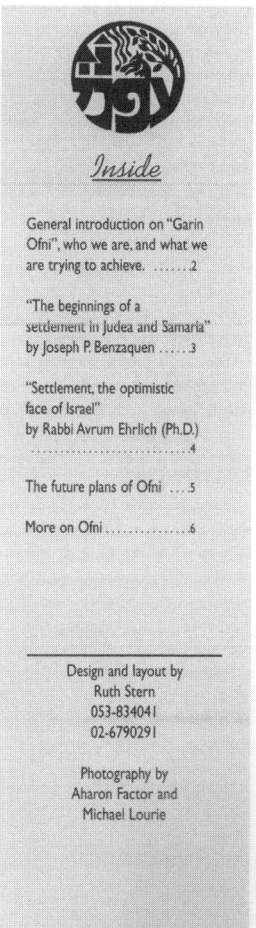

Inside

General introduction on "Garin
Ofni", who we are, and what we
are trying to achieve. 2

"The beginnings of a
settlement in Judea and Samaria"
by Joseph P. Benzaquen 3

"Settlement, the optimistic
face of Israel"
by Rabbi Avrum Ehrlich (Ph.D.)
...........................4

The future plans of Ofni 5

More on Ofni...............6

Design and layout by
Ruth Stern
053-834041
02-6790291

Photography by
Aharon Factor and
Michael Lourie

FIGURE 5.1. Cover page of a brochure produced by Garin Ofni, 1998. (Pnei Kedem
Archive.)

shortly after David reached out to the secretariat, one of its members contacted officials at the Civil Administration and informed them about the illegal outpost. The members of Garin Ofni were quickly forced out of their containers. Ironically, the first attempt to establish a new settlement failed not because of international pressure or complaints from Palestinians, but because they were ratted out by other settlement activists.

David and his collaborators, however, refused to give up. Over the next few months, they searched for an alternative site, preferably at a distance from Ofra, the settlement that had betrayed them. Sarah, an observant woman who had grown up in New York and joined the group after meeting her husband, Moshe, told me about her experience traveling with the men across the West Bank in search of an appropriate site. "I didn't hold strong Right-leaning views," she admitted. "I was a Zionist, but definitely not a settler." But she wanted to be in the company of her new partner, who was totally committed to the cause. It was actually Sarah who would spot the site where Pnei Kedem would be built. One day she was driving with Moshe and David to a valley located about 20 kilometers south of Jerusalem, where a friend had suggested they might find a suitable location. The valley ended up being dark and it lacked the sweeping vistas characteristic of the West Bank. But as they were leaving, Sarah noticed some electricity poles on a nearby hilltop. The maps they had with them indicated the place was empty. Curious to see what was there, they drove to the strange hilltop. To their surprise, they found about forty abandoned mobile homes, all in a dilapidated state (figure 5.2). Some had door signs in Hebrew. But no one was there.

The abandoned mobile homes were the ruins of a religious boarding school named Metzudat David. The school catered to troubled ultra-Orthodox youth who had dropped out of other educational institutions. It had been founded by Mordechai Goldstein, an American who, upon immigrating to Israel in the 1960s, opened the Diaspora Yeshiva in Jerusalem. In 1984, Goldstein founded the settlement of Meitzad for a loyal group of followers that consisted mostly of American-born Jews who had abandoned the hippie culture of the 1960s for Jewish ultra-Orthodoxy. The school was built about 1 kilometer outside the settlement, and it was an important foothold in a small kingdom Goldstein was trying to create in the West Bank. But despite Goldstein's hopes, the school failed to attract students, and after a couple of years, the place was abandoned.[33]

Now, David and the other members of Garin Ofni agreed, it was time to reinhabit the site. Over the next few months, David reached out to government officials, the Settlement Division, and the regional council to seek their support. The government refused to grant an authorization, but the Garin

FIGURE 5.2. The abandoned mobile homes found by Garin Ofni members while searching for a settlement site south of Jerusalem, 2000. (Pnei Kedem Archive.)

Ofni did receive the support of the head of the regional council. This gave them the confidence to set a move-in date: Wednesday, August 30, 2000.[34]

On that morning, the five couples and four bachelors who made up the Garin Ofni, together with between ten and twenty supporters, drove in a caravan of two dozen cars to the hilltop.[35] When they arrived at the site, the young settlers began preparing the place for their first Shabbat two days later. They surveyed the abandoned mobile homes, allocating those in the best shape for housing and transforming two others into a communal kitchen, a dining hall, and a synagogue. In the remaining time, the settlers began cleaning the surroundings. By Friday, when a group of supporters arrived to celebrate Shabbat, the settlement was established. The evening prayers, Sarah told me, felt especially festive. They were followed by an equally festive communal dinner the women had prepared. On Saturday, after the morning prayers, some of the men went on a hike. To the young settlers, it seemed that they had succeeded.

But on their return from the hike, the men found Rabbi Goldstein waiting for them, and he was not happy. He insisted that the site and the abandoned mobile homes belonged to him, and he demanded that they leave immediately. In an attempt to calm the raging sixty-eight-year-old rabbi, the settlers suggested he join the dinner they had prepared so that they could discuss the issue. The rabbi agreed and sat down. But things took a turn for the worse when the women began singing. In some interpretations of the Jewish tradition, the sound of a woman's voice is considered sensual, and therefore men are prohibited from listening to women sing. So when the women began singing, the rabbi was outraged. He stood up and shouted: "This place, a place where females sing next to a rabbi, will be destroyed and a curse will sit on it!" He then picked up one of the tables and threw it, with all the food that was on it, at the women. One of them was injured. In response, her husband pushed the table back at the rabbi.[36] Goldstein had been accompanied by a couple of pupils, and one ran back to Meitzad to report what was happening. The men of Meitzad, worried about the safety of their spiritual leader, ran to the new outpost, where they started fighting with David and his friends, vandalizing the mobile homes, and smashing their cars. Sarah and the other women of Garin Ofni took shelter in one of the mobile homes as the violence continued to escalate. At one point, Rabbi Goldstein's son had his arm and leg broken. Only after thirty police officers arrived at the site did the fighting come to an end.[37]

Over the next couple of weeks, Goldstein and his disciples continued to demand that the Garin Ofni leave the site. They insisted that anyone who wished to live in the vicinity of Meitzad must be a follower of Goldstein. "I do not mind having two, even three hundred new families," Goldstein's son told a reporter who covered the conflict. "The only condition we have is that they will live under our rule, and accept the authority of Rabbi Mordechai (Goldstein) on all public matters."[38]

The stand-off shifted to the media (figure 5.3). One resident of Meitzad told reporters that the ultra-Orthodox settlement had a good relationship with the neighboring Palestinians, and that the new young settlers associated with the religious Zionist faction would ruin that relationship by instigating unprovoked fights with the Palestinians.[39] But, as one news report observed, it was not the Palestinians that the residents of Meitzad were worried about. According to government plans, the area of Meitzad was to be evacuated and returned to the Palestinians within a few years. The residents of Meitzad were promised a generous compensation package: an expensive plot of land near Rabbi Goldstein's yeshiva in Jerusalem. For years they had been waiting for this moment to come. Life on the remote hilltop was difficult. They had moved there only because it was affordable. The government had offered them a way out, but David and his friends were likely to ruin it all: as nationalists, they would undoubtedly resist evacuation orders and might ultimately force the government to keep this remote area under Israeli control. Good-bye to that premium piece of Jerusalem real estate that had been promised to the residents of Meitzad.[40]

The efforts of Goldstein and his followers were in vain. The Garin Ofni members did not leave, and a few days after the skirmish with the residents of Meitzad, they renamed the site. It had been called Meitzad Bet by

Friday

Unsettled territory

The residents of Metzad Alef
and Metzad Bet square off.

Leora Eren Frucht visits two Jewish communities in Gush Etzion
whose ideological differences have led to violent confrontation

FIGURE 5.3. Newspaper article reporting on the conflict between members of Garin Ofni and Meitzad's residents. (*Jerusalem Post*, September 2000.)

Goldstein's followers. But after letting go of the name Ofni, which referred to an ancient town kilometers away—and briefly considering a proposition from Moshe that they name the settlement "Kan Garoo," which alludes to his home country, Australia, and also means "Here They [Once] Lived" in Hebrew—the group decided on Pnei Kedem, which means "Facing East."[41] Having given a name to the hilltop, they moved on to planting over two hundred trees.[42] Soon after, they began repairing the mobile homes that had once served the yeshiva students. The hill was their home now.

THE MOBILE HOME NEIGHBORHOOD

Mobile homes—commonly referred to as caravans—are the most common building type in outposts (figure 5.4). As in most other outposts, the mobile homes that became home to the people of Pnei Kedem were arranged in a

FIGURE 5.4. Mobile homes in an outpost north of Jerusalem. Arranged in rows, they loosely follow the natural slope, 2013. (Photograph by author.)

couple of rows with only small gaps separating one mobile home from another. There were no fences that defined the limits of private property, nor were there sidewalks or street names. This arrangement, Sarah explained to me, fitted the needs of the twenty or so young settlers who found themselves surrounded by hostile neighbors, both Palestinian and Jewish. Having all the houses tightly clustered next to one another provided a sense of security. With time, it also helped generate a strong sense of community. Even though each couple lived in a separate mobile home, they usually left their doors open and passed the hours outside. Since the mobile home was just too small, many also extended their domestic space out into the shared space between the mobile homes.

This semipublic space has become a common feature in many outposts, and residents seem to appreciate the social setting it creates. When a young couple from the outpost of Avigail, 20 kilometers south of Pnei Kedem, built a permanent home with a fenced-in backyard, some of their neighbors felt uncomfortable with the new house. It was at odds with the sense of community that prevailed in the mobile home neighborhood with its shared in-between space.

The interior space of most mobile homes, in Pnei Kedem and elsewhere, follows a simple, rather rudimentary layout: two bedrooms, one on each

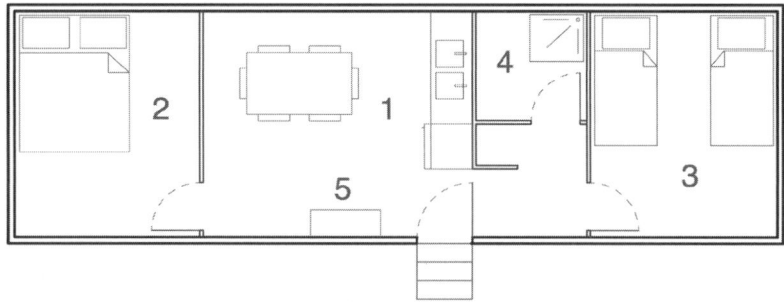

FIGURE 5.5. Floor plan of a typical mobile home with (1) a living room and kitchen, (2) a parents' bedroom, (3) a children's bedroom, and (4) a restroom. If the residents are religious Zionists, holy scriptures would usually be displayed in a bookcase (5) next to the entrance. (Drawing by author.)

FIGURE 5.6. Semipublic front yard with an inflatable swimming pool attached to a mobile home, in an outpost built near the settlement of Eli, 2013. (Photograph by author.)

end of the house, flank a small, multipurpose living room (figure 5.5). Inside the living room, next to the entry door, a modest kitchen sink is mounted to the wall. A couch or a sofa and a small dining table are usually placed in front of the sink. Often, residents try to customize their mobile homes.

FIGURE 5.7. Mobile home with an extra room and a wooden porch, Pnei Kedem, 2015. (Photograph by author.)

Since all lack a door that leads to the back side of the house, they focus their efforts on the front side, installing artificial grass lawns, setting up inflatable swimming pools, or putting out patio furniture to create an inviting semi-public front yard (figure 5.6). Some build wooden patio coverings to create shaded spaces where they can have dinners and other social events. A few go a step further and add a small room, made of metal panels, to the mobile home (figure 5.7).

At first, the mobile homes and these informal additions were welcomed in Pnei Kedem. They were seen as a natural stage in the development of the outpost. Mobile homes had in fact been a common sight in West Bank settlements since the 1970s. They usually served as temporary housing for settlers waiting for work on their permanent homes to be completed. Most settlements had such temporary neighborhoods of mobile homes, and the availability of this interim form of housing facilitated their growth by allowing Israelis to move to settlements before they were finished. Associated with the founding years of most settlements, when infrastructure was not always available and living conditions were harsh, the mobile home has come to signify pioneering bravery and commitment among settlers.[43]

But with time, David began to resent the mobile homes in Pnei Kedem. He worried that they would become a permanent housing solution rather than a transitional one. The illegal status of the outpost discouraged people in Pnei Kedem from building permanent homes. Without government authorization, they were unable to apply for bank mortgages or get building permits. Anything they built, they feared, at least in the early days, could be subjected to a demolition order. The same had happened in almost all other outposts. Fearing home demolitions, residents would rent mobile homes from Amana or the secretariat of the outpost for a modest monthly fee ($60–$75 a month for a mobile home in Pnei Kedem in 2001) and stay there for years.[44] But without permanent homes to anchor them, David and some of his friends worried, residents would leave the minute a better opportunity came their way. In addition, the mobile home, with its metal panels and crude design, was at odds with the environmentally conscious lifestyle many of the residents aimed for. "It is terrible! It is terrible for nature. It is so not sustainable or recyclable," one resident complained to me. It looks foreign to the place, completely removed from its immediate surroundings, she added. The mobile home, a structure that once signified bravery, had come to represent weakness and stagnation.

THE LIMITS OF TOP-DOWN PLANNING

David and core members of Pnei Kedem soon came to realize that they needed a professionally drawn master plan to secure the future of the outpost. Creating a master plan that they could submit to the Civil Administration was a necessary step in the process of legalization, and once that step had been taken, David thought, residents would be able to start building permanent homes in the outpost.

Before contacting a professional architect, David and the settlers of Pnei Kedem first debated what kind of a settlement they wanted to create. In those early days, everyone on the hill seemed to share David's dream of what might be called a "green" settlement.[45] By the end of 2001, they had drafted a two-page document outlining their vision. Entitled "Pnei Kedem—A Program for the Founding of an Ecological Neighborhood," the text opened with a critique of the community settlement model introduced by Ofra:

Since 1980, more than 100 community settlements have been erected, the majority of them exhibit clear suburban characteristics. . . . Although it allows a small parcel of land for each residential unit, this planning conception [the community settlement] does not allow, in most cases, a real form of rural life that is integrated into the landscape, one in which a small agricultural field is attached to each house. Instead, it creates an urban system in the midst of a rural environment, which is not integrated into the natural surroundings and may increase the sense of alienation between the residents and the environment. In addition, it does not create, nor does it encourage, a local social fabric typical of rural lifestyles.[46]

To overcome the gap between the built environment and the natural landscape, the text proposed developing "an ecological neighborhood." Laying out the principles of such a neighborhood, the settlers wrote:

> We propose that the outward appearance of the settlement would resemble that of a rural village that had developed over time, gradually, without infrastructure that deforms the landscape in irreversible ways. We do not want repetitive symmetric [private] land parcels. . . . Instead, a preference should be given to clusters of 6–8 houses, with an open field, a garden or a park, in between the houses, and an open field attached to the back of each house, allowing a garden and an agricultural field, like an orchard, serving the family's needs. . . . Planning will include a network of trails for pedestrians and bicycles . . . as well as narrow rural routes paved with stone and tiles and flanked by trees and flowerbeds, in place of customary asphalt ring roads.

In the following sections, the settlers outlined guidelines for the construction of private houses. All should be built using local materials and incorporate green technologies like photovoltaic cells. The construction company, they suggested, could design three to four prototypes according to these guidelines from which the residents could choose. In aggregate, the settlers concluded, such a housing scheme "is appropriate for rural development; it looks aesthetic and encourages a sense of community."[47]

In addition to drafting planning guidelines, the settlers sent a letter to the Ministry of the Environment requesting its endorsement. In the letter, Amos, a member of Pnei Kedem's Building Committee, laid out their ideas and explained: "Our desire to develop, with the help of God (and of the authorities), an ecological settlement grows in light of the awareness that our country is struggling with severe environmental problems. We assume that these problems will only worsen with the expected steep population growth. Pnei Kedem [therefore] aspires to become an 'exemplary settlement' that may pave the way for developing other regions in the country in an ecological way."[48] The "ecological settlement," they believed, would revolutionize residential construction not only in the West Bank but also in Israel proper by setting new building standards.

Soon after, in November 2001, David met with the Tel Aviv–based architect Rachel Walden, who had been assigned by the Settlement Division of the World Zionist Organization to draw a master plan for Pnei Kedem. During that meeting, held at the offices of the Settlement Division in Jerusalem, David shared the settlers' vision with Walden.[49] Walden already had extensive experience working in settlements. After graduating from the architecture program at the Technion, she worked for a couple of Tel Aviv–based firms, including Thomas Leitersdorf's office, where she took part in the planning of the settlements of Immanu'el and Ma'ale Adumim. After opening her own practice in the early 1980s, she received planning commissions in other West Bank settlements, such as Ari'el, Karne Shomron, and Bet Arye. She therefore had knowledge not only about settlement design but also about navigating the bureaucratic intricacies of the Settlement Division, the Ministry of Construction and Housing, and the Civil Administration. Equally important, she was an observant Jew and a supporter of the settlement movement who would soon move her office to the settlement of Revava.

Walden took note of the planning principles David and his friends had outlined and began working on a master plan for a one-hundred-unit settlement.[50] Twenty of these units, it was agreed, were designated as affordable units, to be partially funded by the state and sold to settlers at a reduced price.[51] By November 2002, after some back and forth with David and with Ministry of Construction and Housing and Settlement Division officials, Walden completed a draft of a master plan for about sixty units as well as plan drawings for affordable units. The master plan addressed the settlers' desire for houses that were more integrated with their natural surroundings: all houses were arranged in two rows that flanked a large open space. Most of the houses were placed on exceptionally large land plots, about twice the standard plot size in community settlements.[52] The affordable units were simple but efficient. Each had two bedrooms, a large dining space that opened onto the living room, and a red-tiled roof.[53]

Walden's drawings, however, left the settlers disappointed. They responded with an annotated copy of the master plan requesting major revisions. These included adding an axis for public buildings, an area for housing for older residents, even larger land plots, a water reservoir, as well as narrowing all the roads and reducing the number of parking spots.[54] At one point, after some of their requests remained unheeded, a resident drew a competing master plan, with clusters of houses, a winery, and an alpine slide. The settlers were also concerned about the affordable units Walden had drawn. From the start, some had opposed the idea. Even though the state-subsidized units would save them a lot of money, several families feared they would ruin Pnei Kedem's ecological vision.[55] In addition, as one of the settlers told me, some feared that Walden's standardized units might discourage people from moving to the remote outpost. "Why should anyone come to Pnei Kedem and have a conventional house he could have anywhere else?" she wondered.[56]

Some of the settlers were so troubled by Walden's designs for the residential units that the very next day after seeing her drawings they drafted a building code mandating the use of "natural materials." "Houses can be built of natural materials (such as stone, wood, mud)," they wrote. "Each house will incorporate wild stone (natural and unrefined) such as an arch at the entrance, a planter, fence, window or door frame, stairs, roof frame, etc." They prohibited materials that they deemed "non-natural," such as concrete, plaster, or metal. In addition, they banned the use of pitched tile roofs, the very roofing element Ofra settlers had fought for two decades before. Instead, they insisted that all houses in Pnei Kedem would have flat roofs.[57] "Mediterranean construction is characterized by flat roofs, and therefore it is recommended to build flat roofs in order to merge into the local landscape," they explained in a subsequent document.[58] Altogether, the building code they drafted made Walden's units impossible to execute on the site.

The settlers' opposition to Walden's work, especially to her master plan, was typical of outpost residents. While visiting other outposts across the West Bank, I often heard residents complain about architects and urban planners, who were usually hired long after settlers had been living on the site. By that point, the settlers had already drafted plans of their own. Architects were thus seen as outsiders, interfering in a process that was already under way. Furthermore, since these architects were usually hired by the regional council, the Settlement Division, or the Ministry of Construction and Housing, outpost residents often felt as if their architects were not loyal to them but to the official bodies that hired them. When I asked Sarah about Walden, for example, she replied: "Rachel Walden is a very nice person. But she doesn't care about this place. She was hired by the Settlement Division. It is not as if we selected her. She never once came here before drawing plans for Pnei Kedem. It is just a matter of money for her. A couple of years ago, after we begged her to come, she made a five-minute visit. It is a job for her. That's it."

There was also a financial interest underlying the residents' opposition to professional planners. Since most outposts were founded without a master plan, those who moved in first usually claimed exceptionally large land plots for themselves. These plots cannot be incorporated into professionally drawn master plans, as they are in conflict with standardized guidelines and budgetary concerns. Any official master plan would mean, therefore, that some residents would have to relinquish part of the plot they had claimed for themselves. Moreover, the legalization process that would follow from the state's approval of a master plan would likely subject residents to new fees, such as a $50,000 development fee (for each household). Considering the relatively low price of construction in outposts, and the high costs legalization would incur, some settlers (as one resident of the outpost of Tkoa Dalet told me) would rather keep the outpost illegal and endure the low risk that their home might be demolished.

This conflict of interests and the settlers' suspicion of outside-appointed planners are not the only challenges faced by architects working in outposts. The High Planning Council at the Civil Administration, the body in charge of approving master plans in the West Bank, has been a source of more serious obstacles to their work. When I met Walden in 2015, she told me that all of her master plans for Pnei Kedem—whether submitted with or without the settlers' support—had been rejected by officials at the Civil Administration. Each time, she was asked to revise the plan in response to newly imposed limitations.[59] In February 2003, she was told that large parts of her plan encroached on a nature reserve.[60] Later, they informed her that the entrance road in her plan crossed through what they had only recently realized was privately owned Palestinian land.[61] Still, the Civil Administration wanted to keep the outpost going and encourage the residents to continue developing it, so rather than reject the plans outright, they repeatedly asked for revisions. A landscape architect who was working on a master plan for the outpost of Havat Ya'ir told me she had encountered similar obstacles.[62]

In Pnei Kedem, as residents reacted to Walden's plans, the initial consensus on "green" design principles fell apart, and some began to argue for a more conventional housing scheme. "Not everyone is willing to make the economic sacrifice environmental principles require," one journalist reported in July 2003, referring to the additional cost of environmentally friendly building materials. "The different opinions in this small settlement indeed create labor pains," he added. "Since everyone feels like they belong, and there is no apathy, tempers get frayed every here and there. . . . The nature [of Pnei Kedem] slowly develops, and each new family that joins inevitably determines how the settlement would look."[63] It was still an open question what form the settlement would eventually take.

While the settlers continued to debate the master plan, their relationship with Walden slowly came to a halt. First, the low-cost units she designed were canceled. Then, in 2004, after one of her master plans was rejected, she took a step back, leaving the residents on their own for a few years.

(Walden continued to serve as the architect of record, but in practice, she was not involved in planning during this time.)[64] In her place, the residents' Building Committee and individual initiatives would take the lead on all design matters.

"SOMETHING THAT FITS THE LANDSCAPE"

In the summer of 2005, one of the couples residing on the hill decided to leave the mobile home neighborhood and build the first permanent home in Pnei Kedem. After paying the settlement's treasury $60 and making a $2,000 deposit, they obtained the settlers' permission to take over one of the plots Walden had outlined in one of the master plans she had submitted to the Civil Administration.[65] A friend helped the couple draw plans for a modest home, and by November of 2005 construction had begun.[66] But then, shortly after the concrete foundations for the house had been poured, the couple received a demolition order from the Civil Administration. They did not know if and when the order would be executed, but they immediately stopped all construction. That same night, everyone in the outpost came to help them cover the foundations with sand and place a mobile home on top of it. When they finished, it looked as if construction had never taken place on the site: it was just another mobile home standing on the bare hilltop. The next day, the couple moved into the mobile home, where they are still living today. For those who were there that night, the event served as a warning sign. It made clear, one resident told me, that whoever was going to build a home in Pnei Kedem would be taking a risk. For years, this fear would haunt them.

David, however, refused to give up. Shortly before that night, he had met Leah, who had just graduated from the Architecture Department at Bezalel Academy of Arts and Design in Jerusalem. They got married, and together they began thinking about building a house in Pnei Kedem. Leah shared David's sense of commitment to the settlement movement. Having grown up in the settlement of Allon Shvut, she had heard many stories about the hardship and the uncertainty settlers had occasionally endured in the 1970s. In fact, her father, an American-born architect who had emigrated from Brooklyn shortly after the Six-Day War, had taken part in the planning and construction of Ofra when it was still a wildcat settlement. Now, she felt, it was her turn to take a risk.

Leah wanted her house, the first permanent house in the settlement, to set an example, something her fellow settlers in Pnei Kedem could draw inspiration from when they designed their own homes. It therefore had to be different from the houses her parents' generation had built in the West Bank, she told me. "[For them,] it was just about having as many units as possible. I always say that they wanted to *populate* Judea and Samaria, instead of *settling* it." Settling, Leah insisted, was a more profound act than simply living somewhere; it entailed forging a connection with the natural surroundings. Only once such a connection with the land had been achieved, she added, could there be a conciliation with the Palestinians. To her mind, a place-based architecture would integrate Pnei Kedem into the natural and the social landscapes of the region.

Leah, however, struggled to find ways of forging that connection between architecture and place. When we met, she explained to me:

> In order to have peace we need to build things so they would fit the place. . . . Now, how do I do it? I look around and I try to find appropriate building forms. I look at the nearby Arab villages. But, you know, I don't see it there anymore. Arabs have abandoned their traditional architectural forms. They gave up on desert architecture. They now do everything with concrete and ornaments that look like Baroque architecture to me. They no longer build things in such a way that would fit the place.

Many settlers of Leah's generation share her views of the Palestinians. As the sociologist Michael Feige has argued, young settlers often complain about what they interpret as the lack of authenticity among young Palestinians.[67] In the early days of the settlement movement, in Hebron during the 1970s, settlers saw the Palestinians as the custodians of ancient Israelite culture, the kind of culture many of them sought to re-create. The outbreak of the First Intifada at the end of the 1980s disabused the settlers—and their architects—of that illusion, and many turned to other formal sources. But now that a younger generation of settlers had turned back to the Palestinians again for architectural models, they found that Palestinian building practices had changed, and that the Palestinians therefore no longer offered a model of how to "settle" the land. Their architecture had become too modern for the settlers' taste.

So Leah found the kind of architecture she was looking for in the work of a New Mexico–based architect named Michael Reynolds. Since the 1970s, Reynolds has been developing what he calls "Earthship" houses. These are passive solar houses made almost exclusively of recycled materials—such as used tires filled with dirt and beer cans—and organized around a U-shaped plan. For a while, Leah thought she might be able to design an Earthship house in Pnei Kedem. She even believed she might be able to get firsthand

FIGURE 5.8. To avoid having his home demolished, the builder of this house in the outpost of Tkoa Dalet went so far as to paint his house in blue and white. State inspectors, he told me, might fail to see a house that blurs into the sky. I didn't meet other settlers who followed his example, and home demolitions in outposts are rare, but I did hear many talk about potential demolitions. (Author's private collection.)

experience working with Reynolds in New Mexico. But after meeting with a few settlers who had recently built permanent homes in the nearby outpost of Sde Boaz, she realized that building an Earthship house would take too much time. The faster she and David could build, the settlers of Sde Boaz told her, the better, because once a home is completed and fully occupied, it is significantly more difficult for the Civil Administration to issue and execute a demolition order. Construction in unauthorized outposts, they told the young couple, must not take more than *six weeks*. Some settlers even used creative tactics, including camouflage and disguising construction facilities, to evade demolition (figure 5.8).

Leah simplified her plans to reduce the time it would take to build. Instead of the U-shaped plan typical of Earthship houses, she designed a square-shaped layout, and replaced the earth-filled used tires and other found materials with lightweight, precast foam concrete blocks. To allow the flow of cool air inside, she organized the rooms around a patio space that opened up toward the valley. In compliance with Pnei Kedem's building code, she insisted that the house would have a flat roof and be painted light brown, the color of the bare hilltop. After she had completed a set of drawings, she found a Jewish contractor willing to work on the site.

But shortly after construction had begun, in 2008, Leah and David encountered a problem: their construction workers were too slow. At the time, the building code stipulated that residents were not allowed to hire Palestinian contractors and construction workers, who were significantly faster. Only Jewish Israelis could be employed in Pnei Kedem.[68] Among settlers, this labor policy is known as "Hebrew labor" (Avoda Ivrit). The term "Hebrew labor" dates back to the first decades of the twentieth century, when Labor Zionists tried to secure a Jewish-only economy in Palestine by encouraging Jewish landlords and plantation owners to favor Jewish laborers over the less-expensive Palestinian ones.[69] About a century later, when the residents of Pnei Kedem adopted the term, they were attempting to identify their settlement activity with that of these early pioneers. It was also the settlers' way of expressing their hostility toward the Palestinians.

A few days into construction, Leah and David realized that their Jewish workers had to be replaced before it was too late. They explained the situation to their neighbors and asked that Palestinian workers be allowed into Pnei Kedem. In the past, residents had refused to discuss the matter. This time, since construction had already begun, and no one wanted to see another unfinished house in the settlement, the people of Pnei Kedem agreed to their request. And once the decision was made, Leah and David's contractor brought in ten Palestinian construction workers; within six weeks, the house was completed (figure 5.9).

As we sat across from her house, some seven years after it was built, Leah couldn't hide her feelings of both frustration and pride. The house, she admitted, is not exactly what she had in mind. It is not ecologically sound, and, aesthetically, it does not really blend into its landscape. "I wish I had the time to build something that fits the landscape better," she confessed. "But you cannot build a house in six weeks. It is just not enough [time]." On the other hand, Leah assured me, the house fulfilled an important purpose in the life of the settlement: it showed others in Pnei Kedem that the risk of building a house was not as great as they thought it was. "We gave others the understanding that they could also build here." And indeed, shortly after the house was completed, others began making plans to build permanent homes in the settlement.

FIGURE 5.9. Leah and David's house, the first permanent house built in Pnei Kedem. (Photograph by author, 2015.)

THE BUILDING COMMITTEE

As more and more settlers became interested in building permanent homes in Pnei Kedem, the Building Committee took on a more important role in the public life of the settlement. As in most other outposts, the Building Committee of Pnei Kedem was formed shortly after the settlers first moved into the mobile homes. Composed of five resident representatives, the committee was in charge of issuing quasi-official building permits, conducting building inspections, and allocating land plots to new residents. Even before anyone had ventured to build permanent homes on the barren hilltop, the committee had drafted a building code. Now that people had begun building homes, the committee's task was to revise the building code, repealing regulations that proved unrealistic and clarifying others that were too vague, in order to offer residents some guidance as they designed their private houses. For a while, Leah served as the unofficial chairperson of the Building Committee, and when I asked her about the original building code, she replied, laughing: "It was something that you could call a 'recommendations document.' It was really nothing. Nothing was enforced. We called it a building code, but it was just a list of random recommendations. You had there things like 'it will be good to have a solar-powered water heater, it will be good to have this or that.' It was very naïve." The master plans prepared by Rachel Walden, on the other hand, had laid out rules regarding building style and size. But her plan was never officially approved, and many of the residents opposed the plan anyway. The Building Committee members had to write a new building code, Leah concluded; otherwise chaos would rule in Pnei Kedem.

As the committee members redrafted the building code, they attempted to involve the other residents. They circulated questionnaires that asked about their aesthetic preferences, they organized consultation meetings to discuss these preferences, and whenever an important building law was about to be decided on, they hosted an open debate that was usually followed by a democratic vote. Any serious new law could be added to the building code only if the majority of the residents supported it.

But these attempts at collaboration were not always productive. As Leah recalls, the questionnaires mainly demonstrated to the settlers the lack of a consensus on some of the most basic issues. This encouraged each person to cling to his or her own vision and to disregard the concerns of others. "The instructions we came up with [based on the questionnaires] simply reflected a collection of individual concerns and interests," she told me. "The people here did not want to be limited in square footage, in building height, or in anything for that matter." The debates the committee held, she added, were too frequent and long and rarely resulted in definitive decisions. And even when a decision was reached, few actually followed it, Leah lamented.

When it came to their homes, the residents did not find it necessary to follow the building code. When I asked Nathan, a resident who was planning to build his house on a plot outside the borders set by the Building Committee, if he was worried about violating the outpost's codes, he immediately dismissed my concerns. "How could they tell me not to build there? It is all illegal here! No one could do anything if I go there and build whatever I want." Even members of the Building Committee showed little respect for the building code. One member was planning a house that exceeded the allowed building size and therefore encountered the opposition of his neighbors. When I asked him about this opposition, he bluntly told me:

> I wrote the building code! So they think they can tell me now how to use it? . . . And, anyway, the building code has no validity. We don't have an approved master plan yet. So I can do whatever I want! . . . [And anyway,] who knows what's going to happen here. Tomorrow someone could come and raze the entire place. Until we have an approved master plan, I am not going to follow a nonvalidated contract.

Given the democratic nature of the Building Committee, he added, the building code in Pnei Kedem is changing constantly. In less than a year, it was changed twice.

To Leah's disappointment, the Building Committee was also unable to control the development of public space in the outpost. At the same time as people were beginning to make plans for their individual homes, debates concerning public buildings also arose. Leah had sketched a preliminary plan with a number of public facilities concentrated in one area, where, in consultation with the committee, she placed the main synagogue, an outdoor theater, a clinic, and other public structures. She showed the plan to some of the residents and to the outpost's secretariat, and they seemed to like the general scheme. It was a good starting point, many agreed, and the committee began working more seriously on the plan.

But even before the plan was finalized, residents had already begun contesting it. While the committee was still debating the plan, one resident, who had received a donation from an American supporter of the settlement movement to build a kids' playground, erected a playground on the highest point in Pnei Kedem (figure 5.10). The playground took less than a day to build. When Leah saw it that evening, after concrete was poured, she was shocked. Considering the high altitude and strong winds in Pnei Kedem, the playground should have been placed at a lower spot, where the children would be protected from the harsh weather conditions of the hilltop. But it was too late, she lamented. Once the concrete was poured, it was virtually impossible to move the playground, which, still today, stands empty for most parts of the year. "Anyone does whatever they want," she told me, recalling that event. "So many mistakes were made here because of this mentality. It is hard for me even to talk about it."

The design of the main synagogue was equally frustrating. For years, the people of Pnei Kedem dreamed of a permanent synagogue to replace the makeshift structure they had cobbled together by joining two mobile homes to each other. In 2001, Moshe, one of the founders, laid out design guidelines for the structure: "It would be erected on the highest point in the settlement . . . [and] built in two stories—the upper level will function as a synagogue and the lower one as an events hall . . . Transparent windows will wrap the synagogue so we would have a 360-degree panoramic view. . . . We should try and use local stone . . . to protect the environment and to beautify the synagogue with natural materials."[70] Without funding to build the synagogue, however, it remained only a dream. Then, in 2015, a rumor began to circulate about a generous donation pledged for the construction of the synagogue, and the Building Committee created a six-member subcommittee

FIGURE 5.10. Playground (left side of the image) located on the highest point in Pnei Kedem, where winds are especially strong, 2017. Permanent homes, built in recent years, can be seen on the bottom right side. (Photograph by author.)

to oversee its design. But a few of the settlers were suspicious of the subcommittee and formed a competing committee that drew different plans for the building. Each group—the Building Committee's subcommittee and the rival synagogue committee—worked independently. Soon, the Building Committee's subgroup itself broke into two opposing camps, as the members couldn't agree on the program for the building or even a set of design principles. While some wanted a relatively conventional structure, others envisioned a gigantic geodesic dome bisected by a rectilinear shape. At one point, it became clear that the rumor about the pending donation was false. There was no money for the synagogue, so the efforts of all three groups were in vain.

Shortly after the playground was erected, Leah, the main force behind the Building Committee and the only trained architect on the hill, decided to resign. Like Walden, she realized that the settlers had little respect for her professional skills or for the authority of the Building Committee. Nor were they able to take part in a democratic planning model. "Democracy works against us here," Leah told me. "No one here cares about anyone else. They only think about their own private worlds." Each, she complained, just builds whatever he wants. "And I care too much. This place is important for me. But here people just don't care."

Not long after Leah left, while I was residing in Pnei Kedem, the Building Committee broke into two groups, as the remaining members proved unable to work together. Unsurprisingly, the Building Committee lost much of the influence it may have had over the residents. The experiment in self-governance and participatory design failed to provide a framework for the development of Pnei Kedem.

UNFULFILLED PROPHECY

In the winter of 2015, three young settlers began building a house 30 meters down the hill from Leah's house. Every morning, they would meet on the site and work until the early afternoon. Work was slow. After a couple of months, there were only a few wooden columns rising up out of an octagon-shaped concrete floor. When I joined the construction team, in February 2015, I found no heavy equipment on the site, only wooden beams, a couple of hammers, saws, and tape measures. "Not using heavy equipment creates an atmosphere," explained Dotan, one of the three settlers, notable for his long dreadlocks, thick beard, and loose clothing (figure 5.11). Detailed plan drawings were also absent from the site. Instead, the three men were making lines on the ground, marking them with sticks and ropes, as in premodern times. These lines, I was told, were loaded with spiritual meaning. The octagonal floor plan, for example, was composed of two interlocking stars of David. "It symbolizes a heavenly encounter," Dotan told me without irony. "Construction is a testament to one's spiritual level."

Construction teams like the one working next to Leah's house have taken over a growing number of building commissions in outposts in recent years, as any attempts to enforce building codes have been pretty much abandoned and residents have been left to do as they will. I met other such teams in the outposts of Tkoa Dalet, Native Ha'avot, and Bnei Adam. Usually, they were composed of two or three young settlers in their twenties and thirties. Some were a one-man show. Almost all were outpost residents. They were not only doing construction but also designing the buildings, despite the fact that they often lacked any architectural training. Unlike their predecessors who settled in Hebron, these young settlers showed little interest in replicating building elements borrowed from the Palestinians. Nor were they interested in the kind of flat roofs that the founders of Pnei Kedem had instituted in the building code a few years ago. Instead, they were fascinated with Jewish iconography: symbols like the Star of David or the Jewish menorah usually decorated the houses they built. Building homes in the West Bank was a matter of religious identity for them.

Eastern spirituality and American counterculture played equally important roles in their designs. The construction teams I met often incorporated

FIGURE 5.11. Dotan by the octagon-shaped house, then under construction, Pnei Kedem, 2015. (Photograph by author.)

mandalas in their projects, and in some cases even built yurts and geodesic domes (figure 5.12). During the time I was conducting fieldwork in Pnei Kedem, Dotan and his team began working on a 10-meter-wide geodesic dome, designed to house a young family that had been living in the mobile home neighborhood for almost a decade (figure 5.13). Geodesic domes are holistic forms, they explained to me. "They are in harmony with the world," the future tenant added. Such comments fitted outpost residents' growing interest in new-age practices and Eastern spirituality that emphasize harmony between humans and the cosmos.

These unconventional forms were often paired with natural building materials. The construction teams I met preferred to work with local stone (figure 5.14). In some cases, the settlers collected these stones from their immediate surroundings. Often, they bought them from local Palestinian quarries. Other popular materials included wood and mud. For the 10-meter-wide geodesic dome in Pnei Kedem, Dotan's team even recruited Shlomi, a twenty-eight-year-old guy living in a nearby settlement, who presented himself as an expert in mud architecture. Mud, just like stone, was a common building material in biblical Israel, Shlomi told me. The

FIGURE 5.12. Two yurts attached to a mobile home in the outpost of Tkoa Dalet, 2015. (Photograph by author.)

FIGURE 5.13. Builder posing by a wooden geodesic dome, then still under construction, in Pnei Kedem, 2015. (Photograph by author.)

FIGURE 5.14. A house made of metal panels covered with local stone in the outpost of Bnei Adam, 2015. (Photograph by author.)

ancient Israelites and the Canaanites, he believed, used both to build their homes.

The builders' interest in unconventional building forms and materials, however, was not just a matter of nostalgia or new-age spirituality. It also stemmed from more immediate economic and competitive concerns. Over the past decade or so, a growing number of settlers in Pnei Kedem, as in other outposts, have been hiring Palestinian contractors and construction workers to build their homes. In Pnei Kedem, Palestinian contractors had built more than half of the fifteen permanent houses completed by 2015. This should come as no surprise. The Palestinians, with a centuries-old heritage of home building in the region, were significantly faster and more skilled. Equally important, their rates were much lower than those charged by Jewish contractors. In 2015, the daily salary of a Jewish construction worker in Pnei Kedem was three times higher than that of a Palestinian. Dotan and his team, however, could not accept their relative inferiority to Palestinian construction workers, and not only because it made it harder for them to make a living. For the zealot builders, it also created a theological problem. "Rabbi Kook said that if you give a piece of land to a Jew in the Land of

Israel, it will generate sacredness," Dotan told me, citing one of the settlement movement's first ideologues. "It would generate beauty." Whatever a person of Jewish faith builds on this land, he added, should be magical; it is his place in the world, and he should know it better than anyone else.[71] Admitting that Palestinians actually build better would mean recognizing that something in the settlers' return to the land had gone wrong—or worse, something in the prophecy itself was untrue. Unconventional structures, such as geodesic domes or mud architecture, gave Dotan and his team an advantage over the Palestinians. He once told me:

> There is not a single Arab who could build such things! No Arab is building stuff like this. . . . They would never even imagine building a geodesic dome. And I am tired of these people in Pnei Kedem . . . and their heavy concrete houses [built by Palestinians]. The dome will open up their minds. It will make them see that there is something else . . . something they cannot get from these Arab contractors!

Building was a matter of competition for young settlers like Dotan, and unconventional building forms were a means of getting a point ahead.

But in this competition, there are no winners. The unconventional forms and building techniques young settlers have chosen to work with often proved too complex. The mud floor built in Pnei Kedem's geodesic dome, for example, ended up tilted and full of cracks; it looked nothing like an actual floor. Soon after those cracks appeared, Shlomi, the "expert" on mud architecture, disappeared, leaving Dotan and his team to deal with the mess he left behind. Meanwhile, Dotan's team was unable to seal the dome itself. After they covered the structure with wood and other materials, water still leaked in. In 2017, two years after it was built, the dome, with a huge Star of David decorating its façade, still stood empty (figure 5.15). In a similar fashion, the octagon-shaped house, the one symbolizing the "heavenly encounter," remained unfinished for a couple of years. Traces of unfinished, odd structures, like Pnei Kedem's geodesic dome, can be found in other outposts as well. Messianic zeal on its own is not enough to make a home.

The Palestinian builders I had met in Pnei Kedem, on the other hand, could hardly be seen as victors in the "competition" over building outposts. They were not worried about having to compete with the messianic builders, of course. Mohammad, a Palestinian contractor who has been working in Jewish settlements since he was a teenager in the 1980s and recently completed four houses in Pnei Kedem, laughed when I asked him about the work of Jewish contractors in the outpost. He thought they still had a lot to learn. In fact,

FIGURE 5.15. Geodesic dome with a large Star of David engraved on its outer shell in Pnei Kedem. In 2017, the dome was uninhabitable because water leaked through the fabric covering the dome. (Photograph by author.)

more than once he had assisted them on the construction site, saving them from making irreparable mistakes. When I asked him about Dotan's geodesic dome, he joked: "Next time I want to pray, I should go there instead of going to the Dome of the Rock." But what Mohammad could not laugh about was the residents' fear of, if not full-on hostility toward, the Palestinians, regardless of their construction skills. Whenever political tensions escalated, Mohammad and his workers were expelled from Pnei Kedem, leaving them without income, at least until tensions subsided. For example, one day in the fall of 2015, at around noon, after a settler was stabbed not far from Pnei Kedem, Mohammad's workers were kicked out of the outpost immediately, without a warning. For about an hour they stood by the gate, in the pouring rain, waiting for a ride home, not knowing when or if they would be able to return to continue their work. In the "competition" over the construction of houses in outposts, they could never win—to say nothing about the devastating impact of places like Pnei Kedem on the long-term prospects of a two-state solution.

As I walked back and forth on Pnei Kedem's main road in the fall of 2015, I could not ignore the eerie feeling of neglect. About a third of the houses along the half-paved road were unfinished. Some, like the geodesic dome, were uninhabitable. Others had been left half completed, waiting for the Palestinian builders to be allowed back into the settlement to continue their work. And houses that had been completed showed no trace of the founders' vision of an "exemplary settlement," a vision they had fought over so fiercely with planning institutions. Nor did their design show much concern for the Building Committee's regulations. This sight of neglect and disarray did not escape Leah's gaze. When we met, she lamented, "Looking back, I think we were wrong. I would have much preferred having a [conventional] plan drawn by planning institutions to what we have here now. It is terrible, each person here just does whatever he wants, and no one actually takes advantage of the landscape. No one is actually building here in a rural style. Some build houses with a floor area ratio of 300 percent, and no one can do anything about it." Taking a deep breath, she later added: "On the one hand, there is the possibility of building a utopia here. I mean this place has so much potential. But on the other hand, time and again, we fall."

CONCLUSION

The architectural history of Pnei Kedem is a history of accidents and contradictions: of a violent clash between religious Zionist and ultra-Orthodox settlers, of plans for "a green settlement" that mandate the installation of heavy infrastructure across vast territories, and of Palestinian builders "threatening" to build the entire outpost by themselves. It is not without cause that Leah told me that there is no "rational planning" in Pnei Kedem.

As with other settlements discussed in this book, Pnei Kedem's contradictory history speaks to the limits of bottom-up design and participatory planning. The residents of the outpost had instituted an exceptionally inclusive design process based on direct participation. Each and every key decision pertaining to the shaping of Pnei Kedem was first negotiated by voluntary committees, and then presented to the general assembly for an open debate followed by a general vote. A consensus, however, has rarely ever been reached in these votes. Different residents have often stuck to different, at times conflicting, aesthetic visions, leaving Pnei Kedem without the kind of master plan needed for authorization for almost two decades. In the absence of a master plan or basic design guidelines, individuals have been making design decisions according to their own preferences, without consulting their fellow settlers, and in ways that have exacerbated tensions in the outpost. The absence of authoritative planning resulted in a lack of any planning that goes beyond the scale of the individual house.

The resulting landscape, in turn, shows how outposts' residents—the vanguard of the settlement movement—struggle to articulate a shared worldview. In previous decades, distinct groups of settlers often shared a worldview that they attempted to inscribe onto their built environment. In Hebron, settlement activists sought to reinhabit a Palestinian landscape they associated with the ancient Israelites. The settlers of Ofra fashioned themselves after early twentieth-century Labor Zionists. The residents of Betar Illit joined forces to have their settlement adapted to the needs of ultra-Orthodox families. The residents of Pnei Kedem, in contrast, are divided among themselves, despite the fact that most of them grew up in settlements and all associate themselves with religious Zionism. Some of the residents wish to break away from their parents' generation by envisioning a settlement that is green; others simply want to live the suburban dream. Meanwhile, those who are engaged in building homes are mainly preoccupied with finding ways to overcome an inferiority complex vis-à-vis their Palestinian counterparts.

That these builders drew on counterculture aesthetics also speaks to the unstable political nature of building styles. When hippies of the 1960s and 1970s experimented with geodesic domes and handmade homes—in Drop City, a commune near Trinidad, Colorado, or in Ananda, a spiritual community in the Sierra Nevada of California, among many other places—they did so with the intention of challenging the American middle-class way of life. The spherical form of the dome and the singular qualities of the handmade home indeed posed an aesthetic alternative to the presumed uniformity of suburban homes and the anonymity of city apartments. But ultimately, as the architectural historian Margaret Crawford has argued, despite their aesthetic qualities, these forms did not really challenge prevailing social norms. Instead, they served as status symbols, allowing privileged counterculture builders to distinguish themselves from the masses and recognize one another.[72] In the West Bank, these same forms accumulated yet another unexpected socio-political meaning: they offered a means of excluding the Palestinians. Pnei Kedem's geodesic dome reminds us with some force that architectural forms have no fixed political meanings.

But despite the tensions among the residents, despite their inability to work with planning institutions, and despite the contradictory landscape they have authored, Pnei Kedem has slowly turned into an indisputable fact on the ground. Since I left Pnei Kedem, it has grown significantly. In 2016, dormitories were built inside the settlement, accommodating about twenty students who attend college in Jerusalem. The following year, one of the residents opened a farm on an adjacent hill, adding another neighborhood to the outpost (if not a whole new neighboring outpost). According to a Peace Now report, in 2018, the Ministry of Construction and Housing was working on the master planning of the settlement.[73] In 2020, *Arutz Sheva*, a news outlet associated with religious Zionism, reported that the Civil

Administration submitted Pnei Kedem's master plan for public review, an important—even if cumbersome and uncertain—step on the path to authorization.[74] Pnei Kedem has become a major political stab, cutting into the prospects of Palestinian sovereignty.

We are used to thinking about architectures of power in terms of large monuments, grand boulevards, or even surveillance mechanisms. The abandoned playground, the leaking geodesic dome, and the disputed master plan of Pnei Kedem are also architectures of power. They are banal, unseemly, and arbitrary. But they demonstrate that power operates not only through discipline and institutions but also through failure and "irrational planning."

POSTSCRIPT

On February 22, 2023, as this book was going to press, the Civil Administration's High Planning Committee approved a master plan submitted on behalf of Pnei Kedem. The outpost is now recognized as an official neighborhood of the settlement of Meitzad even though the two communities operate separately. The authorization came just days after the recently elected government, arguably the most nationalist in Israeli history, announced that it would authorize nine other outposts. While I had not anticipated that Pnei Kedem's master plan would be approved so soon, its authorization underscores my conclusions: Pnei Kedem is a stubborn fact on the ground, and the exercise of power does not necessarily require architectural order or even a coherent vision.

CONCLUSION

In 2021, Kass Group, a development company owned by an ultra-Orthodox settler, stunned the media when it opened two entertainment centers, called Magic Kass and DCITY, in the outskirts of the settlement of Maʿale Adumim. These projects hardly seemed to fit the public image of the broader settlement enterprise. Magic Kass is a three-story indoor amusement park—the fourth largest in the world—built in the shape of an oversized metallic orb. Among its cutting-edge facilities are a 22-meter-high "looper," a sky tower, four carousels, 150 video games, bumper cars, and eight restaurants, as well as two roller coasters, one of which lifts visitors some 10 meters above the roof to offer glimpses of the Judean Desert. DCITY, located just a few minutes down the road from Magic Kass, is a fancy mall boasting some two hundred furniture and home-decor stores, alongside restaurants and kiosks; all are organized around indoor and outdoor plazas. DCITY's main attraction is "the piazza," an atrium inspired by the Venetian Resort in Las Vegas, capped with artificial sky (the largest in the Middle East) and surrounded by faux Renaissance building façades, bordering a small river with toy gondolas (figure 6.1). The two centers, as a *Haaretz* reporter noted, are the first stage in the developers' larger plan of transforming the site into a major tourist destination, with additional recreational facilities such as a water park and go-kart center. "This is quite a dizzying vision," the reporter concluded.[1]

The chapters of this book, spanning some five decades of settlement design, could not have anticipated the construction of Disney World– and Venetian-styled entertainment centers in the occupied West Bank. And yet, if uncertainty and heterogeneity are the common threads of this architectural history, then Magic Kass and DCITY certainly follow the pattern of their precedents. They are merely the latest addition to a haphazard history, and to the heterogeneous landscape it has produced. This landscape—which, by 2022, had come to house almost half a million Israelis—does not conform to the common caricature of settlements as composed of single-family houses perched on remote hilltops, topped with pitched red-tiled roofs, and surrounded by lush lawns. The settlement landscape in fact takes many forms: modest community settlements next to large suburbs; cities with tall apartment buildings; modernist housing blocks and cooperative villages; and scores of outposts built around clusters of mobile homes with, occasionally, some counterculture structures. And now, that landscape also includes two jaw-dropping entertainment centers.

FIGURE 6.1. "The piazza," DCITY's main attraction, designed by Shlomo Gertner. (Photograph by author, 2022.)

Understanding this heterogeneous landscape has been the main goal of this book: examining how it came into being and what it tells us about the settlement movement, about changing Israeli identity and priorities, and, more broadly, about the relationship between politics and the built environment. Contrary to the dominant understanding that the architecture of settlements reflects policy or advances military strategy, by acting as an arm of the Israeli army, this study has revealed a far messier relationship between the design of the settlements and state power—one that involved numerous actors, working from above or below and promoting different ideologies and aesthetic visions, some barely formulated. Over the course of five decades, these actors alternately fought and collaborated over the design of settlements. Each adopted different strategies and tactics. None of them was able to maintain exclusive agency over the design of settlements for extended periods of time or see their own vision fully realized.

The settlers associated with Gush Emunim were the most vocal and arguably the most ambitious of all the actors. Yet even they could not force· their aesthetic vision—nebulous as it was—on the majority of settlers. Only a fraction of settlers today reside in Palestinian towns or in kibbutz-like settlements. In fact, the attempt to model Gush Emunim settlements after the kibbutz was often viewed with cynicism by the broader Israeli public. Few Israelis failed to see the gap between the early twentieth-century Labor Zionists and the settlers. The pragmatists among the pious settlers, however, were open to other settlement models and visions, as long as they would help attract more Israelis to the West Bank. To a degree, this has indeed happened, as more and more Israelis moved to the West Bank in subsequent decades. The introduction of a suburban-style settlement, for example, drew a substantial number of people during the 1980s. Many of these newcomers had little interest in the idea of the whole Land of Israel, much less in the coming of the messiah.[2] But even once these new models were adopted, the core ideological settlers have not been able to attract masses of Israelis to the West Bank or to erase the pre-1967 border.[3] By 2020, settlers constituted only 5 percent of Israeli citizens (and 7 percent of Jewish Israelis), making up 14 percent of the population of the West Bank (not including East Jerusalem).[4] In 2015, almost 90 percent of the population growth in settlements was the product of natural reproduction rather than migration from Israel to the West Bank. Some settlements have even experienced population decline in recent years.[5] Architecture as a tactic or a strategy has not been able to attract most Israelis.

The experience of other groups of settlers, particularly more secular and ultra-Orthodox Israelis, was different. For the most part, they had been drawn not by ideology but by the promise of affordable housing and of design types difficult to build in Israel proper. They bought their houses at bargain prices. But they also had strong ideas about the kind of place they wanted to live in, and they were able to exercise some degree of agency in shaping their built environment. Nevertheless, they rarely saw their desires or visions fully realized, either because of political upheavals or because the economic model was unviable. Those seeking the calm of suburban life were jolted out of their daydream whenever political tensions escalated, especially during the first and second Palestinian uprisings. Many were prepared to leave, if offered compensation. In some cases, the lax regulatory environment of the West Bank resulted in instances of fraud in which homebuyers lost property, got caught in dubious land deals, and were left with unfinished units or in half-built settlements poorly connected to basic infrastructure.

The role of officials and urban planners in official planning institutions shifted over time. Initially, their role was somewhat reactive. The absence of a clear policy regarding the administrative status of the West Bank had sometimes left state officials ham-fisted in the face of mounting pressure from civilian groups to build settlements. It was only after settlement construction became official government policy, following the election of the Likud Party in 1977, that ministry officials and planners at the Settlement Division were in a position to fully oversee the planning process. But the "agency" they had secured was quickly undermined by economic constraints, by the dubious practices of private developers, by unruly homebuyers, and by the stirring of the Palestinian elephant in the room that many in Israel seemed to have forgotten about.

In recent years, the political scene in Israel has shifted to the Right. A number of settlement activists, who previously worked outside state institutions, have obtained positions of power in the Knesset and the Ministry of Construction and Housing.[6] Moshe Merhavia, one of the founders of the settlement of Ofra, is now the head of the Jerusalem region of the Ministry of Construction and Housing. Uri Ariel, an ally of Merhavia and a resident of the settlement of Kfar Adumim, served as the minister of Construction and Housing between 2013 and 2015. Israel's prime minister from 2021 to 2022, Naftali Bennett, not only lived in the settlement of Bet Arye for a short while but also acted as the director general of Yesha Council, a central settler advocacy group, between 2010 and 2012. Simcha Rothman, a resident of Pnei Kedem, entered the Knesset in 2021 and is now chairing the Knesset's Constitution, Law, and Justice Committee. With settlers' growing presence in the government, planning institutions have arguably become more favorably inclined toward the settlement movement. Nevertheless, in a repetition of a pattern they themselves helped set, they have not always had much control over the shaping of the so-called unauthorized outposts that have mushroomed in the first two decades of the twenty-first century.

For architects, whether hired through the Ministry of Construction and Housing, the Settlement Division, or private developers, the history of settlement construction has been anything but satisfying. Since at least the 1980s, Israeli architects have been fully aware of the negative effects that settlements would have on the Palestinians. The majority of them accepted design commissions in settlements because they struggled to keep their practices afloat. Some of them were young and lacked the economic security to turn down work. To express political dissent by refusing to accept commissions was a luxury they felt they could not afford. In fact, the few Israeli architects who did express dissent quickly understood that their efforts did little to arrest the construction of settlements. Perhaps the most notable act of protest carried out by Israeli architects was a 1988 petition that called on planning and design professionals to decline building commissions in settlements. Signed by 103 professionals and aired in local newspapers, it was unprecedented.[7] But, as the architect Karen Wainer, who helped draft the petition, explained to me, it didn't do much. "It wouldn't matter if I refuse to plan a villa or an individual building," she concluded. "The mechanism [of settlement construction] is huge, it is so well-oiled."[8] Meanwhile, architects who—in contrast to the petition signees—were swayed by the possibility of designing complete communities in record time rarely saw their ideas fully realized in the settlements. Their designs could simply be redrawn by the settlers, altered by politicians, overtaken by political events, or subverted by the work of real estate developers.

The messiness of this history—with architectural agency distributed across a wide range of actors, so that the resulting designs (the room layouts, building façades, and public spaces) couldn't possibly reflect a coherent military strategy—does not, of course, redeem the settlement enterprise. Nor can it excuse the negative effects that the settlements have had on the Palestinians. Redemption is not the goal of this book. On the contrary, by exploring the full range of actors and intentions involved in the design and construction of settlements, we can see not only the weird and contradictory character of the settlement enterprise but also how deeply implicated it is in Israeli society across a spectrum of constituencies. Changing the course of the settlement enterprise would require profound changes in Israel itself.

Few sites are as contentious as the occupied West Bank, and comparing one contested site to another is a tricky endeavor. Nevertheless, I believe that the story of this complex web of actors and the heterogeneous (indeed sometimes contradictory) landscape of settlements they produced do offer a broader lesson. It shows the difficulties entailed in trying to use the built environment to represent a single political ideology or to advance specific political intentions. The inhabitants are likely to use the built environment in unexpected ways. Its design and construction must engage a wide range of actors: architects and consultants, state officials, real estate developers, and construction workers, among others. With each pulling in a different direction, and all constantly adjusting their strategies and tactics amid shifting social, political, and economic forces, the built environment can almost never be a stop-frame image of politics. When Michel Foucault was asked in 1982 about the possibility of instilling a predetermined political meaning into a built form, he was pessimistic: "There are only reciprocal relations, and the perpetual gaps between intentions in relation to one another."[9] This is still true.

USERS ON UNEQUAL GROUNDS

The research I presented in this book also complicates accounts that celebrate the triumph of the user in shaping and managing the built environment. On the one hand, by developing separate, even insular, urban and rural forms, settlers indeed made the Israeli housing system more plural. Certain groups of Israelis—most notably, the ultra-Orthodox—have developed community forms that allow them to follow distinct ways of life, apart from the dominant culture, which, for the most part, disdains them. If we consider that until the 1970s the Israeli housing system, under the labor parties, deliberately ignored individual preferences, sometimes with the intention of effacing identities deemed too "diasporic," then the ultra-Orthodox city and community settlement, as planning models, could be seen as a welcome corrective to a previously insensitive and out-of-touch housing system.

On the other hand, the right to transform space in settlements sometimes gave rise to an imaginary of autonomous space where difference is forbidden. More often than not, mechanisms like admission committees or informal police agencies that were instituted in community settlements or ultra-Orthodox city-settlements excluded, sometimes even disciplined, anyone they deemed unfit, even when that person posed no threat to any particular way of life.[10] And, regardless of such mechanisms, all settlements described here exclude the Palestinians.[11] All trod on Palestinian territory. In fact, through squatting, protests, and design interventions, some of the settlers have more firmly entrenched the Israeli occupation. Most notably, Gush Emunim activists have sometimes drawn the government into erecting settlements in heavily populated areas of the West Bank it would have preferred to leave alone.[12]

The settlements, however, are not a cautionary lesson illustrating a dark side latent in user-led design. For one thing, there is no reason to assume that Palestinians would have been welcomed in Jewish settlements in any case. Over the years, Israel has applied a two-tier legal system, applying Israeli laws to settlers and military or Jordanian laws to Palestinians; thus, having both reside in the same community would practically be impossible.[13] It would at least make municipal governance unsustainable. In fact, in 1997, the Israeli military commander of the West Bank issued an order defining settlements as areas closed off to Palestinian residents of the West Bank.[14] (And, regardless of these obstacles, even inside Israel, Palestinian citizens of Israel—who make up 21 percent of the Israeli population—and Jews tend to live apart, in separate towns, neighborhoods, and villages, despite their shared citizenship.)

No less important, the activities of the settlers did not take place on neutral ground. The military occupation of the West Bank created an imbalanced power equation, obviously tilted in favor of the settlers. Even the most radical settlers—who built unauthorized settlements, clashed with state officials, and undermined the rights of the Palestinians—still sometimes received various government services, including funding, security, and physical planning. The settlers of Ofra, for instance, have worked "from below," in defiance of the law, for a relatively long period of time, but at pivotal moments they also enjoyed easy access to key actors in the establishment. Equally important, they rarely paid a price for their illegal activities. According to the geographers Oren Yiftachel and Erez Tzfadia, government agencies in Israel, as happens in countries across the global south, intentionally "launder" and sometimes facilitate the informal activities of favored groups to achieve or maintain control, territorial or otherwise.[15] To be sure, the Israeli government hasn't been consistent enough in its settlement policies to consciously allow such a strategy, certainly not over the course of five decades. Nevertheless, the pattern of intermittent collaboration and contestation with settlers clearly resulted in excessively empowered users, who enjoyed the benefits of both formal and informal status. The architectural history of the settlements thus presents an important case showing the kinds of spaces that may be produced where the law is not applied uniformly or democratically, and how users may themselves participate in the engendering of spatial domination, despite their seemingly disadvantaged position.

BETWEEN ISRAEL AND THE WEST BANK

Although questions about the relationship between politics and the built environment were central to this book, questions about Israeli society also played an important part. Despite the fact that settlements house some 475,000 Israelis (not including East Jerusalem) of various religious and ideological convictions, scholarly attention has traditionally focused on the fundamentalist settler group of Gush Emunim and on its alliances with high-profile politicians.[16] Media representations, for the most part, have been equally narrow. The image of a young religious male settler dangling an M-16 rifle from his shoulder has become emblematic of the settlement enterprise.[17] Only recently has a new generation of scholars begun to consider the diversity of settlers' identities and worldviews.[18] This book adds to this growing body of literature by exploring an even greater diversity of actors who have been involved in the design and evolution of the settlements. Their identities and their (often conflicting) worldviews are inscribed, to some extent, onto settlements' streets, squares, home layouts, and building façades.

And yet settlers' identities and the landscapes they have forged for themselves are not only diverse but also not as removed from those found in Israel proper as some have imagined. As this book has shown, more often than not, settlers—even the most radical ones, who are often seen as radical in their break with secular Israeli society—drew on mainstream architectural culture to fashion their identities. The settlers of Hebron drew on regionalist architecture promoted by avowedly secular Tel Aviv–based architects, while their peers in Ofra were inspired by the architecture of the kibbutz. The settlers, regardless of their ideological affiliation, may have reinterpreted and transformed building forms to fit their own needs and specific worldviews, but they were in constant dialogue with mainstream architectural currents, both in Israel and globally.

This dialogue was not one-directional. The West Bank became a testing ground of sorts, where settlers and design professionals conceived new urban and architectural forms. Among these new forms were the community settlement and the ultra-Orthodox city-settlement. Both were later embraced inside Israel. Hundreds of thousands of Israelis, who have never spent a day in a West Bank settlement, now reside in community settlements and in the ultra-Orthodox city of El'ad, just west of the Green Line, or in the ultra-Orthodox neighborhoods of Ramat Bet Shemesh, near Jerusalem. West Bank settlements have transformed the built environment inside Israel.

As much as this architectural history reveals interconnections between West Bank settlements and Israeli architectural culture, it also emphasizes historical discontinuities between West Bank settlements and pre-1967 Zionist settlements. Although both are products of settler-colonial activity, each is characterized by different physical forms and planning processes.[19] None of the settlement patterns that this book introduced, not even the community settlement, actually resembles the kibbutz or the moshav—Labor Zionists' most cherished settlement forms. Despite some arbitrary parallels, notably the aesthetic reference of the red-tiled roof (which many communities do not mandate anyway), the community settlement marks a radical break from these earlier rural forms. It is significantly denser, it caters to commuters, it lacks serious agricultural production, and, as a result, it has a much smaller footprint. Equally important, the multiplicity of actors that had animated the design and construction of the community settlement and most other settlement patterns in the West Bank is at odds with the state-led centralized building sector that characterized construction in Israel in the first two decades following independence. More often than not, settlers precipitated the decentralization of the building sector. Despite the fact that settlement activists often see themselves as the forebearers of earlier forms of Zionism, their built environments and the planning processes they have promoted spelled the abandonment of that legacy.

CODA

When I met with Elinoar Barzaki, who, as the head of the Jerusalem region at the Ministry of Construction and Housing between 1977 and 1989, had overseen the construction of many settlements, she wondered about the future of the settlements. As a leftist, she was hesitantly optimistic:

> Settlements, as a form of habitation, their right to exist is very much dependent on geo-political conditions. By geo-political conditions I refer to economic, cultural, and social givens. Now, yes it could be that all these things might remain there forever. But it could also be that at one point settlements would lose their raison d'être and that they would dry out and fall down. Let's take the kibbutz as an example. Many kibbutzim [in recent decades] have either changed their form once their raison d'être was gone, or otherwise they became sad places of cemeteries and old people. . . . So let's take a scenario . . . that all of a sudden this idea that we need to keep the [occupied] territories, that our ancestral origins are here, that there is redemption—all these things would become irrelevant, just like the ideology of the kibbutz became irrelevant. Would people in settlements stay there? . . . Do these places [settlements], as we are taught in the university, have the right to exist economically, geographically, topographically? No, not according to modernity. They require too much infrastructure. . . . You won't do it unless there is a political ideology behind it. It does not matter whether this ideology comes from the government or from the settlers. You need some kind of ideological justification to embark on such a suicidal undertaking. And ideologies, they come and go.

But then I think of the abandoned playground at the top of Pnei Kedem, and the children who do not play on it because the winds are too strong. The truth may be that architecture does not need ideology, that sometimes concrete becomes its own justification.

ACKNOWLEDGMENTS

I am grateful for the guidance, support, and friendship of many individuals and institutions without which this book would not have been written. I am especially thankful to Margaret Crawford, Greg Castillo, and the late Paul Rabinow, who provided rigorous criticism and friendly encouragement from the start, when this book was a dissertation project at the University of California, Berkeley. Their intellectual mentorship was invaluable. At Berkeley, I would also like to thank Yuval Ben-Bassat, Daniel Boyarin, Teresa Caldeira, the late Paul Groth, Andrew Shanken, and Jeffrey Skoller for the advice they provided at early stages of this research. At the Princeton-Mellon Initiative in Architecture, Urbanism, and the Humanities, where I was a fellow in 2018–2019, I thank Alison Isenberg, Mario Gandelsonas, Nasser Abourahme, Christine Boyer, Zachary Lamb, Aiala Levy, Aaron Shkuda, and Meredith TenHoor for their insightful feedback. My colleagues Eran Neuman and Ayala Ronel, at Tel Aviv University, provided a supportive environment during the last four years.

At various stages, I benefited from the feedback of multiple audiences. I presented sections of this book at meetings of the Society of Architectural Historians, the Vernacular Architecture Forum, the European Architectural History Network, and the Association for Art History; the Program in Judaic Studies, the School of Architecture and the Princeton-Mellon Initiative at Princeton University; the Center for Jewish Studies at Fordham University; the Urban Planning and Policy program at Hunter College; the Leibniz-Zentrum Moderner Orient; the Architecture Roundtable at UC Berkeley; the landscape architecture program at the University of Toronto; and the Interdisciplinary Program in the Arts and the David Azrieli School of Architecture at Tel Aviv University. On these occasions, I received insightful comments that enriched this manuscript from a number of scholars, including Ben Baruch Blich, Karen Burns, Georges Farhat, Ignacio G. Galán, Mohammad Gharipour, Ralph Ghoche, Philip Goad, Jaime Gómez, Janina Gosseye, Jonathan Gribetz, Joseph Heathcott, Farhan Karim, Kıvanç Kılınç, Roy Kozlovsky, Matthew G. Lasner, William Littmann, Talia Margalit, Daniel Monk, Alona Nitzan-Shiftan, Magda Teter, Paul Walker, and Stathis G. Yeros. No less important have been the conversations and feedback I received from other colleagues and friends: Fatina Abreek-Zubiedat, Eliana Abu-Hamdi, Shaked Afik, Amina Alkandari, Shaikha Al-Mubaraki, Menashe Anzi, Dorit Aviv, Roy Fisher, Giuseppina Forte, Anat Geva, Noam Gidron, Dana Gordon, Shai Gortler, Julia Grinkrug,

Micha Levin, Erez Maggor, Daniel Meir, Trine Mygind Korsby, Juliana Ochs Dweck, Thomas Oommen, Valentina Rozas-Krause, Avigail Sachs, Alberto Sanchez Sanchez, Naomi Simhony, Alec Stewart, Yotam Tsal, and Shira Wilkof. Saleem Al-Bahloly read and commented on the entire manuscript; I cannot imagine having a better friend and interlocutor.

At the University of Texas Press, Robert Devens has been especially supportive and accommodating. I am also indebted to the Lateral Exchanges series editors, Felipe Correa, Bruno Carvalho, and Alison Isenberg, for supporting the project; to Adrienne Gilg, who helped navigate the final steps before publication; and to copyeditor Nancy Warrington. Clare Wolfowitz also helped sharpen the text. Special thanks also go to the anonymous reviewers, whose thoughtful suggestions made this book so much better.

For their generous financial support of this project, I thank the Israel Institute, the Princeton-Mellon Initiative, Fordham and Columbia Universities, the Vernacular Architecture Forum, Tel Aviv University, the Ambassador J. Christopher Stevens Program for Middle Eastern Studies, the Center for Right-Wing Studies, the John L. Simpson Memorial Research Fellowship in International and Comparative Studies, and the Graduate Division at the University of California, Berkeley.

In addition, I am indebted to many archivists. The staff at the Israel State Archives, the Central Zionist Archives, the Jewish Agency for Israel Archives, Yad Tabenkin Archives, the Azrieli Architectural Archive, and the Avie and Sarah Arenson Built Heritage Research Center provided me with kind assistance. I am especially thankful to the staff at Ofra Archives, Alfe Menashe Archive, and the Gush Etzion Archives.

Equally important, I thank the many Israeli architects and urban planners who shared their memories and occasionally also their private collections of photographs and drawings with me: the late Arnona Axelrod, Elinoar Barzaki, David Cassuto, Gideon Charlap, Raphael Dankner, Zalman Deutch, Rita Dunsky-Feuerstein, Daniel Eyal, the late Eli First, Uzi Gdor, Lou Gelehrter, Israel Goodovitch, Haim Katseff, Gavriel Krien, the late Thomas Leitersdorf and Saadia Mandel, Moshe Margalith, Avishai Meiron, Bella Nudelman, Erol Paker, Yonatan Shiloni, Yossi Sivan, Rachel Walden, Karen Wainer, Aviv Yaar, Yaakov Yaar, and Uri Zerubavel. In the occupied West Bank, numerous Israeli settlers have shared their life stories and opened their houses and communities to me, despite our differences. I thank them for their time and patience. I also thank Alon Peled for explaining the intricacies of the Civil Administration to me.

Last but not least, I thank my family, whose love and support have always accompanied me, even when this project took me to places they would not want me to be.

APPENDIX: PLANNING, DESIGN, AND DEVELOPMENT AGENCIES MENTIONED IN THE BOOK

Amana: Gush Emunim's settling movement, founded in 1976. Like other settling movements (see below), Amana is mostly concerned with pragmatic matters such as the budgets and physical development of the settlements under its auspices. Although it was not the sole settling movement working in the West Bank, it has had a dominant role. In 1987, fifty-four settlements operated under its auspices, housing some 2,500 families.

Civil Administration in Judea and Samaria (informally, the Civil Administration): Headed by an Israeli military general, it was founded in 1981 to manage civilian affairs of both Palestinians and Israelis in the West Bank. Among other things, it manages state lands (through the Custodian for Government and Abandoned Property) and oversees planning procedures. It is home to the High Planning Council, the highest planning authority in Area C of the West Bank, which has responsibility for approving master plans for settlements.

Custodian for Government and Abandoned Property: An arm of the Civil Administration, it manages "state lands" and "absentees' lands" in the West Bank. It surveys ownership records, decides on the legal status of lands, and occasionally allocates lands for settlement construction.

Jewish National Fund: A nongovernmental organization founded in 1901 that purchased land in Palestine in the name of the Jewish people during the prestate era. After the Six-Day War, until 1979, it was the sole agency allowed to purchase lands in the West Bank for Israeli interests, using a subsidiary company, Himanuta. It had also been involved in developing land in the West Bank for settlement and infrastructure.

Joint Settlement Committee of the Israeli Government and the World Zionist Organization (also known as the Ministers Committee for Settlement): First convened in January 1970, it guided the establishment of new settlements in both Israel and the occupied territories. It decided on the location and type of new settlements and delegated their physical planning to official planning agencies.

Local council: An independent municipal entity created to manage the affairs of a local community. Local councils can grant building permits based on detailed plans and master plans (after approval by the regional council or by the High Planning Council, respectively). They cannot issue or make changes to master plans.

Ministry of Construction and Housing: A government ministry established in November 1961 as the Ministry of Housing and renamed in 1977 as the Ministry of Construction and Housing. Two of its arms played key roles in the settlement enterprise: (1) The Division of Rural Planning (founded in the late 1960s, transformed into the Rural Building and New Settlements Administration in 1975) was entrusted with detailed planning and construction of housing units and communal spaces in rural settlements, usually based on layout plans created by the Settlement Division. (2) The ministry's city planning units oversaw the planning of larger, more urban settlements in the West Bank. In the early years, the ministry usually employed in-house planners and architects; by the late 1970s, it began to outsource much of the planning process.

Movement for New Urban Settlements: A nongovernmental organization founded in 1975. It represented a number of Jewish settlements in the occupied territories, lobbying for them and overseeing their development. Under the leadership of Uzi Gdor, an Israeli urban planner, it played a significant role in developing the model of the community settlement. It stopped operating by 1977.

Private developers and private initiative settlements: In 1982, private development companies were granted the right to establish Jewish settlements in the West Bank, using mostly private funds. Developers enjoyed some government support, usually in the form of infrastructure installation and the construction of public buildings. They were allowed to purchase lands and to work with architects of their choice.

Regional councils: There are six regional councils in the West Bank. Each governs a number of small settlements (each with its own local committee). The regional council is entrusted with approving detailed plans for settlements within its area of jurisdiction.

Settlement Department of the Jewish Agency (or the Settlement Department): A nongovernmental organization affiliated with the Jewish Agency, a key political institution during the British Mandate period. It planned scores of rural settlements in Israel immediately following independence, training their residents in agricultural work and offering them favorable loans. Although not officially involved in the West Bank, Settlement Department staff played important roles in planning West Bank settlements, working under the guise (and budget) of the Settlement Division.

Settlement Division of the World Zionist Organization (or the Settlement Division): Founded in 1971, it plans and develops rural settlements in the West Bank for Israeli settlers. It acts as an arm of the World Zionist Organization, a nongovernmental organization founded in 1897 to promote Jewish nationalism, originally named the Zionist Organization. The Settlement Division's funding comes from the state budget. Much of its work was contracted out to the Settlement Department until the early 1990s.

Settling movements: Umbrella organizations devoted to creating settlements in Israel and the West Bank. Each is aligned with an Israeli political movement and is usually responsible for a number of rural settlements: recruiting residents, overseeing the development of each settlement, and representing it vis-à-vis settlement authorities. To settle, a settlement group (or "seed") usually needs to be associated with a settling movement.

Yesha Council: An umbrella settlers' association founded in 1979 by Gush Emunim activists. (Yesha is an acronym for Judea, Samaria, and Gaza.) Although it is not directly involved in planning and design, the Yesha Council advocates and mobilizes to pressure decision makers to install infrastructure and expand settlement activity.

NOTES

INTRODUCTION

1. According to Peace Now, an NGO that monitors West Bank settlements, there are 132 settlements the Israeli government authorized and 147 settlements it did not authorize. Peace Now estimates that in 2021, settlements housed 465,400 Israelis, living next to 2,816,004 Palestinians (not including East Jerusalem). The Israeli Central Bureau of Statistics lists the same number of settlers. According to the Yesha Council, however, in early 2022 there were 491,923 settlers living in some 150 settlements. See "Population" (Peace Now, 2021), https://peacenow.org.il/settlements-watch/matzav /population; "Population by District, Sub-District and Religion" (Central Bureau of Statistics, September 15, 2022); "Do"h Netunei Uhlusiya Beyehuda Shomron Vebik'at Hayarden—Nahon Leyanuar 2022" (Yesha Council, March 6, 2022), http://myesha .org.il/?CategoryID=335&ArticleID=10249.

2. Meirav Moran, " 'Ele Hitnahaluyot? Ze Retzef Hole Shel Parvarim Amerikaim Shemahriv Et Atzmo,' " *Haaretz*, March 31, 2021, https://www.haaretz.co.il/magazine /.premium.HIGHLIGHT-MAGAZINE-1.9671136. Unless otherwise noted, all translations are my own.

3. "The Architecture of Violence," *Rebel Architecture* (Al Jazeera English), September 2, 2014, https://www.youtube.com/watch?v=ybwJaCeeA9o. Weizman has made a relatively similar statement in an essay he coauthored with Alessandro Petti and Sandi Hilal, stating: "There are hundreds of thousands of Israeli-built structures in the West Bank, but . . . the number of typologies in settlements and military bases are limited—variations on the single-family dwelling in settlements and concrete prefabricated barracks on military bases." This statement also appears on the website of Decolonizing Architecture Art Research (DAAR), an architectural collective Weizman cofounded with Petti and Hilal. See Alessandro Petti, Sandi Hilal, and Eyal Weizman, "The Morning After: Profaning Colonial Architecture," in *Sensible Politics: The Visual Culture of Nongovernmental Activism*, ed. Meg McLagan and Yates McKee (Brooklyn, NY: Zone Books, 2012), 456–457; Decolonizing Architecture Art Research, "Jabel Tawil/P'sagot—Introduction," *Decolonizing Architecture Art Research* (blog), accessed September 1, 2021, http://www.decolonizing.ps/site /introduction/. Elsewhere, in support of this statement, Petti, Hilal, and Weizman added: "Investigating ways to transform this repetitive semi-generic structure [the single-family house] may open up ways to transform the entire geography of occupation." See Alessandro Petti, Sandi Hilal, and Eyal Weizman, *Architecture after Revolution* (Berlin: Sternberg Press, 2013), 116. In his earlier writings, Weizman acknowledged the existence of several "settlement typologies." See, for example, Rafi Segal and Eyal Weizman, "The Mountain," in *A Civilian Occupation: The Politics of Israeli Architecture*, rev. ed., ed. Rafi Segal and Eyal Weizman (Tel Aviv: Babel; London and New York: Verso, 2003), 80–82.

4. The interpretation of settlements' design as a reflection of a quick land grab is popular among religious Zionist settlers, particularly second-generation settlers. Time

and again, my informants in Pnei Kedem (and elsewhere) would lament previous settlements' disregard for design. This complaint was also aired in the media. See, for example, Moran, " 'Ele Hitnahaluyot?' "; Daniel Shalit, "Amhe"l," *Nekuda*, July 1992, 14–15. It should be noted that land seizure has indeed been key to the Israeli occupation. As I mention in note 41 of this introduction, Israel claimed vast lands in the West Bank as "state lands." However, the built-up area of the settlements takes a small portion of these. In 2012, according to the political commentator Shaul Arieli, the main "settlement blocks," housing 85 percent of the settlers, occupied less than 6 percent of the West Bank's lands. The built-up area of settlements built outside these "settlement blocks" occupied less than 0.4 percent. In other words, as the sociologist Erez Maggor has noted, although land seizure is a prerequisite for the construction of settlements, it cannot fully explain the settlements. Nor can it fully explain their design. See Shaul Arieli, "Lehipared Misheker Hahitnahaluyot," *Haaretz*, October 3, 2012, https://www.haaretz.co.il/opinions/1.1834490; Erez Maggor, "State, Market and the Israeli Settlements: The Ministry of Housing and the Shift from Messianic Outposts to Urban Settlements in the Early 1980s" [in Hebrew], *Israeli Sociology* 16, no. 2 (2015): 146.

5. See, for example, "The Architecture of Violence"; Petti, Hilal, and Weizman, "The Morning After," 459; Segal and Weizman, "The Mountain," 84–87.

6. Yiram Netanyahu, Shlifot im Noam Arnon, *NRG Maariv*, June 6, 2006, https://www.makorrishon.co.il/nrg/online/1/ART1/431/330.html.

7. The Israeli Central Bureau of Statistics defines community settlements as non-agricultural settlements of no more than 2,000 residents who are organized as a cooperative union. In Ofra, however, there were 3,012 residents in 2020. "Thunot Demografiyot—Hagdarot Vehesberim" (Central Bureau of Statistics), accessed October 27, 2021, https://www.cbs.gov.il/he/subjects/Pages/%D7%AA%D7%A4%D7%A8%D7%95%D7%A1%D7%AA-%D7%92%D7%90%D7%95%D7%92%D7%A8%D7%A4%D7%99%D7%AA-%D7%94%D7%92%D7%93%D7%A8%D7%95%D7%AA-%D7%95%D7%94%D7%A1%D7%91%D7%A8%D7%99%D7%9D.aspx; "Regional Statistics: Ofra" (Central Bureau of Statistics, 2020), https://www.cbs.gov.il/he/settlements/Pages/default.aspx?mode=Yeshuv.

8. Aharon Halamish, "Habniya—Vehabe'aya Hayehudit," *Nekuda*, November 14, 1980, 7.

9. I discuss religious Zionism in greater detail in chapters 1 and 2. For now, however, it should be noted that religious Zionists are not a monolith. Various subgroups (and conflicts) exist within religious Zionism. On different theological views among religious Zionist settlers, see Assaf Harel, "Beyond Gush Emunim: On Contemporary Forms of Messianism among Religiously Motivated Settlers in the West Bank," in *Normalizing Occupation: The Politics of Everyday Life in the West Bank Settlements*, ed. Marco Allegra, Ariel Handel, and Erez Maggor (Bloomington: Indiana University Press, 2017). By 2023, a few apartment buildings were built in Ofra.

10. On the number of religious Zionists in Israel and why it is difficult to estimate their number, see Nissim Leon, "Self-Segregation of the Vanguard: Judea and Samaria in the Religious-Zionist Society," *Israel Affairs* 21, no. 3 (July 3, 2015): 348–360; Tamar Hermann et al., *The National-Religious Sector in Israel 2014* [in Hebrew] (Jerusalem: Israel Democracy Institute, 2014), 23–45; Yoav Peled and Horit Herman Peled, *The Religionization of Israeli Society* (London: Routledge, 2020), 53-56. It

is also difficult to estimate the exact number of religious Zionists in the West Bank. Some of them live in "mixed" settlements alongside secular Israelis. Some oscillate between secular and religious lifestyles. In 2015, only 100,000 of the then 380,000 settlers resided in explicitly religious Zionist settlements. According to a 2002 study by Peace Now, 40 percent of West Bank settlers identified as religious Zionists. In a report conducted by Pew Research Center in 2016, 36 percent of the settlers identified as religious (but not ultra-Orthodox or "traditional"). Similarly, according to the Yesha Council, 36 percent of the settlers were religious Zionists by the end of 2020. These estimates do not include Israeli settlers living in neighborhoods built in East Jerusalem. See Yotam Berger, "Mifkad Hamitnahalim," *Haaretz*, June 9, 2017, Nadav Shragai, "Seker 'Shalom Ahshav,'" *Haaretz*, July 25, 2002, 3A; Pew Research Center, *Israel's Religiously Divided Society* (Washington: Pew Research Center, 2016), 37; "Netunei Uchlusiyat Yehuda, Shomron Vebikat Hayarden Beshnat 2020" (The Yesha Council, January 21, 2021), http://myesha.org.il/?CategoryID=335&ArticleID=10135.

11. Uri Yavlonka, "Ahuzot Al Hagva'ot," *Maariv*, September 3, 2004. The Israeli author Nir Baram published a book describing his journey through the West Bank in 2016. The book's title, *In a Land Beyond the Mountains*, resonates with Levy's observation. Nir Baram, *In a Land Beyond the Mountains* [in Hebrew] (Tel Aviv: Am Oved, 2016).

12. To protect the anonymity of Akiva, Esti, Shani and Yotam (whom I mention in the following paragraph), their names are pseudonyms.

13. Danny Gutwein, "The Settlements and the Relationship between Privatization and Occupation," in *Normalizing Occupation: The Politics of Everyday Life in the West Bank Settlements*, ed. Marco Allegra, Ariel Handel, and Erez Maggor (Bloomington: Indiana University Press, 2017); Danny Gutwein, "He'arot al Hayesodot Hamaamadiyim Shel Hakibush," *Theory and Criticism* 24 (Spring 2004): 203–211.

14. On the evolution of "unauthorized outposts" and how government support reaches them despite their illegality, see Talia Sasson, "Havat Da'at (Beynayim) Benose Maahazim Bilti Hukiyim" (Office of the Prime Minister, 2005).

15. See, for example, Michel Foucault, "Space, Knowledge, and Power," interview by Paul Rabinow, in *The Foucault Reader*, ed. Paul Rabinow (Penguin Books, 1984), 245–247 and 255; Gwendolyn Wright, *The Politics of Design in French Colonial Urbanism* (Chicago: University of Chicago Press, 1991), 312; Gwendolyn Wright, "Cultural History: Europeans, Americans, and the Meanings of Space," *Journal of the Society of Architectural Historians* 64, no. 4 (December 2005): 436–440; Gevork Hartoonian, "An Interview with Mary McLeod," *Architectural Theory Review* 7, no. 1 (April 2002): 66–67 and 76, https://doi.org/10.1080/13264820209478445; Lawrence J. Vale, *Architecture, Power, and National Identity*, 2nd ed. (London: Routledge, 2008), ix.

16. Settlements contravene the ban prohibiting an occupying power from transferring its civilians to the occupied territory. The ban is stated in Article 49 of the Fourth Geneva Convention Relative to the Protection of Civilian Persons in Times of War. Israel, however, considers most settlements founded by the 1990s as legal. See Orna Ben-Naftali, Michael Sfard, and Hedi Viterbo, *The ABC of the OPT: A Legal Lexicon of the Israeli Control over the Occupied Palestinian Territory* (Cambridge: Cambridge University Press, 2018), 200–217.

17. On the semantic differences between these terms and their respective levels of moral legitimacy, see Joyce Dalsheim and Assaf Harel, "Representing Settlers," *Review of*

Middle East Studies 43, no. 2 (Winter 2009): 230; Joyce Dalsheim, *Unsettling Gaza: Secular Liberalism, Radical Religion, and the Israeli Settlement Project* (Oxford: Oxford University Press, 2011), 24.

18. On agricultural settlement forms Zionists developed in the prestate era, see S. Ilan Troen, *Imagining Zion: Dreams, Designs, and Realities in a Century of Jewish Settlement* (New Haven, CT: Yale University Press, 2003), 3–81.

19. On Labor Zionist parties' preference for the kibbutz and the moshav, see Erik Cohen, *The City in the Zionist Ideology* (Jerusalem: Hebrew University, Institute of Urban and Regional Studies, 1970), 1–9.

20. Yael Zerubavel, *Recovered Roots: Collective Memory and the Making of Israeli National Tradition* (Chicago: University of Chicago Press, 1995), 29. On the longer history of the term *yishuv* and why it gained traction in the early twentieth century, see Yair Wallach, "Rethinking the *Yishuv*: Late-Ottoman Palestine's Jewish Communities Revisited," *Journal of Modern Jewish Studies* 16, no. 2 (May 4, 2017): 282–285, https://doi.org/10.1080/14725886.2016.1246230.

21. On how the legacy of Zionist settlement activity continued to inform Israelis, especially in the aftermath of the Six-Day War, see Gershom Gorenberg, *The Accidental Empire: Israel and the Birth of the Settlements, 1967–1977* (New York: Times Books, 2006).

22. Tom Segev, "Review: A Bitter Prize: Israel and the Occupied Territories," *Foreign Affairs* 85, no. 3 (2006): 149, https://doi.org/10.2307/20031975; Aharon Kellerman, *Society and Settlement: Jewish Land of Israel in the Twentieth Century*, SUNY Series in Israeli Studies (Albany: State University of New York Press, 1993), 27–28. According to the sociologist Gershon Shafir, most Zionist colonizers sought, at first, to settle across Palestine. Their willingness to make territorial concessions—and, by extension, to secure Jewish majority—evolved over time and was largely the result of economic concerns. See Gershon Shafir, "Karka, Avoda Veuchlusiya Bakolonizatziya Hatziyonit: Heibetim Klaliyim Veyihudiyim," in *Israeli Society: Critical Perspectives*, ed. Uri Ram (Tel Aviv: Breirot, 1993), 114–115.

23. Troen, *Imagining Zion*, 70–71; Kellerman, *Society and Settlement*, 9–10, 28. While Jews were settling in the coastal plains and valleys, it should be noted, Muslims were also settling in these regions. See Seth J. Frantzman and Ruth Kark, "The Muslim Settlement of Late Ottoman and Mandatory Palestine: Comparison with Jewish Settlement Patterns," *Digest of Middle East Studies* 22, no. 1 (Spring 2013): 74–93, https://doi.org/10.1111/j.1949-3606.2012.00172.x.

24. Benny Morris, *1948: A History of the First Arab-Israeli War* (New Haven, CT: Yale University Press, 2008), 396; Arie M. Dubnov and Laura Robson, "Introduction," in *Partitions: A Transnational History of Twentieth-Century Territorial Separatism*, ed. Arie M. Dubnov and Laura Robson (Stanford, CA: Stanford University Press, 2019), 12.

25. "Divrei Haknesset: Hayeshiva Ha'esrim shel Haknesset Harishona," April 4, 1949, 807, The Knesset, https://fs.knesset.gov.il/1/Plenum/1_ptm_250098.pdf.

26. On the events leading to the Six-Day War and how the fighting progressed, see Avi Shlaim, *The Iron Wall: Israel and the Arab World* (New York: Norton, 2000), 236–250; Avi Shlaim, "Israel: Poor Little Samson," in *The 1967 Arab-Israeli War: Origins and Consequences*, ed. William Roger Louis and Avi Shlaim (Cambridge and New York: Cambridge University Press, 2012), 22–55, https://doi.org/10.1017/CBO9780511751431.

27. According to the historian Zeev Sternhell, the commitment of that Zionist leadership to socialism was skin-deep and secondary to nationalism. See Zeev Sternhel, *The Founding Myths of Israel: Nationalism, Socialism, and the Making of the Jewish State* (Princeton, NJ: Princeton University Press, 1999).

28. Religious Zionist parliament members, for instance, were rarely involved in foreign policy decisions. Meanwhile, Mizrahim constituted 40 percent of the population in 1960, but made up less than 10 percent of the Knesset's members. Ari Shavit, *A New Israeli Republic* [in Hebrew] (Rishon LeTsiyon, Israel: Yedioth Ahronoth Books, 2021), 29.

29. Small protests of Mizrahi Jews took place already in the 1950s. In 1971, with the founding of the Black Panthers, a protest group named after the American movement, they became significantly more vocal.

30. Lee Cahaner, Nikola Yozgof-Orbach, and Arnon Soffer, *Haharedim Beyisrael: Merhav, Hevra, Kehila* (Haifa: University of Haifa, 2012), 33.

31. Gilad Malach and Lee Cahaner, "Statistical Report on Ultra-Orthodox Society in Israel 2020" [in Hebrew] (Jerusalem: Israel Democracy Institute, 2020), 11.

32. On experimentation in social and spatial forms in the French colonies, see Wright, *The Politics of Design in French Colonial Urbanism*; Paul Rabinow, *French Modern: Norms and Forms of the Social Environment* (Chicago: University of Chicago Press, 1995).

33. Dan Horowitz and Moshe Lissak, "Authority without Sovereignty: The Case of the National Centre of the Jewish Community in Palestine," *Government and Opposition* 8, no. 1 (1973): 48.

34. A leasehold system was already instituted in the prestate era. It was applied to lands purchased by the Jewish National Fund. On how the Israeli leasehold system evolved from the early twentieth century to the early statehood period, see Jacob Metzer, "Land Regimes in Nation-Building Processes and Nation-States: The Case of Israel in Comparative Perspective," in *Nationalism and the Economy: Explorations into a Neglected Relationship*, ed. Stefan Berger and Thomas Fetzer (Budapest and New York: Central European University Press, 2019), 101–107. After independence, three bodies owned national lands: the State of Israel, the Jewish National Fund, and the Development Authority. Together they owned the vast majority of land in the country. In subsequent decades, land has only been leased to Israelis. In 2002, only 7 percent of the country's total land was privately owned. On Israel's leasehold system and how it had gradually come to accommodate private market needs, see Rachelle Alterman, "The Land of Leaseholds: Israel's Extensive Public Land-Ownership in an Era of Privatization," in *Leasing Public Land: Policy Debates and International Experiences*, ed. Steven C. Bourassa and Yu-Hung Hong (Cambridge, MA: Lincoln Institute of Land Policy, 2003); Amiram Gonen, *Between City and Suburb: Urban Residential Patterns and Processes in Israel* (Aldershot, UK: Avebury, 1995), 57. Nationalizing vast lands was a prerequisite for launching a massive housing project and for dispersing the population. According to the legal scholar Haim Sandberg, however, keeping these vast lands in public hands also speaks to a three-fold goal: to emphasize the connection between the Jewish people and the Land of Israel, hinder its transfer to foreigners, and, to a certain degree, advance equality among citizens. See Haim Sandberg, *Land Law and Policy in Israel: A Prism of Identity*, Perspectives on Israel Studies (Bloomington: Indiana University Press, 2022), 45–71.

35. At first, newcomers rented the units at subsidized rates. Most units were eventually sold to the migrants, who enjoyed subsidies and generous mortgages. Hadas Shadar, *Avnei Habinyan shel Hashikun Hatsiburi: Shisha Asorim shel Beniyah Ironit Beyozmah Tsiburit Beyisrael* (Tel Aviv: Ministry of Construction and Housing, 2014), 40–41.

36. The Israeli new towns had another goal that proved unnecessary: providing urban services for agricultural villages. Kellerman, *Society and Settlement*, 73, 78–79. Regardless, it should be noted that the Israeli new towns policy grew out of an international trend that originated in Great Britain and gained force in the postwar years in various countries, including Sweden, France, and Finland. Troen, *Imagining Zion*, 187–189.

37. Haim Drabkin-Darin, "Megamot Kalkaliyot Vehevratiyot shel Hashikun Beyisrael Betkufat Ha'asor," in *Hashikun Hatziburi: Skirot Veha'arahot al Hashikun Hatziburi Beyisrael Betkufat Ha'asor 1948–1958*, ed. Haim Drabkin-Darin (Tel Aviv: Sifrei Gadish, 1959), 25.

38. On 1950s public housing projects in Israel and how they grew out of state-led, top-down efforts, see Rachel Kallus and Hubert Law-Yone, "Habayit Hale'umi Vehabayit Ha'ishi: Tafkid Hashikun Hatziburi Be'itzuv Hamerhav," in *Space, Land, Home*, ed. Yehouda Shenhav (Jerusalem: Van Leer Institute, 2003), 166–193.

39. Patrick Wolfe, *Settler Colonialism and the Transformation of Anthropology: The Politics and Poetics of an Ethnographic Event*, Writing Past Colonialism Series (London: Cassell, 1999), 163; Patrick Wolfe, "Settler Colonialism and the Elimination of the Native," *Journal of Genocide Research* 8, no. 4 (December 2006): 388, https://doi.org/10.1080/14623520601056240.

40. On government debates concerning the West Bank in the aftermath of the Six-Day War, see Shlaim, *The Iron Wall*, 250–258. Also see chapter 1 of this book.

41. By 1992, Israel declared some 25 percent of West Bank lands as "state lands" (i.e., public lands). Prior to the 1967 war, there were only 527,000 dunams (1 dunam = 1,000 square meters) of "state lands" in the West Bank. By 1992, Israel tripled that amount to 1.44 million dunams. Between 1992 and 1997, Israel claimed no more "state lands." There are no data about lands claimed between 1997 and 2002. Between 2003 and 2009, Israel declared 5,114 more dunams as "state lands." In addition, between 1967 and 1979, Israeli authorities captured 31,000 dunams via military orders. See Arieli, "Lehipared Misheker Hahitnahaluyot"; Maggor, "State, Market," 146; Nir Shalev, *Beetztala Shel Hukiyut: Hahrazot Al Admot Medina Bagada Hamaaravit* (Jerusalem: B'Tselem [NGO], February 2012), 11–12, https://www.btselem.org/download/201203_under_the_guise_of_legality_heb.pdf.

42. See, for example, Teresa Pires do Rio Caldeira, *City of Walls: Crime, Segregation, and Citizenship in São Paulo* (Berkeley: University of California Press, 2000); John Leighton Chase, Margaret Crawford, and John Kaliski, eds., *Everyday Urbanism*, expanded ed. (New York: Monacelli Press, 2008); Jennifer Mack, *The Construction of Equality: Syriac Immigration and the Swedish City* (Minneapolis: University of Minnesota Press, 2017).

43. In 1997, a military order defined West Bank settlements as areas closed off to Palestinian residents of the West Bank. Dror Etkes, A Locked Garden: Declaration of Closed Areas in the West Bank (Jerusalem: Kerem Navot, March 2015), 51–53. In 2020, a few hundred Palestinians holding Israeli citizenship ("Israeli Arab") resided

in settlements (not including East Jerusalem). "Kovetz Hayeshuvim 2020" (Central Bureau of Statistics, Israel, August 2021), https://www.cbs.gov.il/he/publications /Pages/2019/%D7%99%D7%99%D7%A9%D7%95%D7%91%D7%99%D7 %9D-%D7%91%D7%99%D7%A9%D7%A8%D7%90%D7%9C.aspx. A larger number of Palestinians, with an Israeli citizenship or a Jerusalem Residency Certificate, was recorded in Israeli-built settlements in East Jerusalem. See Wendy Pullan and Haim Yacobi, "Jerusalem's Colonial Space as Paradox: Palestinians Living in the Settlements," in *Normalizing Occupation: The Politics of Everyday Life in the West Bank Settlements*, ed. Marco Allegra, Ariel Handel, and Erez Maggor (Bloomington: Indiana University Press, 2017).

44. Dan Horowitz, "Before the State: Communal Politics in Palestine under the Mandate," in *The Israeli State and Society: Boundaries and Frontiers*, ed. Baruch Kimmerling, SUNY Series in Israeli Studies (Albany: State University of New York Press, 1989), 29; Troen, *Imagining Zion*, 50.

45. Moran Azoulay, "Netanyahu Yehalek et Bet Shemesh? 'Degel Lavan Lara'ayon Hatziyoni,'" *Ynet*, December 28, 2011, https://www.ynet.co.il/articles/0,7340,L-4167910,00 .html; Shai Pausner, "Netanyahu Mahye et Ra'ayon Halukat Bet Shemesh," *Calcalist*, March 1, 2012, https://www.calcalist.co.il/real_estate/articles/0,7340,L-3563862,00 .html.

46. On how the segregated nature of the community settlement model shelters religious Zionists from secularization processes, see Leon, "Self-Segregation of the Vanguard," 356–357.

47. Mack, *The Construction of Equality*.

48. Troen, *Imagining Zion*, 149.

49. Yaacov Yaar, *Life and Architecture* (Haifa: Architectural and Landscape Heritage Research Center, The Faculty of Architecture and Town Planning, The Technion, 2016), 199, 230.

50. Rita Dunsky-Feuerstein, phone interview by author, December 15, 2015.

51. On a petition by Architects and Planners for Justice in Palestine (APJP) urging Israeli architects to avoid working on projects that involve seizing Palestinian lands, see "Campaigners Urge Israeli Architects Not to Design 'Illegal' Settlements," *Architects' Journal*, May 24, 2007. On a petition drafted by Israeli architects, see Noam Shoked, "'This Is the Hour': When Architects Protest," *PLATFORM*, April 26, 2021, https:// www.platformspace.net/home/this-is-the-hour-when-architects-protest. On APJP's attempts to pressure the International Union of Architects to suspend the Israeli association (via the Royal Institute of British Architects), see Abe Hayeem, "RIBA Votes to Suspend Israeli Architects' Association from International Body," APJP, March 20, 2014, http://apjp.org/riba-votes-to-suspend-israeli/; Naama Riba, "Irgun Haadrihalim Habriti Kore Lehahrim et Haamuta Hayisraelit," *Xnet*, March 2014, https://xnet.ynet.co.il/architecture/articles/0,14710,L-3105239,00.html.

52. Rafi Segal and Eyal Weizman, "Introduction," in *A Civilian Occupation: The Politics of Israeli Architecture*, ed. Rafi Segal and Eyal Weizman, rev. ed. (Tel Aviv: Babel; London and New York: Verso, 2003), 25; Eyal Weizman, "The Evil Architects Do," in *Content: Triumph of Realization*, ed. Rem Koolhaas and Brendan McGetrick (Cologne: Taschen, 2004), 60–63.

53. On the first wave of scholarship on settlements and its focus on Gush Emunim and strategic considerations, see Dalsheim and Harel, "Representing Settlers"; Marco

Allegra, Ariel Handel, and Erez Maggor, "Introduction: The Politics of Everyday Life in the West Bank Settlements," in *Normalizing Occupation: The Politics of Everyday Life in the West Bank Settlements*, ed. Marco Allegra, Ariel Handel, and Erez Maggor (Bloomington: Indiana University Press, 2017), 1–18. Important exceptions to this rule include the work of the geographers Juval Portugali and David Newman, who analyzed settlement expansion as part of the metropolitan expansion of Tel Aviv and Jerusalem, as well as Meron Benvenisti, who emphasized the role played by government subsidies in attracting Israelis without ideology to settlements. See Juval Portugali, "Jewish Settlement in the Occupied Territories: Israel's Settlement Structure and the Palestinians," *Political Geography Quarterly* 10, no. 1 (January 1991): 26–53, https://doi.org/10.1016/0260-9827(91)90025-P; Meron Benvenisti, *1986 Report: Demographic, Economic, Legal, Social and Political Developments in the West Bank* (Jerusalem: Jerusalem Post, 1986).

54. See, for example, Gutwein, "The Settlements"; Maggor, "State, Market"; Sara Yael Hirschhorn, *City on a Hilltop: American Jews and the Israeli Settler Movement* (Cambridge, MA, and London: Harvard University Press, 2017); Hadas Weiss, "Immigration and West Bank Settlement Normalization," *PoLar: Political and Legal Anthropology Review* 34, no. 1 (May 2011): 112–130; Rivi Gillis, "The Question of Ethnic Identity in the Israeli Settlements" [in Hebrew], *Theory and Criticism* 47 (Winter 2016): 41–62.

55. Paul Groth, "Frameworks for Cultural Landscape Study," in *Understanding Ordinary Landscapes*, ed. Paul Groth and Todd W. Bressi (New Haven, CT: Yale University Press, 1997), 1.

56. According to Shaul Arieli, by the end of 2020, there were 7,618 settlers living in twenty-six settlements in the valleys along the Jordan River and north of the Dead Sea, making up about 1.6 percent of West Bank settlers. According to a Peace Now report that was published in March 2020, however, there were 12,788 settlers living in the area. In either case, as Udi Dekel and Noa Shusterman argue, it housed less than 3 percent of the settlers. Shaul Arieli, "Hamitnahalim Hozrim Habayta Leyisrael," *Haaretz*, August 19, 2021, https://www.haaretz.co.il/opinions/.premium-1 .10132723; "Habniya Behitnahaluyot Be'ezor Habik'a Beshnat 2019" (Peace Now, March 18, 2020), https://peacenow.org.il/construction-in-jordan-valley-2019; Udi Dekel and Noa Shusterman, "Annexation of the West Bank: Where Does It Lead?" (Institute for National Security Studies, June 14, 2020), https://www.inss.org.il /publication/annexation-convention-summary/.

57. On the design of the settlement of Yamit in the Sinai Peninsula, see Fatina Abreek-Zubiedat, "Architecture in Conflict beyond the Green Line: Gaza and Yamit Cities 1967–1982" (PhD diss., Haifa, Technion—Israel Institute of Technology, 2018), esp. 229–273.

58. Scholarship has sufficiently addressed the design and evolution of Jerusalem under Israeli rule. Notable here is Alona Nitzan-Shiftan's groundbreaking work on the construction boom in East Jerusalem during the first decade following the Six-Day War. See Alona Nitzan-Shiftan, *Seizing Jerusalem: The Architectures of Unilateral Unification* (Minneapolis: University of Minnesota Press, 2017); Alona Nitzan-Shiftan, "Seizing Locality in Jerusalem," in *The End of Tradition*, ed. Nezar AlSayyad (London and New York: Routledge, 2004), 231–255; Alona Nitzan-Shiftan, "Frontier Jerusalem: The Holy Land as a Testing Ground for Urban Design," *Journal of Architecture*

16, no. 6 (2011): 915–940; Shira Wilkof and Alona Nitzan-Shiftan, "'An Historical Opportunity': Landscape, Statism and Competition in the Creation and Planning of the Walls of Jerusalem National Park, 1967" [in Hebrew], *Cathedra* 163 (May 2017): 163–190. On the impact of the Israeli-Palestinian conflict on everyday life in an Israeli housing estate in East Jerusalem, see Rachel Kallus, "The Political Role of the Everyday," *City* 8, no. 3 (December 2004): 341–361.

59. On the possibilities and blockages faced by Israelis studying Palestinians under Israeli occupation, see Ariel Handel and Ruthie Ginsburg, "Israelis Studying the Occupation: An Introduction," *Critical Inquiry* 44, no. 2 (Winter 2018): 331–342, https://doi .org/10.1086/695362.

CHAPTER 1: URBAN TRANSPLANTS

1. Zehava Nativ, "Sipura Ha'ishi shel Mishpaha Mitnahelet," in *Kiryat Arba Hee Hevron: Kovetz Ma'amarim Vetmunot Bemeliat Asor Lehidush Hayeshuv Hayehudi Behevron*, ed. Moshe Ozeri (Hebron: Minhelet Kiryat Arba, 1978).

2. Gershon Nativ, "Qiriat Arba : Una Scelta," in *Quest'anno a Gerusalemme: Gli Ebrei Italiani in Israele*, ed. Angelo Pezzana, Collana Storica 25 (Milan: Corbaccio, 1997), 118-121.

3. Yossef Tzuriel, "Bekiryat-Arba Sha'alu: 'Ha'im Zo Hadereh Lehehaletz Mehagetto?,'" *Maariv*, December 16, 1979, 3.

4. Elisha Efrat, *Judea and Samaria: Guidelines for Regional and Physical Planning* (Jerusalem: Ministry of Interior, Planning Department, 1970), xiii. For Efrat's reflection on the gap stretching between the planning guidelines drafted in the immediate years after the Six-Day War and what ultimately was built in the West Bank, see Elisha Efrat, *Geography of Occupation: Judea, Samaria and the Gaza Strip* [in Hebrew] (Jerusalem: Carmel, 2002), 28–29.

5. Efrat, *Judea and Samaria*, xii–xiii. On Jordan's neglect of the West Bank, also see Zev Vilnay, *Yehuda Veshomron* (Tel Aviv: Sifriyat Hasade, 1968), 3.

6. Efrat, *Judea and Samaria*, xxvii–xxix.

7. For estimates of the number of Palestinians who fled the West Bank during and right after the 1967 war, see Efrat, *Geography of Occupation*, 17; William Wilson Harris, *Taking Root: Israeli Settlement in the West Bank, the Golan, and Gaza-Sinai, 1967–1980*, Geographical Research Studies Series 1 (Chichester, UK: Research Studies Press, 1980), 17–24; Tom Segev, *Israel in 1967* [in Hebrew] (Jerusalem: Keter, 2005), 431. According to the geographer Zev Vilnay, in 1961, there were 805,450 people living in the West Bank. Vilnay, *Yehuda Veshomron*, 3. On the eve of the Six-Day War, according to William Harris, there were about 840,000 people living in the West Bank. Harris, *Taking Root*, 7. After the war, according to census data Israel collected in 1967, there were some 600,000 Palestinians in the West Bank. See Efrat, *Judea and Samaria*, 87.

8. The tribe of Judah, one of the twelve tribes of the ancient Israelites, settled in the southern areas of the West Bank (and parts of Israel) in the thirteenth century BCE. King David made Jerusalem the capital of the Israelite state in the tenth century. Yohanan Aharoni, *Eretz Israel in Biblical Times: A Geographical History* [in Hebrew], rev. ed. (Jerusalem: Yad Izhak Ben-Zvi, 1987), 171–172 and 226.

9. Aharoni, *Eretz Israel in Biblical Times*, 257.

10. Benny Morris, *Righteous Victims: A History of the Zionist-Arab Conflict, 1881–2001* (New York: Vintage Books, 2001), 4; Morris, *1948*, 2.

11. On fears of the impending conflict, shared by many Israelis in 1967, see Segev, *Israel in 1967*, 302–307.

12. Oded Avishar, *Sefer Hevron: Ir Haavot Veyeshuvah Beryi Hadorot* (Jerusalem: Keter, 1970), 468; Tzvi Lavie, "Mohammad Ali Jaber Honeh et Hado'ar Hashlishi Betoldotav," *Maariv*, July 10, 1967.

13. On tours Israelis took to the West Bank in the months following the Six-Day War, see Tom Segev, *1967: Israel, the War, and the Year That Transformed the Middle East* (New York: Metropolitan Books, 2007), 424–429.

14. Gadi Taub, *The Settlers: And the Struggle over the Meaning of Zionism* (New Haven, CT: Yale University Press, 2010), 37–38; Aviezer Ravitzky, *Messianism, Zionism, and Jewish Religious Radicalism* (Chicago: University of Chicago Press, 1996).

15. See Shlomo Avineri, "Zionism and the Jewish Religious Tradition: The Dialectics of Redemption and Secularization," in *Zionism and Religion*, ed. Shmuel Almog, Jehuda Reinharz, and Anita Shapira (Hanover, NH: University Press of New England, 1998), 3–4; Yosef Salmon, "Zionism and Anti-Zionism in Traditional Judaism in Eastern Europe," in Almog, Reinharz, and Shapira, *Zionism and Religion*, 29; Taub, *The Settlers*, 37–41; Eli Holzer, *A Double-Edged Sword: Military Activism in the Thought of Religious Zionism* [in Hebrew] (Jerusalem: Shalom Hartman Institute, 2009), 63–87.

16. See Gideon Aran, *Kookism: The Roots of Gush Emunim, Jewish Settlers' Sub-Culture, Zionist Theology, Contemporary Messianism* [in Hebrew] (Jerusalem: Carmel, 2013), 73–87.

17. See Taub, *The Settlers*, 41–46; Aran, *Kookism*, 178–265.

18. Taub, *The Settlers*, 41–46.

19. Gorenberg, *The Accidental Empire*, 22.

20. Taub, *The Settlers*, 42–43.

21. Dov Goldstein, "Lo Nevater al Shum Shaal!," *Maariv*, August 31, 1967, 11.

22. In 1967, the movement circulated a petition signed by poets such as Nathan Alterman, Uri Zvi Greenberg, and Haim Gouri. See Hatenua Lemaan Eretz Yisrael Hashlema, "Lema'an Eretz Yisrael Hashlema," *Maariv*, September 9, 1967, 24. Also important was *Zot Haaretz*, the official biweekly journal of the movement.

23. Jacob Shavit and Mordechai Eran, *The Hebrew Bible Reborn: From Holy Scripture to the Book of Books: A History of Biblical Culture and the Battles over the Bible in Modern Judaism* (Berlin: Walter de Gruyter, 2007), 487. On the Canaanites, see Jacob Shavit, *The New Hebrew Nation: A Study in Israeli Heresy and Fantasy* (London: Frank Cass, 1987); Nitzan-Shiftan, *Seizing Jerusalem*, 54–67; Sarah Hinsky, "Shtikat Hadagim: Mekomi Veuniversally Besiah Haomanut Hayisraeli," *Theory and Criticism* 4 (Fall 1993): 105–122.

24. Yair Sheleg, "Canaanim Lema'an Yisrael Hashlema" (includes an interview with Aharon Amir), *Nekuda*, August–September 1987, 37.

25. Shlaim, *The Iron Wall*, 243–246.

26. The cabinet decision regarding returning territories to Egypt and Syria was formally canceled in October 1968. Shlaim, *The Iron Wall*, 253–254.

27. Shlaim, *The Iron Wall*, 255.

28. Gorenberg, *The Accidental Empire*, 130.

29. Shlaim, *The Iron Wall*, 255–256.
30. Avraham Mosseri, "Strategic Spatial Planning and National Strategy in Israel" [in Hebrew] (Haifa: Technion—Israel Institute of Technology, 1996), 178–185; Shlaim, *The Iron Wall*, 256–258.
31. The cabinet adopted Dayan's plan for military bases. Shlaim, *The Iron Wall*, 256–258.
32. Gorenberg, *The Accidental Empire*, 127.
33. On the authorization of Kfar Etzion, see Gorenberg, *The Accidental Empire*, 102–115.
34. Yossi Katz, *Jewish Settlement in the Hebron Mountains and the Etzion Bloc: From "Nahalat Herzog" to Gush Etzion* [in Hebrew], 2nd ed. (Ramat Gan, Israel: Bar-Ilan University, 1992), 99.
35. Meir Ben Uri, *Tohnit shel Kfar Etzion Kv' Avraham*, map (Haifa, 1944), Gush Etzion Archives; Katz, *Jewish Settlement in the Hebron Mountains and the Etzion Bloc*, 124–125.
36. Kfar Etzion's survivors had settled in Nir Etzion, a cooperative village inside Israel proper, after the 1948 Arab-Israeli War. Idith Zertal and Akiva Eldar, *Lords of the Land: The War over Israel's Settlements in the Occupied Territories, 1967–2007* (New York: Nation Books, 2007), 5.
37. Hagay Huberman, *Keneged Kol Hasikuyim: 40 Shnot Hahityashvut Biyehudah Veshomron, Binyamin Vehabikah, Tashka"z-Tashsa"z* (Ariel: Sifriyat Netsarim, 2008), 26–28.
38. Gorenberg, *The Accidental Empire*, 108. According to the historian Tom Segev, Prime Minister Eshkol began considering the resettlement of Jews in the Etzion Bloc the day after the Six-Day War ended, but on the advice of Yosef Weitz, he decided to wait. See Segev, *1967*, 452.
39. Gorenberg, *The Accidental Empire*, 112–116; Segev, *1967*, 577.
40. Israel Cohen, "Ga'rin Naha"l Ala Lehityashvut al Admat Kfar-Etzion," *Davar*, September 28, 1967, 1–2.
41. Hagay Huberman, *Hanan Porat—Biography* [in Hebrew] (Tel Aviv: Yedioth Ahronoth Books and Chemed Books, 2013), 51.
42. Freddy Kahana, *Neither Town nor Village: The Architecture of the Kibbutz 1910–1990* [in Hebrew] (Ramat Efal: Yad Tabenkin, 2011), 512–539.
43. There are conflicting accounts regarding the exact date when the Division of Rural Planning—which, in 1975, became the Rural Building and New Settlements Administration—was founded. According to Yehezkel Lein, it was founded in 1968. The architectural historian Hadas Shadar noted that it was founded in 1969. According to Shlomo Avni, former head of the Rural Building and New Settlements Administration, however, the Ministry of Housing began to take care of rural settlements already in 1967. The historian Freddy Kahana noted that in 1967 it was *decided* to allocate certain areas that were previously in the hands of the Jewish Agency to the Division of Rural Planning, which, he explained, began to plan and erect new rural settlements only in 1969. See Yehezkel Lein, *Land Grab: Israel's Settlement Policy in the West Bank* (Jerusalem: B'Tselem, May 13, 2002), 19; Shadar, *Avnei Habinyan shel Hashikun Hatsiburi*, 125; Kahana, *Neither Town nor Village*, 89 and 535; Shlomo Avni, "Habniya Bahityashvut Hakafrit," in *Israel Builds 1977*, ed. Amiram Harlap (Tel Aviv: Ministry of Housing, 1977), 255. Roughly, the Ministry of Housing's Division of Rural Construction was charged with detailed planning of the residential units and communal spaces, whereas the Settlement Department

was entrusted with master planning (i.e., drafting the general physical plan of the settlement), designing agricultural or industrial buildings, and aiding settlements until they reached self-sufficiency. Gavriel Krien, interview by author, November 26, 2015; Avshalom Rokach, *Rural Settlement in Israel* (Jerusalem: Jewish Agency for Israel, Rural Settlement Department; The World Zionist Organization, Rural Settlement Division, 1978), 67–71 and 73.

44. Israel Goodovitch, interview by author, March 31, 2015. A number of politicians, including Minister of Defense Moshe Dayan, argued that the occupation would bring economic prosperity to the Palestinians. On Moshe Dayan and the notion of "enlightened occupation," see Boaz Neumann, "Moshe Dayan, Hakibush Hanaor Vehatoda'a Hatzinit," *Panim* 18 (2001): 10–22. On Israel's "developmental" approach toward the occupied territories in the first two decades after the Six-Day War, see Neve Gordon, "From Colonization to Separation: Exploring the Structure of Israel's Occupation," *Third World Quarterly* 29, no. 1 (February 2008): 25–44. On how the occupation had increased the income of Palestinians in the first two decades after the war, see Shlomo Swirski, *The Price of Occupation* [in Hebrew] (Tel Aviv: ADVA Center and MAPA Publishers, 2005), 18–20.

45. Israel Goodovitch, "Planning and Development in Rural Areas in the Developing Urban Society" (Jerusalem: Ministry of Housing, 1970), p. 3.47; Amiram Harlap, ed., *Israel Builds 1977* (Tel Aviv: Ministry of Housing, 1977), 248–249.

46. Michael Chyutin and Bracha Chyutin, *Architecture and Utopia: Kibbutz and Moshhav* [in Hebrew] (Jerusalem: Magnes Press, 2010), 114–118; Elissa Rosenberg, "Landscape Modernism and the Kibbutz: The Work of Shmuel Bickels (1909–1975)," in *Israel as a Modern Architectural Experimental Lab, 1948–1978*, ed. Inbal Ben-Asher Gitler and Anat Geva (Bristol, UK: Intellect, 2020), 100.

47. Harlap, *Israel Builds 1977*, 248–249.

48. On Israeli architects' interest in vernacular architecture, see Nitzan-Shiftan, *Seizing Jerusalem*, 45–78.

49. Harlap, *Israel Builds 1977*, 248–249.

50. Yehoshua Altman, interview by author, July 13, 2015.

51. Altman, interview by author. In 1969, two other Jewish strongholds, Rosh Tsurim and Allon Shvut, were established near Kfar Etzion.

52. Sharon Architects (Kfar Etzion team) to Haim Epshtein, "Beit Sefer Sade Kfar Etzion," November 15, 1970, Folder 965000062968, Azrieli Architectural Archive.

53. Altman, interview by author.

54. Israel (resident and archivist at Kfar Etzion's archive), conversation with author, July 5, 2015.

55. Rabbi Eliezer Waldman, a settlement activist and founder of Nir Yeshiva in Kiryat Arba, complained he was rejected by the people of Kfar Etzion because of his old age. See Moshe Levinger, "Kah Hakol Hethil," Moatza Mekomit Kiryat Arba Hevron, accessed April 18, 2018, http://www.kiryat4.org.il/?CategoryID=402 (link no longer active); Huberman, *Keneged Kol Hasikuyim*, 36; Pinhas Valershtein, interview by author, June 28, 2015.

56. On the number of Palestinians in Hebron and other West Bank cities, see Shmuel Shaked and Amos Livnat, "Urban Settlement in Mount Hebron," January 29, 1969, 5, -112/2A, Israel State Archives, Jerusalem (hereafter cited as ISA); Efrat, *Judea and Samaria*, 94.

57. Shmuel Naftali, "Kah Hitnahalnu Behevron: Re'ayon im Harav Moshe Levinger," *Davar*, September 5, 1975, 21; David Cassuto, interview by author, December 13, 2015.

58. Jerold S. Auerbach, *Hebron Jews: Memory and Conflict in the Land of Israel* (Lanham, MD: Rowman and Littlefield, 2009), 40.

59. Gershon Bar-Kochva, "The Old Hebron Jewish Quarter: Layout, Way of Life and Remains" [in Hebrew], *Cathedra* 169 (September 2018): 45–74.

60. Auerbach, *Hebron Jews*, 60; Avishar, *Sefer Hevron*, 50–58; Bar-Kochva, "The Old Hebron Jewish Quarter," 47. Because of its enclosed layout, resembling that of Jewish ghettos in Europe, it was sometimes referred to as the Ghetto. Bar-Kochva, "The Old Hebron Jewish Quarter," 46. Sephardic Jews referred to the compound as El Cortiyo, "the court of the Jews." Auerbach, *Hebron Jews*, 40.

61. According to the geographer Ghazi Falah, in 1834, there were 241 Jews residing in Hebron; in 1881, there were between 1,000 and 1,200; by 1931, their number had dropped to 135. See Ghazi Falah, "Recent Jewish Colonisation in Hebron," in *The Impact of Gush Emunim: Politics and Settlement in the West Bank*, ed. David Newman (London and Sydney: Croom Helm, 1985), 246–248.

62. On the 1929 riots and the events leading to the evacuation of Jews from Hebron in 1936, see Morris, *Righteous Victims*, 111–120, 128–131; Josef Lang, "The 1929 Riots: Three Viewpoints" [in Hebrew], *Cathedra* 47 (March 1988): 134–154; Auerbach, *Hebron Jews*, 75–76. Sixty-seven Jews were killed in the 1929 riots. See Gorenberg, *The Accidental Empire*, 137.

63. Some twenty plots of land and twenty-four buildings were registered under the names of exiled Jews in Hebron. Avishar, *Sefer Hevron*, 471; Falah, "Recent Jewish Colonisation in Hebron," 248.

64. "Va'ad Peula Leshikum Hayeshuv Hayehudi Behevron," *Maariv*, July 2, 1967, 8; Yisrael Cohen, "Harisat Hamivnim Shehekimu Hayardenim Bebeit Hakvarot," *Davar*, January 26, 1968, 14; A. H. Elhanani, "Yehudei Hevron Bein Etmol Lemahar: Siha im Avraham Franko," *Davar*, May 6, 1968, 7; K. Yisrael, "Behazara Lehevron," *Davar*, January 19, 1968, 11.

65. Yisrael, "Behazara Lehevron," 11; Moshe Levinger, "Yemei Hahitnahalut Harishonim," in Ozeri, *Kiryat Arba Hee Hevron*, 16.

66. Yisrael, "Behazara Lehevron."

67. Levinger, "Yemei Hahitnahalut Harishonim," 16–18.

68. Israel Cohen, "100 Talmidim Miyeshivat New York Muhanim Lehitztaref Lamitnahalim Behevron," *Davar*, April 24, 1968; Levinger, "Yemei Hahitnahalut Harishonim," 18. On the settlers' interactions with Mayor Jabari, and on government ministers' reactions to the settlers' presence in the Park Hotel, see Gorenberg, *The Accidental Empire*, 147–152.

69. On the different approaches of various groups—including religious Zionists—to monuments and history, see Alona Nitzan-Shiftan, " 'Yesh Avanim im Lev': Al Monumentim, Modernism Veshimur Bakotel Hama'aravi," *Theory and Criticism* 38–39 (2011): 65–100. On religious Zionists' interest in the Bible, see Gideon Aran, "Return to the Scriptures in Modern Israel," in *Les retours aux écritures: Fondamentalismes présents et passés*, ed. Evelyne Patlagean and Alain Le Boulluec, Bibliothèque de l'Ecole Des Hautes Études, vol. 99 (Louvain, Belgium: Peeters, 1993). On Palestinians as custodians of a biblical landscape, see Nitzan-Shiftan, *Seizing Jerusalem*, 63–67.

70. Quoted in Avishar, *Sefer Hevron*, 480.

71. Quoted in Yisrael Cohen, "Hazara Lehevron Aharei 39 Shana," *Davar*, April 26, 1968, 11.
72. David Cassuto, "Beit Lehem: Seker Architectoni," *Tvai* 5 (1968): 3–4.
73. See David Cassuto and Israel Levitt's plan in David Cassuto to Yigal Allon (minister of Labor), April 18, 1968, 15/Allon/18/4, Yad Tabenkin Archive, Ramat Efal.
74. Cassuto, interview by author.
75. Cassuto, interview by author; Cassuto to Allon, April 18, 1968.
76. Cohen, "100 Talmidim Miyeshivat New York Muhanim Lehitztaref Lamitnahalim Behevron."
77. In January 1968, Yigal Allon proposed to the cabinet that a Jewish neighborhood be erected "in the immediate vicinity of Hebron." Allon, according to Gershom Gorenberg, often acted as the "settlers' patron," arranging for them to receive weapons for self-defense and helping them obtain a permit to set up a business in Hebron. See Gorenberg, *The Accidental Empire*, 139, 144, 148, 158–159; Joel Beinin, "Mixing, Separation, and Violence in Urban Spaces and the Rural Frontier in Palestine," *Arab Studies Journal* 21, no. 1 (Spring 2013): 31.
78. Cassuto, interview by author. Cassuto and Levitt, it seems, remained in touch with the settlers for a while after sending the plan to Minister Allon. In April 1969, a settlers' representative informed government officials that the two had expressed a willingness to assist with the planning process. See Benjamin Katzover (on behalf of the settlers' secretariat) to Ministers Committee on Hebron, April 16, 1969, 7311/10-A, ISA.
79. Cassuto, interview by author.
80. Government and military officials researched old Jewish properties in other parts of Hebron, along with Palestinian-owned plots near the Tomb of the Patriarchs. See Rural Center in Gush Etzion and Hebron Settlement Ministers Committee, "Merkaz Kafri Begush Etzion Vehahityashvut Behevron," September 30, 1968, 7900/26-A, ISA; Binyamin Lubetkin to Aharon Harsina (senior officer, Israel Defense Forces), October 11, 1968, 6610/6-G, ISA.
81. Aharon Harsina to Moshe Dayan (minister of Security), October 16, 1968, 6610/6-G, ISA.
82. Aharon Harsina to Moshe Dayan, "Hevron," October 16, 1968, 6610/6-G, ISA.
83. Rural Center in Gush Etzion and Hebron Settlement Ministers Committee, "Tohnit Ba'ir Hevron," December 10, 1968, 7900/26-A, ISA. See correspondence regarding the planning commission in Yehuda Tamir to Shmuel Shaked, "Hazmanat Tihnun," January 5, 1969, 10768/14-G, ISA.
84. Shmuel Shaked, former chief architect at the Ministry of Housing, led the team, which included among its members Amos Livnat and Rita Dunsky-Feuerstein.
85. Shaked and Livnat, "Urban Settlement in Mount Hebron."
86. Shaked and Livnat, "Urban Settlement in Mount Hebron, 3."
87. Shaked and Livnat, "Urban Settlement in Mount Hebron," 33.
88. For an account detailing important dates in the evolution of Kiryat Arba, specifying when lands were seized and when the master plan was commissioned, see "Hakamat Kiryat Arba Vehaf'alata," December 1974, 9482/2-GL, ISA.
89. Rita Dunsky-Feuerstein, interview by author, December 24, 2015.
90. Amiram Harlap, ed., *Israel Builds 1973* (Tel Aviv: Ministry of Housing, 1973), 126.
91. Artur Glikson, "Be'ayot Tihnun-Hamegurim Be'arim Ubeshchunot Hadashot," in

Hashikun Hatziburi: Skirot Veha'arahot al Hashikun Hatziburi Beyisrael Betkufat Ha'asor 1948–1958, ed. Haim Drabkin-Darin (Tel Aviv: Sifrei Gadish, 1959), 82.

92. On British new towns and their origins, see Peter Hall and Mark Tewdwr-Jones, *Urban and Regional Planning* (Abingdon, UK: Routledge, 2011), esp. 28–42 and 55–77. On the neighborhood unit, see Benjamin Looker, *A Nation of Neighborhoods: Imagining Cities, Communities, and Democracy in Postwar America* (Chicago and London: University of Chicago Press, 2015), 51–69; Clarence Arthur Perry, *Housing for the Machine Age* (New York: Russell Sage Foundation, 1939), 49–82.

93. On how Israeli planners were influenced by British new towns, see Troen, *Imagining Zion*, 187–189; Hadas Shadar, "Mekehilatiyut Me'uletzet Lindividualizm Babinui Ha'ironi Hatziburi," *Iyunim Btekumat Yisrael* 23 (2013): 212; Shadar, *Avnei Habinyan shel Hashikun Hatsiburi*, 33.

94. Dunsky-Feuerstein, interview by author.

95. Dunsky-Feuerstein, interview by author.

96. Benjamin Mazar, "Kiryat Arba he Hevron," in *Cities and Districts in Eretz-Israel* (Jerusalem: Mossad Bialik and Hahevera Lehakirat Eretz Israel, 1975), 53.

97. Mazar, "Kiryat Arba he Hevron," 53–63. Jehoshua Grintz argues that the name "Kiryat Arba" refers to an ancient family that resided in the place; the Israelites later changed it to Hebron. See Jehoshua M. Grintz, *Motz'ei Dorot: Mehkarim Bekadmoniyut Hamikra Vereshit Toldot Yisrael Vesifruto* (Tel Aviv: Hakibbuts Hameuhad, 1969), 328.

98. The architects Shmuel Shaked and Yaacov Ventura directed the master plan. A team of architects, working under Bitush Comforti, designed the first neighborhood. See A. AI. Robinson (deputy head of the Physical Planning Department at the Ministry of Housing) to Yehuda Tamir, May 18, 1970, 5648/11-GL, ISA. In December 1970, Shmuel Shaked's firm was asked to design eight hundred more units; see "Pirtei-Kol Miyeshivat Ve'adat Hevron Shehitkayma Bemisradei Hamenahel Haklali Beyerushalayim," December 2, 1970, 5648/11-GL, ISA.

99. Nitzan-Shiftan, *Seizing Jerusalem*, 30–31.

100. See Tzvi Gluzman (manager of the Jerusalem region at the Ministry of Housing) to A. Ulnik (head of the Planning and Engineering Department at the Ministry of Housing), A. AI. Robinson, architect A. Levi (Public Buildings Division at the Ministry of Housing), D. Ben-Elul, and Bitush Comforti, October 13, 1970, 5648/11-GL, ISA.

101. Eli Gvirtzman, telephone conversation with author, November 30, 2015.

102. See Moshe Ravid, "Housing for East Jerusalemites at Wadi el Joz, Jerusalem," in *Israel Builds 1970*, ed. Yehonatan Golani and Gersom Schwarze Dieter (Tel Aviv: Ministry of Housing, 1970), p. 4.100. For the decision to replicate housing units from Wadi el Joz, see "Pirtei-Kol: Miyeshiva Shehitkayma Beyom 8.6.70 Bemisradei Hamenahel Haklali Beyerushalayim Vebeatar Habniya Hamutza Behveron," June 8, 1970, 70, 8352/4-GL, ISA.

103. Ravid, "Housing for East Jerusalemites," 4.100.

104. Aharon Dolev, "Hamitnahalim Hanetzurim," *Maariv*, May 31, 1968, 12.

105. The architects had refused to enlarge the units even after government officials urged them to do so. See M. Shtrum (in charge of prefabricated construction at the Ministry of Housing) to Tzvi Gluzman, December 6, 1970, 4948/2-GL, ISA.

106. According to traditional Jewish laws, one could erect the sukkah on the rooftop or in a nearby yard. However, it is far less convenient. See Royi Shamir, "The Halakhic

Space—Halakha as a Planning Method: Spatial Design Methods in Recently Transformed Ultra-Orthodox Neighborhoods in Jerusalem" [in Hebrew] (Technion—Israel Institute of Technology, 2019), 66. On the requirements of sukkah construction and the diversity of sukkot forms and decorations, see Gabrielle Anna Berlinger, "From Ritual to Protest: Sukkot in the Garden of Hope," *Buildings & Landscapes: Journal of the Vernacular Architecture Forum* 24, no. 1 (2017): 4–8, https://doi.org/10.5749/buildland.24.1.0001.

107. Ravid, "Housing for East Jerusalemites," p. 4.100.

108. See "Sikum Veadat Hevron 25.10.71 Shehitkayma Bekiryat-Arba," October 25, 1971, 5648/11-GL, ISA.

109. Quoted in Aharon Dolev, "Im Ifretzu Ha'aravim Lakirya—Hitgonenu Bemaklot," *Maariv*, November 22, 1974, 29. Rabbi Levinger observed that "not much thought was given to beauty and diversity" in the design of Kiryat Arba, and he expressed hope that "in future neighborhoods, prettier and less homogeneous housing models will be offered," quoted in "Hagiga Bekiryat-Arba," *Davar*, June 2, 1972, 15.

110. "Sikum Yeshiva Ve'adat Hevron Me-15.3.71 Yerushalayim," March 17, 1971, 5648/11-GL, ISA; "Sikum Ve'adat Hevron Beyeshiva Miyom 16/3/72 Betel Aviv," March 17, 1972, 5648/11-GL, ISA; Ministry of Housing, Jerusalem District, "Sikum Benose Ihlus Kiryat-Arba Miyom 18.4.71," April 23, 1971, 8352/4-GL, ISA.

111. See Ministry of Housing, Jerusalem District, "Sikum Benose Ihlus Kiryat-Arba Miyom 18.4.71," 71; "Protocol Ve'adat Hevron," December 6, 1971, 5648/11-GL, ISA.

112. See Hebron Settlers Secreteriat to Ze'ev Sherf, July 11, 1971, 6501/27-G, ISA.

113. For settlers' complaints about religious facilities in Kiryat Arba, see Moshe Levinger to Yosef Sharon (director of the Ministry of Housing), January 20, 1971, 8352/4-GL, ISA; Shmaryahu Cohen (head of the Hebron team) to Kiryat Arba Religious Committee, July 12, 1972, 8352/6-GL, ISA; Ministry of Housing, "Sikum Yeshivat Ve'adat Hevron Hitkayma Beyerushalayim Be-26.6.72," June 28, 1972, 8352/6-GL, ISA.

114. A. Yifrah (head of Kiryat Arba Religious Committee) to Prime Minister Menachem Begin, January 1, 1978, 12852/12-GL, ISA.

115. On the legal difficulties of selling units in Kiryat Arba, along with the attorney general of Israel's proposal for overcoming these difficulties, see Attorney General of Israel, "Bniya Bekiryat Arba" (Ministry of Justice, July 31, 1973), 8352/6-GL, ISA. For meeting transcripts and correspondences regarding the matter, see, for example, A. Shtraus to Meir Shamgar (attorney general of Israel), "Hesderei Bniya—Kiryat Arba," August 7, 1973, 8352/6-GL, ISA; Shmaryahu Cohen and Ze'ev Sherf (minister of Housing), "Kiryat Arba—Mehirat Dirot Vehahkarat Karkaot," May 15, 1973, 8352/6-GL, ISA; "Sikum Yeshiva Ve'adat Hevron Shehitkayma Beyerushalayim Be-30.4.73," May 6, 1973, 8352/6-GL, ISA.

116. Gvirtzman, telephone conversation with author; Dunsky-Feuerstein, interview by author; "Protokol Miyeshivat Have'ada Leinyanei Bikoret Hamedina Shitkayma Beyom Gimel, K"A Beshvat, Hatashm"a, 12.2.85, Sha'a 12:30," February 12, 1985, 9–15, 1423/26-K, ISA.

117. See Yair Shtern, "Rabim Me'unyanim Lehitnahel Behevron ah Ein Tohnit Lepituah Nosaf," *Maariv*, January 25, 1972, 15; "Gush Emunim Daf Kesher," ca. 1976, folder DD1/2309, Central Zionist Archives, Jerusalem; "Betazkir Lerosh Hamemshala: Mitnahalei Hevron Mevakshim Lageshet Miyad Lebitzu'a Tohnit-Ha'av She'ushra," *Davar*, February 3, 1972; Moshe Mayevski (head of Kiryat Arba administration) to

Prime Minister Menachem Begin, "Tazkir," June 23, 1977, 6755/4-G, ISA; Moshe Mayevski (head of Kiryat Arba administration) and Moshe Nahalony (secretary of Kiryat Arba administration), Minhelet Kiryat Arba, "Skira Mesakemet Lepeulot Haminhala Bahodashim Tishrei Tashla"z-Nisan Tashla"h," May 7, 1978, National Library of Israel Archives; "Hahlatat Asifat am shel Toshvei Kiryat Arba," August 25, 1979, 12852/12-GL, ISA.

118. Annotated drawing by a Kiryat Arba settler, ca. 1979, 12852/12-GL, ISA.

119. See Elyakim Haetzni, "Toshvei Yisrael Nehshavim 'Nifkadim' Legabei Hashtahim," letter to the editor, *Maariv*, February 2, 1972, 10.

120. Harlap, *Israel Builds 1973*, 138–139, 145–150; Shadar, *Avnei Habinyan shel Hashikun Hatsiburi*, 128–130 and 132–135.

121. On ministry architects' early attempts to consult future residents and account for their needs during the 1970s, see Oryan Shachar, Alona Nitzan-Shiftan, and Rachel Sebba, "Gvulot Veptahim shel Kdusha: Hakirya Hahasidit Behatsor HaGlilit," in *Living Forms: Architecture and Society in Israel*, ed. Shelly Cohen and Tula Amir (Tel Aviv: Xargol Books and Am Oved, 2007), 65–91; Nitzan-Shiftan, *Seizing Jerusalem*, 116–123.

122. See Aharon Dolev, "Betahbulot Ta'ase Leha Yeshuv," *Maariv*, April 15, 1977, 23; Israel Levitt and Ofra's Building Committee, "Giv'at Ofra," April 1977, folder 46, box 4, Ofra Archives; Pinhas Valershtein, interview by author, June 28, 2015.

123. Baruch Nachshon (settlement founder), telephone interview by author, October 11, 2015; Efraim Segal (settlement activist), conversation with author, September 14, 2015; Cassuto, interview by author; "Gush Emunim Daf Kesher." The settlers' suspicions were bolstered when Minister of Housing Avraham Offer described the national-religious settlers' movement as "a cancer in the heart of the nation." See "Hasartan Mihu?," *Maariv*, October 10, 1976, 15.

124. See Levinger to Sharon, January 20, 1971; Settlers Secretariat to Ze'ev Sherf (minister of Housing), March 26, 1971, 8352/4-GL, ISA; Moshe Levinger to Ze'ev Sherf, May 23, 1971, 6501/27-G, ISA; Hebron Settlers Secretariat to Ze'ev Sherf, July 11, 1971, 6501/27-G, ISA. See also Elyakim Haetzni to Ze'ev Sherf, February 19, 1973, 8352/6-GL, ISA; Eli Eyal, "Bein Hakirya Shebehevron Lebein Hakirya Beyerushalyim," *Maariv*, February 11, 1972, 66–67; Kiryat Arba–Hebron Local Committee, "Tazkir al Ikuvei Habniya Bekiryat Arba," November 25, 1974, 6722/28-G, ISA; Settlers of Hebron to Golda Meir, April 21, 1971, 6501/27-G, ISA; Edri Meir to Secretary of the Prime Minister, May 24, 1971, 6501/27-G, ISA; Edri Meir to Prime Minister Golda Meir, October 31, 1971, 6501/27-G, ISA. Settlers also requested that the name "Hebron" be added to the name "Kiryat Arba." See Yitzhak Gvirtz to general manager, Judea and Samaria military headquarters, August 30, 1972, 47113/13-GL, ISA.

125. See, for example, "Sikum Ve'adat Hevron Beyeshiva Miyom 16/3/72 Betel Aviv"; "Sikum Yeshivat Ve'adat Hevron Shehitkayma Beyerushalayim be-26.6.72," June 26, 1972, 2, 5648/11-GL, ISA; Dolev, "Im Ifretzu Ha'aravim Lakirya," 29.

126. Danny Rubenstein, "Hanhalat Hakoalitizya Tadun Behishtatfut Rosh"ham Betzurat Hamemshal Hamekomi Bekiryat Arba: Mahrif Hama'avak Bein Tomhei Levinger Lemisrad Hashikun," *Davar*, December 31, 1971, 1; Danny Rubenstein, "Atida Hamonitzipali shel Kiryat Arba: Ma'avak al Ha'inyanim Bashhuna Hayehudit shel Hevron," *Davar*, January 6, 1972, 10.

127. "Mitnahalei Kir'-Arba Shavtu Neged Bo Hakatzin Hamemune," *Davar*, March 17, 1972, 2.

128. See "Mefunei Kiryat Arba Pathu Beshvita Leyad Batei Haplisha: Hitnagdu Lepinui Harihut Biyedei Aravim," *Maariv*, January 31, 1972, 7; Rubenstein, "Hanhalat Hakoalitizya Tadun Behishtatfut"; Danny Rubenstein, "G. Meir Hezhira Mitnahalei Hevron Mipnei Plishot," *Davar*, February 2, 1972; Naftali, "Kah Hitnahalnu Behevron"; Minhelet Kiryat Arba, "Kiryat Arba he Hevron," 1977, folder V2569/17, National Library of Israel Archives.

129. Rubenstein, "Hanhalat Hakoalitizya Tadun Behishtatfut," 1; Rubenstein, "Atida Hamonitzipali shel Kiryat Arba," 10.

130. Danny Rubenstein, "Mi Yishlot Bahitnahalut Behevron: Mahloket Bein Misrad Hapnim Vehashikun al Nihula shel Kiryat Arba," *Davar*, November 16, 1971, 9.

131. Rubenstein, "G. Meir Hezhira Mitnahalei Hevron," 2.

132. Danny Rubenstein, "Kiryat Arba—Havtahot Bli Kisui," *Davar*, March 21, 1973, 9.

133. Zertal and Eldar, *Lords of the Land*, 28.

134. See Elyakim Haetzni to Yehiel Kadishai (secretary to Prime Minister Menachem Begin), "Kiryat Arba," September 6, 1977, 12852/12-GL, ISA. Attesting to the radicalization of Kiryat Arba was the decision made by the Brooklyn-born ultranationalist Rabbi Meir Kahane to open his election campaign center there. According to the political scientist Ehud Sprinzak, Kahane and his followers "played a crucial role in worsening the relations with the Arabs of Hebron." See "Mateh Habhirot shel Harav Kahana Yukam Bekiryat Arba," *Davar*, February 11, 1977, 3; Ehud Sprinzak, *Every Man Whatsoever Is Right in His Own Eyes: Illegalism in Israeli Society* [in Hebrew] (Tel Aviv: Sifriat Poalim, 1986), 143.

135. Zertal and Eldar, *Lords of the Land*, 28. The settlers disputed this, arguing that in January 1978 there were only 130 empty units. The remaining ones were either occupied or still under construction. See Ronni Shtarsberg (Kiryat Arba administration), "Tazkir al Kiryat Arba," January 1978, 12852/12-GL, ISA.

136. Mayevski to Begin, "Tazkir"; Teddy Froyes, "Gush Emunim o Tur Ve'ale," *Davar*, October 6, 1977, 11.

137. Moshe Levinger to Prime Minister Menachem Begin, "Kiryat Arba–Hevron," June 1978, 12852/12-GL, ISA.

138. A market space and public restrooms were erected on the compound's ruins. Houses on the northern edge of the compound and adjacent Arab-owned houses were not demolished. Bar-Kochva, "The Old Hebron Jewish Quarter," 46. According to Ghazi Falah, two-thirds of the abandoned buildings were demolished by 1967. The remaining ones were leased out. See Falah, "Recent Jewish Colonisation in Hebron," 248.

139. Cassuto, interview by author.

140. Cassuto, interview by author. One of Cassuto's collaborators gave a relatively similar account in a newspaper article he wrote for the daily *Maariv*. See Professor Hirshfeld (Bar-Ilan University), "Hilul Hakodesh Behevron," *Maariv*, June 27, 1973.

141. For settlers' complaints about the synagogue's desolate condition and demands to have it restored, see Binyamin Mandel (Kiryat Arba) and Eliezer Waldman (Kiryat Arba) to Prime Minister Yizhak Rabin, May 15, 1975, 12465/12-GL, ISA; 132 signees (many of whom identified as Kiryat Arba settlers) to Prime Minister Yizhak Rabin, June 15, 1975, 12465/12-GL, ISA.

142. Tavger was working as a guard in the nearby Jewish cemetery in Hebron that was a site of rioting in 1929 and was reopened after a settlement activist buried her baby there in 1975. See Auerbach, *Hebron Jews*, 98–102; Michael Feige, "Jewish Settlement of Hebron: The Place and the Other," *GeoJournal* 53, no. 3 (2001): 328; Ben Zion Tavger, *Hevron Sheli* (Jerusalem: Shamir, 1999), 86–87.

143. Noam Arnon, "Beit Haknesset Avraham Avinu Behevron," in Ozeri, *Kiryat Arba he Hevron*, 38–39; Tavger, *Hevron Sheli*, 127–132.

144. Noam Arnon, interview by author, July 30, 2017. On the excavation of the Avraham Avinu Synagogue, see Arnon, "Beit Haknesset Avraham Avinu Behevron," 36–40; Tavger, *Hevron Sheli*, 100–138, 156–162.

145. Cassuto, interview by author. See one of Cassuto's petitions regarding the matter in David Cassuto to Yitzhak Rephael (minister of Religion), "Beit Haknesset Haatik Behevron," June 18, 1975, 12465/12-GL, ISA.

146. "Hitkablu Hahatza'ot Ha'operativiyot shel Sar Habitahon Legabei Hevron," *Maariv*, October 11, 1976, 3; Arnon, "Beit Haknesset Avraham Avinu Behevron," 39; Tavger, *Hevron Sheli*, 179–180.

147. Cassuto, interview by author.

148. Cassuto, interview by author.

149. Haim Zilber (contractor of Avraham Avinu Synagogue), interview by author, August 1, 2017; Tavger, *Hevron Sheli*, 185, 188, and 190.

150. Arnon, "Beit Haknesset Avraham Avinu Behevron," 40.

151. Arnon, interview by author. An inauguration ceremony took place in May 1981. See Tavger, *Hevron Sheli*, 23–27.

152. Danny Rubenstein, " 'Hashihrur Ha'amiti' shel Hevron," *Davar*, February 8, 1980, 14.

153. One settler told Minister of Agriculture Ariel Sharon: "Abraham our father came to Hebron, not to Kiryat Arba. King David came to Hebron, not to Kiryat Arba. So did we [the settlers] come to Hebron, to build it from its ruins, not to live in a fenced ghetto called Kiryat Arba." Quoted in Aharon Dolev, "Neshot Hadasa Bematzor," *Maariv*, May 4, 1979, 33.

154. First, in February 10, 1980, the government made an initial decision stating that "there is no hindrance to having Jews live in Hebron or anywhere in the Land of Israel." See Hasbara/thanim (Ministry of Foreign Affairs) to the representatives (of the ministry), "Hevron," February 15, 1980, 8411/10-MFA, ISA. Then, in March 23, 1980, it decided to "act to develop the fabric of the court of the Jews in the Jewish quarter in Hebron . . . in this framework, a branch of Kiryat Arba hesder yeshiva will be founded in Hebron, and in Beit Hadassa a field school will be founded." See Aryeh Naor (Secretariat of the Government) to Minister of Construction and Housing, April 3, 1980, 15421/2-GL, ISA. In March 24, 1980, it was reported that according to Minister of Housing David Levy, the yeshiva near the synagogue would have dormitories for eighty students, two faculty housing units, storage spaces, classrooms, administration offices, a library, and a dining hall. The other educational center was to include classrooms, a dining hall and kitchen, several guest rooms, a faculty unit, offices, a library, and a synagogue. See Yosef Waxman, "Kol Ha'atarim Sheyibanu—Bahoveret shel David Levi," *Maariv*, March 24, 1980. On the Ministry of Housing preparation work that followed the initial decision from February 1980, see Dalia Mazori, "Huhal Betichnun Yishuv Harova Hayehudi Behevron,"

Maariv, March 6, 1980, 3; "Habatim Behevron Yibadku Hayom Likrat Ihlusam," *Davar*, March 6, 1980, 2.

155. Akiva Eldar and Idith Zertal, *Adonei Haaretz: Hamitnahalim Vemedinat Yisrael 1967–2004* (Or Yehuda: Kineret, 2004), 354–355. It is unclear when exactly the government commissioned the restoration of Avraham Avinu Quarter as a housing compound. According to a news report, it was decided in a meeting between Prime Minister Begin and Minister Levy in October 1982. Aryeh Avneri, "Harova Hayehudi shel Hevron Yibane Mehadash," *Yediot Aharonot*, October 26, 1982, 15421/2-GL, ISA. By that point, according to Levinger, there were three families (with a total of nineteen people) living in the synagogue's vicinity, and the synagogue itself had functioned as a yeshiva, accommodating twenty-two students. Some guest rooms for students and soldiers as well as a dining hall were on the site. See Moshe Levinger and Ezra Efrati, "Taktziv Shotef Leshnat 82/83," June 3, 1982, 47140/14-GL, ISA.

156. Erol Paker, interview by author, August 10, 2017; Saadia Mandel, interview by author, November 23, 2015.

157. For photographs and drawings of Mandel's designs for Jerusalem, Acre, and Safed, see "A Cluster of Buildings in the Jewish Quarter," *Tvai* 22 (1984): 9–11; "Harova Hayehudi—Pituah Kikar Batei Mahase ('Haduytchfeltz')," *Architectura* (1986): 22; "Proyekt Leshikun Be'ako Ha'atika," *Tvai* 7 (1969): 74–76; "Housing in Jewish Quarter of Safad," *Alef Alef* 3 (1974): 12–13.

158. Aryeh Naor (Secretariat of the Government) to Minister of Construction and Housing, April 3, 1980.

159. Mandel, interview by author.

160. See Nitzan-Shiftan, *Seizing Jerusalem*, esp. 45–78; Nitzan-Shiftan, "Seizing Locality in Jerusalem."

161. Paker, interview by author. See also Saadia Mandel, "Israeli Architecture," *Architecture of Israel* 2 (May 1988): 4–5.

162. Mandel, interview by author.

163. Mandel, interview by author; Paker, interview by author.

164. Mandel, interview by author; Paker, interview by author.

165. On the design of Gilo and Israeli architects' use of inner courtyards, see Nitzan-Shiftan, *Seizing Jerusalem*; Aba Elhanani, *Hama'avak Le'atzmaut shel Ha'adrikhalut Hayisra'elit Bame'ah ha-20* (Tel Aviv: Ministry of Defense, 1998), 160–173; Kallus, "The Political Role of the Everyday," 341–361.

166. For master plans and planning guidelines in Hebron, see *Renewing the Jewish Settlement in Hebron* (Jerusalem: Ministry of Construction and Housing, 1983), Erol Paker private collection; Saadia Mandel et al., *Sikum Tihnun Hayeshuv Hayehudi Behevron: Hamlatzut Lehemsheh Hatihnun* (Jerusalem: Ministry of Construction and Housing, September 1984), Erol Paker private collection.

167. Paker, interview by author.

168. In 1946, members of the Jewish community prepared a list of Jewish-owned properties in Hebron and presented it to the Registrar of Lands in Hebron. The registration process, however, was interrupted by the 1948 Arab–Israeli War. See Shabtai Teveth, *The Cursed Blessing: The Story of Israel's Occupation of the West Bank* (London: Weidenfeld and Nicolson, 1970), 269; Avishar, *Sefer Hevron*, 510–511. The problem of property rights in the site of Avraham Avinu Quarter (and the possibility of having to follow original subdivision lines) had preoccupied legal consultants at least since

March 1980. See, for example, Plia Albeck and Yoram Barsela to Attorney General of Israel, "Binnui Behevron," March 14, 1980, 8411/10-MFA, ISA; Batya Evlin to Minister (unspecified), "Harova Hayehudi Behevron," July 22, 1983, 15421/2-GL, ISA.

169. Mandel, interview by author; Paker, interview by author.

170. Mandel, interview by author.

171. Paker, interview by author.

172. Mandel, interview by author.

173. Paker, interview by author.

174. "Hanukat Habayit Behatzer Hayehudim Behevron" (Ministry of Housing, 1989), Municipal Committee of Hebron's Collection.

175. Mandel, interview by author.

176. Cassuto, interview by author.

177. By 1995, thirty-two Palestinians and thirteen Jews had been killed in violent clashes between settlers and the Palestinians in Hebron. Beinin, "Mixing, Separation, and Violence in Urban Spaces," 33.

178. Paker, interview by author.

179. "Protocol Concerning the Redeployment in Hebron," January 17, 1997, https://www .gov.il/en/Departments/General/protocol-concerning-the-redeployment-in-hebron; Eyal Hareuveni, *Beksut Bithonit: Hamediniyut Haisraelit Behevron Ke'emtzai Leha'avara Bekfiya* (Jerusalem: B'Tselem, September 2019), 6, https://www.btselem. org/sites/default/files/publications/201909_playing_the_security_card_heb.pdf.

180. Ophir Foyershtein, *Ir Refa'im: Mediniyut Hahafrada Haisraelit Vedhikat Ragleihem shel Hafalestinim Memerkaz Hevron* (Jerusalem: B'Tselem, May 2007), 9.

181. Restrictions on the movement of Palestinians in Hebron have changed over the years. In September 2019, there were twenty-two checkpoints controlling the movement of Palestinians in the areas surrounding the Jewish compounds in Hebron. See "List of Military Checkpoints in the West Bank and Gaza Strip: Restrictions on Movement," B'Tselem, updated September 25, 2019, http://www.btselem.org /freedom_of_movement/checkpoints_and_forbidden_roads.

182. Foyershtein, "Ir Refa'im," 11-14 and 29–32. According to United Nations Office for the Coordination of Humanitarian Affairs, in 2015, some 1,079 apartments in the areas surrounding the settler compounds were abandoned. Drawing on that survey, B'Tselem estimates that about 5,500 Palestinians had moved out of the area in recent years. Hareuveni, "Beksut Bithonit," 19; "The Humanitarian Situation in the H2 Area of Hebron City: Findings and Assessment" (United Nations Office for the Coordination of Humanitarian Affairs, Occupied Palestinian Territory, April 2019), 16.

183. Chiara De Cesari, "Hebron, or Heritage as Technology of Life," *Jerusalem Quarterly*, no. 41 (Spring 2010): 6–28.

184. The exact number of Israeli soldiers stationed in Hebron is unclear. See Harriet Sherwood, "A Ghost City Revived: The Remarkable Transformation of Hebron," *Guardian*, June 29, 2015, https://www.theguardian.com/cities/2015/jun/29/hebron-old-city -west-bank-palestinian-ghost-city-revived-transformation; "Israeli Settlers Occupy Palestinian Home in Hebron," *Al Jazeera*, July 28, 2017, http://www.aljazeera.com /news/2017/07/israeli-settlers-occupy-palestinian-home-hebron-170728080215824 .html; Sarah Adamczyk, *Driven Out: The Continuing Forced Displacement of Palestinian Residents from Hebron's Old City* (Oslo: Norwegian Refugee Council,

2013), https://www.nrc.no/globalassets/pdf/reports/driven-out-the-continuing-forced-displacement-of-palestinian-residents-from-hebrons-old-city.pdf.

185. The Israel Central Bureau of Statistics' town rankings, which indexes municipalities on a scale of 1 to 10, placed Kiryat Arba in the third cluster, alongside some of Israel's poorer towns. See "Ifyun Yehidot Geographiyot Vesivugan Lefi Harama Hahevratit-Kalkalit shel Ha'uhlusiya Beshnat 2017" (Central Bureau of Statistics, August 2021). On the social life of Kiryat Arba, see Feige, "Jewish Settlement of Hebron." On Kiryat Arba's negative migration rates, as recorded in 2018, see Shaul Arieli, "Moetzet Yesh"a, Nihshaltem," *Haaretz*, December 31, 2020, https://www.haaretz.co.il/opinions/2020-12-31/ty-article-opinion/.premium/0000017f-f2b2-d223-a97f-ffff938c0000.

186. "Regional Statistics: Kiryat Arba" (Central Bureau of Statistics, 2020), https://www.cbs.gov.il/he/settlements/Pages/default.aspx?mode=Yeshuv.

187. On settler violence in Hebron, see "Special Focus: The Closure of Hebron's Old City" (United Nations Office for the Coordination of Humanitarian Affairs, July 2005), 2, https://www.ochaopt.org/sites/default/files/ochaHU0705_En.pdf; Hareuveni, "Beksut Bithonit," 16–18.

188. Gorenberg, *The Accidental Empire*, 160.

CHAPTER 2: COMMUNITY SETTLEMENTS

1. "New 2018 Population Data for Israelis in the West Bank" (Peace Now, October 2, 2019), https://peacenow.org.il/en/population-data-in-israel-and-in-the-west-bank.

2. Four of the villages built along the Jordan River were kibbutzim, and seven were moshavim. Yehiel Admoni, *Decade of Discretion: Settlement Policy in the Territories, 1967–1977* [in Hebrew] (Tel Aviv: Hakibbutz Hameuchad, 1992), 203–204. In addition to the new kibbutz in the Etzion Bloc, by the early 1970s, the settlement of Allon Shvut was founded to house Har Etzion Yeshiva.

3. See, for example, Aharon Dolev, "Haholhim Lehityashev Beshhem Ha'asura," *Maariv*, June 14, 1974, 24.

4. Yehuda Etzion, interview by author, August 17, 2015.

5. Shmuel Horwitz, "The Community Oriented Model: A New Type of Settlement in Israel," in *Israel Builds 1988*, ed. Amiram Harlap (Ministry of Construction and Housing, 1988), 415–417.

6. Within the Ministry of Housing, it was the Rural Building and New Settlements Administration that was responsible for rural settlements. Other important bodies involved in the planning of rural settlements included the Joint Settlement Committee of the Government and the WZO; the Ministry of Agriculture, which provided agricultural knowledge and guidance to rural settlements; Israel Land Authority, which, among other things, guided settlement activity according to land ownership; and the Israel Defense Forces, which were especially involved in Naha"l outposts. See Avshalom Rokach, *Rural Settlement in Israel* (Jerusalem: Jewish Agency for Israel, Rural Settlement Department; World Zionist Organization, Rural Settlement Division, 1978), 9 and 62–76.

7. Gadi Taub, *Hamitnahalim Vehama'avak al Mashma'uta shel Hatziyonut* (Tel Aviv: Yedioth Ahronoth Books and Chemed Books, 2007), 59.

8. Ian S. Lustick, *For the Land and the Lord: Jewish Fundamentalism in Israel* (New York: Council on Foreign Relations, 1988), 44.

9. On the founding of Gush Emunim and how its origins could be traced to earlier periods, prior to the Yom Kippur War, see Michael Feige, *Settling in the Hearts: Jewish Fundamentalism in the Occupied Territories*, Raphael Patai Series in Jewish Folklore and Anthropology (Detroit: Wayne State University Press, 2009), 21–38; Aran, *Kookism*.

10. Rachel Havrelock, "The Two Maps of Israel's Land," *Journal of Biblical Literature* 126, no. 4 (2007): 651 and 655, https://doi.org/10.2307/27638460.

11. Yossef Shilhav, "Interpretation and Misinterpretation of Jewish Territorialism," in *The Impact of Gush Emunim : Politics and Settlement in the West Bank*, ed. David Newman (London: Croom Helm, 1985), 114.

12. On how the concept of the whole Land of Israel evolved over the course of the twentieth century, see Nadav G. Shelef, "From 'Both Banks of the Jordan' to the 'Whole Land of Israel': Ideological Change in Revisionist Zionism," *Israel Studies* 9, no. 1 (Spring 2004): 125–148.

13. Lustick, *For the Land and the Lord*, 83–85. On disputes concerning the idea of conquering the whole Land of Israel within Gush Emunim, between 1982 and 1987, see Lustick, *For the Land and the Lord*, 105–110.

14. Taub, *Hamitnahalim*, 62.

15. Akiva Eldar and Idith Zertal, *Adonei Haaretz*, 245–246. On Gush Emunim's mixture of rationalism and messianism, also see Feige, *Settling in the Hearts*, 31–33.

16. On government settlement policy according to geographic areas between 1967 and 1977, see David Newman, *Population, Settlement, and Conflict: Israel and the West Bank, Update* (Cambridge: Cambridge University Press, 1991), 26–27.

17. Yosef Waxman, "Tzaha"l Nishlah Lefanot 100 Mitnahalim Behar Baal Hatzor," *Maariv*, March 11, 1975, 1–2; Yosef Waxman, "Behol Hamoed Nahazor Im Revavot Hitnahamu Hamefunim Mibaal Hatzor," *Maariv*, March 12, 1975, Ofra Archives.

18. After a couple of squatting attempts, in 1974, Elon Moreh merged with Gush Emunim. See Zertal and Eldar, *Lords of the Land*, 30–32; Hoberman, *Keneged Kol Hasikuyim*, 71–75; Lustick, *For the Land and the Lord*, 45; Aharon Dolev, "Haholhim Lehityashev Beshhem Ha'asura," *Maariv*, June 14, 1974, 24.

19. Sharon Rotbard, "Wall and Tower (Homa Umigdal): The Mold of Israeli Architecture," in *A Civilian Occupation: The Politics of Israeli Architecture*, ed. Rafi Segal and Eyal Weizman, rev. ed. (Tel Aviv: Babel; London and New York: Verso, 2003), 42–43.

20. Troen, *Imagining Zion*, 69.

21. Rotbard, "Wall and Tower," 42.

22. Aharon Kellerman, "Settlement Myth and Settlement Activity: Interrelationships in the Zionist Land of Israel," *Transactions of the Institute of British Geographers* 21, no. 2 (1996): 375, https://doi.org/10.2307/622486.

23. Yaacov Rabi, "Hamotzi'im et Shem Hahalutziyut Lashav," *Al Hamishmar*, August 1, 1974, 3.

24. Zertal and Eldar, *Lords of the Land*, 32.

25. Hoberman, *Keneged Kol Hasikuyim*, 95.

26. Etzion, interview by author; Hemdat Shani, "Mekimei Hagader—Hasipur Hamale," 2005, Ofra Archives. The yeshiva was moved to the nearby settlement of Allon Shvut when Etzion was still a student.

27. Yehuda Etzion, "Interviews with Four of Ofra's Founders," interview by Inbal Yisraeli (Weiner), April 2005, Ofra Archives.

28. Hoberman, *Keneged Kol Hasikuyim*, 87; Zertal and Eldar, *Lords of the Land*, 33–34; Shani, "Mekimei Hagader"; Etzion, "Interviews with Four of Ofra's Founders."

29. Sprinzak, *Every Man Whatsoever Is Right*.

30. Shani, "Mekimei Hagader."

31. Shani, "Mekimei Hagader"; Menahem Michelson, "Hasod shel 'Ofra,'" *Yediot Aharonot*, June 8, 1975, 21. According to Gershom Gorenberg, Moshe Netzer, settlement adviser to Minister of Defense Shimon Peres, gave the activists a permit to do the work. Gorenberg, *The Accidental Empire*, 306.

32. Shani, "Mekimei Hagader."

33. Hoberman, *Keneged Kol Hasikuyim*, 92; "Gush Emunim: Dapei Meida" (Gush Emunim, May 1975), folder 46, box 4, Ofra Archives.

34. There are different accounts of how Defense Minister Shimon Peres reached the decision to let the settlers stay. According to most accounts, Peres first ordered the immediate evacuation of the activists. After some negotiations and a visit from Porat, Peres changed his decision. The army will not help the settlers, he explained, but will also avoid hindering their efforts. On Peres's decision and motivations, see Zertal and Eldar, *Lords of the Land*, 34–35; Hoberman, *Keneged Kol Hasikuyim*, 92; Yehiel Limor, "Peres: Ani Natati Ha'ishur Lehakamat Mahane Ha'avoda 'Ofra' Leyad Rammalla," June 18, 1975, Ofra Archives; Yosef Harif, "Mishulhan Hamemshala," *Maariv*, December 5, 1975, Ofra Archives; Admoni, *Decade of Discretion*, 150–154.

35. Ester Valershtein, "Interviews with Four of Ofra's Founders," interview by Inbal Yisraeli (Weiner), April 2005, Ofra Archives; Miriam Tan'ami, "Interviews with Four of Ofra's Founders," interview by Inbal Yisraeli (Weiner), April 2005, Ofra Archives; Haya Etzion, Sipuro shel Makom: Proyekt Re'ayonot Im Vatikei Hahityashvut Bebinyamin, interview by Ofra Erlih, January 1, 2013, Ofra Archives.

36. Etzion, "Interviews with Four of Ofra's Founders."

37. The name Ofra was proposed prior to April 1975. See Gorenberg, *The Accidental Empire*, 312. On the biblical significance of Ofra, see Zertal and Eldar, *Lords of the Land*, 32.

38. Hoberman, *Keneged Kol Hasikuyim*, 94; Admoni, *Decade of Discretion*, 151; Etzion, "Interviews with Four of Ofra's Founders."

39. Zalman Deutch, phone interview by author, July 25, 2016.

40. Zalman Deutch, interview by author, April 27, 2015; Deutch, phone interview by author.

41. Deutch, phone interview by author.

42. Deutch, phone interview by author.

43. Admoni, *Decade of Discretion*, 154.

44. See Admoni, *Decade of Discretion*, 36–37; Lein, *Land Grab: Israel's Settlement Policy in the West Bank*, 21.

45. Admoni, *Decade of Discretion*, 154.

46. Ran Abramitzky, *The Mystery of the Kibbutz: Egalitarian Principles in a Capitalist World* (Princeton, NJ: Princeton University Press, 2018), 43. The share of Jewish Israelis living in kibbutzim had also been declining, from almost 5 percent in 1952 to less than 3.5 in the early 1970s. See Ran Abramitzky, "Lessons from the Kibbutz on the Equality–Incentives Trade-Off," *Journal of Economic Perspectives* 25, no. 1 (Winter 2011): 186–187, https://doi.org/10.1257/jep.25.1.185.

47. Yoske Manor (resident and former head of Ofra's construction committee), interview by author, June 11, 2015; Levia Applebaum and David Newman, *Between Village and Suburb: New Settlement Patterns in Israel* [in Hebrew] (Rehovot, Israel: Hamerkaz Leheker Hityashvut Kafrit Ve'ironit, 1989), 25.

48. "Protokol Aseifat Haverim Shehitkayma Bemotza"sh Pr' 'Truma' Tashla"z," 1977, 2–3, resident assemblies transcripts, Ofra Archives.

49. Pinhas Valershtein, interview by author, June 28, 2015; "Soda shel Ofra," *Nekuda*, June 13, 1980, 6; "Aseifat Haverim Beta'arih U"G Tamuz Tashl"a (22.6)," June 22, 1975, resident assemblies transcripts, Ofra Archives.

50. Uzi Gdor, interview by author, August 4, 2015; Yoel Bin-Nun, interview by author, July 25, 2015.

51. Danny Tzidkoni, "Hitnahalut Betzeadei-Tzav," *Lamerhav*, August 22, 1969, 4.

52. Uzi Gdor, interview by author; Danny Tzidkoni, "Mehinim Tochnit Av Lepituah Haretzu'a Vetzfon Sinai," *Davar*, January 19, 1972, 6.

53. Valershtein, interview by author.

54. Uzi Gdor, interview by author, August 13, 2015; Gdor, interview by author, August 4, 2015. In September 1975, a news article reported on the founding of the new agency. The agency represented six settlements located in the West Bank, the Sinai Peninsula, and the Golan Heights. See Danny Tzidkoni, "Ve'ada Lehityashvut Ironit Bashtahim," *Davar*, September 17, 1975, 2. According to David Newman, the official decision to establish the agency took place at another meeting held at the house of the then president of Tel Aviv University, Professor Yuval Neeman. The first official meeting of the agency was carried out in Tel Aviv on August 17, 1975. Newman, "The Role of Gush Emunim," 237–240.

55. Gdor, interview by author, August 4, 2015. See a copy of the text in Uzi Gdor to Aharon Uzan, "Hayeshuv Hakehilati," October 19, 1975, 4141/12-A, ISA.

56. Some moshav residents in the prestate era, it should be noted, were not employed in agriculture. On the so-called "labor settlements" and their significance, see Erik Cohen, *The City in the Zionist Ideology* (Jerusalem: Hebrew University, Institute of Urban and Regional Studies, 1970); Troen, *Imagining Zion*, 17; Newman, "The Role of Gush Emunim," 172–182 and 192.

57. Gdor, interview by author, August 4, 2015. Planners, including Ra'anan Weiss from the Settlement Department, had in fact been preoccupied with finding alternatives to the kibbutz and the moshav. Notably, Weiss drafted plans for nonagricultural rural settlements in the Galilee prior to 1967, designed to "Judaize" the area. He placed each settlement on a hilltop so it would overlook Arab settlements. Weiss's plan was executed only after 1977, when thirty such settlements, which came to be known as *mitzpim*, were built on the hilltops of the Galilee and the Golan Heights. Troen, *Imagining Zion*, 226.

58. Abramitzky, *The Mystery of the Kibbutz*, 50. On industrialization processes in the kibbutz and the moshav, see David Newman, "The Role of Gush Emunim and the Yishuv Kehillati in the West Bank 1974–1980" (PhD diss., Durham University, 1981), 190–198, http://etheses.dur.ac.uk/9372/.

59. Joseph Zeira, *The Israeli Economy: A Story of Success and Costs* (Princeton, NJ: Princeton University Press, 2021), 41–42. The share of Jewish Israelis living in rural settlements had also decreased, dropping from 23.3 percent in 1955 to 9.2 percent in 1975. See Kellerman, *Society and Settlement*, 68–69.

60. On industrial settlements in Israel, see Applebaum and Newman, *Between Village and Suburb*, 14–37.

61. At the time, there were already Israelis who resided in rural settlements and worked in city centers. However, they were usually granted the right to do so only because their income from agriculture was insufficient. Newman, "The Role of Gush Emunim," 245–246.

62. Newman "The Role of Gush Emunim," 230–236.

63. Bin-Nun, interview by author.

64. Gdor, interview by author, August 4, 2015; Uzi Gdor to Shmuel Ofan (Ofra), "Hayeshuv Hakehilati," October 17, 1975, 2–3, Ofra Archives; Danny Tzidkoni, "Ma Ze Yeshuv Kehilati," *Davar*, November 14, 1975, 14.

65. Gdor to Ofan, "Hayeshuv Hakehilati," October 17, 1975, 2; Uzi Gdor, "Tipuah Ma'arahot Kehilatiyot Ke'emtzaee Le'idud Me'oravut Hevratit," 1975, Uzi Gdor's private collection.

66. Gdor to Ofan, "Hayeshuv Hakehilati," October 17, 1975, 1; Gdor, interview by author.

67. Gdor, interview by author, August 4, 2015.

68. Matthew Gordon Lasner, *High Life: Condo Living in the Suburban Century* (New Haven, CT: Yale University Press, 2012), 37–38, 52, and 79–82.

69. Yehuda Don, "The Kibbutz: Issues of Existence and Models of Survival," *Journal of Rural Cooperation* 26, no. 1–2 (1998): 124; Abramitzky, *The Mystery of the Kibbutz*, 120–121.

70. Gdor, interview by author, August 4, 2015. In a letter he wrote, Gdor noted that the residents' association would be the body entrusted with "keeping on the character of the settlement, examining physical plans in the areas of construction and development." See Gdor to Ofan, "Hayeshuv Hakehilati," October 17, 1975, 2.

71. Kallus and Law-Yone, "Habayit Haleumi Vehabayit Ha'ishi," 178.

72. "Pgishat Hamazkirut im Uzi Gdor Mitnuat Hayeshuvim Haironiim Hahadashim: 16.11.75 Sha'a 18:00," November 16, 1975, resident assemblies transcripts, Ofra Archives.

73. Gdor, interview by author, August 4, 2015.

74. Gdor, interview by author, August 4, 2015; Gdor, interview by author, August 13, 2015.

75. Gdor, interview by author, August 13, 2015.

76. Gdor, interview by author, August 13, 2015.

77. It is unclear when exactly Levitt was recruited to the project. The first plan Levitt had drawn for the settlers in Ofra's archives is dated "1975/6." Pinhas Valershtein confirmed to me that this was indeed the time when Levitt was recruited. The earliest mention of the collaboration between the settlers and the Jerusalemite architect I found in a daily newspaper dates to April 1977. Valershtein, interview by author; Aharon Dolev, "Betahbulot Ta'ase Leha Yeshuv," *Maariv*, April 15, 1977, 23; Israel Levitt and Ofra's Building Committee, "Givat Ofra," April 1977, folder 46, box 4, Ofra Archives.

78. *Mi Vami Bein Musmahei Hatehniyon* (Haifa: Irgun Musmahei Hatehniyon, 1965), 51.

79. Yonatan Shiloni, interview by author, November 29, 2015; Lou Gelehrter (architect in charge of landscaping and development at Ofra), interview by author, August 8, 2016.

80. Levitt collaborated with two other architects, Y. Perlshtein and Y. Sheinberg, on the

project. Amiram Harlap, ed., *Israel Builds 1973* (Tel Aviv: Ministry of Housing, 1973), 132–137; Yehonatan Golani and Dieter Gershom V. Schwarze, eds., *Israel Builds 1970* (Jerusalem: Ministry of Housing, 1970), pp. 4.23–4.31.

81. Nitzan-Shiftan, *Seizing Jerusalem.*

82. David Cassuto, interview by author, January 22, 2019.

83. Neve Gordon, "Of Dowries and Brides: A Structural Analysis of Israel's Occupation," *Israeli Sociology* 9, no. 2 (2008): 283–287; Gordon, "From Colonization to Separation," 30.

84. Levitt and Ofra's Building Committee, "Givat Ofra." By 1976, Levitt had completed an earlier draft that was significantly more rudimentary. See Israel Levitt, "Tohnit Binui," 1976, folder 18, box 2, Ofra Archives.

85. Levitt and Ofra's Building Committee, "Givat Ofra."

86. On the Joint Settlement Committee, see "Protokol Miyeshivat Have'ada Leinyanei Bikoret Hamedina Shitkayma Beyom Gimel, K"A Beshvat, Hatashm"a, 12.2.85, Sha'a 12:30," February 12, 1985, 2–3, 1423/26-K, ISA; Lein, *Land Grab*, 20; Rokach, *Rural Settlement in Israel*, 63–64.

87. A. Lishanski (prime minister's secretary), "HT/20, HT/21," July 26, 1977, 7006/12-A, ISA.

88. "Protocol: Yeshivat Have'ada Leinyanei Hityashvut Hameshutefet Lamemshala Velahistadrut Hatziyonit," August 2, 1977, 7006/12-A, ISA.

89. For settlers' complaints about being turned down by state officials prior to government authorization, see, for example, Ofra's Secretariat to Prime Minister Yizhak Rabin, "Bakasha Lepgisha," August 14, 1975, 6723/68-G, ISA.

90. Yosef Waxman, "Ma'ale Adumim Ihiyeh Yeshuv Ironi; Elon-Moreh Veofra-Kfarei Ta'asiya," *Maariv*, August 3, 1977.

91. See Gavriel Krien to S. Tzukerman (Ha'agaf Letihnun Hityashvuti), "Ofra," September 30, 1977, 104338, Jewish Agency for Israel Archives (hereafter JAIA).

92. "Soda shel Ofra," 15.

93. Lou Gelehrter, interview by author.

94. Bin-Nun, interview by author.

95. Gavriel Krien to Israel Levitt, "Heskem Avoda Letihnun Ofra," December 19, 1977, 104338, JAIA; Israel Levitt to Gavriel Krien, "Heskem Avoda Letihnun Ofra," December 21, 1977, 104338, JAIA; World Zionist Organization and Israel Levitt, "Heskem," December 21, 1977, 104338, JAIA.

96. The lands were seized from the nearby Palestinian villages of Yabrud and Silwad. Nir Shalev, *Hahitnahalut Ofra: Ma'ahaz Bilti-Murshe* (Jerusalem: B'Tselem, December 2008), 15-20.

97. Israel Levitt, "Ofra: Tohnit Mit'ar," January 1978, S15M205275, Central Zionist Archives (hereafter CZA); Israel Levitt, "Ofra: Tohnit Mit'ar," January 1978, S15M205271, CZA.

98. Etzion, Sipuro shel Makom: Proyekt Re'ayonot im Vatikei Hahityashvut Bebinyamin; Etzion, interview by author.

99. Prior to presenting his final drawings, Levitt had a meeting with state planners in January 1978 where they discussed the plans. See transcription by Gavriel Krien, "Sikum Ve'ada Miktzoit Ofra Miyom 5.1.78," January 18, 1978, JAIA. At the same time, the regional planner Yossi Sakoza and the geographer Ilana Ben conducted a study of the environmental conditions of Ofra's area for the Settlement Department.

See Yossi Sakoza and Ilana Ben, "Do"h Lemikumei Keva," February 1978, 104338, JAIA.

100. "Sikum Ve'ada Shiput—Ofra Miyom 6.3.78" (World Zionist Organization, March 15, 1978), 103242, JAIA.

101. Yossie Naim to Ofra secretariat, September 13, 1979, 104338, JAIA. According to B'Tselem, Ofra nevertheless lacked a legally valid detailed master plan, at least until 2008. Shalev, "Hahitnahalut Ofra," 10-12.

102. David Newman, "Settlements as Suburbanization: The Banality of Colonization," in *Normalizing Occupation: The Politics of Everyday Life in the West Bank Settlements*, ed. Ariel Handel, Marco Allegra, and Erez Maggor (Bloomington: Indiana University Press, 2017), 38.

103. Gdor, interview by author, August 4, 2015.

104. Gavriel Krien, interview by author, November 26, 2015.

105. Levitt and Ofra's Building Committee, "Givat Ofra."

106. Valershtein, interview by author.

107. Moshe Merhavia (first secretary of Ofra), interview by author, December 24, 2015; Valershtein, interview by author.

108. Manor, interview by author. As a government-approved rural settlement, Ofra was eligible for state funding. In other rural settlements, the government would usually fund the construction of all houses. The houses were then either handed over to the residents for as long as they remained there, or sold to them on favorable terms. On the financing of houses in rural settlements in Israel and its effects on community settlement residents, see Newman, "The Role of Gush Emunim," 322–324.

109. Levitt and Ofra's Building Committee, "Givat Ofra." At first, the settlers also discussed with ministry officials the possibility of applying a Build Your Own Home scheme in Ofra. Valershtein, interview by author; Newman, "The Role of Gush Emunim," 322–324; Y. Margalit (head of the new settlements and rural administration and rural construction engineer at Jerusalem region), "Programa Lebniya—Ofra: Tohnit 1978," December 13, 1978, 104338, JAIA; Haggai Eshed, "Sharon: Hushlema Hamisgeret Layeshuvim Hadashim Bashomron," *Davar*, August 8, 1978.

110. On Zionist iconography of rural landscapes, see Yael Zerubavel, *Desert in the Promised Land*, Stanford Studies in Jewish History and Culture (Stanford, CA: Stanford University Press, 2019), 69.

111. Yossi Ben-Artzi, "Nof Vezehut: Hagag Ha'eretz Yisraeli Bemerutzat Hadorot," in *A Century of Israeli Culture*, ed. Israel Bartal (Jerusalem: Magnes Press, 2002), 266–272.

112. Newman, "Settlements as Suburbanization," 37.

113. Merhavia, interview by author. Other activists I interviewed confirmed Merhavia's comments. Yoske Manor, for example, emphasized the fact that the red roofs offered uniformity. Manor, interview by author.

114. Etzion, interview by author.

115. Aaron Halamish (Ofra secretary in 1980–1981), interview by author, May 18, 2015.

116. Notably, in 1980, two deadly attacks against settlers took place in Hebron. Prior to that, starting in 1975, skirmishes between Jews and Palestinians around the Tomb of the Patriarchs became commonplace. Ehud Sprinzak, *The Ascendance of Israel's Radical Right* (New York: Oxford University Press, 1991), 90–91. Altogether, 495 violent acts occurred in the West Bank between 1968 and 1977. Meron Benvenisti,

1986 Report: Demographic, Economic, Legal, Social, and Political Developments in the West Bank (Jerusalem and Boulder, CO: American Enterprise Institute, West Bank Data Base Project; Westview Press, 1986), 63.

117. On Gush Emunim's changing and multifaceted attitude toward the Palestinians, see Feige, *Settling in the Hearts*, 112–130.

118. Merhavia, interview by author. On how violent clashes with the Palestinians have influenced the architectural discourse in Israel, see Alona Nitzan-Shiftan, "On Concrete and Stone: Shifts and Conflicts in Israeli Architecture," *Traditional Dwellings and Settlements Review* 21, no. 1 (Fall 2009): 51–65.

119. The houses the Ministry of Construction and Housing built in rural settlements usually measured 68 square meters. Settler representatives explained they needed larger houses because they were older and had more kids. The selected model home was 72 square meters. Settlers had the option of adding one or two bedrooms. Manor, interview by author; Merhavia, interview by author; Y. Margalit (head of the new settlements and rural administration and rural construction engineer at Jerusalem region), "Programa Lebniya—Ofra: Tochnit 1978," December 13, 1978, JAIA.

120. Hemdat Shani, conversation with author, May 5, 2015; Valershtein, interview by author; Aaron Halamish, interview by author.

121. Halamish, interview by author.

122. Valershtein, interview by author.

123. Halamish, interview by author.

124. Yehoram Rasis-Tal, interview by author, May 12, 2015.

125. Valershtein, interview by author; Pinhas Valershtein, interview by Hemdat Shani, December 12, 2007, Ofra Archives.

126. Haggai Segal, "Shchunat Keva Rishona Be'ofra," September 23, 1981, Ofra Archives.

127. Haggai Segal, "Im Hapanim Lebinyamin," *Nekuda*, August 13, 1983, 12.

128. For kibbutz members' criticism of settlements, see, for example, Kalman Kleiman, "Hityashvut—O Hitnahalut," *Maariv*, May 15, 1986, 11; Yitzhak Ben-Aharon, "Hamitpatmim Mehahon Haleumi," *Davar*, April 6, 1987 (reprinted in *Nekuda*, vol. 110); Reuma Ziskind, "Mi Shemehapes Hayey Shituf Yeleh Lakibutz Velo Lehitnahaluyot," *Maariv*, February 16, 1987, 13; Oved Tzur (Kibbutz Malkiya), "Shuvu Habayta, Alu Artza!," *Nekuda*, May 15, 1988; Eyal Kafkafi, "Hayeshuvim Beyo"sh Lo Tormim Labitahon," *Nekuda*, November 1987, 4. Also see Amos Oz, *In the Land of Israel*, trans. Maurie Goldberg-Bartura (San Diego: Harcourt Brace, 1993), 134.

129. Settlers adhered to these rules even after Ministry of Construction and Housing officials requested that they avoid doing so. See a Ministry request to remove the settlers' insistence on pitched red-tile roofs and stone cladding in D. Ben-Yishai (Jerusalem region engineer) to Yossie Naim, September 28, 1979, 104338, JAIA. For Ofra's building code, see Ofra's Building Committee, "Taktzir Takanot Habniya Be'ofra Venohalei Hagashat Habakashot Le'ishurei Bniya," January 1993, folder 26, box 2, Ofra Archives.

130. I was told that, in subsequent years, when working on other projects, Levitt would refer back to the red-roofed homes Ofra's settlers had commissioned as a negative example. "Just not Ofra houses again," he would say. Shiloni, interview by author.

131. Israel Levitt, "Synagogue Plans," 1981, folder 28, box 2, Ofra Archives.

132. Jabo (Ze'ev Hanoh Erlih), "Tohnit Hadasha Lebeit Haknesset Hakavua," August 21, 1982, Ofra Archives.

133. Yehuda Etzion, "Beit Hatfila," *Et Ofra*, December 10, 1982, 10–11, Ofra Archives.

134. Yehuda Etzion on behalf of the synagogue committee, "Leromem Et Beit Elokeinu," *Et Ofra*, June 11, 1983, 11–12, Ofra Archives.

135. Etzion, "Beit Hatfila," 10–11.

136. Etzion, interview by author; Jabo, "Tohnit Hadasha Lebeit Haknesset Hakavua."

137. Yehuda Etzion on behalf of Yoel Bin-Nun and Jabo, "Mikdash Me'at," *Et Ofra*, October 29, 1982, 3–4, Ofra Archives. The term *mikdash me'at* appears in the Book of Ezekiel (11:16) and is sometimes used to denote a synagogue.

138. Etzion, "Mikdash Me'at," 3–4.

139. See Yehuda Etzion on behalf of Yoel and Jabo to Gideon Charlap, October 1983, Gideon Charlap private collection.

140. Oz Almog, *The Sabra—A Profile* [in Hebrew] (Tel Aviv: Am Oved, 1997), 252–254, 265; Anita Shapira, *New Jews Old Jews* [in Hebrew] (Tel Aviv: Am Oved, 1997), 219.

141. See Shapira, *New Jews*, 226–232. On the encounter between Israeli nationalism, the biblical imaginary, and modern architecture, see Nitzan-Shiftan, *Seizing Jerusalem*, 36–44. On secular Zionists' selective reconstruction of the past, see Zerubavel, *Recovered Roots*, esp. 13–36; Nitzan-Shiftan, "On Concrete and Stone."

142. On settlers' use of biblical archaeology and geography and its effects, see Michael Feige, *One Space, Two Places: Gush Emunim, Peace Now and the Construction of Israeli Space* [in Hebrew] (Jerusalem: Magnes Press, 2002), 75–100. On secular and religious Zionists' use of the Bible, see Aran, "Return to the Scriptures in Modern Israel."

143. Jabo, "Tohnit Hadasha Lebeit Haknesset Hakavua."

144. Gideon Charlap, interview by author, August 23, 2016.

145. Etzion, "Beit Hatfila."

146. Etzion, "Leromem Et Beit Elokeinu."

147. Etzion, interview by author.

148. Etzion, interview by author; Etzion, "Leromem Et Beit Elokeinu."

149. On the Jewish Underground, see Haggai Segal, *Dear Brothers* [in Hebrew] (Jerusalem: Keter, 1987).

150. Etzion, interview by author.

151. Meiron Poliakin, phone conversation with the author, 2015.

152. For criticism of Ofra's synagogue, see, for example, *Nekuda* team, "Harutinizatzya shel Hahagshama," *Nekuda*, October 1987, 42; Hava Pinhas-Cohen, "Livroah min Haklishaot: Re'ayon im David Cassuto," *Nekuda*, September 21, 1984, 37. For a special issue of *Et Ofra* that was dedicated to the inauguration of the synagogue (and had some words of praise), see Tzipi and Hava, eds., "Et Ofra," October 1987, Ofra Archives.

153. Gush Emunim, "Tohnit Av Lehityashvut Beyehuda Veshomron," 1978, Hovrot, Ofra Archives.

154. "Settlements and Outposts Numbers and Data" (Tel Aviv: Peace Now, June 2009).

155. Newman, "The Role of Gush Emunim," 108, 135–138, and 446. According to Shaul Arieli, only a small portion of Drobles's plan was executed. Shaul Arieli, "Meshihiyut Al Sela Hametzi'ut: Mif'al Hahitnahaluyot Beyehuda Vershomron, Hazon o Ashlaya, 1967–2016" (Israel, November 2017), 28–31 and 61, https://www.shaularieli.com/wp-content/uploads/2018/08/%D7%94%D7%9E%D7%A9%D7%99%D7%97%D7%99%D7%95%D7%AA-%D7%A2%D7%9C-%D7

%A1%D7%9C%D7%A2-%D7%94%D7%9E%D7%A6%D7%99%D7%90%
D7%95%D7%AA-191117.pdf, 28–31 and 61.

156. Valershtein, interview by author.

157. Among those who assumed leading roles in the settlement movement are Israel Harel (who founded *Nekuda* magazine and the settlers' representative council, Yesha) and Pinhas Valershtein (who became secretary of Mateh Binyamin Regional Council). Some of Ofra's residents helped sketch a couple of master plans that Gush Emunim proposed to the government in subsequent years. Notable among Gush Emunim's plans was a master plan from 1978 for some two million residents scattered across Israel and the occupied territories: 750,000 of them were to be settled in the West Bank within less than twenty-five years. To ensure Jewish presence in each and every corner of the West Bank, the plan proposed erecting some 120 community settlements (alongside other settlement forms). The community settlement model, they emphasized, had the power not only to scatter the population across the West Bank but also to fill what they envisioned as a deeply rooted social need—to move from urban to rural environments. However, Gush Emunim's master plan was not accepted by official planning agencies. According to Meron Benvenisti, it inspired Matityahu Drobles, from the World Zionist Organization, and was somehow incorporated into his plan. See Gush Emunim, "Tohnit Av Lehityashvut Beyehuda Veshomron," 1978, Hovrot, Ofra Archives; Meron Benvenisti and Shlomo Khayat, *The West Bank and Gaza Atlas* (Jerusalem: WBDP, 1988), 64.

158. Gabriel Schwake, "The Community Settlement: A Neo-Rural Territorial Tool," *Planning Perspectives* 36, no. 2 (March 4, 2021): 237–257; Newman, "Settlements as Suburbanization."

159. Leon, "Self-Segregation of the Vanguard," 356–357.

160. Horwitz, "The Community Oriented Model," 30; Shmuel Horwitz, "Hadegem Hakehilati Bemisgeret Hityashvut Hadasha," in *Leket Hartzaot Benos'ei Tihnun, Binui Ve'ihlus*, ed. Zehava Bar-Yosef (Jerusalem: Ministry of Housing, 1985), 6–20.

161. According to Peace Now's data sheet, in 2011 there were some eighty community settlements. According to B'Tselem's report, however, in 2002 there were only sixty-six officially designated community settlements. According to Newman and Applebaum, by 1992, there were seventy-four. This gap probably stems from the fact that the Central Bureau of Statistics considers any settlement with more than two thousand residents "urban," leaving out some settlements that in practice operate as community settlements. (According to Peace Now's data, in 2011, there were about sixty-seven community settlements with fewer than two thousand residents.) See "Settlements Database" (Peace Now, 2011); Lein, *Land Grab*, 24; David Newman and Levia Applebaum, "Hayeshuv Vehakfar Hakehilati Mera'ayon Lemetziot," in *Ascent to the Mountains: Renewal of Jewish Settlement in Judea and Samaria* (Jerusalem: Sifriyat Beit El, 2022).

162. On the politics and the significance of commemoration, see M. Christine Boyer, "Collective Memory Under Siege: The Case of 'Heritage Terrorism,'" in *The SAGE Handbook of Architectural Theory*, ed. Greig Crysler, Stephen Cairns, and Hilde Heynen (London: SAGE, 2013), 325–339.

163. To a degree, these two design projects—the synagogue on the one hand, and the model home on the other—speak to the tension the sociologist Michael Feige identified in Ofra between religious fundamentalism and normative daily life. See Feige, *Settling in the Hearts*, 181–195.

164. On the transformation of community settlements into suburban ones, see Schwake, "The Community Settlement," 244–248. According to the architectural historian Yael Allweil, flexibility is the defining principle of the community settlement model, which, she writes, is "a unique settlement model capable of producing tiny, isolated outposts as well as large, urban, populous settlements based on the single-family home as a building block." It "is both *city* and *village*," she adds. The community settlement model is indeed more flexible than the kibbutz, but Allweil's argument strikes me as an exaggeration. While some community settlements adopted a suburban façade, none, so far, is "large, urban, populous." Allweil's exaggeration may stem from the fact that some of the settlements she uses as evidence of the community settlement's flexibility (like the settlement of Ma'ale Adumim) are not, in fact, community settlements, and altogether her account lacks historical detail. (For instance, she claims that professional planners were not involved in the conception of the community settlement, failing to account for Gdor's role.) Yael Allweil, "Both City and Village: The West Bank 'Communal Settlement' as Architecture and Planning Lab," in *Israel as a Modern Architectural Experimental Lab, 1948–1978*, ed. Inbal Ben-Asher Gitler and Anat Geva (Bristol, UK: Intellect, 2020), 71–93.
165. Etzion, interview by author.

CHAPTER 3: QUALITY-OF-LIFE SETTLEMENTS

1. Israel Goodovitch, interview by author, March 31, 2015.
2. According to B'Tselem, by the end of 1977, there were thirty-one settlements, and by the end of 1983, there were seventy-six. Lein, *Land Grab*, 18.
3. Goodovitch, interview by author.
4. Benny Avni, "Sar Lekol Rohesh," *Ha'ir*, April 1, 1983, 9.
5. Although construction accelerated rapidly in 1981, under the Likud, Marco Allegra has argued that the Likud government merely continued processes that the Labor government had set in motion prior to 1977. See Marco Allegra, "'Outside Jerusalem—Yet so Near': Ma'ale Adumim, Jerusalem, and the Suburbanization of Israel's Settlement Policy," in *Normalizing Occupation: The Politics of Everyday Life in the West Bank Settlements*, ed. Marco Allegra, Ariel Handel, and Erez Maggor (Bloomington: Indiana University Press, 2017); Marco Allegra, "Habanaliyut shel Hakibush Vahapolitika shel Haparvar: Hamikre shel Ma'ale Adumim," *Theory and Criticism* 47 (Winter 2016): 95–99.
6. A Peace Now database from 2011 divided authorized settlements into three categories: "ideological," "quality-of-life," and "ultra-Orthodox." Of the eighty-one settlements Peace Now qualified as community settlements, about fifteen were defined as "quality-of-life" settlements, and eight were marked as "quality-of-life/ideological." Meanwhile, fifty-eight community settlements were defined as "ideological," and the remaining two as "ultra-Orthodox." "Settlements Database" (Peace Now, 2011).
7. Lein, *Land Grab*, 18.
8. Seventy-three percent of the units built between 1979 and 1984 in settlements were in so-called urban settlements (rather than rural ones). Maggor, "State, Market," 156. In 1986, 84.8 percent of the settlers resided in the metropolitan areas of Jerusalem and Tel Aviv. Benvenisti and Khayat, *The West Bank and Gaza Atlas*, 33.
9. According to Benvenisti (who presented slightly different numbers), "The annual

increase [in settlers' population in 1986] was 14.2 percent compared with 20 percent in 1985 and about 60 percent in 1984." In 1981–1983, it was about 30 percent. See Meron Benvenisti, *The West Bank Data Base Project 1987 Report: Demographic, Economic, Legal, Social and Political Developments in the West Bank* (New York: Routledge, 2019), 52–55. According to Eldar and Zertal, about 14,000 Israelis moved into settlements between 1984 and 1985, and, on average, only 5,000 joined them every year between 1986 and 1989. The decline in settlement construction, they argue, was also an outcome of an economic recession. Eldar and Zertal, *Adonei Haaretz*, 140–143; "Settlements Database."

10. Lein, *Land Grab*, 18.

11. Eldar and Zertal, *Adonei Haaretz*, 143. Already in mid-1986 and April 1987, violent incidents had slowed sales in settlements. Benvenisti, *The West Bank Data Base*, 65.

12. According to Peace Now, in 1987, there were 60,300 settlers. According to B'Tselem, there were 57,900. "New 2018 Population Data for Israelis in the West Bank" (Peace Now, October 2, 2019), https://peacenow.org.il/en/population-data-in-israel-and-in -the-west-bank; Lein, *Land Grab*, 18.

13. The initial decision to erect a settlement was made by the Joint Settlement Committee and not by the Ministry of Construction and Housing. But, as the sociologist Erez Maggor has shown, the ministry was the main governmental authority charged with settlement construction at the time. Maggor, "State, Market," 147.

14. Avni, "Sar Lekol Rohesh," 9.

15. On the Likud government's early declarations and activities, see Newman, "The Role of Gush Emunim," 125–129; Eldar and Zertal, *Adonei Haaretz*, 83–89.

16. Talia Sasson, "Havat Da'at," 60–61.

17. Maggor, "State, Market," 145–146.

18. Sasson, "Havat Da'at," 52.

19. Palestinian residents of the village of Rujeib, whose lands were taken to make space for the settlement of Elon Moreh, filed the petition that led to the 1979 court ruling. After Gush Emunim activists and a former IDF chief of staff argued that Elon Moreh was not built to advance Israel's security, the Supreme Court ordered it dismantled and the land returned to its Palestinian owners. Lein, *Land Grab*, 49–50.

20. Sasson, "Havat Da'at," 61.

21. The government could claim two types of lands as "state lands": "Miri" and "Mawat" lands. See Lein, *Land Grab*, 52.

22. See Plia Albeck, "Karka'ot Beyehuda Veshomron: Tadpis Hartza'ata shel O"d Pliya Albeck," May 28, 1985, S136/3770, CZA; Eyal Weizman, *Hollow Land: Israel's Architecture of Occupation* (London: Verso, 2007), 116–120; Benvenisti and Khayat, *The West Bank and Gaza Atlas*, 61; Maggor, "State, Market," 145–146.

23. By 1992, some 25 percent of West Bank lands were designated as "state lands" (not including lands seized in East Jerusalem). Nir Shalev, *Be'etztala shel Hukiyut: Hah-razot al Admot Medina Bagada Hama'aravit* (Jerusalem: B'Tselem, February 2012), https://www.btselem.org/download/201203_under_the_guise_of_legality_heb.pdf. According to Maggor, mapping and land appropriations were mostly made between 1980 and 1984. Maggor, "State, Market," 146. According to a Peace Now report, 1,400,000 dunams were designated as "state lands" in the West Bank by 2018. Less than half of these lands were allocated for any use. Of those allocated, only 0.24 percent (about 1,625 dunams) were given to Palestinians. See "State Land Allocation

in the West Bank—For Israelis Only" (Peace Now, July 17, 2018), https://peacenow
.org.il/en/state-land-allocation-west-bank-israelis.

24. Maggor, "State, Market," 147.
25. On ministry budgets allocated to settlements, see Maggor, "State, Market," 149–153.
26. Danny Gutwein, "He'arot," 203–211. On changes at the Ministry of Housing following the 1977 elections, see Hadas Shadar, *Avnei Habinyan shel Hashikun Hatsiburi*, 162–167.
27. Erez Maggor, "State, Market," 151.
28. Gutwein, "He'arot," 206–208.
29. Shanee Shiloh, "Vilot Tzena: Adrichalut, Itzuv Pnim Vema'amad Hevrati Beyisrael (1948–1967)" (colloquium talk, Tel Aviv University, 2020).
30. Gonen, *Between City and Suburb*, 120.
31. Joseph Zeira, *The Israeli Economy: A Story of Success and Costs* (Princeton, NJ: Princeton University Press, 2021), 39.
32. On how increasing wealth is likely to influence sprawl, see Robert Bruegmann, *Sprawl: A Compact History* (Chicago: University of Chicago Press, 2005), 10.
33. Gonen, *Between City and Suburb*, 116.
34. Gonen, *Between City and Suburb*, 114 and 117.
35. Gonen, *Between City and Suburb*, 121.
36. The geographer Juval Portugali took this argument a step further, contending that "Jewish colonization of the West Bank was mostly part of the metropolitan expansion of the Tel-Aviv region and the metropolization of Jerusalem." Portugali, "Jewish Settlement in the Occupied Territories," 33.
37. Shmaryahu Cohen to Gideon Patt (minister of Housing), "Ma'ale Adumim," February 6, 1978, 15429/9-GL, ISA; Mahon Urbani, "Bdikat Itur Vepotenzial Pituah shel Yeshuv Be'ezor Ma'ale Adumim," May 1977, 13 and 118, 14538/8-G, ISA.
38. Mahon Urbani, "Bdikat Itur."
39. Mahon Urbani, "Hanhayot Veprograma Lepituah Ma'ale Adumim," March 1978, 6, Ma'ale Adumim Archives (hereafter MAA).
40. Mahon Urbani, "Bdikat Itur," 146, 4.
41. Yosef Waxman, "Rashei Halikud Kvar Hevtihu: Yeshuv Ironi Yukam Bema'ale Adumim," *Maariv*, June 20, 1977.
42. David Ovadiya to Colonel Feldman, "Ma'ale Adumim—Itur Hashetah Lebinyan Ha'ir," April 2, 1978, 15429/9-GL, ISA.
43. Elinoar Barzaki, interview by author, December 23, 2015.
44. Thomas Leitersdorf, "Ir Hadasha Bema'ale Adumim: Gisha Ra'ayonit Veirgunit Lebitzua Avodot Hatihnun," October 20, 1977, 2–3, 15484/4-GL, ISA.
45. Daniel A. Barber, "Experimental Dwellings: Modern Architecture and Environmental Research at the M.I.T. Solar Energy Fund, 1938–1963," in *A Second Modernism: MIT, Architecture, and the "Techno-Social" Moment*, ed. Arindam Dutta (Cambridge, MA: MIT Press, 2013), 263–284; Daniel A. Barber, *A House in the Sun: Modern Architecture and Solar Energy in the Cold War* (New York: Oxford University Press, 2016).
46. On the history of building climatology in Israel between the 1940s and 1970s, see Or Aleksandrowicz, "Appearance and Performance: Israeli Building Climatology and Its Effect on Local Architectural Practice (1940–1977)," *Architectural Science Review* 60, no. 5 (September 3, 2017): 371–381.
47. Harlap, *Israel Builds 1977*, 301.

48. Harlap, *Israel Builds 1977*, 301–302.

49. Nachum Granot to Thomas Leitersdorf, "Ma'ale Adumim: Yeutz Vetihnun Ma'arachot Energiya," November 10, 1977, 15484/4-GL, ISA.

50. Other team members included Nachum Granot, Aryeh Bitan, Ezra Zohar, and Y. Tamir. See decision to commission a special climate consulting team in "Sikum Pgisha Me-20.10.77 Benose Ma'ale Adumim," October 1977, 15425/13-GL, ISA.

51. On Givoni's research experience in Pittsburgh, Cleveland, and Massachusetts, see Baruch Givoni, "Creativity and Testing in Research," *Journal of Architectural Education* 32, no. 4 (May 1979): 26, https://doi.org/10.2307/1424381.

52. Baruch Givoni, *Man, Climate and Architecture* (Amsterdam: Elsevier, 1969).

53. Nachum Granot to Shmaryahu Cohen, "Ir Bema'ale Adumim—Pirteikol: Yeshivat Avoda Meshutefet shel Tzevet Yiutz Aklimi im Tzevet Hametachnenim Shehitkayma Beyom 1.1.78," January 5, 1978, 15484/4-GL, ISA; Ezra Zohar to Nachum Granot, "Yeshuv Ironi Bema'ale Adumim," December 18, 1977, 15484/4-GL, ISA.

54. In an interview he gave to the architect Eran Tamir-Tawil in 2002, Leitersdorf recalled a meeting with Ariel Sharon, during which he also emphasized the strategic advantage of the site, arguing that it overlooked an important route to Amman. I was unable to find transcripts of that meeting. See Eran Tamir-Tawil, "To Start a City from Scratch: An Interview with Architect Thomas M. Leitersdorf," in *A Civilian Occupation: The Politics of Israeli Architecture*, rev. ed, ed. Rafi Segal and Eyal Weizman, (Tel Aviv: Babel; London and New York: Verso, 2003), 153–154.

55. Benny Dvir, "Rikuz He'arot Ledo"h Beynayim Shehugash A"Y Adrihal Thomas Leitersdorf," January 25, 1978, MAA.

56. "Sikum Diyun Benose Hakamat Yeshuv Ironi Mizraha Leyerushalayim," February 1, 1978, 15429/9-GL, ISA; Shmaryahu Cohen to Shlomo Avni, "Ma'ale Adumim—Itur Ironi," February 14, 1978, 15429/9-GL, ISA.

57. Amiram Harlap, ed., *Israel Builds 1988* (Jerusalem: Ministry of Housing, 1988), 167; Mahon Urbani, "Hanhayot Veprograma," 4–5.

58. Mahon Urbani, "Hanhayot Veprograma."

59. David Margalit et al., "Ma'ale Adumim: Tahbura Tziburit Pnimit," August 10, 1978, 15484/4-GL, ISA; Thomas Leitersdorf, "Ir Hadasha Bema'ale Adumim," January 21, 1981, 15428/10-GL, ISA; Harlap, *Israel Builds 1988*, 164; Thomas Leitersdorf, "Atar A Hanhayot Klaliyot Lemetahnenei Hamithamim," November 1978, 15484/4-GL, ISA; S. Powsner, G Powsner Architects, and T. Leitersdorf, J. Goldenberg Architects, "Ma'ale Adumim Town Center" (Ministry of Construction and Housing, 1981), 15428/13-GL, ISA. Also, on the trolley system, see "Ma'arehet Hakvishim Hapnimit Vehakroniyot," *Bema'ale Adumim*, July 1981, MAA.

60. Ayala Levin, *Architecture and Development: Israeli Construction in Sub-Saharan Africa and the Settler Colonial Imagination, 1958–1973* (Durham, NC: Duke University Press, 2022), 209–210.

61. See experts' report on the proposed transportation system and correspondence with Chance Manufacturing Co. in "Bhina Kalkalit shel Mashmaut Haf'alat Ma'arehet Tahbura Tziburit Pnimit Nifredet Bema'ale Adumim: Do"h Mesakem" (Economic Consulting and Planning [Y.C.A.] Ltd., April 18, 1980), 15415/10-GL, ISA; [Name unreadable] to Benny Dvir, "Sunliner (Price List and Specifications)," February 11, 1980, 15484/4-GL, ISA. Also see Terry Jessup to Gittit Jakobovitz, "Sunliner," January 28, 1980, 15415/10-GL, ISA.

62. Baruch Givoni, "Hamlatzot Rishoniyot Le'ekronot Habinui Vetihnun Habinyanim Bema'ale Adumim," April 1978, 1–2, 15484/4-GL, ISA.

63. Abraham Rabinovich, "Scramble for Homes in New Town," *Jerusalem Post Weekly*, November 1, 1981.

64. Mahon Urbani, "Hanhayot Veprograma," 7; "Emtza'im Leyisum Hara'ayon [Subheading]" (Ministry of Housing, ca. 1977), 4, 15429/9-GL, ISA.

65. Harlap, *Israel Builds 1988*, 166; Thomas Leitersdorf, "Ir Hadasha Bema'ale Adumim," January 21, 1981, 5, 15428/10-GL, ISA.

66. Thomas Leitersdorf, "Kavim Letihnuna shel Ha'ir," *Bema'ale Adumim*, July 1981, 2, MAA.

67. Harlap, *Israel Builds 1988*, 166.

68. Leitersdorf, "Atar A," 1–2; Leitersdorf, "Ir Hadasha," 5.

69. Thomas Leitersdorf, "Ir Hadasha Bema'ale Adumim: Din Veheshbon Al Hitkadmot Ha'avoda Vepeulot Lebitzua," November 8, 1977, 15484/4-GL, ISA; Thomas Leitersdorf, "Ir Hadasha Bema'ale Adumim: Gisha Ra'ayonit Veirgunit Lebitzua Avodot Hatihnun," October 20, 1977, 15484/4-GL, ISA.

70. Ten construction companies were involved in the development of the first phase of construction. Harlap, *Israel Builds 1988*, 164.

71. See Yaacov Yaar, *Life and Architecture* (Haifa: Architectural and Landscape Heritage Research Center, Faculty of Architecture and Town Planning, The Technion, 2016), 94–108 and 247–257.

72. Nitzan-Shiftan, *Seizing Jerusalem*, 53.

73. Yaar, *Life and Architecture*, 230.

74. Harlap, *Israel Builds 1988*, 172–173; Yaar, *Life and Architecture*, 230–233.

75. Dror Haruvi, "Gan Yeladim Solari Bema'ale Adumim," *Alef Alef*, December 1983.

76. Harlap, *Israel Builds 1988*, 168–169; S. Powsner, G. Powsner Architects and T. Leitersdorf, J. Goldenberg Architects, "Ma'ale Adumim Town Center."

77. Max Wolfson and Azgad Feldi, "Tifroset Habinui Beyeshuv Ironi Hadash—He'arot Mitoh Tazpiyot Ma'akav Bema'ale Adumim," June 1981, 44986/2-GL, ISA.

78. On Israelis' desire for privacy, see Gonen, *Between City and Suburb*, 114–118.

79. For unit prices and government funding, see, for example, "Lihyot Tov Bema'ale Adumim," *Maariv*, October 17, 1980, 15428/10-GL, ISA; "Hoda'a al Mehirot Dirot Bemivnanim d/9 (Ramat) g/6 (Goldstein)" (Ma'ale Adumim Local Council, March 4, 1981), 15425/5-GL, ISA.

80. P. Sefer, "Ma Osim Hahevere Hatovim Bema'ale Adumim?," *Al Hamishmar*, October 22, 1980, 15428/10-GL, ISA.

81. Leitersdorf, "Ir Hadasha."

82. Mahon Urbani, "Hanhayot Veprograma," 7; "Emtza'im Leyisum Hara'ayon," 4.

83. Moshe Bar Natan to Ehud Tayar, "Do"h Sikum Hagralot Ledirot Ma'ale Adumim Shene'erhu Beyom Alef' 28.12.80 Bemtzaut Hev' 'Yuval-Gad,'" January 1, 1981, 15425/5-GL, ISA; Moshe Bar Natan to Ehud Tayar, "Do"h Sikum Hagralot Dirot Shene'erhu Bemisgeret Mehirat Dirot 'Bema'ale Adumim' shel Hevrat Remet Vehev' 'Goldstein' Be'emtzaut Sho"p," April 5, 1981, 15425/5-GL, ISA.

84. Yossi Rivlin, "Histayem Shalav Rishon Beihlus Ma'ale Adumim," *Bema'ale Adumim*, December 1983, 1, MAA. According to the Peace Now database, by 1985 there were 9,340 Israelis living in Ma'ale Adumim. "Settlements Database."

85. In 1983, the average age in Ma'ale Adumim, according to the head of the local

council, was thirty. See Yossi Rivlin, "Ma'ale Adumim—Mifal Atzum," *Bema'ale Adumim*, December 1983, MAA.

86. Iris Kaplan, "Ibuyi Hahityashvut hu Ya'ad Leumi," *Bema'ale Adumim*, May 1984, 6, MAA.

87. Uri Cohen and Nissim Leon, "The New Mizrahi Middle Class: Ethnic Mobility and Class Integration in Israel," *Journal of Israeli History* 27, no. 1 (March 2008): 51–64, https://doi.org/10.1080/13531040801902823.

88. Rafi Vaknin, "Bemo Yadeinu Mananu Hityashvut Masivit Beyesh"a," *Nekuda*, July 26, 1985; Rivi Gillis, "The Question of Ethnic Identity in the Israeli Settlements," 51–54. The Israeli Central Bureau of Statistics conducted partial surveys in settlements in 1983 and 1995. Neither survey, however, provides accurate information concerning the ethnic composition of the settlers. For one thing, the surveys registered Israelis whose parents were born in Israel as "Israeli-born," without specifying their grandparents' ethnic background. In addition, in the case of children of "mixed" parents, the surveys used the father's ethnic identity. Lastly, many settlements were not surveyed at all. In the 1983 survey, which covered only thirty-eight settlements, Mizrahim made up 31 percent of settlers, Ashkenazim made up 36 percent, and "Israeli-born" amounted to 34 percent. In the 1995 survey, 24 percent of West Bank settlers were Mizrahim, 26 percent were Ashkenazim, 34 percent were "Israeli-born," and 11 percent were immigrants from the former Soviet Union. The 1995 survey included a settlement-based breakdown according to these categories. Only 7 percent of the surveyed settlements had a Mizrahi majority, according to the sociologist Rivi Gillis, while 52 percent had an Ashkenazi majority. (The rest were "mixed.") This may suggest that Mizrahi Jews may have indeed been largely excluded from settling in large numbers in community settlements, which make up the largest number of settlements, and instead settled in large suburban settlements. On the Central Bureau of Statistics' surveys and the ethnic breakdown of the settlers, see Rivi Gillis, "The Ethnic Morphology of the Israeli Settlements" [in Hebrew] (master's thesis, Tel Aviv University, 2009), esp. 19–31.

89. Mizrahim, according to Cohen and Leon, amounted to about 30 percent of Israelis in 2008. (This estimate, it seems, does not include those the Central Bureau of Statistics identifies as "Israeli-born," though they may identify as Mizrahim.) Cohen and Leon, "The New Mizrahi Middle Class," 54. According to the 1995 survey, 32 percent of Ma'ale Adumim's residents were Mizrahim, 37 percent were "Israeli-born" (who could be identified as either Ashkenazim or Mizrahim), 15 percent were Ashkenazim, 15 percent were immigrants from the former Soviet Union, and 1 percent were Ethiopian Jews. Gillis, "The Ethnic Morphology," 59.

90. Accurate data on Mizrahim in the settlements is unavailable, as I explained in the previous notes. Nevertheless, in 2017, the *Haaretz* reporter Ron Cahlili suggested that Mizrahim might very well constitute the majority of people residing in suburban settlements like Ma'ale Adumim and Ari'el. See Ron Cahlili, "Bahura Ashkenaziya im Tzama Vetana"h," *Haaretz*, July 30, 2017, 13.

91. "Mish'al: Eih [Ha]Hargasha Bema'ale Adumim," *Bema'ale Adumim*, December 1983, MAA. On residents' complaints concerning the lack of public facilities, see Amos Levav, "Ir Besiman She'ela," *Maariv*, October 10, 1986. On how residents perceived the settlement and its role as a suburb of Jerusalem, see Allegra, "Outside Jerusalem," 53–56.

92. Levav, "Ir Besiman She'ela," 17.
93. "Mish'al," 5.
94. "Settlements Database."
95. Barzaki, interview by author.
96. In April 1979, Defense Minister Ezer Weizman proposed allowing Israelis to purchase lands in the West Bank. Avinoam Bar-Yosef, "'25 Elef Dunamim Shenimkeru Beyo"sh Nisharu Bemodaot Hapirsomot,'" *Maariv*, December 10, 1985, 13. On September 16, 1979, the government allowed Israelis to buy lands in the West Bank. See Yitzhak Zamir (government's legal consultant) to Ezer Weizman (minister of Defense), "Hanhayot Lekniyat Mekarkein Be'ezor Yehuda Veshomron," November 8, 1979, 7006/12-A, ISA. In April 1982, a statement allowing private developers to erect settlements in the West Bank was made. See "Protokol Ms' 31 Miyeshivat Have'ada Leinyanei Bikoret Hamedina Shehitkayma Beyom G', K"A Beshvat, Hatashm"a, 12.2.85, Sha'a 12:30," February 12, 1985, 3, 1423/26-K, ISA. Likud officials believed this was an easy way to complement and accelerate settlement activity. See Plia Albeck to the director of the Settlement Implementation Committee, September 23, 1983, 11, 7618/5-A, ISA; Michael Dekel (vice minister of Agriculture), "Tazkir," July 5, 1983, 8193/5-A, ISA. On settlements erected by private developers in Israel and the West Bank, see Levia Applebaum and David Newman, "The Private Sector Settlements in Israel: Developmental Process and Local Government Status" [in Hebrew] (Rehovot: Development Study Center, 1991).
97. Yaacov Norodetzky (founder of a group of Israel Aerospace Industry employees that settled together in the settlement of Bet Arye), interview by author, July 9, 2015; Effi Barshaf (among the core members of the group that settled in Bet Arye), interview by author, July 29, 2015. These groups usually worked under the auspices of a so-called settlement movement. Among these settlement movements were Gush Emunim's Amana and Mishkei Heirut Beitar. See Lein, *Land Grab*, 22.
98. Yaron Balslev, "The First Decade of the Development of Tel Aviv Neighborhoods across the Yarkon, 1947–1958" [in Hebrew], *Iyunim: Multidisciplinary Studies in Israeli and Modern Jewish Society* 23 (2013): 248; Haim Drabkin-Darin, *Shikun Veklita Beyisrael: Tash"ah—Tasht"av* (Tel Aviv: Sifrei Gadish, 1955), 91–92. Between 1949 and 1958, government agencies supported the construction of 6,088 apartments for military personnel, military veterans, and those with military service–related disabilities. Some received government loans to contract private developers to build their communities. Haim Drabkin-Darin, "Megamot Kalkaliyot Vehevratiyot shel Hashikun Beyisrael Betkofat Ha'asor," 27–28.
99. Gonen, *Between City and Suburb*, 131; Balslev, "The First Decade," 248–249.
100. In 1986, a Housing Administration (Minhelet Hamegurim) was founded to manage housing projects catering to Israel Defense Forces personnel. On the Housing Administration, and how national and local planning administrations considered military officials to be prize homebuyers and a stepping stone for further development in the 1980s, see Gabriel Schwake, "An Officer and a Bourgeois: Israeli Military Personnel, Suburbanization and Selective Privatization," *Planning Perspectives* 36, no. 1 (January 2, 2021): 183–194; Tamar Berger, *Autotopia: Suburbian* [sic] *In-between Space in Israel* [in Hebrew] (Tel Aviv: Hakibbutz Hameuchad, 2015), 78–79.
101. On the Los Angeles–based group Community Homes and their attempt to create a racially integrated community of single-family houses, see Anthony Denzer, "Community

Homes: Race, Politics and Architecture in Postwar Los Angeles," *Southern California Quarterly* 87, no. 3 (Fall 2005): 269–285, https://doi.org/10.2307/41172271. On two racially integrated cooperative housing developments in the San Francisco Bay Area that were sponsored by labor unions, see Hilary Botein, "Labor Unions and Race-Conscious Housing in the Postwar Bay Area: Housing Projects of the International Longshoremen's and Warehousemen's Union and the United Automobile Workers," *Journal of Planning History* 15, no. 3 (August 2016): 210–229, https://doi.org/10.1177/1538513215608096. On postwar veterans' co-ops, see Matthew Gordon Lasner, *High Life: Condo Living in the Suburban Century* (New Haven, CT: Yale University Press, 2012), 130–134.

102. Shlomo Amar to Tova Alinson (Ministry of Interior), "Bakashat Hayeshuv Alfe Menashe Lehakamat Mo'atza Mekomit," November 4, 1984, 56775/2-GL, ISA.

103. Yair Sheleg, "Vehem Alfe Menashe," *Nekuda*, May 27, 1987, 22–23.

104. D. Ish Shalom (manager of internal inspection at the Ministry of Housing) to Asher Weiner (general manager at the Ministry of Housing), "Hakamat Alfe Menashe—Do"h 34," February 26, 1984, 14616/10-GL, ISA.

105. "Do"h Tikun Likuyim," n.d., 14616/10-GL, ISA; State Comptroller of Israel, "Hakamat Alfe Menashe," n.d., 4, 14616/10-GL, ISA; Ish Shalom to Weiner, "Hakamat Alfe Menashe—Do"h 34," February 26, 1984, p. (3)7. At the time, the settlement was referred to as Karnei Shomron C, after the nearby settlement of Karnei Shomron. The name was changed to Alfe Menashe after planning and construction were allocated to Tzavta. Aryeh Dayan, "Bayit Im Gina," *Koteret Rashit*, May 16, 1984.

106. Ish Shalom to Weiner, "Hakamat Alfe Menashe—Do"h 34," February 26, 1984, esp. pp. (5)7 and (1)7.

107. On the agreements between the Ministry of Housing and Tzavta, see Ish Shalom to Weiner, "Hakamat Alfe Menashe—Do"h 34," February 26, 1984; D. Ish Shalom to H. Eliad (inspection manager at the State Comptroller's Office), "He'arotenu Letyotat Do"h Hakamat Alfe Menashe," February 2, 1984, 14616/10-GL, ISA; "Do"h Tikun Likuyim," n.d.; State Comptroller of Israel, "Hakamat Alfe Menashe"; Dayan, "Bayit Im Gina."

108. Ish Shalom to Weiner, "Hakamat Alfe Menashe—Do"h 34," February 26, 1984, p. (2)7.

109. Ish Shalom to Eliad, "He'arotenu Letyotat Do"h Hakamat Alfe Menashe," February 2, 1984.

110. "Do"h Tikun Likuyim"; Yossi Sivan, interview by author, December 10, 2015. According to some documents, the decision to hire Yaski was made before Tzavta took over the project. See State Comptroller of Israel, "Hakamat Alfe Menashe," 2; Ish Shalom to Weiner, "Hakamat Alfe Menashe—Do"h 34," February 26, 1984, p. (4)7. In either case, Yaski had two partners with whom he shared the office at the time: Yossi Sivan and Yaakov Gil.

111. On Avraham Yaski and his work in the settlement of Gilo, in East Jerusalem, see Nitzan-Shiftan, *Seizing Jerusalem*, 104–116. For a comprehensive account of Yaski's projects, excluding those built in the West Bank, see Sharon Rotbard, *Avrahm Yasky, Concrete Architecture* [in Hebrew] (Tel Aviv: Babel, 2007).

112. On the sabra generation of architects and their worldview, see Nitzan-Shiftan, *Seizing Jerusalem*, 45–78.

113. Sivan, interview by author.

114. Nitzan-Shiftan, *Seizing Jerusalem*, 45–78.

115. Sivan, interview by author.

116. Unit prices for security personnel were as follows: 4.5 million (old) shekels for small units, and 8.7 million (old) shekels for big units. State Comptroller of Israel, "Hakamat Alfe Menashe," 16.

117. According to a decision of the Joint Settlement Committee from July 1981, settlers could lease land plots for 5 percent of their value. The land's value was to be decided on by a government appraiser. The 5 percent counted as 80 percent of the land's total value, as long as the person purchasing the land stayed put for at least five years after construction was completed. See "Protokol Yeshivat Have'ada Lehityashvut Hameshutefet Lamemshala Velahistadrut Hatziyonit Haolamit," July 26, 1981, 7618/1-A, ISA.

118. More than 90 percent of lands in Israel are public. On the Israeli leasehold system, see note 34 of the introduction. In the West Bank, homebuyers signed a renewable forty-nine-year lease. According to Eyal Weizman, the lease included a clause emphasizing that the lease would lose its validity in the case of military withdrawal. Eyal Weizman, *Hollow Land: Israel's Architecture of Occupation* (London and New York: Verso, 2007), 103.

119. According to some sources, 112 units were purchased by security personnel. See Ish Shalom to Weiner, "Hakamat Alfe Menashe—Do"h 34," February 26, 1984, pp. (4)7 and (13)7; Sheleg, "Vehem Alfe Menashe," 23; Alfe Menashe Local Council, "Alfe Menashe—Kah Hakol Hethil," n.d., Alfe Menashe Archive.

120. Apartments sold to random Israelis who were not affiliated with the Ministry of Defense were more expensive. The cheapest units went for 6.66 million (old) shekels, and the most expensive ones went for 9.8 million (old) shekels. State Comptroller of Israel, "Hakamat Alfe Menashe," 14 and 16. At around the same time, on November 15, 1982, Alfe Menashe was moved from the Rural Building and New Settlements Administration at the Ministry of Housing to the Department of Urban Construction at the Ministry of Housing. See Ish Shalom to Weiner, "Hakamat Alfe Menashe—Do"h 34," February 26, 1984, p. (4)7.

121. See, for example, "Helkat Elohim Ktana—Be'alfe Menashe," *Maariv*, November 29, 1985, 146; "Tzavta Be'alfe Menashe—Sipur Htzlaha," *Maariv*, December 27, 1985.

122. In (old) shekels, in November 1983, houses in Alfe Menashe ranged from 6.6 to 9.8 million. Average income of households whose main breadwinner was an employee in 1983 was 513,900 (old) shekels. During *The Achievements of the Settlement of Judea and Samaria Exhibition*, homebuyers needed to put down only $10,000 (equivalent to US$26,000 in 2020 dollars) to secure a house. For house prices, see Sheleg, "Vehem Alfe Menashe," 23; "Meot Batim Bealfe Menashe Bemilyonei Shkalim," *Davar*, June 10, 1983, 5; Ish Shalom to Weiner, "Hakamat Alfe Menashe—Do"h 34," February 26, 1984, p. (15)7. For average household income, see "Income Surveys," *Monthly Bulletin of Statistics: Supplement* (Central Bureau of Statistics, September 1984), 138. Since inflation rates in Israel soared in 1983, conversion to dollars is approximated.

123. The settlement opened in September 1983. By mid-May 1984, according to a news report, there were 478 units completed, and only 325 were sold. State Comptroller of Israel, "Hakamat Alfe Menashe," 16; Dayan, "Bayit Im Gina." Five months later, in October 1984, there were some 290 families residing in Alfe Menashe, leaving

about 210 unoccupied. See Amar to Alinson, "Bakashat Hayeshuv," November 4, 1984, 1. Not until 1989, according to a news report, would there be 510 families living in Alfe Menashe. Ran Kislev, "Ahrei Yeruham, Ahrei Kfar Saba," *Haaretz*, February 17, 1989.

124. Dayan, "Bayit Im Gina."
125. Edna Blepolsky and Orly Kalinski, "Hahalom Veshivro," *Alfe Menashe*, n.d., 6, Alfe Menashe Archive.
126. Ran Kislev, "Ahrei Yeruham, Ahrei Kfar Saba," 7.
127. Nitzan-Shiftan, "On Concrete and Stone," 51–65; Alona Nitzan-Shiftan, "Israelizing Jerusalem: The Encounter Between Architectural and National Ideologies, 1967–1977" (PhD diss., Massachusetts Institute of Technology, 2002), 190–192.
128. Yossi Ben-Artzi, "Nof Vezehut," 272.
129. Archivist of Alfe Menashe, interview by author, July 8, 2015. On how religious settlers had altered their views of the Palestinians in light of violent clashes, see Feige, *Settling in the Hearts*, 124–127.
130. Ran Kislev, "Ahrei Yeruham, Ahrei Kfar Saba," 7.
131. On the "separation fence" and its impact on the Palestinians, see Ben-Naftali, Sfard, and Viterbo, *The ABC of the OPT*, 43–59; Shaul Arieli and Michael Sfard, *The Wall of Folly* [in Hebrew] (Tel Aviv: Yediot Aharonot Books, 2008).
132. "Regional Statistics: Alfe Menashe" (Central Bureau of Statistics, 2020), https://www.cbs.gov.il/en/settlements/Pages/default.aspx?mode=Yeshuv.
133. After trouble emerged in settlements erected by private developers, in April 1983, the Ministry of Housing was required to examine more thoroughly each private initiative to confirm its suitability. H. Eliad (inspection manager at the State Comptroller's Office) to Asher Weiner, "Peulot Misrad Habinui Vehashikun Beyishuv Yehuda Vehashomron," January 5, 1984, 3, 14616/9-GL, ISA.
134. Amos Levav, "Yisraelim Kvar Rahshu 1/2 Milyon Dunam," *Maariv*, December 14, 1982, 45-46.
135. Lein, *Land Grab*, 62–63. Land prices ranged according to the plot's proximity to the Green Line. In the beginning of 1981, according to the daily *Maariv*, homebuyers paid $500–$1,000 for a dunam in Kedumim. By the end of 1982, it went for $3,-000–$6,000. In the settlement of Elon Moreh, located farther east, a dunam would go for $300–$500 in 1981, and $1,500–$2,000 by the end of 1982. A dunam in the settlement of Sha'are Tikva, located closer to the Green Line, sold for $15,-000–$20,000 in December 1982. Dolev, "Hamahapah Bemapat Hashomron," 34.
136. Levav, "Yisraelim," 45. Also see Yair Kotler, "Bulmus Bniya Beyehuda Veshomron—Bemehirim Marki'im," *Maariv*, October 1, 1982, 17.
137. Eliad to Weiner, "Peulot," January 5, 1984, 3.
138. Moshe Meizles, "Ha'im Mutar Lehevrot Histadrutiyot Livnot Beyehuda Veshomron?," *Maariv*, December 24, 1982, 25; Yaron London, "Halakoah Sheli haya Rotze Lagur Behertzeliya," *Koteret Rashit*, May 4, 1983, 22.
139. Levav, "Yisraelim," 45.
140. Haim Katseff, interview by author, December 8, 2015.
141. Yitzhak Axel, "Do"h Hatzevet Habein Misradi Lebdikat Hamismahim Hamishpatiyim—Hev' Nofim Mifalim Kalkaliyim Baa"m," November 5, 1982, 4146/3-A, ISA. In correspondence from April 1982, the number of units was five hundred. See Yehuda Nahari (in charge of "government and abandoned property in

Judea and Samaria") to Danny Mif'alim Kalkaliyim (Danny Weinmann's company), "Yakir Bet—Shtahim Lepituah Vebniya," April 30, 1982, 4146/3-A, ISA; Daniel Hoffer to Yehuda Nahari, "Yakir Bet—Shtahim Lepituah Vebniya," April 30, 1982, 4146/3-A, ISA.

142. Katseff, interview by author.

143. Ben-Artzi, "Nof Vezehut," 272.

144. "Nofim—Kedai Ahshav," *Maariv*, December 24, 1982, 146.

145. On Build Your Own Home, see Dikla Yizhar, "Build Your Own Home Project: The Built Space at a Social, Cultural, and Professional Turning Point" [in Hebrew] (master's thesis, the Technion—Israel Institute of Technology, 2008).

146. Danny Rubenstein, "Shilton Hakitch Vehakiur," *Davar*, February 4, 1983.

147. Rubenstein, "Shilton Hakitch Vehakiur."

148. Tula Amir, "Hazman Shekafa Bebeit Hamegurim: Villa Toskanit Provansalit," in *Living Forms: Architecture and Society in Israel*, ed. Shelly Cohen and Tulah Amir (Tel Aviv: Xargol Books and Am Oved, 2007), 258–261.

149. "Protokol Ms' 31 Miyeshivat Have'ada Leinyanei Bikoret Hamedina," February 12, 1985, 16.

150. Boaz Evron, "Tfos Bearnakha," *Yediot Aharonot* (reprinted in *Nekuda*, vol. 72, April 16, 1984), March 30, 1984. For an equally harsh critique, see Rubenstein, "Shilton Hakitch Vehakiur," 17.

151. The company offered help to those unable to procure the down payment. "Nofim—Kedai Ahshav." House prices ranged according to size. In 1982, a 130-square-meter house went for $100,000, of which $15,000 was to be paid upfront. It went for $95,000 if the entire amount was paid upfront. "Nispah Tashlumim," 1982, 4146/3-A, ISA. With time, prices were reduced. In January 1984, the price of the smallest house was $65,000; the down payment was $5,000. "Nofim—Ahshav Hazman," *Maariv*, January 3, 1984, 34.

152. "Nofim—Kedai Ahshav."

153. "Kah Ota, he Shelha Bematana!," *Yediot Aharonot, 7 Yamim*, April 1, 1983.

154. Miri Levy, interview by author, November 24, 2015. In April 1983, the sales campaign won the "Israeli Oscar Award for Advertising." Niva Lanir, "Jabotinsky Over Lasoher 'Baruah Haaza Parah min Hadegel Hamagen-David," *Davar*, April 22, 1983, 2.

155. In December 1982, it was reported that 250 units were sold in Nofim. Levav, "Yis-raelim," 45. In February 1984, however, it was reported that only 220 units were sold. Elazar Levin, "Ma Kore Be'Nofim'," *Haaretz*, February 13, 1984, 9.

156. Katseff, interview by author.

157. Levy, interview by author.

158. Levav, "Yisraelim," 45.

159. "Kvutzat Avi Dudai Mevakeshet Lirkosh Hashlita Be'Nofim'," *Maariv*, February 10, 1984, 3.

160. For Weinmann's requests, see Danny Weinmann to David Levy (minister of Housing), December 14, 1983, 14616/8-GL, ISA; Danny Weinmann to David Levy (minister of Housing), "Michtavenu Miyom 14.12.83," December 27, 1983, 14616/8-GL, ISA.

161. Baruch Na'e and Amiram Fleisher, "Halom Hahayim Hayafim Be'Nofim' Hitnapetz: Konei Havilot Bashomron Mehakim Le'Moshia'," *Maariv*, February 17, 1984, 3; Baruch Na'e, "'Nofim' hem Lifamim Gaagu'im Lavilla Shenagoza," *Maariv*, September 3, 1986, 13.

162. Aya Orenshtein and Aharon Priel, "Konei Batim Benofim Tov'im Peiruk Hahevra," *Maariv*, February 27, 1984, 2.
163. Oron Meiri, "Yazam Nofim—Baereh Lemishpat," *Hadashot*, December 18, 1986, 4; Eli Danon and Ilan Bahar, "Ne'etzar Danny Weinmann Manka"l Nofim Leshe'avar; Hashud Shekibel Bemirma Milyonei Dolarim Memishtaknim," *Maariv*, September 1, 1986, 1.
164. Na'e, "'Nofim' Hem Lifamim," 13.
165. Uri Urbah, "Makom Tov Ba'emtza," *Nekuda*, August 13, 1986, 12. Already in 1983, after warnings about the risks these construction projects entailed were aired in the media, Israelis began to retract previous arrangements they had made with private developers working in settlements. See Michael Dekel (deputy minister of Agriculture) to Prime Minister Menachem Begin, "Hityashvut Beyo"sh," June 19, 1983, 8193/5-A, ISA.
166. Plia Albeck to the director of the Settlement Implementation Committee, September 23, 1983; Plia Albeck to Head of the Ministers' Committee for Settlement, May 8, 1983, 7618/2-A, ISA; Plia Albeck to Minister of Justice, "Bidiya—Sheih Tzabah—Elkana D'," May 15, 1983, 7618/2-A, ISA.
167. Haggai Segal, "Ma Kara Letohnit Hame'a?," *Nekuda*, December 9, 1986, 9–10.
168. Oron Meiri, "Veshuv Honhim et Nofim," *Hadashot*, August 11, 1987, 6; "Hasar Levi Hodi'a al Hidush Habniya Benofim'," *Yated Ne'eman*, August 12, 1987.
169. Katseff, interview by author.
170. By August 1987, two units in Nofim were occupied. By June 1990, twenty units were occupied. See Robert Shteiner, "Nofim—Sof Sof Hayim Yafim," August 28, 1987, 44994/7-GL, ISA; Efraim Mariansky, "Nofim: Nispah Sanitari," June 13, 1990, 4, 44994/7-GL; Levy, interview by author.
171. According to Eldar and Zertal, the intifada reduced Israelis' demand for units in the occupied territories. Eldar and Zertal, *Adonei Haaretz*, 143.
172. "Settlements and Outposts Numbers and Data" (Tel Aviv: Peace Now, June 2009).
173. "Regional Statistics: Nofim" (Central Bureau of Statistics, 2018), https://www.cbs.gov.il/he/settlements/Pages/default.aspx?mode=Yeshuv.
174. Yitzhak Ben-Ner, Alex Anski, and Eldar Sharon, "Architectura shel Tohu Vavohu," *Yediot Aharonot*, April 1, 1983, sec. Seven Days, 22.
175. For example, see Aba Elhanani, "Al Siyur Noge Beyehuda Veshomron," *Tvai* 22 (1984): 64–65.
176. Nitzan-Shiftan, "Israelizing Jerusalem," 88.
177. Maggor, "State, Market," 149; Segal, "Ma Kara Letohnit Hamea?," 9.
178. Moshe Merhaviya, "Habniya Ha'atzmit: Sh'at Hamivhan shel Hahityashvut Hahadasha," *Nekuda*, January 30, 1981.
179. "Tarbut, Dibur," *Nekuda*, November 7, 1986, 82. Originally published in *Nekuda*, vol. 65.
180. Yehuda Etzion, "Hal'a Hakibush Hamashhit," *Nekuda*, May 27, 1987, 18–21.
181. Vaknin, "Bemo Yadeinu," 27.
182. Uri Ariel, "Marbit Habniya Beyo"sh Mitbatza'at Bethumei Tohnit Allon," *Nekuda*, November 25, 1983, 5.
183. Segal, "Ma Kara Letohnit Hamea?," 9. According to Benvenisti, the total population growth in the ten larger settlements of Gush Emunim between 1984 and 1986 was

only 510 persons. Benvenisti, *The West Bank Data*, 52. In 1985, only 110 families joined community settlements. Benvenisti, *1986 Report*, 59.

184. In 1985, 14,700 settlers resided in "semi-rural settlements" (community settlements and kibbutzim, only some of which were associated with Gush Emunim) and 37,000 in "urban settlements." See Benvenisti, *1986 Report*, 47.

CHAPTER 4: FAITHFUL CITIES

1. According to Eitan Regev and Gabriel Gordon, in 2017, 98.3 percent of Modi'in Illit residents were ultra-Orthodox. I estimate that the remaining 1.7 percent were not actually residing in Betar Illit or were adolescents. Eitan Regev and Gabriel Gordon, "The Haredi Housing Market and the Geographical Distribution of Israeli Haredim," report [in Hebrew] (Jerusalem: Israel Democracy Institute, 2020), 28.

2. For estimates of Haredim's portion of Israelis in 1995, see Eli Berman, "Sect, Subsidy, and Sacrifice: An Economist's View of Ultra-Orthodox Jews," *Quarterly Journal of Economics* 115, no. 3 (August 2000): 942; Momi Dahan, "The Ultra-Orthodox Jews and Municipal Authority: Part 1—Income Distribution in Jerusalem" (Jerusalem: The Jerusalem Institute for Israel Studies, 1998), 7.

3. In 2013, according to Lee Cahaner and Yossef Shilhav, ultra-Orthodox Jews made up 30 percent of West Bank settlers (not including East Jerusalem). In 2017, according to Regev and Gordon, they amounted to 35 percent. Lee Cahaner and Yossef Shilhav, "Ultra-Orthodox Settlements in Judea and Samaria" [in Hebrew], *Social Issues in Israel* 16 (2013): 41; Regev and Gordon, "The Haredi Housing Market," 26. According to Dror Etkes and Lara Friedman, in 2005, more than half of all construction in settlements took place in Betar Illit and Modi'in Illit. In 2019, as noted in a Peace Now report, 39 percent of construction starts of housing units in settlements was recorded in ultra-Orthodox settlements. Dror Etkes and Lara Friedman, "Ha'uhlusiya Haharedit Bahitnahaluyot" (Peace Now, October 29, 2005), https://peacenow.org.il/ultra-orthodox; "Settlement Construction Report 2019" (Peace Now, March 18, 2020), 2 and 5, http://peacenow.org.il/wp-content/uploads/2020/03/2019-Construction-Report_Peace-Now.pdf.

4. Samuel C. Heilman, *Defenders of the Faith: Inside Ultra-Orthodox Jewry* (Berkeley: University of California Press, 2000), 14–21; Michael K. Silber, "The Emergence of Ultra-Orthodoxy: The Invention of a Tradition," in *The Uses of Tradition: Jewish Continuity in the Modern Era*, ed. Jack Wertheimer (New York: Jewish Theological Seminary of America, 1993), 23–84.

5. Silber, "The Emergence of Ultra-Orthodoxy," 23–84; Menachem Friedman, *The Haredi (Ultra-Orthodox) Society: Sources, Trends and Processes* [in Hebrew] (Jerusalem: Jerusalem Institute for Israel Studies, 1991), 9–13.

6. Friedman, *The Haredi*, 9; Heilman, *Defenders of the Faith*, 11–13.

7. Cahaner and Shilhav, "Ultra-Orthodox Settlements," 42–43.

8. Moving to settlements involved transgressing another religious commandment that prohibits Jews from residing in a hostile environment where their safety is endangered. See Yosseph Shilhav, *Ultra-Orthodoxy in Urban Governance in Israel* (Jerusalem: Floersheimer Institute for Policy Studies, 1998), 43; Aviva Luri, "Immanu'el Lo Mitpashetet," *Mussaf Haaretz*, November 13, 1998, 38.

9. A couple of small settlements that cater to national Haredi Jews—a branch of

Judaism that at least until recently was considered marginal, if not external, to ultra-Orthodoxy—were built in the early 1980s. See Cahaner and Shilhav, "Ultra-Orthodox Settlements," 46–49. On the opposition of Ovadiya Yossef, chief Sephardic rabbi of Israel, to the Israeli occupation of the West Bank, see "A Chief Rabbi Makes It Clear," *Los Angeles Times*, February 8, 1980, sec. II, 7.

10. Shilhav, *Ultra-Orthodoxy*, 1, 6–7.

11. In the early 1980s, on average, Haredi Israeli women had 6 children. Between the mid-1980s and late 1990s, they had 7, on average. Between 2019 and 2021, that number decreased to 6.5. Gilad Malach and Lee Cahaner, "Statistical Report on Ultra-Orthodox Society in Israel 2022" [in Hebrew] (Jerusalem: Israel Democracy Institute, 2022), 14.

12. Shilhav, *Ultra-Orthodoxy*, 128. On poverty rates among ultra-Orthodox people, see Hagai Levin, *Hamigzar Haharedi Beisrael: Ha'atzama toh Shiluv Bata'asuka* (Jerusalem: National Economic Council, Prime Minister's Office, 2009), 10.

13. Lee Cahaner, "Between Ghetto-Politics and Geopolitics: Ultraorthodox Settlements in the West Bank," in *Normalizing Occupation: The Politics of Everyday Life in the West Bank Settlements*, ed. Marco Allegra, Ariel Handel, and Erez Maggor (Bloomington: Indiana University Press, 2017), 114; Cahaner and Shilhav, "Ultra-Orthodox Settlements," 50; Shilhav, *Ultra-Orthodoxy*, 3–6.

14. Y. Ben Moshe, "Siha Im Manka"l Agudat 'Mishkenot Yerushalayim': 'Betar' —Ir Legaon Uletiferet," *Hamodia*, September 29, 1989; Cahaner and Shilhav, "Ultra-Orthodox Settlements," 51.

15. On the government decision to allow private developers to work in settlements, see Shlomo Gazit, *Trapped Fools: Thirty Years of Israeli Policy in the Territories* [in Hebrew] (Tel Aviv: Zmora Beitan, 1999), 244–245; "Protokol Ms' 31 Miyeshivat Have'ada Leinyanei Bikoret Hamedina," February 12, 1985, 3; Bathia Avlin to David Libai, "Do"h Mevaker Hamedina-Ms' 35-Ishur Hevrat 'Kohav Hashomron Ba"m' Kehevra Meshakenet," June 10, 1985, 14616/12-GL, ISA.

16. On the city's projected population and how the numbers had changed over the course of the design process, see "544 Yehidot Diyur Bebniya," *Immanu'el: Iton Ha'ir Immanu'el. Ir Shehe Ba'it*, vol. 1, 1982, National Library of Israel; Star of Samaria/ Gal. Beit-El, "Immanu'el: Ha'ir Hagdola," ca. 1982, Star of Samaria Officers in Emmanuel; Amiram Harlap, ed., "Emmanuel—A New Town in Samaria," in *Israel Builds 1988* (Jerusalem: Ministry of Housing, 1988), 147; Thomas Leitersdorf and Y. Goldenberg, "Immanu'el: Ir Shehe Bayit. Tohniyot Nispahot Lesefer Taktziv Minhelet Ha'ir 1983–4," 1983, City Planning Division of Immanu'el.

17. Avlin to Libai, "Do"h Mevaker Hamedina," June 10, 1985.

18. Avlin to Libai, "Do"h Mevaker Hamedina." In August 1982, a ceremony was held on the site, celebrating the construction of a road leading to Immanu'el. See Kokhav Hashomron Ba"am and Ministry of Construction and Housing, "Hazmana Letekes Hanukat Hakvish Le'irenu Immanu'el," 1982, 14615/9-GL, ISA; Pinhas Arenreich and Yaacov Kaufman to Asher Weiner, September 30, 1982, 14615/9-GL, ISA.

19. Thomas Leitersdorf, interview by author, August 24, 2016.

20. Shilhav, *Ultra-Orthodoxy*, 18. To a degree, the lack of planning guidelines for the Haredi population continued into the 1990s. A 1995 Ministry of Construction and Housing report noted that "to date, there are no defined guidelines or clear criteria [needed] for the unique planning of [the] Haredi neighborhood, especially [missing

is] a public institutions' program." See Programs Department, "Mediniyut Shikun Lamigzar Haharedi" (Ministry of Construction and Housing, May 18, 1995), 9, 43698/7-GL, ISA.

21. On the design of the Hassidic neighborhood in Hatsor HaGlilit, see Oryan Shachar, "From A-Locality to Locality: The Gur Neighbourhood in Hatzor HaGlilit," in *Israel as a Modern Architectural Experimental Lab, 1948–1978*, ed. Inbal Ben-Asher Gitler and Anat Geva (Bristol, UK: Intellect, 2020), 43–68. Other examples of early construction projects geared toward Haredim include Shomrie Emunim neighborhood and several other neighborhoods built along the Green Line in Jerusalem since the early 1960s. According to Yossef Shilhav, however, the government's involvement in the development of these neighborhoods was limited. Shilhav, *Ultra-Orthodoxy*, 18.

22. Leitersdorf, interview by author.

23. "Tohniyot Meyuhadot Lehavtahat Eihut Hayim Letoshvei Immanu'el," *Immanu'el: Iton Ha'ir Immanu'el. Ir Shehe Bayit*, vol. 1, 1982, National Library of Israel.

24. Leitersdorf, interview by author.

25. Eli First, interview by author, January 24, 2019.

26. On sabra architects' interest in the architecture of the Palestinians, see Nitzan-Shiftan, *Seizing Jerusalem*, 45–78.

27. "18 Batim Bodedim—Shhuna A,' " undated, City Planning Division in Immanu'el.

28. Noah Zvuluni, "Haredim Beyerushalayim Mohim al Hakamat 'Kollel' Bashtahim," *Davar*, April 15, 1983, 5.

29. Noah Zvuluni, "Bituah Mipnei Hahzarat Shtahim," *Davar*, July 17, 1983, 9; Noah Zvuluni, "Hametihut Bekerev Meyasdei Hair Immanu'el Yigrom Lepeiruk Hev' 'Kokhav Hashomron,' " *Daver*, April 9, 1985, 3.

30. "Tzfuyim Revavot Besimhat Beit Hasho'eva," *Immanu'el: Iton Ha'ir Immanu'el. Ir Shehe Bayit*, vol. 2, September 1982, National Library of Israel; Pinhas Arenreich and Yaacov Kaufman to David Levy, "Hatzagat Tohnit Hapeula shel Imma-nu'el Le'aviv-Kayitz Tashma"g Vebakasha Lematan Hasut," November 2, 1982, 14615/9-GL, ISA; Haim (manager of Star of Samaria, founders of Samaria), interview by author, December 22, 2015.

31. Pinhas Arnreich, quoted in Yedidiya Meir, "Ir Nidahat," *Haaretz*, December 16, 2001, B3. Arnreich made a similar statement in Amos Nevo, "Arnreich Ay"h," *Yediot Aharonot*, June 14, 1985, 21. This promise was also mentioned in Luri, "Immanu'el Lo Mitpashetet," 34.

32. "Hanesi'a Leimmanu'el Mimerkaz Haaretz Tekutzar Le-20 Dakot," *Immanu'el: Iton Ha'ir Immanu'el. Ir Shehe Bayit*, vol. 2, September 1982, National Library of Israel.

33. For example, see "Immanu'el Nivnet Belev Eizor History-Dati," *Immanu'el: Iton Ha'ir Immanu'el. Ir Shehe Bayit*, vol. 2, September 1982, National Library of Israel.

34. Equally important were low unit prices and generous funding packages. On prices and funding, see Tzabar Azriel to custodian of government property, "Haktza'at Karka Lebniya—Immanu'el," September 20, 1983, 14616/1-GL, ISA; Pinhas Arn-reich to Eli Nataf, "Mehirei Dirot Beimmanu'el," November 28, 1983, 14616/1-GL, ISA; "Hashefel Beshuk Hadirot Kimat lo Heshpia al Hamehirim," *Immanu'el: Iton Ha'ir Immanu'el. Ir Shehe Bayit*, vol. 2, September 1982, National Library of Israel; "Rohshei Hadirot Beimmanu'el Yohlu Lekabel Mashkantaot Vehalvaot Ad 95% Mimehiran," *Immanu'el: Iton Ha'ir Immanu'el. Ir Shehe Bayit*, vol. 1, 1982, National Library of Israel.

35. David Nofar, phone conversation with the author, December 3, 2015.
36. Yona Ginsberg, "Nashim Harediyot Be'ir Hadasha: Yahasei Hagomlin Bein Hasviva Hafizit Lebein Dfusei Hitnahagut Ve'emdot" (Tel Aviv: Pinhas Sapir Center for Development, Tel Aviv University, June 1988), 12–13.
37. On the requirement to sleep in separate beds, see Haim Zicherman, *Black Blue-White: A Journey into the Charedi Society in Israel* [in Hebrew] (Tel Aviv: Yedioth Ahronoth Books and Chemed Books, 2014), 207.
38. See some of the residents' complaints on the units in Immanu'el (along with some praise of the settlement, noting the fresh air and beautiful views it afforded) in Ginsberg, "Nashim Harediyot," 10–16. See town officials' note acknowledging the need to find ways to expand the units that were too small in Raziel Pri-Gan, "Mihtav Galuyi Latoshav," *Immanu'el: Beta'on: Mo'atza Mekomit "Immanu'el,"* vol. 2, July 1985, 1, National Library of Israel.
39. Shmuel Shteiner to Asher Weiner, March 15, 1984, 14616/10-GL, ISA; Shmuel Shteiner to Asher Weiner, "Bniyat Yh"d Beimmanu'el—Programa 1984," March 21, 1984, 14616/10 GL, ISA.
40. On tensions between Immanu'el's developers, see Rakezet Hameyda, "Ha'ir Immanu'el Bashomron," June 3, 1985, 14616/12-GL, ISA; Aryeh Lavie, "Zrihato Vedeihato shel Kokhav Hashomron," May 3, 1985, 14616/12-GL, ISA; Nevo, "Arnreich Ay"h." The company went into receivership in July 1985. Construction and sales had stopped a few months prior to that. See Asher Weiner to Hahashav Haklali, "Dhiyat Pir'on Hov shel Bank 'Tfahot' Begin Mimun Helki Lehevrat Kokhav Hashomron Ba"m," June 13, 1985, 14616/12-GL, ISA; Baruch Na'e, "Bniya: Moshe Haim Shienfeld Muamad Letafkid Manka"l 'Kohav Hashomron,'" *Maariv*, June 10, 1985, 8; Baruch Na'e, "Yaacov Ne'eman—Kones Nihsei 'Kokhav Hashomron,'" *Maariv*, July 12, 1985, 8. For correspondences regarding the company's collapse, see Yaacov Ne'eman to David Levy, "Kokhav Hashomron Ba"m (Bekinus Nehasim)—Ha'ir Immanu'el," November 28, 1985, 14616/12-GL, ISA; David Ben Yehuda to Yaacov Ne'eman, July 26, 1985, 14616/12-GL, ISA.
41. Luri, "Immanu'el Lo Mitpashetet," 36; Noa Vaserman, "Yozma Bemisrad Hamishpatim Letashlum Lekokhav Hashomron Shebanta et Immanu'el," *Globes*, December 8, 1996, https://www.globes.co.il/news/article.aspx?did=126542.
42. Yaacov Ne'eman to Levi, "Kokhav Hashomron Ba"m," November 28, 1985; Plia Albeck, "Do"h Mevaker Hamedina—Immanu'el," July 26, 1985, 14616/12-GL, ISA.
43. Meirav Eliyahu to Asher Weiner, "Mo'atza Mekomit Immanu'el," March 11, 1985, 14616/12-GL, ISA; Baruh Ovitz to Asher Wiener, "Gimur Kvish Mis. 35 Sheshmo Reh' Hagr"a Ba'ir Immanu'el Shebashomron," July 7, 1985, 14616/12-GL, ISA. For interviews with residents, see Luri, "Immanu'el Lo Mitpashetet," 32–38.
44. Baruh Ovitz to Eitan Soroka, "Hei'ader Kvish Vemidraha Berhov Hatam Sofer Beimmanu'el," November 6, 1985, 14616/12-GL, ISA.
45. Eliyahu Meirav to Tzvi Amir, May 30, 1985, 14616/12-GL, ISA.
46. Avner Maatuf, Yizhak Anki, and Yoav Mehasri to David Levy (minister of Construction and Housing), "Hashlamat Mivne Byhak"n 'Rahel' Beimmanu'el," July 3, 1985, 14616/12-GL, ISA.
47. M. Shienfeld to Yaacov Ne'eman, "Tviot Tfahot + Msb"s Neged Dayarim," November 12, 1985, 14616/12-GL, ISA.
48. In 2020, there were 4,128 people residing in Immanu'el. "Regional Statistics:

Immanu'el" (Central Bureau of Statistics, 2020), https://www.cbs.gov.il/EN/settlements/Pages/default.aspx?mode=Yeshuv.

49. Y. Ben Moshe, "Siha Im Manka″l; Meir Rabinowitz, "Behehsher Harav Shah," *Nekuda*, November 1990, 13.

50. See the initial decision to erect a settlement on the site in "Protokol Yeshivat Have'ada Lehityashvut Hameshutefet Lamemshala Velahistadrut Hatziyonit Haolamit," August 8, 1982, 7618/2-A, ISA. For correspondences regarding Hadar Betar, see Uri Bar On to Yehuda Nahari, "Haktza'a Leyeshuv Beita″r," November 7, 1982, 46701/4-GL, ISA; Yehuda Nahari to Yeshuv Beita″r Ba″m, "Hoda'a al Ishur Tihnun," March 27, 1983, 46701/4-GL, ISA; Uri Bar On to Yehuda Nahari, "Moked 'Hadar-Beita″r,' " September 2, 1984, 46701/4-GL, ISA.

51. Moshe Leibovitz, interview by author, May 11, 2015.

52. Uri Urbah, "Erez Bimkom Dardar," *Nekuda*, November 22, 1985, 6–7, 38.

53. Rosenberg died from a stroke in 1987, dealing yet another blow to Hadar Betar. Leibovitz, interview by author. On the rise and fall of Hadar Betar, also see Shilhav, *Ultra-Orthodoxy*, 14–17.

54. State planners began making their plans for the settlement while Rosenberg was still alive, in tandem with his plans for Hadar Betar. See Shilhav, *Ultra-Orthodoxy*, 17. On the preliminary discussions concerning the city-settlement and for the invitation to the stone-laying ceremony, see Nadav Shragai, "Ha'ir Hahadasha Betar Teyoad Leharedim," *Haaretz*, March 25, 1987; Ministry of Construction and Housing, Department of Planning and Engineering, "Betar Illit—Tohnit Mit'ar," December 23, 1985, Yaar collection, 77 Betar, Avie and Sarah Arenson Built Heritage Research Center, The Technion (hereafter ASABHRC); Ministry of Construction and Housing, "Hazmana Letekes Hanahat Even-Pina La'ir Betar," March 1987, Yaar collection, 77 Betar, ASABHRC.

55. Two hilltops were to be allocated for Haredim and one for religious Zionists. "Protokol Ms' 2/88 shel Ve'adat Ha'ishurim Shehitkayma Beyom 18.1.88 Bemshb″s Yerushalayim," February 12, 1988, Folder Betar 77, ASABHRC; "Tyota Letadrih Tihnun Leshluha C Ba'ir Betar Illit," ca. 1988, Yaar collection, 77 Betar, ASABHRC.

56. Rabinowitz, "Behehsher," 15.

57. Yaar, *Life and Architecture*, 199.

58. According to the master plan, 3,400 units were to be built on the first hill, 4,000 on the second hill, and 800 on the third hill. See Binyamin Weil (department head at the Ministry of Housing), "Betar—Tihnun Haharhavot Hamizrahiyot: Tadrih Tihnun + Programa Lemosdot Tzibur," March 20, 1994, 43698/7-GL, ISA.

59. Nan Ellin, *Postmodern Urbanism*, rev. ed. (New York: Princeton Architectural Press, 1999), 27–36.

60. Ellin, *Postmodern Urbanism*, 30.

61. Yaar, *Life and Architecture*, 124–125.

62. In his memoir, when discussing Pisgat Ze'ev, Yaar also mentioned Christopher Alexander's essay "A City Is Not a Tree," and Bernard Rudofsky's book *Streets for People*. Yaar, *Life and Architecture*, 218.

63. Amiram Harlap, ed., *Israel Builds 1988* (Jerusalem: Ministry of Housing, 1988), 95.

64. Aba Elhanani, "Perek K″h: Hab'ayatiyut shel Harehov Hayisraeli Hamatzyui," *Tvai* 29–30, 1992. On the Yaars' turn to postmodernism, see Alona Nitzan-Shiftan and Shanee Shiloh, "Aherim Bamerkaz: Al Ora Veyaacov Yaar," foreword to Yaar, *Life*

and *Architecture* (Haifa: Architectural and Landscape Heritage Research Center, Faculty of Architecture and Town Planning, The Technion, 2016), 13.

65. Ministry of Housing, Jerusalem District, "Betar Illit," September 8, 1985, Yaar collection, 77 Betar, ASABHRC.

66. Yaar, *Life and Architecture*, 200.

67. Aviv Yaar and Yaacov Yaar, interview by author, April 20, 2015.

68. A. Yaar and Y. Yaar, interview by author. In his memoir, Y. Yaar argued that some of their ideas, designed to accommodate the needs of the Haredim, were rejected by the project's chief engineer. Yaar, *Life and Architecture*, 201–202.

69. "Re'ayon, Ha'adrihal Yaacov Yaar, Metahnen Ha'ir: Betar Tihiyeh Ir Yafa Im Eihut Hayim Vehat'ama Meiravit Letzurhei Hatzibur Haharedi," *Hadshot Betar*, December 1989, 8.

70. Y. Ben Moshe, "Siha Im Manka"l." For more details on buying options that were available for homebuyers in 1989, see Mishkenot Yerushalayim, "Heikef Hamashkantaot Lelo Ribit Bebetar," *Hadshot Betar*, October 1989, 11; Moshe Cohen, " 'Moreh Nevohim' Besugiyat Hamashkantaot," *Hadshot Betar*, December 1989, 11; "Betar Hamovila Betnaei Hamashkanta," *Hadshot Betar*, March 1991, 5. According to a report that appeared in a Haredi weekly newspaper in December 1988, two-bedroom apartments were to cost $56,000, of which $47,000 was financed with no-interest loans. Three-bedroom apartments were to be sold for $66,000. "Betar: Reshamei Bikur," *Hamahane Haharedi*, December 7, 1988, 44986/5-GL, ISA. With time, prices went up. In 1994, Nahum Freeman, the chairperson of Mishkenot Yerushalayim, told a reporter that three-bedroom units were sold for $90,000. Each homebuyer received a grant in the amount of $17,500 that was deducted from the sale price, in addition to favorable government loans. See H. Dovrat, "Betar: Mehalom Le'ir," *Mishpaha: Hashavuon Labayit Hayehudi*, vol. 167, 1994.

71. "Eser Shnot Pitronot," *Hadshot Betar*, April 1992, 6–7; Y. Ben Moshe, "Siha Im Manka"l."

72. Leibovitz, interview by author. The committee members worked voluntarily and, among other things, negotiated unit prices, mortgage conditions, and the allocation of synagogues and other public facilities. See "Yoter Me-700 Pitronot Hadiyur shel 'Mishkenot Yerushalayim,' " *Hadshot Betar*, March 1991, 12.

73. "Sukka Rishona Hukma Bebetar: 'Ushpizin' Rabim Tzfuyim Behoham"s," *Hadshot Betar*, October 1989, 14; "Alafim Yevakru Behoha"m Sukot Ba'ir Betar," *Hamodia*, October 13, 1989, 2.

74. "Simhat Beit Hashoeva Rishona Bebetar," *Hadshot Betar*, December 1989, 14.

75. In 1990, Betar Illit was designated as a "local council," a status given to Israeli settlements that are smaller than cities. In 2001, it received a "city" status. Leibovitz's responsibilities and activities nonetheless matched those that would have been given to a mayor. On Betar Illit's municipal status, see Lee Cahaner, "The Development of the Spatial and Hierarchic[al] Structure of the Ultra-Orthodox Jewish Population in Israel" (University of Haifa, 2009), 161.

76. Leibovitz, interview by author.

77. The three largest Haredi groups in Israel are the Hasidim, Lithuanians, and Sephardim. Subgroups include different Hasidic "courts" formed around a specific religious leader, among others. See Benjamin Brown, *The Haredim: A Guide to Their Beliefs and Sectors* [in Hebrew] (Tel Aviv: Am Oved; Jerusalem: Israel Democracy Institute,

2017), 17–18. A study conducted by the Israeli Democracy Institute divided the residents of Betar Illit into five main groups: Hasidim (making up 55.4 percent of the town in 2017), Lithuanians (20.8 percent), Sephardim (16.5 percent), Sephardim with a Lithuanian education (3.6 percent), and Chabad (3.8 percent). See Regev and Gordon, "The Haredi Housing Market," 30. On the tapestry of ultra-Orthodox identities, see Zicherman, *Black Blue-White*, 21–129.

78. Raphael Dankner, interview by author, July 22, 2015.

79. For Leibovitz's request to add green spaces and playgrounds, and his concern about the lack thereof, see Yahal Mehandesim, "Proyect Betar: Diyun Ms' P-BI-247," August 22, 1990, Yaar collection, 77 Betar, ASABHRC; "Yeshivat Mo'atza Ms' 9," July 16, 1991, Yaar collection, Betar Binder 1, ASABHRC; Yigal Margalit to David Ovadiya, "Betar A1—Shinuyi Hesderei Tnu'a Bekvishei Hashhuna," December 21, 1992, Yaar collection, Betar Binder 1, ASABHRC.

80. In 1991, Leibovitz, the Yaars, and ministry officials debated alternative uses for the commercial spaces. See Z. Gluzmann to Yaacov Yaar and Z. Ovadiya, January 8, 1991, Yaar collection, 77 Betar, ASABHRC; Adi Shrist, "Proyekt Betar—Sikum Diyun Ms' PI-B-355," October 27, 1991, Yaar collection, Betar Binder 1, ASABHRC.

81. Leibovitz, interview by author. On the difficult site conditions at the industrial area, see "Yeshivat Mo'atza Ms' 9."

82. Leibovitz, interview by author.

83. Tamar, interview by author, June 26, 2015.

84. Dankner, interview by author.

85. At a 1992 planning meeting, it was noted that the units did not allow building additions. Nevertheless, Ashtrum was asked to explore possible ways to allow some expansions. See "Proyekt Betar: Sikum Diyun Ms' P-B-387," May 13, 1992, ASABHRC.

86. Avishai Meiron, interview by author, June 6, 2015.

87. Leibovitz, interview by author.

88. Leibovitz, interview by author.

89. For meeting transcripts where such changes were raised, see "Yeshivat Mo'atza Ms' 9"; Aliza Kaviti, "Sikum Diyun Shehitkayem Beyom 7.12.92: Hanose: Itur Shta-him Lebatei Knesset Bebetar," December 8, 1992, Yaar collection, Betar Binder 1, ASABHRC; Yaar, Yaacov to Adi Shrist, "Betar A-1: Shinuyi Taba Lediyun," May 27, 1991, Yaar collection, Betar Binder 1, ASABHRC. Also see Avirama Golan, "Hem Yaviu Keves, Anahnu Navi Shohet," *Haaretz*, November 13, 1994, 2.

90. See revised drawings with clusters in Yaar to Yair Eshel, September 3, 1993, Yaar collection, Betar Binder 1, ASABHRC. The planners had, in fact, considered arranging the houses around inner courts in the initial stages of design, but due to the harsh topographical conditions, they abandoned the idea. See "Protokol Ms' 2/88," 5.

91. Leibovitz, interview by author; Golan, "Hem Yaviu," 2; Ofer Petersburg, "Yalla Betar Yalla," *Maariv*, August 30, 1994, 10; Koby Bleih, "Alilot Moshe Ba'ir Haktana," *Maariv*, May 23, 1995, 16.

92. Some Haredim use "Shabbat elevators," which stop automatically at each floor, and therefore, according to some, do not violate Shabbat laws. Many of Betar Illit's residents, however, reject Shabbat elevators.

93. Meiron, interview by author.

94. Leibovitz, interview by author. Leibovitz's battles with the planners can partially be found in his correspondence with the architects. See, for example, Moshe Leibovitz

to Aviv Yaar, "Mihtavha Lemar Aziza Me-7/1/93 Betar A2 Shdeira Rashit," January 17, 1993, 47136/3-GL, ISA.

95. Petersburg, "Yalla," 10.

96. Golan, "Hem Yaviu," 2.

97. Meiron, interview by author.

98. Sarit Tzolshein (manager of the City Planning Division in Modi'in Illit), interview by author, June 10, 2015.

99. Meiron, interview by author.

100. Reizi (a young ultra-Orthodox female designer working in Betar Illit), interview by author, June 18, 2015; Tamar, interview by author. For correspondence with the Yaars regarding the building additions, see Eli Aziza to Yaar Architects, "Tohniyot Harhava—Betar Illit," February 28, 1993, Yaar collection, Betar Binder 1, ASABHRC; Yaacov Yaar to Eli Aziza, "Betar—Harhavot Diyur," March 2, 1993, Yaar collection, Betar Binder 1, ASABHRC; Yaacov Yaar to Eli Aziza, "Planning Housing Expansion in Beita"r—Communications Proposal," June 21, 1993, Yaar collection, Betar Binder 1, ASABHRC.

101. Reizi, interview by author. According to the local newspaper *Kore Bebetar*, between 2008 and 2009 the City Planning Division had approved some two hundred building additions with a total area of some 10,000 square meters. "Karov Le-200 Tosfot Bniya," *Kore Bebetar*, January 24, 2011, 5.

102. Tzolshein, interview by author.

103. Meiron, interview by author. On the industrial area, see "Nehtam Hoze Lehakamt Eizor Hataasiya Harishon Bebetar Illit," *Zo Irenu*, November 9, 2003; "Haya'ar Ha'angli Huhnas Lethum Hashiput Hamoniciplay shel Betar Illit," *Zo Irenu*, February 23, 2006.

104. Menachem Friedman, "The Ultra-Orthodox Woman," in *A View into the Lives of Women in Jewish Societies*, ed. Yael Azmon [in Hebrew] (Jerusalem: Zalman Shazar Center for Jewish History, 1995), 281.

105. Friedman, "The Ultra-Orthodox Woman," 284.

106. Friedman, "The Ultra-Orthodox Woman," 278–288.

107. On Haredi women's appropriation of various occupations and the outcomes of this process, see Friedman, "The Ultra-Orthodox Woman"; Yossef Shilhav, "Nashim Harediyot Bein Shnei Olamot," *Mifne: Bama Le'inyanei Hevra* 46–47 (May 2005): 53–55.

108. Michal Zernowitski, "Klalei Hashuk Haglobali Megi'im Lebetar Illit," *Eretz Acheret*, October 1, 2009, 76–81; Gadi Algazi, "Matrix Bebil' in: Sipur al Capitalism Coloniali Beisrael shel Yameinu," *Theory and Criticism* 29 (2006): 173–192.

109. "Pahot Mishana Meha'ihlus: Lemaala Me'esrim Batei Knesset Beshhunat Hagefen," *Zo Irenu*, May 13, 2003, 3.

110. "Ushru Haktzaot Veshiryunim shel Kehamishim Karkaot Berahvei Ha'ir Lehakamat Batei Knesset Vemosdot Hinuh," *Zo Irenu*, September 19, 2002, 3.

111. "Likrat Shabbat Lehu Vanelha: Behoraat Raboteinu Mari Deatara Shalit"a: She'arei Haknisa Lebietar Illit Yinaalu Beyemei Vav' 40 Dakot Lifnei Hashki'a," *Zo Irenu*, December 29, 2002.

112. Avishai Ben Haim, "Haredim Le'iram: Ve'adot Hakabala Yotzot Meha'asiron Ha'elyon Vemegiot Gam Lamigzar Haharedi," *Maariv*, July 9, 2007, 16; Akiva Novik, "Ir Ktana Veyeladim Ba Harbe," *Yediot Aharonot: Mamon*, August 28, 2013, 9;

"Moda'a Vebakasha," *Hadshot Ha'ir*, July 1, 2001, 5. Populating committees were formed in several other places where Haredi people settled. See Shahar Ilan and Daniel Aviv, "Haredim Mekimim Ve'adot Ihlus Bematara Limnoa Mehirat Dirot Lehilonim Veleolim," *Haaretz*, February 13, 1995, 5. On Modi'in Illit's Populating Committee, see Cahaner, "The Development," 169.

113. Ben Haim, "Haredim Le'iram," 16.

114. Novik, "Ir Ktana," 9.

115. In 2007, someone leaked the names of the committee members. They resigned quickly afterward. Tamar Rotem, "Ata Lo Tagur Kan," *Haaretz*, February 8, 2008, 7.

116. "Lamazhir Velanizhar," *Kore Bebetar*, February 5, 2008, 6; "Hahel Miyom A Hakarov: Hatahbura Hatziburit Tuf'al Bematkonet Mehadrin Mele'a," *Kore Bebetar*, February 5, 2008; Yosef Pe'er, "Hamishtara: Hakirat Rubenstein Veparashat Mishmarot Hatzniut Timasheh," *Kikar Hashabat*, February 18, 2013; Akiva Peled, "Kah Pa'ala Mishmeret Hatzniut Bebetar Illit," *Kooker*, May 22, 2013.

117. Akiva Novik and Yaron Doron, "Mishmarot Tzniut Behasut Ha'iriya," *Yediot Aharonot*, February 19, 2013, 20. See Betar Illit (male) rabbis' comments on clothing stores and dress codes in "Hahlatot Hakinus: Hukreu A"y Hever Habada"tz Hagara"tz Braverman Shalit"a," *Zo Irenu*, February 7, 2007, 4.

118. Ben Haim, "Haredim Le'iram," 16.

119. Yoel (resident of Modi'in Illit), interview by author, June 21, 2015.

120. For rules and regulations in Betar Illit as announced in 2007, see "Hahlatot Hakinus," 4.

121. Novik and Doron, "Mishmarot"; Novik, "Ir Ktana," 9.

122. Yoel, interview by author.

123. Ben Haim, "Haredim Le'iram," 16.

124. Rotem, "Ata Lo Tagur Kan," 7.

125. In June 1983, the Palestinian residents of Husan submitted an appeal, arguing that some of the lands allocated to Betar Illit were privately owned. The appeal was dismissed on January 9, 1985. See "Arar 23/83: Mahmud Hayun, Ali Shvahin et al. Vebein Hamemune Al Harehush Hamemshalti," n.d., 46701/4-GL, ISA; Joe Rosenberg, "Betar—Yeshuv Ironi Be'ezor Gush Etzion," January 21, 1985, 46701/4-GL, ISA.

126. See, for example, Amira Hass, "Pitom Hakav Hayarok Hitkarev Letoshvei Hussan," *Haaretz*, December 19, 2000, B3.

127. Petersburg, "Yalla," 10; Golan, "Hem Yaviu," 2.

128. Bleih, "Alilot Moshe Ba'ir Haktana," 16.

129. Cahaner, "Between Ghetto-Politics and Geopolitics," 119.

130. Cahaner and Shilhav, "Ultra-Orthodox Settlements," 57; Cahaner, "Between Ghetto-Politics and Geopolitics," 118–120; Nissim Leon, "Rabbi Ovadia Yosef, the Shas Party, and the Arab-Israeli Peace Process," *Middle East Journal* 69, no. 3 (2015): 394. For an estimate of Haredi settlers' portion of Israeli Haredim, see Regev and Gordon, "The Haredi Housing Market," 25.

131. Tamar Rotem, "Anahnu? Mitnahalim? Has Veshalom," *Haaretz*, September 23, 2003, https://www.haaretz.co.il/misc/1.912534.

132. "Seker Geocartographia: 80% Mitoshvei Betar Illit Sve'ei Ratzon Bemida Raba ad Raba Meod Min Hamegurim Bebetar," *Zo Irenu*, July 14, 2005, 1.

133. "Rov Toshvei Betar Illit Sve'ei Ratzon Mehamegurim Ba'ir, Mehasherutim Ha'ironiim Vemetifkud Ha'iriya Bihlal," *Zo Irenu*, October 5, 2006, 3.

134. In 2002, Betar Illit won "five stars" in a national competition organized by the Council for a Beautiful Israel. See "Betar Illit Zachta Behamisha Kokhvey Yofi Mehamoʻatza Leisrael Yaffa," *Zo Irenu*, December 15, 2002, 4. In the following year, it won the same award and was crowned as "The Prettiest Haredi City." See "Betar Illit Zachta Behamisha Kokhvei Yoffi Vemithaderet Batoar 'Haʻir Haharedit Hayafa Beyoter,'" *Zo Irenu*, December 11, 2003, 3. In 2006, it won "the beauty flag" and in 2007, a "Golden Star" for having won "five stars" for five years in a row from the Council. "Betar Illit-Haʻir Haharedit Harishona Shezoha Be'Kokhav Hazahav' shel 'Hamoatza Leyisrael Yaffa,'" *Zo Irenu*, January 4, 2007, 2.
135. Mack, *The Construction of Equality*.
136. Margaret Crawford, "The Garage Sale as Informal Economy and Transformative Urbanism," in *The Informal American City: Beyond Taco Trucks and Day Labor*, ed. Vinit Mukhija and Anastasia Loukaitou-Sideris, Urban and Industrial Environments (Cambridge, MA: MIT Press, 2014), 21–38; Margaret Crawford, "Blurring the Boundaries: Public Space and Private Life," in *Everyday Urbanism*, expanded ed., ed. John Chase, Margaret Crawford, and John Kaliski (New York: Monacelli Press, 2008), 22–35.
137. "Regional Statistics: Betar Illit" (Central Bureau of Statistics, 2021), https://www.cbs.gov.il/he/settlements/Pages/default.aspx?mode=Yeshuv.
138. "Regional Statistics: Modiʻin Illit" (Central Bureau of Statistics, 2021), https://www.cbs.gov.il/he/settlements/Pages/default.aspx?mode=Yeshuv.
139. "Tel Zion" (Binyamin Regional Council), accessed February 17, 2022, https://www.binyaminregion.org.il/tel-zion/; Cahaner and Shilhav, "Ultra-Orthodox Settlements," 53.
140. Shaul Arieli, "Mifal Hahitnahaluyot Nihshal," *Haaretz*, June 16, 2016, https://www.haaretz.co.il/opinions/.premium-1.2977962.

CHAPTER 5: OUTPOSTS

1. Talia Sasson, "Havat Daʻat," 19–20.
2. "Hamaʻarav Haparua, Girsat Hashtahim," *Channel 2 News*, March 3, 2017, https://www.mako.co.il/news-military/israel-q1_2017/Article-982be108da59a51004.htm; Danny Halamish (resident and founder of Maʻale Rechavʻam), interview by author, October 16, 2015; Haim Levinson, "Bishvil Meyasdei Hama'ahazim, Hahsharatam He lo Tamid Hadashot Tovot," *Haaretz*, June 11, 2015, https://www.haaretz.co.il/news/politics/.premium-1.2770226.
3. To protect informants' anonymity, all of their names, excluding those of public figures, are pseudonyms.
4. Zertal and Eldar, *Lords of the Land*, 129.
5. According to the agreements, work on all master plans that hadn't been approved would be stopped. There was, however, an "exempt committee" that had the power to promote certain plans. Eldar and Zertal, *Adonei Haaretz*, 176–178; Huberman, *Keneged Kol Hasikuyim*, 255; Sasson, "Havat Daʻat," 19.
6. The Palestinian Authority assumed responsibility for providing all Palestinians, regardless of the area where they live in the West Bank, civil services such as health care and education. In Area A, the Palestinian Authority received responsibility for law and public order. In Area B, it received responsibility for public order, while Israel

maintained responsibility over security. In Area C, Israel maintained full control over issues of security and public order as well as civil issues relating to territory (zoning and planning, among others). See Gordon, "From Colonization to Separation," 35–36; Ben-Naftali, Sfard, and Viterbo, *The ABC of the OPT*, 525–526.

7. Sasson, "Havat Da'at," 19. After a Right-leaning government was formed in 1996, construction resumed in existing settlements. New settlements, it was agreed, were to be founded only according to a government decision. Settlement Watch, Peace Now, "Shitat Hama'ahazim Hozeret: 17 Ma'ahazim (Hitnahaluyot) Hukmu Bashanim Ha'aharonot," March 2018.

8. Sasson admitted that, because some data was missing, her estimate was probably inaccurate. Sasson, "Havat Da'at," 21 and 104. Sasson's report was submitted in 2005. By 2008, according to the political geographer Erez Tzfadia, there were 132 outposts. Erez Tzfadia, "Informality as Control: The Legal Geography of Colonization of the West Bank," in *Cities to Be Tamed? Spatial Investigations across the Urban South*, ed. Francesco Chiodelli, Beatrice De Carli, and Maddalena Falletti (Newcastle, UK: Cambridge Scholars Publishing, 2013), 200.

9. Talia Sasson, *On the Brink of the Abyss: Is the Triumph of the Settlements the End of Israeli Democracy?* [in Hebrew] (Jerusalem: Keter, 2015), 41.

10. Sasson, "Havat Da'at," 19.

11. Sasson, "Havat Da'at," 20–21.

12. Niv Ya'ari, interview by author, April 15, 2015.

13. Ronni Shaked, Itamar Eichner, and Tzvi Zinger, "Arafat: Nagen Berovim Al Zhuy-oteinu Beyerushalayim," *Yediot Aharonot*, November 16, 1998, 6.

14. Ya'ari, interview by author.

15. Sasson, *On the Brink*. While reviewing archival material, I stumbled upon a document indicating that Gush Etzion Regional Council and the Settlement Division supported Pnei Kedem in its early days. See "Sikum Mosadot Shetomhim Bayeshuv Pnei Kedem," September 24, 2001, Pnei Kedem Archive (hereafter PKA).

16. Eli Tobeli, interview by author, April 12, 2015.

17. Settlement Watch, Peace Now, "Shitat Hama'ahazim Hozeret: 17 Ma'ahazim (Hitnahaluyot) Hukmu Bashanim Ha'aharonot."

18. Tobeli, interview by author.

19. On how outpost residents are generally perceived, and how they differ from these perceptions, see Erez Tzfadia, "Informal Outposts in the West Bank: Normality in Gray Space," in *Normalizing Occupation: The Politics of Everyday Life in the West Bank Settlements*, ed. Marco Allegra, Ariel Handel, and Erez Maggor (Bloomington: Indiana University Press, 2017), 102–105.

20. Hagar Shizaf, "Hatzatat Mishpahat Dawabshe Bedoma: Amiram Ben Uliel Hursha Beshalosh Aveirot Retzah," *Haaretz*, May 18, 2020, https://www.haaretz.co.il/news/law/.premium-1.8852683; Hagar Shizaf, "Rotzeah Mishpahat Dewabshe, Amiram Ben Uliel, Nidon Leshlosha Ma'asarei Olam," *Haaretz*, September 14, 2020, https://www.haaretz.co.il/news/law/1.9153447; Haim Levinson, "Parashat Doma: Amiram Ben-Uliel Muasham Beretzah Mishpahat Dawabshe," *Haaretz*, January 3, 2016, https://www.haaretz.co.il/news/politics/2016-01-03/ty-article/0000017f-e676-d62c-a1ff-fe7f5bea0000.

21. Nehama Dwek and Yuval Karni, "Ulmert: Lo Nisbol Blokim al Shotrim," *Yediot Aharonot*, February 2, 2006, 2.

22. Quotations of residents in this chapter are drawn from conversations and interviews I conducted in 2015.

23. On the culture of illegality in Israel, see Sprinzak, *Every Man Whatsoever Is Right.*

24. On the increase in housing prices in Israel and authorized settlements, and how that increase pushed some to unauthorized outposts, see Tzfadia, "Informal Outposts," 103.

25. Feige, *Settling in the Hearts*, 237–241.

26. On the so-called cohousing groups in the United States, see Lucy Sargisson, "Second-Wave Cohousing: A Modern Utopia?," *Utopian Studies* 23, no. 1 (April 1, 2012): 28–56, https://doi.org/10.5325/utopianstudies.23.1.0028.

27. On German construction groups, see Florian Urban, "Berlin's Construction Groups and the Politics of Bottom-up Architecture," *Urban History* 45, no. 4 (November 2018): 683–711, https://doi.org/10.1017/S0963926817000694. On cohousing groups' nonradical attitude, see Sargisson, "Second-Wave Cohousing," 51.

28. "Ofni: Building for the Future," ca. 1998, PKA.

29. "Ofni: Building for the Future."

30. "The Future Plans for Ofni," ca. 1998, PKA.

31. "Sipura shel Mishpaha," *Pninei Kedem: Alon Pnei Kedem*, June 3, 2005, PKA.

32. On Amana's support, see "Ofni: Building for the Future."

33. When the people of Ofni settled in the place, there were 36–38 ultra-Orthodox families living in Meitzad. Goldstein himself resided in Jerusalem, but to maintain control over Meitzad and the yeshiva, he had his son live there. On Goldstein, his yeshiva and followers, and on Metzudat David, see Haggai Sari, "Goldshtein Neged Goldshtein," *Makor Rishon*, September 8, 2000, 28; Nava Cohen-Tzuriel, "Meizad Ehad Meizad Sheni," *Kol Hazman*, September 8, 2000, 74–76; Sayed Kashua, "Meizad Ehad Ledaber, Meizad Sheni Lehahtif," *Kol Ha'ir*, September 8, 2000; Leora Eren Frucht, "Unsettled Territory," *Jerusalem Post*, September 8, 2000, B5. The settlement of Meitzad, it should be noted, was first founded by the Israeli Defense Force as a Naha"l outpost in 1983. The government intended to transform it into a community settlement housing some 250 families. See "Protokol Yeshivat Have'ada Lehityashvut Hameshutefet Lamemshala Velahistadrut Hatziyonit Haolamit," October 5, 1983, 7618/5-A, ISA. See a news report announcing that Meitzad had evolved into a civilian settlement (and was no longer a Naha"l outpost) in "Nir'e Lemerhakim," *Nekuda*, 1984, 30.

34. "Pnei Kedem," ca. 2001, PKA.

35. A video footage of the caravan of cars heading toward the hilltop is available on YouTube. See *The First Day in Pnei Kedem YOM HAALIYA 29th Menachem Av 5760 30th August 2000*, accessed May 28, 2018, https://www.youtube.com/watch?v=8m0elSsqLX4&app=desktop.

36. Sari, "Goldshtein Neged," 25; Kashua, "Meizad Ehad Ledaber"; Cohen-Tzuriel, "Meizad Ehad Meizad Sheni."

37. Cohen-Tzuriel, "Meizad Ehad Meizad Sheni."

38. Sari, "Goldshtein Neged," 28.

39. Yuval Karni, "Mitnahalim Neged Mitnahalim," *Yediot Aharonot*, August 31, 2000, 12; Eren Frucht, "Unsettled Territory."

40. Cohen-Tzuriel, "Meizad Ehad Meizad Sheni," 74. Also see "What Is Really Happening at Meitzad?," *Israel Wire*, September 10, 2000.

41. David Shteinman, "Route 165: Where Life Goes On," *Australian Jewish News*, June 22, 2001, 15; "Rosh Hashana Hatshs"a Bepnei Kedem," September 30, 2000, PKA.

42. "Growing with Meitzad Bet," *Voices*, October 2000, 3, PKA.

43. Feige, *Settling in the Hearts*, 79.

44. An old mobile home went for 250 shekels; a new one for 310 shekels. Mordechai Yeul and Naomi Sapir to residents of Pnei Kedem (Meitzad Bet), May 6, 2001, PKA.

45. See Alon Hadar, "Pnei Kedem: New-Age," *Malabes*, November 1, 2002, PKA.

46. Pnei Kedem Secretariat, "Pnei Kedem: Programa Lehakamt Shhuna Ekologit," 2001, PKA.

47. Pnei Kedem Secretariat, "Pnei Kedem."

48. Amos to Ministry of the Environment, "Bakashat Yeutz Vetmiha Bepituah Hayeshuv Pnei Kedem Keyeshuv Ekology," n.d., PKA. (Pnei Kedem's Building Committee was sometimes referred to as the Planning and Development Committee, as is the case in this letter.)

49. "Dvar Hamazkirut," November 16, 2001, PKA; "Protokol Yeshivat Mazkirut—Gimel Kislev Hatashsa"b 18/11/2001," November 18, 2001, PKA.

50. "Programa Lepnei Kedem: Meitzad Bet: Shhuna Ekologit Al Sfar Hamidbar" (Settlement Division at the World Zionist Organization, November 6, 2001), PKA; "Sikum Yeshiva Benose Tihnun Pnei Kedem Miyom 11/3/2002," March 12, 2002, PKA.

51. "Sikum Yeshiva Benose Tihnun Pnei Kedem."

52. Pnei Kedem's Building Committee, "Hatza'a Leshinuyim Betohnit Hamit'ar Vemadrih Lemikum Atarim Ktanim Bayeshuv," November 14, 2002, PKA. In March 2002, Walden showed sketches to David and Moshe and officials from the Ministry of Housing, Amana, and the Gush Etzion regional council. See "Sikum Yeshiva Benose Tihnun Pnei Kedem."

53. Rachel Walden to Amos, "Pnei Kedem—Bniya Taktzivit," June 16, 2002, PKA.

54. Pnei Kedem's Building Committee, "Hatza'a Leshinuyim."

55. "Protokol Yeshivat Mazkirut—Gimel."

56. Amos made a relatively similar argument in a letter he sent to the Gush Etzion regional council. See Amos to Shaul Goldshtein, "Mazkir Layeshuv Pnei Kedem," January 4, 2002, PKA.

57. "Takanon Bniya (Helek Alef)," June 17, 2002, PKA.

58. "Takanon Bniya Pratit," n.d., PKA.

59. Rachel Walden, interview by author, March 12, 2015. Walden submitted two master plans between 2001 and 2004 and another one in 2011.

60. "Mishulhana shel Ve'adat Bniya Atidit," *Pninei Kedem: Alon Pnei Kedem*, February 2003.

61. Walden, interview by author.

62. Bella Nudelman, interview by author, August 5, 2013.

63. Meir Tzeri, "Pnei Kedem," *Gushpanka—PirsuMeyda*, February 7, 2003, 22, PKA.

64. Walden was called in again in 2011 to draw and submit another iteration of the master plan to the Civil Administration.

65. On plot pricing and procedures in the early days of Pnei Kedem, see "Takanon Bniya Pratit."

66. Ben Shahar Family, "Ratzinu Lomar," *Pninei Kedem: Alon Pnei Kedem*, November 18, 2005, PKA.
67. Feige, *Settling in the Hearts*, 241–243.
68. "Takanon Avoda Ivrit: Beyozmat Akiva Yonatan Shapiro," n.d., PKA.
69. On the "conquest of labor" and "Hebrew labor," see Gershon Shafir, *Land, Labor, and the Origins of the Israeli-Palestinian Conflict, 1882–1914* (Berkeley: University of California Press, 1996); Andrew Ross, *Stone Men: The Palestinians Who Built Israel* (London: Verso, 2019), 21–41; Anita Shapira, "The Struggles for the Employment of Jewish Labour" [in Hebrew] (PhD diss., Tel Aviv University, 1974), esp. 12–19.
70. Moshe (pseudonym), "Tihnun Atidi shel Beit Haknesset Bepnei Kedem," December 4, 2001, PKA.
71. Dotan, who was speaking informally, probably drew on the first chapter of Kook's *Orot* ("Lights" in Hebrew), where Kook glorifies the wonders of the Land of Israel and its unique effects on Jewish personhood and creativity. See Abraham Isaac Kook, *Orot* (Jerusalem: Degel Yerushalayim, 1920), 1–6.
72. Margaret Crawford, "Alternative Shelter: Counterculture Architecture in Northern California," in *Reading California: Art, Image, and Identity, 1900–2000*, ed. Stephanie Barron, Sheri Bernstein, and Ilene Susan Fort (Los Angeles: Los Angeles County Museum of Art; Berkeley: University of California Press, 2000), 249–270.
73. Settlement Watch, Peace Now, "Shitat Hama'ahazim Hozeret."
74. "Tza'ad Mahri'a Badereh Lehasdarat 'Pnei Kedem,'" *Arutz Sheva*, October 15, 2020, https://www.inn.co.il/news/454023.

CONCLUSION

1. Yonatan Englender, "Park 'Magic Kass': Kemo Tzalahat Meofefet Shenahta Bamidbar," *Haaretz*, November 8, 2021, https://www.haaretz.co.il/gallery/trip/.premium.HIGHLIGHT-MAGAZINE-1.10361798.
2. According to the political scientists Sivan Hirsch-Hoefler and Cas Mudde, in 2020, more than two-thirds of the settlers had "*no* ideological zeal" and did "not truly *believe* in the idea of Eretz Yisrael." Sivan Hirsch-Hoefler and Cas Mudde, *The Israeli Settler Movement: Assessing and Explaining Social Movement Success* (Cambridge: Cambridge University Press, 2020), 232–233, https://doi.org/10.1017/9781316481554.
3. Arieli, "Mif'al Hahitnahaluyot Nihshal."
4. "Population" (Peace Now, 2020), https://peacenow.org.il/en/settlements-watch/settlements-data/population.
5. Arieli, "Mif'al Hahitnahaluyot Nihshal"; Shaul Arieli, "Hahitnahaluyot, Lo Ma Shehashavtem," *Haaretz*, March 2, 2017, https://www.haaretz.co.il/opinions/.premium-1.3901515. In 2019, growth rates in settlements, standing at 3.2 percent, were nevertheless much higher than those inside Israel, which stood at 1.9 percent. Eyal Hareuveni and Dror Atkes, *Ze Shelanu, Ze Gam Ken: Medinuyut Hahitnahalut Hayisraelit Bagada Hama'aravit* (Jerusalem: B'Tselem, March 2021), 8.
6. According to the sociologist Shlomo Swirsky, in 2017, settlers associated with Gush Emunim's ideology amounted to 60,000 to 80,000, or roughly 1 percent of the Israeli population. Nevertheless, they enjoyed a much greater representation in the parliament and in government ministries. Between 2013 and 2015, out of 120 parliament

members, 12 were settlers; between 2015 and 2019, 10 were settlers. Shlomo Swirski, "Eretz Ahat vela Shnei Me'iyonim Elyonim," *Haaretz*, July 5, 2017, https://www.haaretz.co.il/opinions/.premium-1.4234048.

7. "Neged Bniya Bashtahim," *Kol Ha'ir*, August 12, 1988; Shahar Ilan, "Adrihalim Neged Bniya Bashtahim," *Kol Ha'ir*, July 29, 1988.

8. Karen Wainer, interview by author, August 3, 2017. On the 1988 petition, see Shoked, "'This Is the Hour.'" Other important protest events and actions carried out by Israeli architects and planners include "Blue Line, Red Lines" (Kav Kahol, Kavim Adumim), a symposium that took place in 1997 in Tel Aviv, and the founding, in 1999, of Bimkom—Planners for Planning Rights, a nonprofit that provides planning services to disempowered communities in Israel and the West Bank. On the 1997 symposium and the events leading to it, see Ester Zandberg, "Hayim Betoh Bua," *Haaretz*, July 3, 1997, D2; Ester Zandberg, "Hamilhama Nimshehet Al Shulhan Hasirtut," *Haaretz*, June 23, 1997, D1; Amira Hass, "Ma'ale Yehudim," *Haaretz*, July 2, 1997, B2.

9. Foucault, "Space, Knowledge, and Power," 247.

10. In recent years, Israeli lawmakers have attempted to mitigate the power of admission committees in community settlements (and elsewhere). In 2011, they prohibited admission committees from evaluating candidates based on their race or religious views, and, in the case of communities of more than four hundred families, they prohibited the use of screening mechanisms altogether. These restrictions, however, were only partially applied. See Hen Ma'anit, "Ve'adot Hakabala Hador Hahadash: Bo'u Lagur Itanu! Ala im ken Atem Datiyim, Aravim, Ravakim, O Stam Nirim Ktzat Shone," *Globes*, February 1, 2019, https://www.globes.co.il/news/article.aspx?did=1001271315; Ofer Petersburg, "Metzaftzefim Al Hahok: Asrot Yeshuvim Mesanenim Toshavim," *Ynet*, May 16, 2019, https://www.ynet.co.il/articles/0,7340,L-5509851,00.html; Matan Shahak, "Ve'adot Kabala Beyeshuvim Kehilatiim Banegev Ubagalil" (The Knesset Research and Information Center, May 2, 2019), https://fs.knesset.gov.il/globaldocs/MMM/8076aeaa-ce01-e911-80e1-00155d0a98a9/2_8076aeaa-ce01-e911-80e1-00155d0a98a9_11_12403.pdf.

11. In 2020, it should be noted, there were a few hundred Palestinian citizens of Israel living in settlements. "Kovetz Hayeshuvim 2020."

12. For a discussion of settlement activists' effect on the geographical distribution and the number of settlements, see Hirsch-Hoefler and Mudde, *The Israeli Settler Movement*, 233–235.

13. Ben-Naftali, Sfard, and Viterbo, *The ABC of the OPT*, 52.

14. Etkes, "A Locked Garden," 51–53.

15. Oren Yiftachel and Erez Tzfadia, "Ir Hamahar Ha'afora," in *Cities of Tomorrow: Planning, Justice and Sustainability Today?*, ed. Tovi Fenster and Oren Shlomo (Tel Aviv: Hakibbutz Hameuchad, 2014), 182; Erez Tzfadia, "Informal Outposts in the West Bank: Normality in Gray Space," in *Normalizing Occupation: The Politics of Everyday Life in the West Bank Settlements*, ed. Marco Allegra, Ariel Handel, and Erez Maggor (Bloomington: Indiana University Press, 2017), 92–111.

16. For estimates of settlers' population, see note 1 of the introduction. For accounts that have focused on Gush Emunim or its alliances with high-profile politicians, see, for example, Feige, *Settling in the Hearts*; Lustick, *For the Land and the Lord*; Zertal and Eldar, *Lords of the Land*.

17. Tzfadia, "Informal Outposts," 102.
18. See, for example, Gutwein, "The Settlements"; Maggor, "State, Market"; Yael Hirschhorn, *City on a Hilltop*; Weiss, "Immigration and West Bank Settlement Normalization"; Gillis, "The Question of Ethnic Identity."
19. For accounts that emphasize the similarities between pre- and post-1967 settlement activity in Israel/Palestine, see, for example, Gershon Shafir, "Land, Labor, and Population in Zionist Colonization: General and Unique Aspects," in *Israeli Society: Critical Approaches*, ed. Uri Ram (Tel Aviv: Breirot, 1993), 104–119; Tzfadia, "Informal Outposts."

INDEX

Page numbers in *italics* refer to figures.

menswear store in staircase, *167*; planning and construction of, 157–160; playgrounds in, 162, 164; Populating Committee, 169, 170–172; population and demographic statistics, 6–7, 174, 176; relations with Palestinian neighbors, 172, 174, 175; residential unit plan for, *160*; residents' satisfaction with, 174–175; steering committee, *161, 173*; synagogues in, 7, 162, 166, 169, *170*; tunnel road near, *173*

Bet Arye, 197, 220, 268n97

Bethlehem, 14, 28, 30, 40

Bet Shemesh, 20, 224

Bin-Nun, Yoel, 87–88

Bnei Adam outpost, 208, *211*

bottom-up design and processes, 18–21, 109, 144, 176, 214, 221–223

British Mandate: Etzion Bloc and, 33; segregation and, 20; settlement history and, 13, 15; stockade and tower settlement method, 69–70, 183

Canaanites (ancient peoples), 211

Canaanites (twentieth-century group), 32, 34, 63

caravans. *See* mobile homes

Cassuto, David, 40–41, 51, 52–53, 59–60, 65, 84

Certeau, Michel de, 19

Charlap, Gideon, 99

Chasani, Michael, 34

checkpoints, 3, 12, *13*, 27, *62*, 172, 251n181

Civil Administration in Judea and Samaria, 110, 181, 188, 195, 197, 199–200, 202, 216

Cohen, Uri, 119

community settlements: critique of, 195–196; definition of, 3, 232n7; exclusion and, 20, 81, 119, 222; "labor settlements" compared with, 224; Likud Party and, 102; Neve Tzuf, 132, *133–134*; origins and history of, 66–67, 78–83; population and demographic statistics, 142, 261n161, 262n6; quality-of-life settlements and,

104, 107, 262n6, 262n164. *See also* Ofra settlement

Crawford, Margaret, 175, 215

Dayan, Moshe, 32–33, 242n44

Deutch, Zalman, 75–76

development towns, 17–18, 119, 131–132

Dome of the Rock, 100, 213

Eban, Abba, 32

Efrat, Elisha, 28

Ein Tzurim, 72

Eshkol, Levi, 32–34, 241n38

Eshkol Heights, 84

Etzion, Yehuda: arrest and imprisonment of, 100, 101; culture of illegality and, 73; Gush Emunim and, 72–74; Ofra and, 76, 88, 91, 96–101; on present state of settlements, 104, 141

Etzion Bloc, 33–34, 66, 241n38; Ein Tzurim, 72. *See also* Kfar Etzion

Feige, Michael, 97, 184, 201

Felix, Menachem, 72

First, Eli, 148, *149*

first Palestinian uprising (First Intifada): architectural impact of, 22, 126–127, 201; demographic impact of, 11, 61, 138–139, 142, 143–144, 156, 219; violence of, 61, 126

Froman, Menachem, 184

Gamerman, Giora, 85

Garin Ofni, 185–191. *See also* Pnei Kedem

Gdor, Uzi, 78–79, 81–83, 84, 86, 88, 104

Gelehrter, Lou, 87

geodesic domes, 207, 209, *210*, 212–213, *213*, 215

Gil, Yaacov, 148

Givoni, Baruch, 113–117, 139

Golan Heights, 1, *25*, 32, 78

Goldstein, Baruch, 61

Goldstein, Mordechai, 188–192; Diaspora Yeshiva founded by, 188, 190–191, 285n33; Meitzad and, 188, 190–191, 285n33

Goodovitch, Israel, 35, 105, 107
Gordon, Neve, 85
Green Line, 86, 111, 157; Alfe Menashe
and, 128; Betar Illit and, 6, 156; land
prices and, 271n135; Nofim and, 5
Groth, Paul, 23
Gush Emunim: Amana settling movement,
142, 186, 195; impact of, 218–219,
222, 223; Likud Party and, 109;
master plans prepared by, 261n157;
Ofra and, 78, 81–84, 90–91, 99,
101, 102, 104; population and
demographic statistics, 273–274n183,
287–288n6; settling tactics and
ideology of, 68–69, 71–73, 97,
140–142; whole Land of Israel
ideology of, 68–69, 104, 219
Gutwein, Danny, 10, 110

Hacohen, Shmuel Avidor, 40
Hadar Betar settlement, 156–157, 278n54
Haetzni, Elyakim, 50–51
halakhah, 68, 150
Halamish, Aharon, 3–4, 9
Halamish, Edna, 3–4, 9
Haredim (ultra-Orthodox Jews), 145–146;
dress code, 171, 175; housing crisis,
146; main groups, 279–280n77; in
Meitzad, 188, 190–191, 285n33;
origins and history of, 145; population
and demographic statistics, 7, 15,
176; religious and cultural views
and practices of, 145–146; Shomrie
Emunim neighborhood and, 276n21;
terminology, 145. See also Betar Illit
settlement; Immanu'el settlement;
Modi'in Illit settlement
Hatsor HaGlilit, 147
Havat Ya'ir outpost, 199
"Hebrew labor" policy, 203
Hebron: 1929 riots, 39, 52; annotated
drawing by Kiryat Arba settler,
50; Avraham Avinu Quarter, 58;
Avraham Avinu Synagogue, 52–55,
54; barriers and checkpoints in, 62;
Beit Hadassah restoration, 59, 61;
closed Palestinian-owned stores, 62,

63, 64; Committee for the Restoration
of Hebron, 39; Park Hotel squatting
activity in, 39–40, 47, 49; playground
in, 3, 4. See also Avraham Avinu
Quarter; Avraham Avinu Synagogue;
Kiryat Arba settlement; Tomb of the
Patriarchs
Hebron Protocol, 61
Hebron Rehabilitation Committee, 62
Hershkovitz, Wladislav, 35–36, 37
Horwitz, Shmuel, 67

Ibrahimi Mosque. See Tomb of the
Patriarchs
illegality, culture of, 72
Immanu'el settlement, 146–156, 197;
apartment buildings in, 148, 151, 153,
154, 155, 156; drawing of Immanu'el
inspired by Old City, 153; financial
collapse of, 155–156, 161; Haredi
community needs and, 148, 151,
153; Haredim's opposition to plans
for, 149–150; marketing campaign
for, 150–151, 152; master plan for,
147; Palestinian-inspired architecture
in, 148, 150, 157; planning and
construction of, 146–151; population
and demographic statistics, 156; Star
of David-shaped synagogue of, 148,
149, 155–156; sukkahs in, 148, 153
Industrial Village settlement model, 79
International Union of Architects, 22, 158
Israel, founding of State of, 14, 15, 17,
73, 77, 168
Israeli Association of United Architects, 22
Israel Land Development Company, 35

al-Jabari, Muhammad Ali, 39, 43
Jabotinsky, Vladimir (Ze'ev), 68–69
Jackson, John Brinckerhoff, 23
Jericho, 65, 66, 111–112, 113
Jewish Agency. See Settlement
Department of the Jewish Agency
Jewish Underground, 100
Johnson, Lyndon, 33
Joint Settlement Committee of the Israeli
Government and the World Zionist

Machsom Watch, *13*
Mack, Jennifer, 21, 175
Mandel, Saadia, *55–59, 58, 59,* 61, 65
Mazar, Benjamin, 44
Meir, Golda, 52
Meitzad settlement, 188–191, 285n33
Merhavia, Moshe, 90–93, 220
Merkaz Harav Yeshiva, 38
mikveh, 49, 75, 143
Ministry of Housing (later Ministry
    of Construction and Housing),
    105, 107–108; architects and, 198,
    220–221; Avraham Avinu Quarter
    renovation and, 55, 56, 59; Betar
    Illit and, 156–158, 160–161, 169,
    171–172, 174; Build Your Own Home
    program, 131–133; Division of Rural
    Planning, 35, 105, 241–242n43;
    Immanu'el and, 147, 155; Kfar Etzion
    and, 35, 38; Kiryat Arba and, 41,
    43–45, 49, 51, 55; Ma'ale Adumim
    and, 111–120; Nofim and, 138; Pnei
    Kedem and, 197, 215; Rural Building
    and New Settlements Administration
    (was Division of Rural Planning), 67,
    122, 241–242n43, 252n6, 270n120
Mitzpe Ramon, *17*
Mizrahi Jews, 15, 17–18, 23, 119,
    235nn28–29, 267nn88–90
mobile homes: with extra room and
    wooden porch, *194;* floor plan, *193;* in
    Hadar Betar, 156–157; in Pnei Kedem,
    8–9, 188–195, *189,* 200, 204, 206,
    209; on slope north of Jerusalem, *192;*
    in Tkoa Dalet, *210;* yurts attached
    to, *210*
Modi'in Illit settlement, 143, 166, 169,
    176, 274n3; apartment buildings in, 7,
    143, *165;* commercial activity in, 166,
    169; Jewish laws in, 171; playground
    in, 7, 143, *165;* population and
    demographic statistics, 143, 176,
    274n1
moshavim, 27; design characteristics of,
    87, 90; immigrant, 119; as inspiration
    for settlement designs, 87, 90–91,
    141; Labor Zionism and, 79, 224;

origins and history of, 13; pitched-
    roof designs of, 90; screening of new
    residents in, 20
Moshav Nehalim, 47
Movement for the Whole Land of Israel,
    31–32, 33–34, 35, 38

Nablus, 28, 33, 38, 65, 69, 72
Nakba, 15, 17. *See also* Arab-Israeli War
    of 1948
Namir, Ora, 132
National Religious Party, 68
Nativ, Zehava, 27, 31, 63
Nekuda (magazine), 102, 119, 135, 138,
    142, 261n157
Netanyahu, Benjamin, 20, 181
Neve Tzuf settlement, 132, *133–134*
Newman, David, 88, 90
Nitzan-Shiftan, Alona, 45, 56, 84, 116,
    123, 126, 238–239n58
Nofar, David, 151, *154*
Nofim settlement, 5–6, 129–139; ad
    promising Fiat to house buyers, *137;*
    "dream homes" in, 10, 132, 136,
    138; financial collapse of, 138–139;
    government authorization for, 130;
    historical background of, 129–130;
    master plan for, 130; model home, *131*

Ofra settlement: aerial view of, *95;*
    government authorization of, 86;
    historical background of, 67, 72–73;
    house design plan for, 90; kibbutzim-
    inspired design in, 3–5, 5, 11, 77–78,
    79, 81, 87–88, 90–93, 104, 141;
    master plan for, 85, 88, 91; occupation
    of abandoned Jordanian military
    camp, 73–76; permanent house design
    and construction in, 89–93; pitched
    red-tile roofs in, 11, 89–93, 102,
    141; replications of, 102; resident
    historicization of, 102–104; resident
    planning of, 77–79, 82–83, 96–97;
    screening mechanisms of, 81; site plan
    for, *85;* social solidarity of, 81, 104;
    synagogue in, 85, 86, 95–102, *96, 98,*
    100, 101, 103; uniformity of, 82, 93